res vera, res ficta: Fictionality in Ancient Epistolography

Trends in Classics – Supplementary Volumes

Edited by
Franco Montanari and Antonios Rengakos

Associate Editors
Stavros Frangoulidis · Fausto Montana · Lara Pagani
Serena Perrone · Evina Sistakou · Christos Tsagalis

Scientific Committee
Alberto Bernabé · Margarethe Billerbeck
Claude Calame · Kathleen Coleman · Jonas Grethlein
Philip R. Hardie · Stephen J. Harrison · Stephen Hinds
Richard Hunter · Giuseppe Mastromarco
Gregory Nagy · Theodore D. Papanghelis
Giusto Picone · Alessandro Schiesaro
Tim Whitmarsh · Bernhard Zimmermann

Volume 149

res vera, res ficta: Fictionality in Ancient Epistolography

Edited by
Janja Soldo and Claire Rachel Jackson

DE GRUYTER

ISBN 978-3-11-221543-2
e-ISBN (PDF) 978-3-11-130812-8
e-ISBN (EPUB) 978-3-11-130849-4
ISSN 1868-4785

Library of Congress Control Number: 2023942334

Bibliographic information published by the Deutsche Nationalbibliothek
The Deutsche Nationalbibliothek lists this publication in the Deutsche Nationalbibliografie;
detailed bibliographic data are available on the Internet at http://dnb.dnb.de.

© 2025 Walter de Gruyter GmbH, Berlin/Boston
This volume is text- and page-identical with the hardback published in 2023.
Editorial Office: Alessia Ferreccio and Katerina Zianna
Logo: Christopher Schneider, Laufen
Printing and binding: CPI books GmbH, Leck

www.degruyter.com

Acknowledgments

This volume originates from a workshop originally held at Sidney Sussex College, Cambridge, in December 2019. We would like to thank all the original speakers, chairs, respondents, and participants from the workshop, in particular Olivia Elder, Andrew Morrison, Antonia Sarri, Tim Whitmarsh, for their involvement. We are especially grateful to Serena Cammoranesi for organising the original workshop with us, and for her insight and enthusiasm which took this idea from our preliminary conversations in a café in Manchester to the workshop in Cambridge to this volume.

We want to express our particular thanks to John Osborn, without whom the workshop from which this volume originated would not have been possible. John's contributions to supporting Classics at Sidney Sussex have been numerous and wide-reaching, and we are very grateful for his generosity which enabled us to take this workshop from idea to reality. We also want to thank everyone at Sidney Sussex who helped make the event happen, and in particular Yannis Galanakis for his support of the original proposal and advice and encouragement throughout. We are also very grateful to the Classical Association for offering additional funding.

Claire Rachel Jackson would like to acknowledge the support of the European Research Council (ERC) under the European Union's Horizon 2020 research and innovation programme (grant agreement No. 819459 – NovelEchoes) during the process of editing this volume, and to express special thanks to Koen De Temmerman and Evelien Bracke for their advice, support, and generosity throughout.

Our thanks to the anonymous reviewers and to Antonios Rengakos for their encouragement and insightful critiques, and to Carlo Vessella and the entire editorial team at De Gruyter for their help and support.

Special thanks go to Irene Peirano Garrison for her participation in the original workshop, her continued encouragement and her enthusiasm for the ideas behind this volume.

Finally, we are immensely grateful to all of our contributors, not just for agreeing to participate in the workshop in the first place, but for then being willing to participate in the volume despite the Covid-19 pandemic which threw everyone's lives and schedules into turmoil. In such a global period of upheaval, both personal and professional, your commitment to this volume has been nothing short of exceptional.

We want to dedicate the volume to Valentina Zdenka who was born in the lockdown of 2021. Without her, this volume would have been published much earlier, but life would be not as joyful.

Contents

Acknowledgments —— V

Claire Rachel Jackson and Janja Soldo
Introduction: Fictions of Genre —— 1

Part I: (Auto)Biographical Fictions

Roy K. Gibson
Fact and Fiction in Pliny's *Epistles*: The Augustan Poetry Book and its Legacies —— 21

Claire Rachel Jackson
Fiction and Authenticity in the *Letters* of Euripides —— 45

Catharine Edwards
Greetings from the Margin: Ovid's *Epistulae ex Ponto* —— 69

Part II: Editorial Fictions

Michael Trapp
Just Some Notes for My Own Use: Arrian's ('Arrian's'?) Letter to Lucius Gellius —— 89

Serena Cammoranesi
Cicero's *Epistulae ad Familiares*: From Authentic Letters to Literary Artefact —— 107

Part III: Pseudepigraphic Fictions

Kathryn Tempest
The Latin Letters of Pseudo-Brutus (Cic. *Brut.* 1.16 and 1.17) —— 131

Janja Soldo
Fictionality and Pseudepigraphy in the Apocryphal Letter Exchange between Seneca and Paul —— 161

Part IV: Ekphrastic Fictions

Ruth Morello
Fictions in the Real World: Language and Reality in Cicero's Letters —— 181

Emilia A. Barbiero
Let's Get Real: Ekphrasis, Reality and Fiction in Pliny's *Epistles* —— 207

List of Contributors —— 239
Bibliography —— 241
General Index —— 259
Index Locorum —— 263

Claire Rachel Jackson and Janja Soldo
Introduction: Fictions of Genre

The place of fiction in ancient epistolography is something of a paradox. Depictions of letters litter classical literary culture and play a key role in the plots of works commonly classified as fictitious, from drama to elegy to the ancient novel. The paradigmatic examples of Bellerophon's tablet in the *Iliad* and Phaedra's suicide note in Euripides' *Hippolytus* testify to an awareness even in some of the earliest literature extant from classical antiquity of the potential of letters to construct false, even deceptive stories.[1] By the imperial period, the variety of letter-collections ascribed to ancient celebrities including Pythagoras, Hippocrates, and Themistocles, but likely written long after their deaths, testify to a widespread interest in letters as a vehicle to embellish and rewrite traditional biographical narratives about famous figures.[2] Early Christian pseudepigraphic letters have, by contrast, been argued to be fiction as a counterweight to accusations of forgery.[3] The label of fictional letters, therefore, covers a multitude of forms, genres, and contexts, ranging from letters within fictional narratives to invented collections neutralised within a generic label and those intended to deceive. And yet the extent to which ancient audiences, both contemporary readers and later compilers, conceptualised fiction as a distinct category is far from clear. While analogies with the early modern epistolary novel are relatively commonplace, this risks implying a generic clarity and fixity for which there is little evidence in

---

Claire Rachel Jackson would like to acknowledge the funding of the European Research Council (ERC) under the European Union's Horizon 2020 research and innovation programme (grant agreement No. 819459 - NovelEchoes) in her contribution to this introduction.

1 On these paradigms see in particular Rosenmeyer 2001, 39–44 and 88–97.
2 On the *Letters* of Themistocles see Penwill 1978. Many of these collections remain understudied and largely inaccessible, since the most recent edition in many cases for Greek collections is the nineteenth-century opus of Hercher (*Epistolographi Graeci*, 1873). The recent work of the AHRC-funded *Ancient Letters Project*, based at the University of Manchester, aims to survey these collections from the fourth century BCE to the fifth century CE in order to increase access to these hitherto obscure collections.
3 See in particular the edited volume of Frey/Herzer/Janßen/Rothschild 2009. On early Christian forgery see Ehrman 2013. See Klauck 2006 for an overview of New Testament letters.

antiquity.⁴ What, then, exactly do we mean when we talk of fictional letters, and what is at stake in this terminology?

Concerns about how to distinguish invented from genuine letters are not new, nor have they ever been uncontroversial. Richard Bentley's late seventeenth-century *Dissertation on the Epistles of Phalaris* is just one intervention in a much wider debate,⁵ but the sharpness and starkness of its argument that the eponymous letters were inauthentic established it as the primary model for later approaches to such pseudepigraphic letter collections.⁶ Throughout the treatise Bentley argues pedantically for the *Epistles*' inauthenticity based on anachronistic details such as mistakes made regarding types of currency or drinking cups easily established by citing standard scholarly reference works of the time. As such, in Haugen's words, 'Bentley's *Dissertation* was thus a spectacular application of compiled collective learning rather than an original piece of research in itself.'⁷ While this kind of pedantic *Echtheitskritik* perhaps reflects more on Bentley than on the *Epistles* themselves,⁸ throughout the course of this debate and others Bentley's central premise, namely that such collections should be understood through the binary lens of authenticity and forgery, remained unchallenged.⁹ The late nineteenth-century rediscovery of the papyri at Oxyrhynchus, including a variety of documentary letters, added to the urgency of this argument.¹⁰ Particularly influential at this time was Gustav Adolf Deißmann's distinction between letters, written for private purposes only, and epistles, written with publication in mind.¹¹ His study of the Pauline letters acknowledged that letters (*Briefe*) and, respectively, epistles (*Episteln*) vary in their degree of authenticity and established a firm opposition between real and fictive letters. Despite various attempts to nuance this distinction in subsequent scholarship,¹² ancient

---

4 For example, Rosenmeyer 2001, *passim*; Morrison 2013. See Jackson forthcoming a and in this volume for critique of such terminology in relation to the *Letters* of Chion and Euripides respectively.
5 Described in more detail by Haugen 2011, 110–123.
6 Discussed briefly by Rosenmeyer 2001, 194–196.
7 Haugen 2011, 113.
8 On *Echtheitskritik* in antiquity see Peirano 2012, 37–42, and into modernity see also Speyer 1971, 99–105.
9 On this controversy in relationship to the *Letters* of Euripides see Hanink 2010, 537–541.
10 On this context see the survey of Rosenmeyer 2001, 5–7.
11 Deißmann 1908.
12 For example, Sykutris 1933 and Stirewalt 1993, who argues even more narrowly for a distinction between fiction and forgery on the grounds that such pseudepigraphic letter collections were not written for financial gain. Rosenmeyer 2001, 8–13 offers further critique of these approaches, among others.

epistolography remained primarily viewed through a binary lens of truth and falsehood, where references to fiction would only signify mendacity or deceit.

These kinds of interventions set the tone for scholarship on epistolary fiction for much of the twentieth century, and it is only recently that analysis has attempted to move beyond these binary oppositions.[13] The volume edited by Niklas Holzberg, *Der griechische Briefroman: Gattungstypologie und Textanalyse*, argues for the category of the epistolary novel and outlines conventions of the genre, subsuming different pseudonymous Greek collections into this category.[14] On this reading, the potentially problematic pseudonymity of collections attributed to Plato, Socrates, Chion, and Euripides can be neutralised within a generic framework through the familiar modern paradigm of the epistolary novel. This approach is developed even further by Patricia Rosenmeyer's *Ancient Epistolary Fictions*. In this work, Rosenmeyer looks both at the depictions of letters in canonical Greek texts and later pseudepigraphic collections not as a derivative imitation of documentary letters, but as a field of study in its own right. Although Rosenmeyer's stated focus is on rehabilitating neglected letter-collections by collating them as a unified although not unitary genre,[15] this nonetheless implicitly reinscribes an opposition between fictional and seemingly genuine letters. The key difference is that the rhetoric of forgery has been sublimated into the more impartial terminology of fiction, which downplays any deceptive intentions and outlines a distinct generic opposition between letters which are what they claim to be and those which are not. This shift in approach has been highly influential for later studies of epistolography, not least because it rightly showcases the value of epistolographic fiction within classical literary culture, but also for its clear focus on letters as a literary form rather than historical documents.[16] As a result, subsequent scholarship has positioned pseudepigraphic letters not as forgeries, but as a category of creative expression which develops from the educational precepts of the imperial era,[17] or the rise of prose fiction in the form of the

---

13 This parallels recent work on literary forgery, which has increasingly moved away from seeing this phenomenon as a binary contrast of authenticity and fraud to considering it as a creative exploration of the limitations of the literary canon. See Grafton 1990.
14 Holzberg 1994b. For further critique of the label of epistolary novel, see Jackson forthcoming a and her contribution in this volume.
15 Most clearly stated at Rosenmeyer 2001, 12–16.
16 For example, Jenkins 2006; Hodkinson/Rosenmeyer/Bracke 2013.
17 Malosse 2005, for example, explores the connection between *ethopoiia*, rhetorical exercises involving literary invention and embellishment, and epistolary fiction. See Peirano 2012 on fakes as part of imperial culture and education more widely.

ancient novel,[18] or the increasing interest in biography in the postclassical world.[19]

And yet, even as such approaches embed pseudonymous letters in the literary, rhetorical, and educational contexts of the ancient world, this essential distinction between authentic and inauthentic letters has not been challenged. The extent to which letters interrogate the boundaries between fiction and historicity has long been recognised and scholars have repeatedly decried an over-reliance upon rigid typologies,[20] but in practice these binary categories have remained stubbornly fixed despite this change of terminology. While the label of fiction inoculates pseudonymous collections against accusations of deception by aligning them within a less charged generic framework familiar to contemporary readers from early modern traditions of the epistolary novel, it nonetheless reinscribes an opposition between documentary and invented letters, even as the criteria for determining this distinction shift. Seen through this lens, it is perhaps not surprising that a key focus of Holzberg's definition of ancient epistolary novels is anachronism.[21] By emphasising the ways in which scholarly *Echtheitskritik* can distinguish pseudonymous letters from genuine ones, the historical value of authentic letters can be protected from any hint of deception and confidently distinguished from their invented counterparts. On such a reading, therefore, fictional letters remain a circumscribed category distinct from historical letters, which are defined by their lack of authenticity, and this generic approach naturalises epistolary fiction as a teleological precursor to the early modern epistolary novel.

One striking consequence of this approach is visible in the bifurcated understanding of fiction across scholarship on Latin and Greek letters respectively. Michael Trapp's epistolary anthology has often been cited as a turning point in contemporary studies,[22] in large part due to its expansive approach and diverse range of letters cited. In contrast to other translations and editions, Trapp's anthology juxtaposes Greek and Latin letters from a variety of periods within functional

---

18 Konstan 1998 traces the invention of fiction to New Comedy and the rise of the novel in the imperial period. On the relationship between novel and fiction in ancient letter collections, see Jackson forthcoming a and Hodkinson 2019 on the *Letters* of Chion of Heraclea.
19 Trapp 2006.
20 For example, as Rosenmeyer 2001, 11 put it, 'every letter is also an artifact purporting to be historically authentic.' Rosenmeyer 1994, 147: 'yet behind the awkward issue of authenticity lies a central feature of letter-writing: epistolary technique always problematizes the boundary between reality and fiction.' See also Gunderson 2007 for an eloquent articulation of this problem.
21 Holzberg 1994a, especially 44.
22 Sogno/Storin/Watts 2017b, 1–2; Morello/Morrison 2007b, v.

rather than generic categories.²³ Trapp rejects the idea that all letters are fictional or that there are unique markers of epistolary fiction in favour of a broader definition of letters which focuses on the similarities between different epistolary texts rather than their differences.²⁴ As such, the anthologised letters are divided not by questions of authentication or fictitiousness, but rather by function and theme, with Cicero alongside Ovid and letters from Oxyrhynchus.²⁵ This wide-ranging approach has repeatedly been reaffirmed in scholarship, often with insight and incisiveness, but the perennial return to such issues testifies to the difficulties of defining letters as a genre.²⁶ In practice, despite this commitment to inclusivity, a stark divide emerges from subsequent scholarship in how fiction is conceptualised across Latin and Greek letters. Discussions of epistolary fiction in antiquity have tended to focus especially, although not exclusively, on Greek collections, where the large number of pseudonymous letters can be more easily grouped as a coherent corpus and assimilated within the label of the epistolary novel.²⁷ As such, recent scholarship has done much to bring more visibility to collections widely accepted to be fictional, such as those of Alciphron, Aelian, Philostratus, and Aristaenetus, as well as the pseudepigraphic collections attributed to Plato and Chion of Heraclea, amongst others, to say nothing of the fictional letters embedded in the ancient Greek novel and the *Alexander Romance*.²⁸ Even as much more ground remains to be covered with regards to the vast corpora of pseudonymous Greek letters, scholarship broadly has reached a consensus that fiction can be applied as a generic label to Greek pseudonymous letters which allows such collections to be quantified, contextualised, and categorised.

---

23 For example, Rosenmeyer 2006 and Costa 2002 only look at Greek letters in their translations. Latin letters are represented in the anthology of Zeiner-Carmichael 2013, which groups them chronologically without much distinction between prose and poetic letters.
24 Trapp 2003, 4.
25 Trapp 2003, 46–47.
26 Gibson/Morrison 2007; Hodkinson 2007; Sogno/Storin/Watts 2017b.
27 Seminally Holzberg 1994a; see also Rosenmeyer 1994; 2001, 133–251. On the coherence of Greek epistolary fiction aside from this terminology of novel, see for example the edited collections of Hodkinson/Rosenmeyer/Bracke 2013; Vox 2013; Marquis 2023.
28 On Alciphron see the essays in Biraud/Zucker 2019; on Aelian Hodkinson 2013 and Drago 2013; on Philostratus Goldhill 2009, Schmitz 2017 and Leonard 2020; and on Aristaenetus Höschele 2012 and Bing/Höschele 2014. On the Platonic *Letters* see Wohl 1998; Morrison 2013; 2014a; 2023; on Chion of Heraclea's *Letters* see Jackson forthcoming a and Hodkinson 2019. On letters in the novel see the overviews of Rosenmeyer 2001, 133–168, Létoublon 2003 and Jackson forthcoming b, and on the *Alexander Romance* see Whitmarsh 2013, 86–100. This is by no means exhaustive, and all contain further valuable bibliography. For a succinct overview see Jones 2017.

By contrast, Latin fictional letters exist in more of a grey area. There are few Latin equivalents for the extensive corpora of Greek pseudonymous letters in the imperial period, with the important exceptions of the letter-exchange ascribed to Seneca and Paul and the pseudonymous letters of Pseudo-Brutus, which are discussed by Janja Soldo and Kathryn Tempest respectively in this volume. Although collections of invented letters are extant in Latin, they are frequently written in verse which challenges attempts to fit them into this teleological model of the epistolary novel.[29] For example, although Ovid's *Heroides* have been shown to be a highly influential ancestor of early modern European novels in letters,[30] they have generally been marginalised from discussions of ancient epistolary fiction due to being too well-discussed elsewhere in scholarship and too poetic to fit the novelistic model.[31] The relative paucity of pseudonymous letters and the increased proportion of verse letters means that by comparison to Greek letters, Latin prose epistolography is more commonly seen as authentic. This is not to say that such letters are believed to be documentary texts, but rather that their more straightforward relationship with authorship and historical context enables a more nuanced spectrum of historicity and fiction. In other words, whereas the ascription of Greek letter collections to a famous author is generally interpreted as a sign of its pseudonymity, Latin letters associated with a well-known author, as the letters of Cicero, Seneca, and Fronto demonstrate, are seen primarily through the lens of authenticity even when the letters are highly literary. Consequently, the label of fictional or, more commonly, literary letters in reference to Latin texts often indicates a more blurred spectrum of rhetorical stylisation and fictionalisation rather than a generic distinction between invented and documentary collections. This continuum of history and fiction, however, also invokes issues of its own, epitomised by Erik Gunderson's question, 'when is a letter literary and hence susceptible to literary analysis?'[32] While this overview is far from

---

29 Notably Horace's *Letters* and Propertius 4.3: on these see the seminal commentaries of Rudd 1989 and Mayer 1994 on Horace and Hutchinson 2006 and Fedeli/Dimundo/Ciccarelli 2015 on Propertius. Freudenberg 2009 is a collection of valuable contributions to Horatian scholarship on the *Letters*: see also Fantham 2013 and Günther 2013. See also the discussions of Gibson and Edwards in this volume. For an overview see Edwards 2005, 274–277; Ebbeler 2010; Salzman 2017, 29–30, although they do not focus specifically on the fictive aspects of poetic Latin letters.
30 As Brownlee 1990 demonstrates.
31 See the wider survey of Hodkinson/Drago 2023b, 1–4. Gibson/Morrison 2007, 4–9 note that various Greek poems were traditionally seen as letters, and note the porousness of these definitions.
32 Gunderson 2007, 4.

universal or rigid,³³ the segregation of inauthentic and documentary letters has facilitated the perception that epistolary fiction is a genre strongly associated with Greek letter collections, whereas Latin literary letters, despite aspects of fictionalisation, are assumed to fall somewhere on a scale of historicity.³⁴

Contemporary approaches to early modern epistolary writing, however, challenge these neat narratives. Epistolary fiction has gained a reputation of being an especially intimate form of writing which allows audiences unfiltered, if not voyeuristic, insight into the private experiences of the purported letter-writer. This view is both enabled and perpetuated by the stereotype that letters are romantic in nature and feminine in character. As Gilroy and Verhoeven put it, 'the most historically powerful fiction of the letter has been that which figures it as the trope of authenticity and intimacy, which elides questions of linguistic, historical, and political mediation, and which construes the letter as feminine.'³⁵ As a result of this reading, novels such as Samuel Richardson's *Pamela* and Frances Burney's *Evelina* have become paradigmatic of epistolary fiction as domestic, private, and female. Yet, as Mary Favret has shown, women in the eighteenth-century moved beyond this 'fiction of letters' to use epistolary writing for political, even revolutionary purposes.³⁶ Thomas Beebee has argued even that epistolary fiction should not been seen as part of the genealogical development of the novel, but rather 'such fiction can be found everywhere, and not just in texts aimed specifically at aesthetic consumption.'³⁷ If ancient epistolary fiction cannot be reduced to simply a generic category or a spectrum of historicity or a by-word for literary stylisation or a precursor to the teleological development of the epistolary novel, how should it be understood? What is at stake in these fictions of authenticity and genre?

The limitations of such approaches to epistolary fiction can be seen in the case of the Platonic *Epistles*, a pseudepigraphic collection ascribed to the eponymous philosopher. The letters describe Plato's journeys to Sicily and relationship with the tyrant Dionysius II, a period of his life tantalisingly unexamined by

---

33 This is not to overlook the various collections dedicated to both Latin and Greek letters, such as Morello/Morrison 2007a and Hodkinson/Drago 2023a, but rather to point out general trends visible across scholarship as a whole. This division is also noted by Hodkinson/Drago 2023b, 3–4.
34 Noted by Nilsson 2023, 30.
35 Gilroy/Verhoeven 2000, 1. On the association of epistolarity with the female voice, see the foundational works of Kauffman 1986 and the essays in Goldsmith 1989.
36 Favret 1993. This fiction of intimacy has been noted in regard to ancient texts, epitomised by Whitmarsh's claim that 'letters both embody the novelistic fiction of access to a hidden world and deconstruct it by exposing its very fictionality' (Whitmarsh 2013, 87).
37 Beebee 1999, 3.

either his own philosophical writings or ancient biographical traditions. Yet, while they offer an autobiographical perspective unparalleled in the Platonic corpus, they in fact offer little in the way of coherent philosophy. Given the long-held Socratic bias towards written philosophy, moreover, the very existence of the letters risks negating their value as Platonic philosophical texts. Debates over the authenticity of the Platonic letters have dominated scholarship, although the current consensus tends towards treating the collection as broadly invented. Cicero's apparent acceptance of the collection as authentic,[38] however, gives us both a *terminus ante quem* for their otherwise debatable dating and also a challenge to this view. If modern scholarship wishes to see the *Epistles* as fictional, their circulation in the Late Republic without any obvious pseudepigraphic predecessors challenges what this means if they cannot be contextualised amongst imperial epistolography.[39] The *Epistles*, however, cannot so easily be dismissed as mere forgeries either, as the letters repeatedly exploit the paradox of their conceit to be Platonic writings in such a way as to thematise their own inauthenticity.[40] As such, the Platonic *Epistles* unsettle these comfortable assumptions of a clearly demarcated category of epistolary fiction, and raise wider questions about what is at stake in such a seemingly innocuous label.

The Platonic letters also, however, raise the question of whether contemporary readers were as preoccupied with the question of authenticity as modern scholars. If this collection can openly flout its inauthenticity while simultaneously being cited as the authoritative voice of its supposed author, would fiction have been an important consideration for ancient audiences? The case-study of Pliny's letters offers a clear example of how the author recognised and exploited this tightrope between authenticity and fiction. In the first letter of the collection, Pliny rejects a chronological ordering of his letters in favour of an (allegedly) random arrangement and explicitly distances himself from historiographical

---

38 McConnell 2014, 36–37, especially n. 14–15. While McConnell rightly notes that Cicero is the earliest testimony we have to the *Epistles*, there is little other evidence to suggest that they were believed to be inauthentic in antiquity. Both Aristophanes of Byzantium (third century BCE) and Thrasyllus (first century CE) include the *Epistles* in their collections of Platonic works, and Diogenes Laertius makes reference to the thirteen letters of the *Epistles*, which suggests that Thrasyllus knew the letters of the collection as we have them today (3.61). For more on this, see Wohl 1998, 87 n. 1.
39 Although the dating of all such collections is difficult to ascertain definitively, no extant pseudepigraphic letter collection has been suggested to predate the Platonic *Letters*.
40 Most fully demonstrated in Wohl 1998: see also Morrison 2013; 2014a; Jackson forthcoming a.

writing.⁴¹ This both establishes expectations of a certain liberty towards historical fact and biographical narrative, and also allows a certain degree of fictionalisation into his letters. Consequently, despite Pliny's claims that he will present each letter as it came to his hand (*ut quaeqe in manus uenerat*), ancient audiences would probably not have expected to read a straightforward account of his life or to get unadulterated access to his letters in their original form.⁴² Despite the long and often tedious debate about whether the letters are real or fictitious,⁴³ it is undeniable that the letters betray careful arrangement, literary sophistication, as well as Pliny's pervading interest in self-fashioning alongside discussion of historical events and identifiable figures, as recent scholarship has shown.⁴⁴ In other words, as the contributions of Gibson and Barbiero to this volume explore in more detail, fiction is a central concern of Pliny's letters not despite its autobiographical focus and historiographic detail but because of them. Even if concerns about authenticity are disregarded as a modern affectation, therefore, the framing of Pliny's epistolary corpus invites active consideration of the relationship between truth and falsehood, history and fiction.

These two collections, therefore – one Greek and one Latin, one marked historically by questions of inauthenticity and one whose authorship is in no way disputed – individually raise questions about fiction, verisimilitude, and authenticity which cannot be reduced to a generic lens. On the contrary, both works testify to at least some level of awareness of fiction even in antiquity, and suggest that ancient writers were more than capable of exploiting issues of invention and even forgery, not as generic categories but as part of the architecture of epistolary writing. This volume aims to explore the implications of such awareness of fiction in ancient epistolary texts, and to bring out the various facets of fiction which underlie epistolography beyond simply novelistic collections and stylised narratives.

But to what extent are such issues simply a consequence of reading letter collections as coherent and continuous narratives? While modern epistolary novels demonstrate how the exchange of letters can structure a lengthy plot, individual

---

41 *Ep.* 1.1: *frequenter hortatus es ut epistulas, si quas paulo curatius scripsissem, colligerem publicaremque. collegi non seruato temporis ordine (neque enim historiam componebam), sed ut quaeque in manus uenerat.*
42 On this phrase, see the more detailed discussion of Barbiero in this volume.
43 On which see Whitton 2013 and Gibson's contribution to this volume.
44 A good example is Pliny's portrayal of his uncle's reaction to the outbreak of Vesuvius which brings together the report of the disaster, the depiction of his uncle's Stoic demeanour and the message to his addressee Tacitus: on this see Marchesi 2008. On the literary qualities of the letters in general see also Ludolph 1997, the essays in Marchesi 2015b, Gibson/Morello 2012, and Gibson and Barbiero's contributions to this volume.

letters seen through this lens become inherently fragmentary snippets of a larger context. If so, however, what then is distinctive about epistolary fiction as opposed to other kinds of extended narrative? Letters are easy to recognise, after all, but notoriously hard to define.[45] Some of the earliest literary depictions of letters are characterised by their unconventional form and mode of transmission, and are not explicitly labelled as letters. Most famously, Bellerophon's letter in *Iliad* 6 is described simply as mournful signs (σήματα λυγρά, *Il.* 6.168) enclosed in a folding tablet, and Herodotean letters are transmitted secretly by being tattooed on the body of their messenger.[46] In these cases the format of the message is directly connected to the secrecy of its contents, but it nonetheless demonstrates the difficulty of formally defining epistolary texts between documentary letters, literary depictions, and the diversity visible amongst ancient letter collections. Despite the number of ancient handbooks theorising letter-writing still extant, within these manuals there is little explicit definition of a letter, much less a fictional letter.[47] Instead, the handbooks are more focused on categorising different types of letters according to their function, and do not distinguish between documentary or invented examples of these various typologies. Even though a writer must know what a good letter is in order to write one, as Libanius concedes, such knowledge must be acquired through experience and examples rather than theoretical reflection (*De forma epistolari* 1). As such, it might be easy to conclude that the distinction between fictional and documentary letters was not important to ancient audiences, since epistolary theorists working across a range of time periods and literary contexts do not explicitly discuss or even acknowledge this distinction.

A closer examination of such handbooks, however, reveals a pervasive view that ancient letters were felt to have a fictionalised component. This is clearest in the recurrent claim that letters should represent half of a dialogue (Demetrius *Eloc.* 223–224):[48]

---

[45] On definitions of letters, see Trapp 2003, 1–5; Gibson/Morrison 2007, all of whom acknowledge the difficulties involved in crafting an inclusive definition.
[46] For example, Hdt. 5.35.3 and 1.123.3–4, where the letter is hidden in the body of a hare. On this see Steiner 1994, 127–185, especially 150–151, and Bowie 2013. Compare also the secretive communications at Hdt. 7.239.3–4 (writing hidden underneath the wax of a tablet), 8.128.1–3 (letters attached to arrows and fired to an agreed location).
[47] Malherbe 1988 collects the most prominent examples of these texts. See also Trapp 2003, 42–46 and Poster 2007.
[48] Text and translation taken from Innes 1995. See also Cic. *Fam.* 12.30.1.

Ἀρτέμων μὲν οὖν ὁ τὰς Ἀριστοτέλους ἀναγράψας ἐπιστολάς φησιν, ὅτι δεῖ ἐν τῷ αὐτῷ τρόπῳ διάλογόν τε γράφειν καὶ ἐπιστολάς· εἶναι γὰρ τὴν ἐπιστολὴν οἷον τὸ ἕτερον μέρος τοῦ διαλόγου. καὶ λέγει μέν τι ἴσως, οὐ μὴν ἅπαν· δεῖ γὰρ ὑποκατεσκευάσθαι πως μᾶλλον τοῦ διαλόγου τὴν ἐπιστολήν· ὁ μὲν γὰρ μιμεῖται αὐτοσχεδιάζοντα, ἡ δὲ γράφεται καὶ δῶρον πέμπεται τρόπον τινά.

Artemon, the editor of Aristotle's *Letters*, says that a letter should be written in the same manner as a dialogue, the letter, he says, is like one of the two sides to a dialogue. There is perhaps some truth in what he says, but not the whole truth. The letter should be a little more formal than the dialogue, since the latter imitates improvised conversation, while the former is written and sent as a kind of gift.

This statement, from likely one of the earliest extant considerations of the theory of letter-writing,[49] exposes the central fictional conceit of letters. The analogy with dialogue frames the exchange of letters as a direct and unfiltered conversation between author and addressee. Yet, as Demetrius admits, the written format of letters undercuts this dialogic conceit, as the very nature of epistolary documents is predicated on the interlocutors' separation and dependence upon texts to mediate their conversation.[50] The treatise goes on to argue that letters essentially reflect the soul of their author, since letters reveal their writer's character more than any other kind of speech (227: σχεδὸν γὰρ εἰκόνα ἕκαστος τῆς ἑαυτοῦ ψυχῆς γράφει τὴν ἐπιστολήν. καὶ ἔστι μὲν καὶ ἐξ ἄλλου λόγου παντὸς ἰδεῖν τὸ ἦθος τοῦ γράφοντος, ἐξ οὐδενὸς δὲ οὕτως, ὡς ἐπιστολῆς).[51] Although this claim makes clear letters' potential to sustain personal intimacy, the description of the letter as an image (εἰκών) foregrounds its status as an artificial representation rather than a window to the reality of the writer's character. While such claims seemingly naturalise letters as straightforward vehicles of their authors' character and relationships, in practice they highlight the artificiality inherent to epistolography, whether individual letters are characterised as authentic or not.

The relationship between the theory and practice of ancient epistolography is far from straightforward, and it is not clear to what extent these handbooks reflect actual epistolary practice rather than an idealised and unattainable view of it.[52] But if we take the conversational and representational nature of letters

---

49 On the question of dating see Innes 1995, 310–319; Malherbe 1988, 2.
50 In a later part of *On Style*, Demetrius even claims that attempts to imitate a conversational tone, such as in Platonic dialogues, are not appropriate to letters as written rather than oral texts (*Eloc.* 226). On this tension in epistolography see Altman 1982, especially the summary at 185–190.
51 See also Sen. *Ep.* 40.1; Cic. *Fam.* 16.16.2.
52 Noted by Sogno/Storin/Watts 2017b, 2. In particular, the relationship between the extant letter collections and these epistolary handbooks is complicated by the issue of relative dating, as examples of both are difficult to date with any accuracy.

seriously, we have to acknowledge that fiction is at least to some extent woven into the structure of ancient epistolography, although this cannot be understood purely in generic terms. While ancient epistolary theorists do not explicitly tackle questions of fiction in these handbooks, the focus both there and in the writings of other epistolographers on typologies of letters as opposed to their authenticity testifies to the difficulties of categorising epistolary texts. These classifications overlap in various ways, but individual authors differ on exactly how many categories of letter there are, from Cicero's two, public and private,[53] to Libanius' forty-one, including letters of thanksgiving, recommendation, accusation, and more.[54] These different approaches even in antiquity make visible the extent to which letters problematise issues of genre. While genre is of course a fluid rather than immutable concept for both ancient and modern texts, letters are particularly visible as a format which has been adopted for all kinds of writing, from philosophical treatises to political administration to theological disputes to domestic intimacy. In Jacques Derrida's famous definition, the letter is 'not a genre but all genres, literature itself.'[55] Yet, the specific nature of letters as a format means that genre is far from the only way to categorise them. As the typologies found in ancient epistolary handbooks demonstrate, while Libanius, among others, distinguishes letters based on their function, Cicero does so based on their intended audience. Modern scholars have also offered a variety of ways to classify epistolary collections, including whether they are written in poetry or prose, Greek or Latin, or whether they were composed in the classical period, broadly defined, or Late Antiquity.[56] This sheer variety of ways to categorise letters testifies to their capacity to cross between different conceptual categories and to invite reassessment of such binaries. In other words, letters are uniquely well-placed to unsettle disciplinary boundaries of fact and fiction, authentic and spurious.

This is further complicated by the role of the editor in ancient letter collections. Although epistolary taxonomies such as Cicero's detailed above categorise letters based on their intended audience, identifying authorial intention in ancient epistolography is a particularly thorny issue, not least due to the lack of

---

[53] Cic. *Pro Flacco* 37.
[54] Surveyed at Malherbe 1988, 12–13.
[55] Derrida 1987, 48.
[56] While these periodisations are inherently arbitrary, a particular difficulty emerges with the advent of Christian letters, in part due to the sheer size of the corpus of, for example, papal letters, and the additional complexities of theological and doctrinal issues surrounding forgery and fiction. On Late Antique letters see Allen/Neil 2020 and Sogno/Storin/Watts 2017a; the essays in Riehle 2020 on Byzantine letters; and those in Høgel/Bartoli 2015 on medieval letters.

formal features distinguishing public from private letters.[57] Whereas we know that Pliny published his own letters and as such exercised total control over his epistolary output, the existence of most other letter collections is due to the providential decisions of a third party, if not parties, to publish correspondence which they may neither have written nor been the direct recipient of. These editors remain largely anonymous, but their impact on the content, form, and reception of ancient letter collections cannot be overstated. By selecting and arranging the letters, these anonymous compilers offer different versions of the narratives implied by the juxtaposition of individual letters, with repercussions for the collection's chronology, cohesion, and the character of its supposed author.[58] As Andrew Morrison has demonstrated, the various different collections of Plato's *Epistles* construct different versions of the philosopher's life by including or excluding particular letters, or even reordering them entirely.[59] The idea that Cicero's letters were edited for publication by his slave and later freedman Tiro has proved irresistible to many scholars, although Cammoranesi's contribution to this volume demonstrates how the *Ad Familiares* have been shaped by a variety of competing editorial agendas.[60] This is even visible in pseudonymous collections. While references to letters missing from the collection ascribed to Chion of Heraclea have been interpreted as an authenticating gesture,[61] given the work's self-consciousness about its inauthenticity throughout it also draws attention to the artificiality of the collection's ordering and narrative.[62] Such editorial interventions or allusions to them, therefore, have the potential to construct new narratives and authorial personae for the collections' purported or actual authors, and add another layer of fiction to an already self-consciously fictionalising form. What then does it mean to label a collection as fictional when perceptions of its truth or falsehood might be manipulated throughout its transmission by the many editors and audiences which reorder it?

---

[57] For example, Seneca's *Moral Epistles*, while addressed to Lucilius, seem to be clearly written with a wider readership in mind (cf. e.g. *Ep.* 8.2; 21). Sogno/Storin/Watts 2017b, especially 3, for example, repeatedly reference authorial intention as key to their definition of letters and their ordering of their volume. On formal features of letter-writing in antiquity, see Ceccarelli 2013, Sarri 2017, and the overview of Trapp 2003, 6–11.
[58] As Gibson 2012 demonstrates, chronology is not the primary motivation behind ancient Latin collections, although it becomes more important for later editors, as Shackleton Bailey's famous edition of Cicero's letters shows. On this see Cammoranesi in this volume.
[59] Morrison 2013.
[60] See also Martelli forthcoming.
[61] Hodkinson 2019; Rosenmeyer 2001, 239.
[62] As argued in more detail by Jackson forthcoming a.

As such, the terminology of fictional letters, while not inaccurate, risks eliding the complexities of the diverse corpora of ancient epistolography. Rather than offering a neat opposition between forgery or genuine letters, this overview suggests that the concept of ancient epistolary fiction as a distinct genre raises more questions than it answers. The value of such approaches was recently reaffirmed with the acknowledgement that a broad definition of epistolary collections is necessary in order to 'nonetheless resist dilution into meaninglessness.'[63] This volume intends to demonstrate that considering fiction as a facet of all letters aside from generic concerns is neither meaningless nor pointlessly provocative. After all, questions of authenticity are indeed significant to ancient readers, particularly in the example of Christian theological letters, where authors face allegations of deceit when these letters are classified as pseudepigraphic.[64] Yet, given letters' potential to cross boundaries and unsettle binaries, from private to public, literary to historical, we contend that this also includes perceptions of authenticity, invention, truth, and fiction. As we have seen, ancient theorists acknowledge the fiction of epistolary writing, which even in the most unimpeachably authentic example involves the conceit that they can conjure a dialogue between absent interlocutors, writing in a present form to be read as an artefact of the past by a future reader.[65] Questions about fiction are thereby implicated in the very format of letters, which are then compounded by how they are arranged and embedded in a collection, the literary paradigms or genres against which they are framed, and the contexts of their reception across a variety of time periods beyond their date of composition. This volume argues that fiction is an inherent and fluid property of letters which ancient writers recognised and exploited, and that appreciating the unique dynamics of epistolary fiction opens up productive ways to understand the breadth and diversity of ancient epistolography holistically. To put it simply, what is at stake in defining letters as fictional or not, and how does this help us understand the nature of these texts themselves?

This volume attempts to tackle these questions directly to interrogate the utility of fictional letters as a category for understanding ancient epistolography. Our approach aims to be as broad as possible to reflect the diversity of letters extant from classical antiquity, crossing Greek and Latin, poetry and prose, and the increasingly blurry boundaries between the Roman imperial period and Late Antiquity. Yet, given the fact that scholarship on fiction in epistolary collections from antiquity has tended to prioritise Greek works due to their perceived

---

63 Sogno/Storin/Watts 2017b, 1.
64 Key here is Ehrmann 2013. See also Allen/Neil 2020, 62–64 on forgery and Van Hoof 2016.
65 For more on this see Morello's contribution to this volume.

proximity to a coherent generic category of epistolary fiction, this volume gives particular space to Latin collections which have not traditionally been seen through this lens. As already discussed, many of the texts most easily labelled as fiction have already been the subject of scholarly attention, and while more remains to be said about many Greek pseudonymous collections, this volume aims to tackle texts and topics traditionally excluded from such academic narratives. As such, the contributions to this volume discuss texts frequently dismissed only as spurious, works considered as fiction without consideration of the implications of such a label, and in particular Latin collections often prized for their historical value and whose fictionality has long been downplayed. By doing so we aim to offer a diversity of readings which respect the individual nuances of context and content while simultaneously dramatising different methodological approaches to the nebulous and broadly-defined landscape of ancient epistolary fiction.

While our nine papers which begin (Gibson) and end (Barbiero) with Pliny's *Epistles* might, together with this introduction, suggest an analogy with the ten books of Pliny's correspondence, the volume is structured in four thematic sections in order to showcase the wider variety of ancient epistolography. The first, **(Auto)Biographical Fictions**, explores the relationship between biographical writings and epistolary formats, and how this form exposes and exploits concerns about fiction. Roy Gibson opens the volume by throwing down the gauntlet to a long-vexed question, namely the tension between biographical fact and literary artistry in Pliny's letters. Different letter collections, Gibson argues, require different strategies to interpret their approach to truth and fiction, and this chapter offers a fresh perspective on this old issue by placing Pliny in dialogue with his Augustan poetic predecessors. In adopting the format of the Augustan poetry book, whose authors so thoroughly problematised the tensions between biographical details and literary fictions, Gibson shows not just how Pliny's collection negotiates these issues, but also how these questions resonate throughout the diverse corpus of ancient epistolography. From there, Claire Rachel Jackson looks at the pseudonymous *Letters* attributed to Euripides, which play with the diverse biographical traditions surrounding the poet in antiquity. As a collection which offers a strikingly idiosyncratic approach to the playwright's life and is the only biographical source to adopt an epistolary format, the work offers a unique insight into the relationship between biography, epistolarity, and fiction. Jackson argues that the Euripidean *Letters* expose the limitations of the terminology of fictional letters and invites us to consider what is at stake in such labels. Finally, Catharine Edwards explores the ways in which Ovid's exile poetry draws attention to the materiality of the letter as a communicative artefact, and how this invites awareness of the fictions underlying the collection. Central to Edwards' argument is the absence of the author, which not only reflects Ovid's exile in the remote area of Tomis, but also justifies the use of letters as a vehicle for the exilic poetry. In this way, as Edwards shows, regardless of the exact details of Ovid's exile, the poems exploit the paradoxes inherent in epistolary fiction as a format rooted in a physical object which relies on the absence of their sender.

The second, **Editorial Fictions**, considers the fictions of authenticity which surrounded collections believed to be genuine, and how this is affected by the vested interests of later readers and editors in the identity of the author and the narratives of the collection. Michael Trapp starts with a single letter, the prefatory letter appended to the writings of Epictetus attributed to Arrian, and explores the scholarly fictions that have been constructed to explain its composition and role. Taking this one letter, Trapp builds outwards to explore how scholarly priorities about authorship and authority, authenticity and fiction, necessitate different 'speculative hypotheses' in order to naturalise the letter's fictional potential. These different critical approaches, as Trapp demonstrates, respond to the ways in which the letter itself invites and frustrates such readings. Although this is just one letter, Trapp argues, the letter is not exceptional in its epistolarity, but is instead a paradigm of it. Picking up on Trapp's discussion of the role of the editor in crafting and sustaining the fictions surrounding the letter, Serena Cammoranesi explores the tension between the documentary qualities of the individual letters of Cicero's *Ad Familiares* and the different fictions their editors have shaped them into. As Cammoranesi persuasively shows, the organisational principles that different editors have used to order the letters within individual books and across the work as a whole create new fictionalised narratives with the historical events recounted in Cicero's letters. Cammoranesi, therefore, offers a significant corrective to simplistic oppositions between fictional and documentary letters by making visible the often-invisible role of the later, largely anonymous, editors of Cicero's collection. In doing so, her work invites awareness of and reflection on modern scholars' own vested interests in reading letter-collections through our own priorities, and how different orders and contexts generate and sustain different narratives.

The third, **Pseudepigraphic Fictions**, tackles invented correspondence and questions about forgery, authenticity, and fiction most directly. Kathryn Tempest takes the letters attributed to Brutus as a case-study in order to explore what is at stake in viewing these works as pseudepigrapha, and how they fit into the wider traditions surrounding Brutus' afterlife in antiquity. While Tempest does make a convincing argument against the authenticity of the letters, this is not the central point of her argument. Tempest neatly deconstructs the paradox at the heart of pseudepigraphic fiction, namely all the markers which can be used to canonise or legitimise a work become aspirational standards for forgers attempting to deceive their audiences. In other words, rather than viewing the letters attributed to Brutus solely through the lens of truth or fiction, Tempest considers exactly what role the letters play in an imperial context and what is at stake in the label of pseudepigraphic fiction. Next, Janja Soldo considers the only Latin pseudepigraphic collection found in classical antiquity, the letters claimed to have been exchanged by Seneca and Paul. As Soldo argues, while the letters cannot be genuine, they position themselves against Seneca's *Epistulae Morales* and exploit the silences and omissions in Seneca's own experiences with imperial power and philosophical dialogue. Soldo shows convincingly that the collection functions not as an incompetent attempt at forgery, but as a commentary on such pseudepigraphic letter-collections, and exposes the potential rewards and pitfalls of such fictional constructions.

The fourth and final section, **Ekphrastic Fictions**, considers the visual, sensory, and temporal aspects of epistolary writing, and how they construct and sustain immersive scenarios within the fiction of the letter. Ruth Morello looks at the ways in which the historical documents which make up Cicero's *Ad Familiares* are tinged throughout with fictionalising 'colour'. As Morello argues, the use of literary paradigms and philosophical models which overlay the descriptions found in the letters offer insight into Cicero's subjective experiences of the events he describes, and heightens the potential for unreality and awareness of fiction within the collection. A theme which runs throughout Morello's chapter is the temporal importance of such epistolary descriptions, where the letter's ability to be situated in a specific and contested historic moment while imagining a variety of possible outcomes entwines fictional futures into Cicero's political forecasts. Fictionalising motifs, in Morello's argument, are not alien to the documentary qualities of the letters, but are instead central to them, as they act as a political strategy which allows Cicero to reflect upon the turbulent nature of his current situation. Finally, Emilia Barbiero's contribution returns to the questions with which the volume opened about literature and history, fact and fiction, in Pliny's correspondence. Barbiero explores the ways in which Pliny's letters adopt ekphrastic strategies to both encourage a sensory, immersive reading but also challenge the different levels of reality inherent in such detailed descriptions. In this way, as Barbiero suggests, such ekphrastic epistles meditate on the ontological problems which reverberate throughout the collection as a whole, and opens up new ways of understanding the literariness of Pliny's collection. In her closing comments, Barbiero provocatively challenges the dichotomy of authenticity and forgery and proposes to reframe this as a 'productive paradox', a model which epitomises the questions at the heart of this volume.

These sections are neither discrete nor comprehensive: this is neither an exhaustive checklist of markers of epistolary fiction nor does it cover the entirety of ancient fictional letters. What it does do, however, is offer a series of paradigmatic snapshots which open up new ways of thinking about epistolary fiction without resorting to either generic assumptions or binary oppositions. As such, we have actively attempted to juxtapose collections which may seem at first glance to have little in common with each other in terms of language, chronology, or function, such as Cicero's *Ad Familiares* with Epictetus' prefatory letter, or Pliny's letters with the pseudonymous *Letters* of Euripides. Similarly, the inclusion of Ciceronian and Plinian collections may seem like an odd choice for a volume on fictional epistolography given the amount of scholarly ink spilled on their value as historical documents. But this, we suggest, demonstrates our point. As we have argued already, fiction is an inherent quality of letter-writing by virtue of its central conceit of representing a conversation at a distance. What we are interested in here is how ancient authors not only recognise this fictional potential but also manipulate it. Consequently, this volume does not offer a comprehensive or unified definition of fiction, as the nebulous nature of the term both in antiquity and modern scholarship renders any attempt to do so inadequate. Instead, by exploring the variety of nuances of fictional letters demonstrated throughout the ancient corpus of letters, we aim to show not only that fiction is an intrinsic feature of ancient letters which their writers understood and consciously used, but also that a more nuanced approach to fiction helps us to understand the vast corpus of ancient letters more holistically.

Part I: **(Auto)Biographical Fictions**

Roy K. Gibson
Fact and Fiction in Pliny's *Epistles*: The Augustan Poetry Book and its Legacies

Abstract: Pliny stands at the intersection between epistolary (biographical) fiction and fact. He is routinely studied by two academic constituencies whose critical assumptions do not necessarily align: ancient historians and literary critics. Statements about biographical fiction in Pliny often proceed from unargued assumptions about 'how literature works' — assumptions generally derived from study of the Augustan poets. I argue that assumptions about autobiographical fiction in Ovid cannot simply be transferred to Pliny. We need to construct individual theories for individual authors, working from the text up to personalized theory, rather than from generalized theory down to text. The Augustan poetry book is central to the development of Latin letter collections (in sharp contrast to the lack of influence from poetry books on the Greek epistolographical tradition). But the poetics of the two Roman forms are fundamentally different. In Ovid's *Amores*, the signifier is centripetal and returns to reflect on its own programmatic status within a collection; but Pliny's letters are centrifugal and generally move outwards from internal signifier to external signified. Prospects for reading events in Pliny's life as primarily instantiations of a literary programme are diminished.

Keywords: Pliny the Younger, letters, biography, fiction, Ovid, Augustan poetry book

In their prospectus for this volume, the editors suggest that 'letters are uniquely well-placed to unsettle disciplinary boundaries of fact and fiction, authentic and spurious', and that it is one of the volume's key insights that 'fiction is an inherent and fluid property of letters which ancient writers recognised and exploited'. Pliny stands right at the intersection between epistolary (biographical) fiction and fact. He is routinely studied by two academic constituencies whose interests and critical assumptions do not (routinely) align: ancient historians

---

I would particularly like to thank Claire Rachel Jackson and Janja Soldo for guidance during the writing of this paper, as well as the audience in Cambridge in 2019, Chris Whitton, Aaron Pelttari, and Johanna Hanink: none should be presumed to agree with its arguments.

and literary critics.[1] If political historians soberly regard *Ep.* 2.1 on the funeral of Verginius Rufus as evidence and context for understanding Nerva's gerontocracy and an averted civil war in 97 CE,[2] literary critics are likely to be distracted by textual allusions to Tacitus' *Agricola* and the *Laelius de amicitia* of Cicero.[3] Divergent conclusions on the nature and significance of the text might follow — pointing to a much larger problem. In the *Cambridge Critical Guide to Latin Literature* (2023), Myles Lavan warns that the broader relationship between literary and historical studies is under threat: 'I think Latinists ought to be worried by the degree of disinterest [*sc.* in their work by historians], which sometimes borders on alienation'. Transformational work on the rhetoricity and literary texture of ancient historians (as on Pliny's letters) risks not being provocative, in Lavan's estimation, but rather evading 'complex questions about the relationship between historiography and history'.[4] What is the value of a text that draws attention to its insistent and sophisticated interplay with other texts? Do truth and meaning reside in intertextuality or in the historical event that the text narrates? Is the latter merely pretext and opportunity for the free play of the former? What then is our understanding of the nature and quality of the narration of the event? To what extent has 'fact' undergone fictionalization beneath the pressure of the literary (however we define that)?

The present chapter looks only at one author, but it does offer an argument of wider significance. Statements about biographical fact and fiction in Pliny often proceed from unstated or unargued assumptions about 'how literature works' — assumptions often derived, in the case of Latin literature, from study of the Augustan poets. Despite clear resemblances between Pliny and the Augustan poets — not least in a shared dedication to the artistic possibilities afforded by a series of single papyrus rolls — I argue that assumptions about autobiographical fiction in Ovid cannot simply be transferred to Pliny. We need to construct individual theories for individual authors, working from the text up to

---

[1] On these two constituencies, see Gibson/Morello 2012, 5; Woolf 2015; Whitton/Gibson 2016, esp. 19–47; Whitton 2019, 37–38.

[2] Syme 1991, 518–519.

[3] Whitton 2013, 65; cf. Smith 2020, 132 arguing that 'ultimately Pliny's artistic, scripted portrait of his wife is largely, if not entirely, a simulacrum. Removing the biographical narrative, it becomes evident that Pliny does not blend the role of husband and lover so much as he, as an author, blends elegy and an elegiac effigy of a woman named Calpurnia into his epistles. I do not intend to suggest that Pliny has wholly invented Calpurnia'.

[4] Lavan 2023 goes on to argue that Latinists can find more common ground with their historian colleagues by taking an interest in the kinds of non-literary texts where skills of close reading remain in demand (inscriptions, the juristic corpora, documentary letters).

personalized theory, rather than from generalized theory down to text. Different texts by different authors establish relations with 'fact' and 'fiction' in different ways and to different degrees. Generalisations about literature (including this one) must be replaced with nuanced individual studies of epistolography in action. Pliny is not Seneca nor Symmachus nor St Paul: each letter-writer requires an individualised grammar; each author generates a different compact of expectations for negotiation with their readers.[5]

1 The disciplinary context: Oxford in the 60s vs Paris in the 20s

Fact and fiction have a long modern history in the study of Pliny. Anne-Marie Guillemin (1868–1963) earned her docteur ès lettres from the Université de Dijon in 1921, and in 1927–8 published a three-volume edition of Books 1–9 of Pliny's letters for the prestigious Budé series of text and translations. Her Latin text was not a critical success,[6] but a combination of translation, notes and affordability ensured that the edition remained long in print. Rather more successful was Guillemin's monograph *Pline et la vie littéraire de son temps*, published in Paris in 1929. This study, in the overview of Chris Whitton, aimed 'to set the *Epistles* in a cultural and intellectual context, with a particular eye to Pliny's "literary influences", in which ... poetry features prominently. Guillemin's arguments ... did not convince all (especially more "historically" minded readers), but they are a signal precursor of interests in recent decades, both specifically in intertextuality (as we now call it) and more broadly in the implicit claim that the *Epistles* merit intensive literary study'.[7]

Although nearly four decades and one world war separate Guillemin's monograph from the publication of Sherwin-White's magisterial commentary on Pliny in 1966, the work had clearly found a place under the Oxford commentator's skin. Sherwin-White subtitled his work 'A Historical and Social Commentary'

---

5 The letter collections of the New Testament perhaps stand in most urgent need of an individualized theory in relation to a cognate area: authenticity and forgery. Ehrman 2013 argues that fourteen out of twenty-one epistles in the New Testament are either forgeries or falsely ascribed to their named authors. On Seneca and Paul's forged correspondence see Soldo in this volume.
6 See Carlsson 1929. An edition of Book 10 and the *Panegyricus* followed in 1947; for the critical context, see Whitton and Gibson 2016, 14–16.
7 Whitton ap. Whitton and Gibson 2016, 16.

on the *Letters*. This was in part a response to Guillemin's avowedly 'literary' project, and he took time in his Introduction to formulate his rejection of the implications of her work and its threat to the foundation of his commentary:[8]

> Pliny certainly writes under strong literary influences... These influences are not generally the subject of this commentary. But Guillemin, in *Pline et la vie littéraire*, ch. iii, musters them for an attack on the truth and accuracy of the letters. Because Pliny writes in the language of his predecessors on themes of Statius or Martial, the whole thing is taken to be a fiction...

Guillemin's name appears over seventy times in the course of the commentary: many of the references are to her Budé edition of the letters and accompanying notes, and Sherwin-White is appropriately respectful or critical of her contributions. The monograph frequently provokes incomprehension and dismay; Sherwin-White is never (quite) discourteous, but his lack of sympathy for Guillemin's approach is plain.[9] Pliny's description of Trajan's new deep-water port at Centum Cellae (modern Civitavecchia) in *Ep.* 6.31 is cited by Sherwin-White as an 'extreme example' of Guillemin's approach:[10] 'Guillemin suggested unconvincingly (*VL* 118) that Pliny's description is a literary cliché without factual value, after the style of Vergil's description of Carthage (*Aen.* 1.159 ff.) used also by Livy (26.42.8) and Lucan (2.616–18). There are verbal echoes of Vergil (s. 16 n.), but the other parallels are not detailed'.[11] In fact Guillemin had merely observed that 'tous les ports "littéraires", en effet, sont identiques', adding 'le modèle copié par Pline est décelé par la resemblance des vocabulaires et des traits, et c'est l'imitation de Virgile que trahit cette resemblance'. The implication that Pliny is more interested in literary imitation than factual description is clear all the same.

Sherwin-White's attack on Guillemin was reprised in 2009–10 by the responses of Eckard Lefèvre and Keith Bradley to Ilaria Marchesi's landmark

---

8 Sherwin-White 1966, 16.
9 E.g. Sherwin-White 1966, 189 on *Ep.* 2.17.1: 'Guillemin, (*VL*, 145) abandons common sense in the hunt for stylization'; 1966, 359 on *Ep.* 6.4: 'she exaggerates the formality of the letters to Calpurnia, and their debt to Cicero'; 1966, 451 on *Ep.* 8.4.2: 'ignoring the precise details, Guillemin (*VL*, 143–4) unconvincingly regards this section as a literary commonplace based on such passages as Horace, *Ep.* 2.1.252–4'. Cf. the acute analysis of Whitton 2019, 38 n. 88, and see also Ma's brilliant 1994 "Black hunter variations" study of two approaches to Plutarch *Cimon* 1–2: a Vidal Naquet-style essay (in French) versus a 'historical commentary' (in English).
10 Sherwin-White 1966, 16.
11 Sherwin-White 1966, 396 on *Ep.* 6.31.15.

monograph, *The Art of Pliny's Letters* (2008).¹² For Lefèvre and Bradley, 'authenticity' tends to preclude sustained literary imitation. The argument has become, in the words of one commentator, 'persistent, and sterile'¹³ — but I am personally invested in it. In 2019 my long-time collaborator Chris Whitton¹⁴ published *The Arts of Imitation in Latin Prose: Pliny's Epistles / Quintilian in Brief*, while in 2020 I published *Man of High Empire: the Life of Pliny the Younger*. On the face of it, the books are doing two very different things. Whitton's book demonstrates — convincingly — that the letters are a work of minute and dense textual artistry; there is no letter of Pliny's, and hardly a paragraph within a letter, that lacks for a rich intertextual weave, encompassing authors from Homer to Tacitus. Two texts emerge as particularly significant, alongside Cicero: the *Institutio Oratoris* of Quintilian and the *Dialogus de Oratoribus* of Tacitus; Pliny keeps up a dialogue with the great optimist of and the great pessimist of Roman rhetorical theory and practice throughout his *Letters*. In *Man of High Empire*, I was trying to do something potentially different: to take the data of the letters and use them to write a biography of Pliny. The publisher did ask me (politely) if I could tone down the emphasis on the *Letters*, and concentrate on giving readers 'the facts', but I was forced to reply that it might be a bit tricky to do that, because the letters were — in a fundamental sense — 99% of the 'facts' we had. And we left it there.

Since I remain committed (yes) to the intellectual project of the recovery of a life from Pliny's letters, and regard Whitton's book as an epochal paradigm shift in our understanding of intertextuality in Latin prose, a question arises: how can a single text allow such two detailed but very different types of reading? The gap between the two books does not reprise Sherwin White vs Guillemin or Lefèvre and Bradley vs Marchesi, since I am not a historian, never deny the importance or reality of intertextual play in Pliny, and have even made careful efforts to make things worse, from the viewpoint of 'Sherwin Whiters'.¹⁵ Whitton never suggests that the vast web of literary play he has uncovered undermines the historicity of the letters.¹⁶ I will not surrender to the trope 'I can see a middle way here', much less participate in the Anglo-Saxon pragmatism of

---

12 Lefèvre 2009, 17–18; Bradley 2010.
13 Whitton 2013, 4–5.
14 Gibson/Whitton 2016; Whitton in Gibson/Morello 2022; Gibson/Whitton 2023.
15 E.g. Gibson/Steel 2010; Gibson 2011; Gibson/Morello 2012; Gibson forthcoming a; forthcoming b.
16 Dubbing the clash one between 'intertextualists' and 'epistoliteralists', Whitton 2019, 38 declares 'I want to fan the flames and yet to reconcile the two caucuses by arguing both for allusive (i.e. ludic) acuity but also for demonstrable influence'.

Sherwin-White's response to the Parisian threat posed by Guillemin: 'Pliny simply uses Virgilian language to describe what he saw with his own eyes'.[17] I want to see if we can achieve more precision in thinking about literature and history, fact and fiction in Pliny.

Key to achieving that precision is thinking harder about critical assumptions imported from Augustan poetry to the study of Pliny's letters. In what follows, I trace the lineage of Roman epistolography to the Augustan poetry book and look at the numerous resemblances between Pliny's letters and his poetic predecessors. This is not literary history for its own sake (although some patience is asked of the reader). It is precisely these parallels that are the ultimate — and unexamined — source of the assumption that aspects of Pliny's textual life, like that of Ovid or Propertius, are in some sense fictional. I argue that the poetics of Pliny's epistles are essentially different from those of Augustan poetry (being centrifugal rather than centripetal in tendency), but still leave considerable room for manoeuvre in a grey area between truth and falsehood.

2 Epistolography and the legacy of the Augustan poetry book

The ancient book unit plays a negligible role within the Greek epistolographical tradition. Despite the growing use of book units as a way of dividing up (and structuring) longer works from at least the Hellenistic era,[18] there is little evidence for their use within Greek epistolography before the collection of Alciphron in the early third century CE and of Libanius in the fourth. Most Greek letter collections prior to these eras are relatively short; but some are certainly long enough to have been amenable to division into books (for instance Plato). Nor do books become a mode of organization in the Greek epistolographical tradition in the era of Libanius and after: they are absent from the manuscript traditions of the often lengthy collections of Gregory of Nazianzus, Julian, Basil of Caeserea, Gregory of Nyssa, John Chrysostom, and Synesius.[19]

---

17 Sherwin-White 1966, 16.
18 Highbie 2010.
19 In Hellenistic poetry, the books of Apollonius Rhodius' epic average around 1700 lines (over twice the length of the Augustan poetry book), while those of Callimachus' *Aetia* appear to have been over 1000 lines (Stover 2022, 266 and 276.). If the huge poetry books of the Hellenistic era were the most recent and most prestigious available models for Greek epistolographers, it is perhaps no surprise that they felt no need to return to the model of the much shorter

No surviving Latin letter collection lacks the book unit as its basic building blocks until the eras of Cyprian, Jerome and Augustine; even then, letter-writers such as Ausonius, Symmachus, Ambrose and later Sidonius continue to use the book unit to structure their collections. Seen from this perspective, Horace and Ovid — far from being irritating or anomalous offshoots from the mainstream of Roman epistolography ('not real letters') — are the founding fathers of the Latin tradition. The Augustan poetry book, from the *Eclogues* to the *Amores* via the elegists and the *Odes* of Horace, evolved an ethic of symmetry, variety and non-linear narration within a unit of roughly 800 lines made up of shorter items of varying length and subject-matter.[20] It has often been remarked that Propertius Book 1 — with its elegies addressed to a series of male addressees (Tullius, Bassus, Ponticus, Gallus) — resembles a letter collection. Letter collections clearly circulated at Rome before Horace published the first book of his *Epistulae* c. 19 BCE; but the publication of this leading poet's letters in the prestigious format of the Augustan poetry book would be decisive for the history of Roman epistolography. This poetic work was joined by Ovid's *Epistulae Heroidum* (about whose original form we can say little since our text is heavily interpolated) and in due course by the four books of his *Epistulae ex Ponto* (before 16 CE). Both Horace and the *Ex Ponto* letters exhibit the symmetry, variety and non-chronological arrangement of letters that is also characteristic of the Augustan poetry book,[21]

Homeric book (Stover 2022, 276–277). A large series of letters might be accommodated without the need for book divisions.

20 Van Sickle 1980a remains a classic contribution on 'the book roll and some conventions of the poetic book'; cf. Van Sickle 1980b on the *Eclogues*. See further Blanck 1992, also the essays collected in Gutzwiller 2005 and in Hutchinson 2008, also Winsbury 2009 and Macedo 2021.

21 The first and penultimate letters of Horace' *Epistulae* address Maecenas (1.1, 1.19) and the second and antepenultimate address Lollius (1.2, 1.18). The pair 1.13 (about the delivery of Horace's *carmina*) and 1.20 (addressed to the *libellus* itself) frame the latter part of the collection; for brief analysis, see Mayer 1994, 48–51. Froesch 1968, 127–144 demonstrated that the letters of Ovid's *Ex Ponto* 1–3 are symmetrically positioned by addressee around a notional axis situated at 2.5–6. Four letters addressed to Cotta Maximus in *Pont.* 1 and 3 (1.5, 1.9 and 3.2, 3.5) are symmetrically placed around this axis, as are two pairs of letters in *Pont.* 2 addressed to Atticus (2.4, 2.7) and again to Cotta Maximus (2.3, 2.8). *Pont.* 1–3 as a whole is framed by letters addressing Brutus (1.1 and 3.9) and Fabius Maximus (1.2 and 3.8). (The authorial design for the heavily interpolated *Epistulae Heroidum* is beyond recovery; see Gibson 2018.) The discovery of such symmetries was also an invitation to critics to become insistently over-demanding in their search for the 'perfect poetry book': see Barchiesi 2005.

and would later be deployed in the epistolary books of Seneca[22] and particularly Pliny,[23] among others.

Why are the letter collections of Cicero not foundational for the Latin epistolographical tradition? For one thing, they were not published until the age of Tiberius at the earliest. The first probable reference to a letter found in a book from our *Ad Familiares* is made by the Elder Seneca (late 30s CE).[24] The first citation of the *Ad Atticum* clearly in public circulation is found in the *Epistulae Morales* of Seneca.[25] Remarkably, it can be shown that it was the Augustan poetry book that influenced the compilers of Cicero's correspondence in their editorial work, for not only did the editors borrow the techniques of the Augustan poetry book in terms of meaningful arrangement of items,[26] but, as Stover has recently shown, there appear to be strong links between the Augustan poetry book and the Ciceronian epistolographical book in terms of length.[27] The length of Cicero's philosophical books and particularly of his rhetorical books is significantly longer than that of the average Ciceronian epistolographical book, while the mean average length of the Ciceronian epistolographical book is not much longer than that of the average Augustan poetry book, and is close to that of the letter books of Seneca and Pliny.[28] In other words, the Ciceronian letter collections are transitional rather than foundational in the Latin epistolographical tradition.

---

[22] Although Seneca would prefer the chronological arrangement that is roughly maintained in Cicero's *Ad Atticum*. On Seneca as book-maker, see esp. Soldo 2021 on Sen. *Ep.* 2.
[23] See esp. the essays collected in Marchesi 2015b.
[24] Sen. *Suas.* 1.1.5: *eleganter in C. Cassi epistula quadam ad M. Ciceronem missa positum*, 'the point is neatly made in a letter of Cassius to Cicero' — followed by an inaccurate quotation of *Fam.* 15.9.4 (which some take as evidence of only indirect access to the letter).
[25] The earliest reference (e.g.) to an *Ad Atticum* collection is found in Nepos' *Life of Atticus* 16.2–4; but the relationship between Nepos' evidently unpublished eleven *uolumina* and the sixteen-book collection of the mss is unclear (Beard 2002, 119 n. 49, 127–128). Various allusions by Ovid to *Ad Atticum* letters have been proposed (e.g. *Att.* 3.5, Ov. *Tr.* 3.7.46–47), but the first certain references to items from the collection are found in Seneca's letters (97.3–6, 118.1–2; cf. 21.4).
[26] See Beard 2002 on *Fam.* Book 16; Grillo 2015 on Book 1; Grillo 2016 on Books 1 and 6; Martelli 2017 on Book 15; Wilcox 2022 on Book 9; Morello 2022 on Book 10; and Gibson 2022 on Book 4; cf. Whitton 2022 on the *Ad Brutum* collection.
[27] Stover 2022.
[28] Stover 2022, 276–282.

3 Pliny and the Augustan poetry book

Pliny's notorious declaration in letter 1.1 that his letters have been arranged in random order makes clear allusion to similar claims made in the closing lines of the third book of Ovid's *Epistulae ex Ponto*.[29] The Ovidian allusion has a precise purpose. Just as the Augustan poet's claim to random order is comprehensively undermined by the careful arrangement of poems in the preceding three books of the Pontic epistles,[30] so Pliny invites his readers to anticipate that this renewed assertion of random disposition of individual letters is likely to be proven false. And not only does Pliny engineer an intricate series of links between the opening and closing suite of letters in Books 1 and 9 of his collection,[31] he also creates symmetries within books. In Book 6, some missing 'Ciceronian' panthers at the end of the book (6.34) correspond to a sorely missed Ciceronian Tiro at its outset (6.1); Pliny's best ever speech in the Centumviral courts in the book's penultimate letter (6.33) matches the death of his greatest rival in the same courts in letter 6.2; and gifts conveyed on women can be discovered in third position at either end (6.3, 6.32). The symmetry here is presented in an understated manner, and receives only delicate signposting; but its presence is unmistakable.[32]

What does this add up to? Pliny confirms the debt that the Roman epistolographical collection owes to the Augustan poetry book. And, like Augustan predecessors such as Propertius and Tibullus or Horace in the *Satires* and *Odes*, Pliny works hard to make his books distinctive from one another. Unlike many of the surviving books of Cicero's *Ad Familiares*, the individual books of Pliny are *not* linguistically very distinct from one another (Book 10 aside).[33] Distinctiveness

---

29 *Ep.* 1.1.1: *collegi non seruato temporis ordine (neque enim historiam componebam), sed ut quaeque in manus uenerat*, 'I have collected them, without preserving the order of dates (since it was not a history that I was compiling), but just as each came to hand'; cf. Ov. *Pont.* 3.9.51–53: *nec liber ut fieret, sed uti sua cuique daretur | littera, propositum curaque nostra fuit. | postmodo conlectas utcumque sine ordine iunxi*, 'Not that a book might come out of it, but to send the appropriate letter to each person – this was my project and my care. These letters I later collected, put them together somehow, without order'. The deliberate reference here to Ovid was first detected by Froesch 1968, 51, and given apparently independent endorsement by Syme in 1985, 176. On the lack of attention shown to the reference in Plinian studies, see Marchesi 2008, 21.
30 See above n. 21.
31 See Gibson 2015, 186–94, with reference to earlier literature.
32 Gibson/Morello 2012, 39–43. For further instances of symmetry in Pliny's books, see Marchesi 2015a.
33 On the idiolect of Book 10, see Coleman 2012.

is achieved for individual books in other ways. Take Book 6: Pliny gives geographical and topographical distinctiveness to this unit by omitting mention of the 'Tuscan' villa so prominent in Book 5 (5.6), by mentioning Comum only once (6.25),[34] and by filling the book instead with venues in central and southern Italy.[35] Campania, which has little visibility elsewhere in the *Epistles*, makes several prominent appearances: Pliny is deliberately creating a suitable home for the two great Vesuvius letters contained in the book (6.16, 6.20), whose action, of course, takes place on the bay of Naples.

In sum, Pliny's books matter. Like the Augustan poetry books on which they are modelled, Pliny's books are enriched by distinctive themes and symmetries created for individual units, and are made up of letters that themselves feature pervasive intertextuality and other literary games designed to draw attention to the artistic interdependence of apparently freestanding items. Is this signalling of an inheritance from and allegiance to the Augustan poetry book a strong hint that we ought to regard Pliny's letters as fundamentally fictional in some sense? Is Pliny providing a grammar for how we ought to read him?

Modern writers have evolved a grammar for allowing us to distinguish between fact and fiction. If we are reading modern prose that relies on concrete description, emphasizes immediate sensory perception at a particular time and place, and prizes a narrative pace that focuses on relatively short periods of time (i.e. hours and minutes) — then we are probably reading fiction. If we are reading a work that tends to downplay some or all of the latter and prefers to offer social generalizations, includes frequent and direct reference to contemporary politics and economics, and features a narrative pace focusing on days and weeks — then we are probably reading a non-fiction genre such as biography.[36] These rough distinctions are hardly infallible (not least when fiction deliberately imitates biography or vice versa), but they are certainly clear enough to be reliable most of the time.

---

34 On the geographical distinctiveness of *Ep.* 6 by comparison with books 5 and 7, see Gibson/Morello 2012, 49.

35 In 6.4 Calpurnia is found recuperating in Campania (and again at 6.7); in 6.10 and 6.31 Pliny is on the coast not far north of Rome at Alsium and Centum Cellae respectively; in 6.14, Pliny arranges a visit to Formiae in Latium; letters 6.16 and 6.20 revisit the scenes on the Campanian coast of 79 CE; in 6.18, Pliny agrees to act as advocate for the Picenum town of Firmum; in 6.25, Pliny is asked to intervene in the case of someone who has gone missing in Umbria not far from Rome; 6.28 relates the visit of Pliny to a friend's villa in Campania; and 6.30 deals with the management of an estate in Campania.

36 See Underwood 2019, 1–33 on the long-term trends separating the Anglophone novel from its non-fiction counterparts.

Is the Augustan poetry book the ancient equivalent of this modern grammar? It is now widely agreed that the first-person statements of the Augustan poets — or at least certainly those of Propertius, Tibullus, Ovid and the Horace of the *Odes* and beyond — cannot be taken seriously as autobiography in the way that the *Res Gestae* was clearly intended as historical record (thoroughly tendentious as it is). Propertius is indeed from Assisi and Ovid from Sulmona, and both spent time in Rome in prestigious literary circles, but what other autobiographical statements or features of their love elegies earn our trust as historically authentic in some sense? Cynthia and Corinna, it is now agreed, are not (thinly) disguised flesh and blood women, but textual constructs — symbols for a series of 'pre-existing erotic, social, moral, legal, political and poetic assumptions'.[37] The poets' own careers of decadence and erotic addiction in Augustan Rome are a statement of socio-political and poetic allegiances and not a matter of potentially verifiable biographical record.[38]

Perhaps the most interesting (and notorious) incident on the road to this consensus was the thesis that Ovid had never gone to Tomis on the Black Sea, and had stayed all along in Rome, writing poetry in protest against the censorship of his poetry by Augustus; Ovid's assertion of banishment from Rome was to be understood as an extended and elaborate metaphor for the unjust exile of his poetry from imperial libraries. A version of the thesis had been proposed as long ago as 1913, and found new life in the scholarship of the 1980s and 1990s as it edged towards creating today's consensus on the essentially textual rather than autobiographical nature of Roman love elegy.[39] Few today stand by a 'hard' version of the 'no exile' thesis (it looks a bit naïve), though it remains at the edge of scholarly consciousness as one among many critical possibilities worth revisiting at some point in the future. It is, after all, consistent with the main thrust of elegiac scholarship.

No one has yet proposed that Pliny never went to his own province on the Black Sea, roughly a century after Ovid's alleged failure to go to Tomis (although it is a fair guess that someone somewhere is contemplating a punt on the idea).[40] Pliny's adoption of the format and technique of the poetry book

---

37 Miller 2013, 178.
38 Sharrock 2013.
39 The thesis was first proposed by J.J. Hartmann during the first world war (van der Velden 2019), and revived by Fitton Brown 1985. For an overview of the course of the debate, see Tissol 2014, 13–16.
40 Cf. Woolf 2015, 144. For Pliny's allusions to Ovid's own journey to the Black Sea, see Gibson/Morello 2012, 259–263; for his references to the symmetries and other textual features of the *Epistulae ex Ponto*, see Gibson 2015.

format invites us to venture further down that path, all the same, towards the embrace of textual games rather than historical reality. Is Pliny telling us that much of his life is to be understood as a textual construct like that of Ovid or Propertius: a statement of largely symbolic socio-political and literary allegiances rather than a *cursus honorum*? The Augustan poetry book is after all associated with unreliable or bogus biography.

4 Plinian inventions?

There are numerous instances where critics have suspected Pliny of invention or manipulation. A short — if far from comprehensive — taxonomy might be useful:

1. Instances where dates and figures in the letters do not match up with other elements in the historical record: for example, an August date for the eruption of Vesuvius (the archaeological record is beginning to point towards a later date),[41] or the death of the daughter of Minicius Fundanus in her fourteenth year (her urn records an earlier date).[42]
2. Instances where Pliny describes landscape and architecture either in language borrowed from poetry (e.g. the harbour at Centum Cellae mentioned earlier) or in other ways that lead critics to suspect literary invention. The overtly ekphrastic elements present in Pliny's descriptions of his Laurentine and 'Tuscan' villas (2.17, 5.6) have prompted readers to understand these villas as literary creations[43] (whatever the presence of brick-stamps bearing Pliny's initials at a site near ancient Tifernum in central Italy might suggest).[44]
3. Instances where mundane details recorded in the letters have been understood to operate as political or social metaphor. For example, Pliny briefly

---

41 At *Ep.* 6.16.4 Pliny supplies an August date, but archaeological evidence is beginning to tip towards the autumn; see Gibson 2020, 77–78 n. 25. Foss 2022 provides an authoritative account.
42 *Ep.* 5.16.2 reads *nondum annos xiiii impleuerat*, 'she had not yet completed her fourteenth year' (with no discrepant readings in the mss); but the girl's rediscovered urn clearly records her age at death as follows: 'D. M. Miniciae Marcellae Fundani f. v(ixit) a(nnos) XII m(enses) XI d(ies) VII.' (*ILS* 1030), i.e. she was in her thirteenth year. For a fascinating account of the discovery of the family crypt of the Minicii at Monte Mario just outside Rome in the late nineteenth century, see Lanciani 1888, 281–3.
43 E.g. Pierre Du Prey, leading authority on the reception of Pliny's villa letters in the architectural designs of later centuries, opines, 'The letters may not refer to any archaeological truth, and the villas may be more or less pure figments of their author's imagination' (2018, 467).
44 See Gibson/Morello 2012, 228–33, with reference to the excavation reports of Braconi and Uroz Sáez 1999, 2008.

narrates a journey through the towns of Ocriculum, Narnia, Carsulae and Perusia: apparently a route towards his Tuscan villa (*Ep.* 1.4.1).[45] Does this passage rather represent a retracing of the scenes of military action that brought the Flavian house to power in 69 CE?[46] The political metaphor potentially negates the literal truth of the journey: the letter documents the foundation of political dynasties not a travel route.
4. Instances where specific biographical details appear to have been manipulated or even invented in order to fulfil a literary agenda or programme.

These categories of course overlap in various ways; but it is the last that is perhaps the most challenging. I want to concentrate on an instance in a letter with strong links to love elegy.

In the early 80s CE, Pliny served in the Roman province of Syria as a military tribune with the legion III Gallica — perhaps based at Samosata on the west bank of the Euphrates, modern south-east Turkey.[47] Instructed to audit the accounts of the cavalry and infantry divisions, Pliny — inevitably — discovered *magnam quorundam foedamque auaritiam*, 'an extensive and filthy rapacity of certain parties' (7.31.2). The time Pliny spent here in his early 20s has left a surprisingly large footprint in the letters, since it is the one period from his early manhood that recurs most insistently throughout the corpus; people that he met or served with during that period recur even towards the end of Pliny's life, in Book 10.[48]

One isolated reminiscence occurs in Book 7. In letter 7.4, Pliny offers his addressee, Pontius Allifanus, his literary biography. Unlike the letters as a whole, which practice chronological disordering (at least within books), this individual letter offers a strict chronological account of Pliny's development as a poet — reading almost as if Pliny were competing for a place in the recently or soon-to-be published *De Viris Illustribus* of Suetonius (which offered potted

---

45 Ocriculum, Narnia, Carsulae all lay on the old via Flaminia and its western branch on the high ground through Carsulae. The mention of Perusia as the final stop indicates that Pliny is probably travelling from Rome to his Tuscan villa, which lay near the top of the valley at whose foot Perusia lay.
46 Hoffer 1999, 52–53: 'The Flavians reached Carsulae, while Vitellius' last significant forces had taken up a stand at Narnia. The peaceful surrender at Narnia led to Vitellius' attempted abdication on 18 December, and the fatal delay at Ocriculum for the Saturnalia led to ... "the worst crime in all of Roman history", the burning of the Capitoline temple'.
47 Gibson 2020, 194 and 223 n. 28–29.
48 Gibson 2020, 194–196.

biographies of men of literary achievement in a range of genres).[49] At the start of the narrative Pliny tells us (7.4.2–3):

> ais legisse te hendecasyllabos meos; requiris etiam quemadmodum coeperim scribere, homo ut tibi uideor seuerus, ut ipse fateor non ineptus. numquam a poetice (altius enim repetam) alienus fui; quin etiam quattuordecim natus annos Graecam tragoediam scripsi. "qualem?" inquis. nescio; tragoedia uocabatur. mox, cum e militia rediens in Icaria insula uentis detinerer, Latinos elegos in illud ipsum mare ipsamque insulam feci. expertus sum me aliquando et heroo, hendecasyllabis nunc primum.

> You say that you have read my hendecasyllables, and you want to know how a serious man like me came to write them; and I am not frivolous, I admit. To start at the beginning, I was always interested in poetry and wrote a Greek tragedy at the age of fourteen. What it was like I can't say—anyway, I called it a tragedy. Later on I was weatherbound in the island of Icaria while on my way home from military service, and wrote some Latin elegiacs with the sea and island for theme. I have also occasionally tried my hand at epic verse, but this is my first attempt at hendecasyllables.

Writing elegiacs on the island of Icaria is something of a literary tradition,[50] as can be seen from an anonymous and undated Greek epigram (*AP* 7.699), beginning 'Icaria, memorial of the disastrous journey of Icarus flying through the newly-trodden air, would he too had never seen you, would that Triton had never sent you up above the expanse of the Aegean sea. For you have no sheltered anchorage...'[51] Likewise the winds of which Pliny complains are a feature of the small, but vibrant literary and historiographical tradition that surrounds this Aegean island, from the first Homeric *Hymn* onwards.[52] As might be expected when a would-be poet talks about his verse, the language in which Pliny writes about his poetry becomes charged, and a school of intertexts rises to the surface. To the Vergilian and Terentian intertexts identified by Ilaria Marchesi

---

49 On the publication of this Suetonian work, see Power 2010. On the purpose and puzzles of the chronological narration in 7.4 (Pliny does not explain his evolution through time), see Marchesi 2008, 78–88.

50 Pliny's poetry, it can be added, is shockingly poor: Michael Reeve has suggested of some lines quoted by Pliny in a nearby letter (7.9.10–11): 'This must be one of the worst couplets ever written' (Whitton 2019, 305 n. 23). The contrast with his eminence as a prose stylist is disturbing.

51 Cited by Hanink 2016, 136–137; cf. *AP* 7.499, 7.651. I owe these references and other information about Icaria to Johanna Hanink.

52 On Icaria in antiquity, see Papalas 1992. Note also that the Attic deme of Icaria was associated with the birth of Athenian tragedy (a genre Pliny claims to have attempted in this letter), thanks to its association with the legendary actor Thespis.

and Chris Whitton, I can add a possible reference to Catullus — Pliny's favourite poet.[53]

But a question arises: did Pliny ever go to Icaria on his return from Syria? Spyridon Tzounakas observes, 'nowhere else does he suggest that he passed through Icaria. Besides there are a number of alternative, briefer routes one could have taken returning from Syria. If his intention was to pass through Corinth, why should he travel as far as Samos and Icaria?'[54] Icaria in fact has a habit of appearing in fictional biographies: as Johanna Hanink has recently shown, the island turns up as a scenario in a third-century BCE life of Euripides, where the tragedian writes an epigram on a family who died from eating poisoned mushrooms.[55] Doubts multiply about the Icarian incident when we reflect that writing an elegy when delayed against one's will on a Greek island *while on military service* is precisely the scenario of the most memorable of Tibullus' elegies: in elegy 1.3, Tibullus writes apparently from Corfu, delayed by illness from travelling with Messalla who is on his way east for military service.[56] Furthermore, Pliny's passing reference to the sea into which the over-daring young Icarus plunged could be a self-mocking comment on the quality of the elegies written by the youthful Pliny; like Icarus, his elegies went down like a lead balloon into the expunging water.[57]

5 The poetics of Pliny's epistles

Pliny is, at the very least, pushing readers hard to think about the role of literary typology and other forms of intertextuality in the framing and communication of a life's narrative — he had, after all, freed himself from the constraints of 'history' in his opening letter (1.1.1: *neque enim historiam componebam*, 'it was not history that I was compiling'). Literary critics, as Lavan notes, like to complicate (i.e. evade) 'questions about the relationship between historiography

---

53 See Marchesi 2008, 80 and Whitton 2019, 40 n. 107 on: Ter. *Heaut.* 77 and Verg. *Georg.* 4.285–6; cf. Catull. 85. On further Catullan and Ovidian intertexts in 7.4.4–6, see Whitton 2019, 305 n. 126, 307 n. 135.
54 Tzounakas 2012, 304 n. 18.
55 Hanink 2016, 135–141.
56 Tzounakas 2012, 303. To judge by the index locorum of Whitton 2019, 531–549, Tibullus — despite endorsement by Quintilian as Rome's leading elegist — never appears in Pliny's intertextual weave; Ovid's elegies rate fourteen citations.
57 Tzounakas 2012, 303.

and history'. Whatever that relationship might be, Pliny has in theory written himself an *exeat*, although he is neither the first nor last author of prose in Latin to confront readers with questions about typological events in autobiographical narrative. Seneca had done so in the *Epistulae Morales*, where episodes from his life sometimes rather neatly fit the Stoic life lessons served up to Lucilius.[58] Augustine's pear tree is the most famous illustration. In the *Confessions*, the saint tells us that in his sixteenth year he and his friends stole the fruit from 'a pear tree in the orchard next to ours', solely 'for the pleasure we had in tasting forbidden fruit', because as a young man he 'was in love with my own ruin and rebellion' (*Conf.* 2.4.9). Is this an actual incident? Or is it a purely metaphorical narrative based on the typology of the Garden of Eden, where the theft of fruit from the tree of good and evil signifies original sin?[59] The readers of Thagaste, Augustine's hometown in north Africa, presumably had a view.

Had the Icaria vignette appeared in Ovid's *Amores*, we would straightaway understand it as a fundamentally metapoetic narrative designed to express the writer's alignment towards Tibullus and the genre of elegy. When Ovid tells us that he has *graciles...artus*, 'slender limbs' (*Am.* 2.10.23), this is a statement of generic allegiance rather than an autobiographical self-description,[60] and similar instances of poetic identity or programme masquerading as autobiographical fact can be found also in the exile poetry.[61] According to Aristotle, Homer had taught poets 'to make false statements in the right way' (*Poet.* 1460a18–19). More to the point, Horace in the *Ars Poetica* views poetic falsehood as essentially an aesthetic problem of overall-unity in a work: *atque ita mentitur, sic ueris falsa remiscet, | primo ne medium, medio ne discrepet imum*, 'and so skilfully does he invent, so closely does he blend facts and fiction, that the middle is not dis-

---

58 On the *status quaestionis*, see Setaioli 2014, 191–194; Mollea 2019.
59 On the episode, its biblical typology, and underlying references to the figure of Catiline, see O'Donnell 1992, II.126–8.
60 But for an expression of dissatisfaction with the mainstream approach to Ovid as fundamentally metapoetical, see Rimmell 2019.
61 Hinds 1989 and Williams 1994 remain foundational in this respect. In exile poems that offer more highly concentrated biography, Ovid adopts a slightly different tack: e.g. in *Tr.* 4.10, the poet selects for emphasis elements of his life that correspond to the biographical self-presentations of his poetic predecessors and (in particular) of the emperor Augustus; see the classic contribution of Fairweather 1987. Pliny too selects for emphasis: reflections on adoption by his uncle are in part designed to align his life with Trajan's adoption by Nerva (Gibson 2020, 16–18); and Pliny's only revelation of his physical appearance — that he was thin — is designed not only to contrast with the corpulent elder Pliny, but to resonate with Cicero's self-description in his youth (Gibson 2020, 25 and 31 n. 81).

cordant with the beginning, nor the end with the middle' (*Ars* 151–2).⁶² Elsewhere in the *Amores*, Ovid himself insists: *nec tamen ut testes mos est audire poetas;* | *malueram uerbis pondus abesse meis*, 'And yet 'tis not the custom to heed the poet's witness; my verses, too, I had preferred should have no weight' (*Am.* 3.12.19–20). Ovid is, as usual, playing with us: his insistence on an association between poetry and falsehood is situated in an episode of paranoia about his own poetry's prostitution of his *puella* to the reading public; it is now in his interest to be thought to be lying about her legendary beauty. Ovid's teasing prevarication about the reality or fiction of his Corinna starts in the *Amores* and — more arrestingly — continues into the exile poetry (where a straight denial might have been called for).⁶³ Ovid knows we suspect it is all fiction; we know he knows we suspect ... (you get the picture); but he won't confirm or deny.

Is the grammar that we apply to understanding Ovid's autobiographical statements in the *Amores* the same in some respects as the grammar we want to apply to Pliny's letters? His adoption of the format and techniques of the Augustan poetry book certainly point in that direction, and the letters do not lack for metapoetic consciousness. In letter 1.3, Pliny urges Caninius Rufus to dedicate himself to the production of some immortal literary work; later, in the letter which lies in third place from the end of the nine-book collection, Pliny writes to a friend celebrating the long-awaited completion of a literary work by their mutual friend 'Rufus' (9.38). These two letters clearly trace the progress of Pliny's own epistolary project from inception in Book 1 to completion in Book 9.⁶⁴ As a collection, the letters also harbour literary ambitions to absorb the content and style of a range of other genres, from satire and epigram to epic and historiography (seen most obviously in the second Vesuvius letter, *Ep.* 6.20).⁶⁵

Pliny also gives us some elements with which to construct a rather different grammar to understand his books of letters. Some are a matter of absences and silences. As Whitton's *Arts of Imitation in Latin Prose* demonstrates in abundance, Pliny persistently engages with — alludes to, incorporates and modifies the diction of — Quintilian's *Institutio Oratoris* and a range of other texts.⁶⁶ Yet if 'the primary colours of Pliny's Latin are brevity, clarity and rhetoricity', where

---

62 On the literary-theoretical background, see Brink 1971, 223–224.
63 Cf. e.g. *Am.* 2.17.29–30; *Ars* 3.538; *Tr.* 2.339–340; 4.10.59–60, Kennedy 1993, 89–90. Such provocations are well suited to the *Tristia*, where the poet encourages a habit of paranoid and suspicious reading; see Hinds 2007.
64 Gibson 2015.
65 On 6.20, see Marchesi 2008, 171–189. On the range of genres absorbed by the epistles more generally, see the collection of essays in Neger/Tzounakas (forthcoming).
66 Whitton 2019.

'*pressus sermo purusque* "succinct and simple language" ... is the professed norm of epistles (7.9.8)', the author never deploys a coherent set of loaded terms to codify a literary programme for his letters — of a sort to match the elegists' (gendered) emphasis on the soft lightness of their poetry (*leuis, tenuis, mollis*) as against the rougher weight of shaggier rival genres (*grauis, durus*). Neither (e.g.) *pressus* nor *purus* act as load-bearing terms for the poetics of Pliny's epistles. *pressus* is found fourteen times in the letters: its frequent use of the spoken and especially written style of self and others renders it ideal to express a literary programme in metaphorical contexts; but Pliny uses it only twice in contexts other than literal descriptions of style.[67] *purus* displays an opposite pattern of usage: found nine times in the letters, it is twice used of literary style (4.20.2, 7.9.8), but otherwise deployed in a wide range of contexts, including silver service, the body of a Vestal virgin, sunny nooks in a villa, climate, the *fons Clitumnus*, and the source of an aqueduct's water in Bithynia.

Here is an important clue to the direction of travel in 'signification' within Pliny's letters. Rather than creating an internal loop, where a signifier is potentially centripetal and returns to reflect on its own programmatic status within a collection, the letters are centrifugal and generally move outwards from internal signifier to external signified. Prospects for reading events in Pliny's life as primarily instantiations of a literary programme are diminished. As literary critics, we can of course choose to ignore the direction of travel in signification, although we do so in the knowledge that we are reading against the grain of the collection.

Augustan poets in fact developed a range of different methods to signal (or limit) the relationship of their text to their own lives. If Propertius evolved a set of programmatic terms whose cumulative effect is to tell the reader that apparently objective observations or facts are simply encapsulations of his generic values and allegiances, Ovid took this approach even further by largely ridding his text even of the limited quantity of *Realien* that Propertius had been prepared to admit.[68] One result is that his programmatic value terms easily swamp the few details present. Where elegy is relatively thin in biographical content, the epistles of Pliny are enormously rich. The superabundance of biographical material supplied by Pliny swamps the needs of any literary programme. Pliny's distinctive interests in accountancy and financial probity, inheritances and

---

[67] *Ep.* 5.6.17 (of the styling of bushes); 8.20.4 (of the colour of lake Vadimon); on *pressus* as a literary term, see Whitton 2013, 265 on *Ep.* 2.19.6

[68] Ovid's exile poetry is the exception, but even here extended biographical content is confined to a relatively small number of poems.

testamentary gifts, senatorial and legal procedure, and the challenges of farm management (including sharecropping and bulk advance purchasing of the vine harvest) — all provide challenges to reading the letters as primarily an exercise in the expansion and codification of a new genre.[69]

Alongside such absences and silences, positive evidence of a grammar for Pliny's letters emerges from his use of a notorious poem. Catullus 16 is a complex text that offers a multiplicity of challenges to interpretation. Like many writers confronting 'strong' predecessors, Pliny simplifies Catullus' text and produces the version he wants to deal with. In letter 4.14, Pliny explains and justifies his publication of a collection of (potentially outrageous and offensive) hendecasyllables (*Ep.* 4.14.4–5):

> *ex quibus tamen si non nulla tibi petulantiora paulo uidebuntur, erit eruditionis tuae cogitare summos illos et grauissimos uiros qui talia scripserunt non modo lasciuia rerum, sed ne uerbis quidem nudis abstinuisse ... scimus alioqui huius opusculi illam esse uerissimam legem, quam Catullus expressit:*
> *nam castum esse decet pium poetam*
> *ipsum, uersiculos nihil necesse est,*
> *qui tunc denique habent salem et leporem*
> *si sunt molliculi et parum pudici.*
>
> But if some of the passages strike you as rather indelicate, your reading ought to tell you how many distinguished and serious writers in dealing with such themes neither avoided lascivious subjects nor refrained from expressing them in plain language. ... I know that the best rule for this kind of thing is the one in Catullus, when he says that 'the true poet should be chaste himself, though his poetry need not be, for it must be relaxed and free from restraint if it is to have wit and charm'.

Here, in the analysis of Ilaria Marchesi, Pliny 'interprets the text as a precept on style. Catullus 16 indicated that the subject-matter of poetry was not to be taken as a clue to construct the extra-textual figure of the author, even in the borderline case of the highly personal poetry of Catullus. Pliny uses the poem as if it contained a recipe for distinguishing the style of poetry from the social dignity of its author'.[70] Catullus 16 offers Pliny the chance to erect a barrier between first-

---

69 Tibullus is different again. Less reliant on a programmatic vocabulary to warn his readers that everything they see is a refraction of the genre of elegy, Tibullus uses the future tense and the potentialities of the subjunctive to describe his actions (Lee 2008): almost nothing actually takes place in the first book of his elegies. Pliny makes no equivalent programmatic use of the future tense or subjunctive mood: his work has a distinct preference for the set-piece narrative (as most obviously in the Vesuvius letters).
70 Marchesi 2008, 77.

person literature and life; he does not take it. Confirmation, apparently, of the direction of the flow of signification in the letters.

Finally, an exemplary instance of the relationship between literature and Pliny's life. Found in the *Panegyricus*, it is presented here as an argument *a fortiori*: if poets since Homer had license to tell falsehoods, the same liberty was afforded even more generously to imperial panegyrists. As professor of rhetoric in Milan, Augustine was tasked with praising the emperor in front of an audience thoroughly familiar with the rules of the game: 'I was preparing to recite a panegyric to the emperor. In that panegyric I would tell many lies, and be applauded for my pains by many who knew that they were lies' (*Conf.* 6.6.9).[71] (Ovid's ideal audience, by the sounds of it.) By Augustine's time, Pliny's own speech to Trajan, delivered on the occasion of his consulship of 100 CE, stood at the head of the collection of late antique orations known as the *Panegyrici Latini*; it was widely admired as a classic of the genre. The license for exaggeration, hyperbole and even falsehood had Latin roots that stretched back beyond Pliny to the imperial confections found in the final book of Horace's *Odes* and the *Epistulae ex Ponto*.

Pliny's record of his own career in a genre that was perhaps valued and even enjoyed for its loose relationship with truth bears examination. Near the end of the speech, Pliny reflects on his accelerated run to a praetorship in 93 or 94 CE under Domitian, and the interval before reaching the consulship under Trajan in 100 CE. Notoriously, Pliny omits mention of a post at the military treasury to which he was appointed by Domitian before his assassination in 96 CE (*Paneg.* 95.3–4):

> *si, cursu quodam prouectus ab illo insidiosissimo principe, antequam profiteretur odium bonorum, postquam professus est substiti <et>, cum uiderem, quae ad honores compendia paterent, longius iter malui.*
>
> If, having been advanced at something of a pace by that most treacherous emperor before he confessed his hatred of good men, I halted once he had confessed it and preferred, when I saw what shortcuts to magistracies lay open, the longer route.[72]

Pliny's implicit claim to have 'halted' in his career after the praetorship is technically correct, since there was a distinction between magistracies on the *cursus honorum*, such as praetor and consul, and lesser administrative offices like the

---

[71] Aug. *Conf.* 6.6.9: *cum pararem recitare imperatori laudes, quibus plura mentirer et mentienti faueretur ab scientibus.*

[72] Text and translation from Whitton 2015b, 2, see n.6 for the conjectured <*et*>.

military treasury post. It would be another six or seven years until Pliny's consulship. The additional assertion that Pliny preferred 'the longer route' begs questions. Pliny could be taken to imply that he preferred a mundane treasury posting with other similar offices in prospect: a 'longer route'. The alternative 'short cut' was an accelerated run to the consulship — presumably through acting as one of Domitian's agents in the final years of his reign. The likelihood of the latter is impossible to prove. As it was, he would reach the consulship in a time well under the decade between praetor and consul that was normal for all except patricians.[73] At any rate, in the analysis of Chris Whitton, Pliny is guilty of failing to spell the matter out, since the prefecture of the military treasury 'goes forgotten, and the inference is all too easy that he held no post at all. Yet if Pliny had really been able in the *Panegyricus* to brandish several years without office, would he have settled for so understated a claim as *longius iter malui*?' He adds, incisively: 'Admire or condemn Pliny's careful footwork as you please: tendentious, yes; dishonest, not quite. ... Take Pliny's word at your peril. But he will not be caught lying'.[74]

6 Hard cases and bad law

Pliny is happy to mislead the unwary, yet will not be found propagating actual falsehoods about his own life. For someone like Pliny so aware of the possible effect of literature on perception of his *dignitas* (as the Catullus 16 letter demonstrates) or his public or private record, it was unwise for him to uphold too firmly the poet's distinction between literature and biography. Pliny will play with words and can deliver less than the whole truth; but he 'will not be caught lying'. Do we have here a rubric for interpreting the biographical data, truth and fiction, of the letters — adopted *a fortiori* from the genre of panegyric (where public falsehood was normal in a way that cannot be held true of epistolography in a simple or uncomplicated way)? It does leave Pliny and his readers considerable room for manoeuvre and play. That Pliny awards himself the right to misdirect (but not to invent or lie) makes sense of the atmosphere of literary suggestion and play that many readers of the letters instinctively detect. Nor has

---

[73] See Syme 1958b, 652–656; 1991, 561–563.
[74] Whitton 2015b, 19, 20. The same rule is not applied, of course, to Trajan's own career: the claim of ten years service for Trajan as military tribune (*Paneg.* 15.3) must count both as egregiously impossible and as an expected part of the panegyrist's task when praising the honorand. Pliny's carefulness in regard to his own career offers a clear contrast.

Pliny set himself the task of maximum misdirection. In the broader context of an apparent tendency not to invent (as such), we can begin to understand Pliny's biographical typologies and love of intertextuality as a form of communication with his audience. If your life begins to resemble literature — if you want to write elegies on an island while on military service — then the parallel is worth pursuing: literature provides the framework for creating a shared narrative with your audience. The promotion of biographical parallels between life and literature, after all, helps soften the risk inherent in speaking as an isolated individual rather than as a representative of the collective.

I close this chapter with one illustration of how far that room for manoeuvre and play might extend: an instance of intertextual play that is the most puzzling I have yet encountered in Pliny. The Vesuvius letters, particularly the second, are intertextual treasure houses.[75] The insistent allusion to Vergil throughout 6.20 is appropriate because much of the action of the letter takes place at cape Misenum — a site with strong Vergilian associations of its own (*Aen.* 6.156–235). Livy also figures as an important intertext in the letter:[76] a fitting choice given that this is the very historian whose work Pliny has been asked by the Elder to 'excerpt' as part of his 'homework' prior to the eruption (6.20.5). Rather more arresting is the reference in the closing paragraphs of *Ep.* 6.20 to the *Satyricon* of Petronius, where Pliny records the anxious night spent by his mother and himself after they had endured the terrors of the terrible black cloud emanating from Vesuvius (*Ep.* 6.20.19):

> regressi Misenum **curatis utcumque** corporibus suspensam dubiamque **noctem** spe ac metu **exegimus**. metus praeualebat; nam et tremor terrae perseuerabat, et plerique lymphati terrificis uaticinationibus et sua et aliena mala ludificabantur.

> We returned to Misenum where we attended to our physical needs as best we could, and then spent an anxious night alternating between hope and fear. Fear predominated, for the earthquakes went on, and several hysterical individuals made their own and other people's calamities seem ludicrous in comparison with their frightful predictions.

---

75 See Marchesi 2008, 171–189; cf. Gigante 1989.
76 *Ep.* 6.20.5: *posco librum Titi Liui, et quasi per otium lego atque etiam ut coeperam excerpo* ('I called for a volume of Livy and went on reading as if I had nothing else to do') includes a Livian turn of phrase (Livy 27.2.10: *spolia per otium legere* ('gathered spoils at their leisure') at the very moment Pliny asks for a copy of Livy; see Marchesi 2008, 188. Cf. also (e.g.) *Ep.* 6.20.12 ~ Livy 26.9.5 (Gigante 1989, 43); 6.20.15 ~ Livy 3.42.6 (Gigante 1989, 47); 6.20.20 ~ Livy 38.29.3 (Berry 2008, 300 n. 14); and see Gibson forthcoming b.

A parallel with an incident in Petronius was spotted in 1958 by Luigi Pepe.[77] Encolpius narrates the aftermath of a shipwreck, at *Sat.* 115.6: *hoc opere tandem elaborato casam piscatoriam subimus maerentes, cibisque naufragio corruptis* **utcunque curati** *tristissimam* **exegimus noctem,** 'When this business was at last completed, we came sadly to a fisherman's cottage, refreshed ourselves more or less with food spoilt by sea-water, and passed a very miserable night'. Alongside strong verbal similarities, a contextual closeness is clear: a night-time disaster survived, the resort to the relative safety of a settlement, the enjoyment of such refreshment as was possible, and the passing of an anxious night.[78] The contextual relationship is even stronger than Pepe realised, because in his next sentence Pliny reveals the purpose of the return to Misenum: *nobis tamen ne tunc quidem, quamquam et expertis periculum et exspectantibus, abeundi consilium, donec de auunculo nuntius*, 'Even then, however, we ourselves did not plan to leave, in spite of our experience and expectation of the dangers, until the message came about my uncle' (6.20.20). In *his* next sentence, the Petronian Encolpius relates the discovery of a corpse on the seashore: *postero die, cum poneremus consilium, cui nos regioni crederemus, repente uideo corpus humanum circumactum leui uertice ad litus deferri*, 'Next morning, as we were trying to decide into what part of the country we should venture, I suddenly saw a man's body caught in a gentle eddy and carried ashore' (Petron. *Sat.* 115.6). Of course, at the time of the Younger Pliny's return to Misenum, the corpse of the Elder Pliny was lying on the seashore, across the bay of Naples at Stabiae; the time is precisely marked at *Ep.* 6.16.18–21.

We could make it easy for ourselves by deciding that we have evidence here for Petronius post-dating Pliny's *Epistulae*.[79] That would be to allow the tail to wag the Plinian dog. What exactly is Pliny trying to tell us here? That his letters do not yield up their full sense until they are read against a range of other texts — even the most unexpected? Is he daring us to doubt the historicity of his account (he certainly didn't invent the eruption of Vesuvius or the death of the Elder)? Or demonstrating the ability of his text to transcend fiction while still producing art? Or is he creating a significant contrast with the evidently neglected corpse reported in Petronius: the body of the Elder was found 'whole and

---

[77] Pepe 1958. Many thanks to Chris Whitton for drawing my attention to this intertext and its bibliography; cf. Whitton 2019, 42 n. 118.
[78] Pepe 1958, 292–293; cf. Ratti 2015.
[79] Roth 2016 argues that Petronius imitates Pliny on the basis of other and unrelated parallels in *Ep.* 10.

uninjured' (6.16.20: *corpus inuentum integrum illaesum*) on the seashore, not left where it might be taken by the waves?[80]

7 Envoi

I started this chapter with the insistence that individual writers need individual theories in terms of their relationship to (biographical) truth and fiction: Pliny is not Ovid. But for all epistolographers who choose to write and collect letters within the format of the Augustan poetry book — from Seneca to Sidonius — the same questions will apply: how will they negotiate the relationship between literature and life that the great Augustans — from Vergil's *Eclogues* to Ovid's *Epistulae ex Ponto* — had so thoroughly problematised in their creation and promotion of Rome's greatest literary invention, the slim volume of first-person poems (and their dubious or bogus biographies). What room for manoeuvre will epistolographers award themselves as they employ the typologies and intertextualities so deeply embedded in this most prestigious of literary formats?

---

80 Pliny's *corpus ... integrum illaesum* already seems designed to scotch the rumour reported in Suetonius' abbreviated life of the Elder Pliny: *ui pulueris ac fauillae oppressus est, uel ut quidam existimant a seruo suo occisus quem deficiens aestu ut necem sibi maturaret orauerat*, '[The Elder] succumbed to the quantity of dust and ash, or as some believe was dispatched by one of his slaves whom he had begged when the heat overwhelmed him to expedite his death'.

Claire Rachel Jackson
Fiction and Authenticity in the *Letters* of Euripides

Abstract: The *Letters* ascribed to Euripides have long been recognised to be inauthentic, and have been characterised variously as a simple forgery, a creative response to the wider biographical tradition surrounding the tragedian, or as some kind of epistolary novel. Yet, the wider consequences of these different labels have not yet been explored. This chapter considers how the Euripidean *Letters* consistently thematise the tensions inherent in their own pseudepigraphic conceit and in doing so challenge any assumptions scholars may have about fictional letters as a familiar or naturalised form of epistolary writing in antiquity. By exploring how this collection aligns itself within and against biographical traditions about Euripides while simultaneously undercutting their own authenticity, this chapter uses the *Letters* to nuance the terminology of fictional letters and to interrogate the boundaries of epistolary fiction as a genre.

Keywords: *Letters* of Euripides, biography, epistolary fiction, letter collections, authenticity

The pseudonymous *Letters* attributed to Euripides seem, at first glance, to be unproblematically fictitious. Comprised of only five letters, the collection details a brief but critical period in the playwright's life, covering his infamous move from Athens to Macedon and relationship with the Macedonian king Archelaus

---

The conference paper on which this chapter is based was written during my time at Sidney Sussex College, Cambridge, and I am very grateful to the college and my colleague Yannis Galanakis for their support, both for my work and the workshop from which this volume has arisen. Special thanks also to Andrew Morrison for his perceptive response at the workshop, and to Émeline Marquis and Heinz-Günther Nesselrath for being willing to share forthcoming work with me. I am incredibly grateful to Koen De Temmerman for his insightful comments, and to Janja Soldo for her support, encouragement, and thoughtful critique throughout. The writing up of this chapter was funded by the European Research Council (ERC) under the European Union's Horizon 2020 research and innovation programme (grant agreement No. 819459 – NovelEchoes).

https://doi.org/10.1515/9783111308128-003

which is the subject of much controversy in other biographical testimonia.[1] Although the authenticity of the *Letters* has rarely been entertained in modern scholarship,[2] with the current consensus being that they likely date from the imperial period,[3] at least one ancient reader, unusually, also questioned the collection's legitimacy.[4] The anonymous author of one of the *Lives* of Aratus, for some time believed to be the novelist Achilles Tatius,[5] attributes the Euripidean *Letters* to a certain Sabirius Pollo, who is also claimed to be the source of some of the letters circulating under Aratus' name (*Vita Arati* I pg. 10.16–19 Martin).[6] The ascription of the *Letters* to the otherwise unknown Pollo explicitly impugns the authenticity of the collection, not least because the obviously Roman name places the composition of the text in a specifically imperial context rather than one contemporary with the historical poet. The anonymous biographer seems not to have been alone in their belief. The Euripidean letters are never transmitted alongside Euripides' plays and are instead collected together with other pseudonymous letter collections, implying that for later readers at least they were not seen as genuine Euripidean works.[7] As such, despite their stated claim

---

[1] Scodel 2017; Tyrrell Blake 2020, and Scharffenberger 2015 offer brief overviews of the Euripidean biographical tradition, with the latter as the most methodologically focused. None of these chapters, however, discuss the Euripidean *Letters* in any detail.

[2] See Hanink 2010, 537–540 for a summary of early modern debates over the *Letters*' authenticity.

[3] Gösswein 1975, 29 building on an earlier discussion at 9–12. See also Jouan/Auger 1983, 186–187, with 194 on their preference for a composition in imperial Athens or their preferred option, Rome, and Poltera 2013, 153.

[4] Such explicit questioning of a collection's legitimacy is not common in antiquity, with one exception being the letter-collection attributed to Plato. The Platonic *Epistles* not only repeatedly thematise their own authenticity, on which see Wohl 1998, but also include a note at the end of *Ep*. 12 that it is believed not to be Plato's (ἀντιλέγεται ὡς οὐ Πλάτωνος), as well a note in one of the manuscripts in *Ep*. 13 that it is inauthentic (νοθεύεται). On the former see Morrison 2013, 107 n. 1 and Isnardi Parente 2002, 272, on the latter Wohl 1998, 83.

[5] Noted by Gösswein 1975, 6 n. 13 and Jouan/Auger 1983, 187. On the confusion between the novelist and the Achilles mentioned at several points in the tradition to Aratus, see Whitmarsh 2020, 3–4 with further bibliography.

[6] μόνος Ἀπολλωνίδης ὁ Κηφεὺς ἐν τῷ ὀγδόῳ περὶ κατεψευσμένης ἱστορίας οὐκ εἶναι αὐτὰς Ἀράτου φησίν, ἀλλὰ Σαβιρίου Πόλλωνος· τοῦ δὲ αὐτοῦ τούτου φησὶν εἶναι <τὰς> ἐπιγεγραμμένας Εὐριπίδου ἐπιστολάς. On this see Gösswein 1975, 6–9 and Jouan/Auger 1983, 187–188, who explore the difficulties of identifying the otherwise unknown Pollo. See also Hanink 2010, 540 n. 10. Gösswein 1975, 9–12 also explores this testimonium's implications for the dating of the *Letters*.

[7] Knöbl 2008, 200–203; Hanink 2010, 560–561. For a comprehensive overview of the manuscript history of the *Letters*, see Gösswein 1975, 31–67, along with the more concise summary of Jouan/Auger 1983, 188–190.

to be written by the historical Euripides, at least some ancient readers appear to have recognised that the *Letters* were fictitious rather than authentic.

But exactly what the categorisation of the *Letters* as fictional means depends on the perspective from which they are viewed. Even if the *Life* of Aratus raises the spectre of the collection's pseudonymity, the anonymous writer mentions only a single speaker (μόνος Ἀπολλωνίδης ὁ Κηφεύς) who claims that the letters attributed to Euripides are inauthentic, suggesting that this may have been at best a minority opinion.[8] By contrast, recent scholarship has described the collection as an 'epistolary novelette'[9] and an 'epistolary short story',[10] appellations which align the *Letters* within the recent trend for treating fictional letters as a genre analogous to that of the early modern epistolary novel.[11] And yet, the *Letters* have not been generally included in such discussions, receiving far less consideration than the portrayal of letters in Euripidean drama.[12] Instead, the majority of critical attention dedicated to the *Letters* has focused on their place within Euripidean biographical traditions, in particular the ways in which the collection challenges and even rewrites other narratives of the playwright's life.[13] All of these approaches presume that the collection is fictional, but in different ways. While the *Life* suggests that the collection is a forgery, the comparison with epistolary novels frames the work as a familiar, if anachronistic, form of fiction which is so ubiquitous as to be naturalised for modern audiences. Similarly, recent scholarship has increasingly moved beyond questions of historical veracity to look at biographical traditions as a kind of creative literary criticism, where such narratives are constructed as a response to the texts

---

8 Jouan/Auger 1983, 187 briefly discuss the possible identity of the unknown Apollonius Cepheus.
9 Poltera 2013, 154.
10 Hanink 2010, 544.
11 Most notably Rosenmeyer 2001: see also the edited volume of Hodkinson/Rosenmeyer/Bracke 2013. Morrison 2014b examines this question explicitly, although we come to different conclusions. This is discussed in more detail in the introduction to this volume.
12 For example, Rosenmeyer 2001 does not mention the Euripidean *Letters* but does devote a chapter to the portrayal of letters in Euripidean drama (61–97). Ironically, the *Letters* are mentioned briefly in the edited volume of Sogno/Storin/Watts 2017a as a paradigmatic example of an imperial fictional letter-collection to lay the groundwork for late antique examples: see Jones 2017, 41–42. Exceptions include Morrison 2014a, which compares the Euripidean *Letters* to other pseudonymous collections, although does not consider them in terms of fiction specifically, and Nesselrath 2023, as part of a volume devoted to epistolary fiction more generally (Marquis 2023).
13 In particular Hanink 2010: see also Jouan/Auger 1983 and Knöbl 2008, 189–258.

attributed to that author.[14] On the one hand, then, considering the *Letters* as fictional letters naturalises them as a generic exemplar where fiction is not just expected but required, while on the other looking through the lens of biography sees the fictional inventions of the collection as a specific response to Euripidean literary and biographical traditions. To describe the *Letters* as fiction encompasses a wide spectrum of meaning, ranging from a creative response to wider biographical trends to a familiar, albeit anachronistic, generic label, to a straightforward recognition of their inauthenticity. What, then, does it mean to label the *Letters* as fiction, and what is at stake in doing so?

This chapter aims to interrogate these various definitions of fiction in the Euripidean *Letters*. As outlined above, the *Letters* sit on the fault lines of different approaches to fiction, but rather than arguing for the collection's inclusion within the recent swell of interest in fictional letters and creative biographies, this article uses the *Letters* as a case-study to challenge the limitations of these definitions of fiction. Instead of subsuming the collection under familiar generic labels or scholarly trends, I aim here to explore how the *Letters* themselves actively explore the tensions inherent in their own inauthenticity and consequently complicate any assumptions we might have about the collection as fiction. In other words, my goal here is not to police the boundaries of epistolary fiction as a category, but rather to interrogate this terminology. As such, this paper aims to offer a more nuanced reading of the Euripidean *Letters* as fictional letters which exposes what is at stake in these various definitions of epistolary fiction for pseudepigraphic collections more widely.

1 Biography and Reputation

The *Letters* situate themselves on the cusp of a major transition in Euripides' biography. The collection begins with the tragedian writing to the Macedonian king Archelaus from Greece, and ends with him at Archelaus' court sending letters to the friends he has left behind in Athens.[15] Many of the testimonia to the life of Euripides focus on his move to Macedon, and given that the Euripidean

---

14 Most significantly, Graziosi 2002; De Temmerman/Demoen 2016; Fletcher/Hanink 2016; Powell/Hardie 2017, amongst others. This 'deductive' method is not however as predominant in ancient biographical anecdotes as sometimes assumed: on this see Hanink 2016, especially 128–133, on other methodologies visible in the sources of Euripidean biographies in particular.
15 See Knöbl 2008, 243–248 on the symbolic geography of the collection. See also Hanink 2010, 546–547.

biographical tradition is one of the most extensive in antiquity, second only to Homer's,[16] the sheer variety of anecdotes which engage with this event suggests that it was a long-contested issue.[17] The *Letters* not only repeatedly demonstrate their knowledge of such traditions, but also attack them as slanderous rumours, to the extent that Jouan and Auger describe the Euripides of the *Letters* as the antithesis of the image of the poet found in other sources.[18] And yet, while the *Letters* position themselves in opposition to other stories about Euripides' infamous move to Macedon, they do not offer a straightforward alternative. This is clear from the very outset of the collection (*Ep.* 1.1):[19]

> τὸ μὲν ἀργύριον ἀνεπέμψαμέν σοι πάλιν, ὅπερ ἡμῖν Ἀμφίας ἐκόμιζεν, οὐ δόξαν κενὴν θηρώμενοι, εἰ μή γε καὶ <σ'> ἀχθεσθήσεσθαι μᾶλλον ἢ ἀποδέξεσθαι ἡμᾶς δι' αὐτὸ ἐνομίζομεν, τοὺς δ' ἄλλους αὐτὸ δὴ τοῦτο καὶ μάλιστα πάντων συκοφαντεῖν ἐπιχειρήσειν ὡς ἐπίδειξιν οὖσαν τὸ πρᾶγμα καὶ πρόσχημα μᾶλλον εἰς τοὺς πολλούς, οὐ μεγαλοφροσύνην οὐδεμίαν. ὥστε τούτοιν μὲν ἀμφοῖν ἕνεκα κἂν ἐδεξάμεθα… ἀλλ' < > ὡς τὸ μὲν αὔταρκες ἡμῖν τε καὶ τοῖς φίλοις παρόν, τὸ δ' ὑπὸ σοῦ πεμφθὲν πλεῖον ἢ ὅσου ἥ τε κτῆσις ἥρμοζε καὶ ἦν ἡμῖν ἡ φυλακὴ ῥᾳδία.

The money which Amphias attempted to deliver I have sent back to you. This was not a quest for idle glory, since I thought that you might even be annoyed with me rather than approve of me for this deed, while others would attempt to slander me for this very thing on the grounds that it was ostentation and pretence before the crowd and no true greatness of spirit. Therefore for these two reasons I might even have accepted it…but <I decided against acceptance>[20] since my friends and I had enough, while your gift is worth more than my property may properly be worth and more than I can easily guard.

---

16 Knöbl 2008, 1, 20–21; Hanink 2010, 547.
17 The testimonia to Euripides' life are collected in Kovacs 1994, of which the key sources are the Euripidean *Vita*, transmitted in some manuscripts of the plays, and a fragmentary Hellenistic dialogue attributed to Satyrus. As Hanink 2010, 546 n. 30 discusses with further bibliography, while the historical accuracy of Euripides' supposed Macedonian exile has been vigorously debated, the story was likely circulating in the third century BCE and is already attested in Aristotle *Pol.* 1311b. On this see also Jouan/Auger 1983, especially 190–194. On the prominence of Macedon in receptions of Euripidean biography and drama, see Revermann 1999–2000; Hanink 2008.
18 Jouan/Auger 1983, 191–192: 'la confrontation entre l'Euripide des biographies et celui des *Lettres* fait surgir en quelques sorte une figure et son exacte antithèse.' On the *Letters*' challenge to and subversion of the wider Euripidean biographical tradition, see Jouan/Auger 1983; Knöbl 2008, 256–258; Hanink 2010. See Gösswein 1975, 23–28 on sources of the *Letters*.
19 Text throughout adapted from Gösswein 1975, translation adapted from Kovacs 1994.
20 Here I follow the emendation in the final clause proposed by Kovacs 1994, 128–129 to reflect Herscher's suspicions of a lacuna.

This opening both establishes the relationship between Euripides and Archelaus which underpins the playwright's move to Macedon and also undercuts it. On the one hand, Archelaus' generous gift, described as worth more than the tragedian's house (τὸ δ' ὑπὸ σοῦ πεμφθὲν πλεῖον ἢ ὅσου ἥ τε κτῆσις ἥρμοζε), makes visible the power dynamics inherent in the relationship between poet and patron, and aligns with accusations found elsewhere in the biographical tradition that Euripides moved to Macedon purely for the money.[21] On the other, however, Euripides' refusal to accept this money subverts both these hierarchies and these allegations. As such, this opening has been interpreted as a programmatic assertion of Euripides' ethical superiority in contrast to the avarice ascribed to him in the more hostile branches of the biographical tradition,[22] and, consequently, the *Letters*' intention to rehabilitate the playwright's reputation.[23]

But rather than offering a moralistic motivation, the Euripides of *Letter* 1 instead gives practical reasons for refusing Archelaus' offer such as his lack of need and the logistics of guarding such a large sum of money.[24] These kinds of pragmatic concerns have been seen in other letter-collections as examples of epistolary verisimilitude, where references to the mundane details of the letter-writer's circumstances are believed to enhance the authenticity of the collection.[25] Here, however, the letter's overarching concern for Euripides' reputation undercuts any appeal to verisimilitude and makes visible the spectre of the collection's inauthenticity. In contrast to his ultimately banal motivations, the letter foregrounds the playwright's insistence that his refusal was driven by a desire for empty fame (οὐ δόξαν κενὴν θηρώμενοι) and his concern that others might falsely interpret it as an act of political theatre rather than a sincere gesture. As Andrew Morrison has argued, such anxieties about how Euripides' actions will be interpreted highlight the fictional nature of the collection, since

---

[21] As Gösswein 1975, 88 puts it with further reference to the ancient sources, 'daß es Euripides während seines Aufenthaltes am Hof des Archelaos gut ging, bezeugen die biographischen Quellen einstimmig'. See also Knöbl 2008, 204–205.
[22] Knöbl 2008, 204.
[23] Gösswein 1975, 22–23; Jouan/Auger 1983, especially 190–194; Knöbl 2008, 248–258; Hanink 2010, especially 548–549; Morrison 2014a, 300–302.
[24] Gösswein 1975, 25 notes the parallels with an anecdote about Xenocrates, who upon receiving fifty talents from Alexander the Great, kept three thousand drachmas and returned the rest on the grounds that Alexander had more dependents to support than himself (Diog. Laert. 4.8). Against other financial motifs in fictional letter collections, on which see Holzberg 1994a, 13–17, the very practical reasons given by Euripides here suggest that the *Letters* are both alluding to and subverting these *Geldmotive*.
[25] Rosenmeyer 2001, 246–248; Morrison 2014a, 294; Hodkinson 2019.

this privileges a later audience aware of the playwright's posthumous reputation and underlines the text's own role in shaping such interpretations.[26] And yet, this complicates the supposedly rehabilitative principle of the *Letters*. If the more moralistic interpretation of Euripides' life is intended to supplant more hostile biographies, this presupposes that the *Letters* are intended to be perceived as a genuine alternative to these other sources, whereas their overt awareness of these later traditions emphasises their anachronistic belatedness.[27] Instead of simply proposing an alternative narrative to rehabilitate Euripides' reputation, therefore, the *Letters*' self-consciousness about their own inauthenticity invites further critical consideration.

Although the *Letters* have been described as 'freestanding letters without any kind of connective narrative,'[28] the subplot involving the young men of Pella which runs across multiple letters most clearly supports an overarching rehabilitative structure to the *Letters*. In the first letter Euripides claims that he has previously written to Archelaus to plead for the release of the wrongfully-imprisoned Pellaeans (*Ep.* 1.2). The lack of any further explanation of who they are or what their apparent crime is might at first glance again be ascribed to epistolary verisimilitude.[29] Their exoneration prompts the third letter, with Euripides profusely thanking Archelaus for his clemency, followed by the fourth using Archelaus' recent act of mercy towards the Pellaeans as the starting point for a more abstract discussion of kingship.[30] This sequence as presented in the *Letters* supports a rehabilitative reading of the collection. Given that the Pellaean saga is unattested elsewhere in the Euripidean biographical tradition,[31] this sequence appears designed to respond to accusations of the tragedian's indifference to the tyrant's reputation for cruelty, since here Euripides' relationship with the tyrant influences him for the better.[32]

---

26 Morrison 2014a, 301–302.
27 On the role of fiction in ancient biographical narratives, see De Temmerman 2016; Hodkinson 2010.
28 Poltera 2013, 154, although his comparison of the *Letters* to the collections attributed to Themistocles and Chion in n. 6, works which have been praised for their coherence as 'epistolary novels,' raises questions about how effective this characterisation is. On criticisms of coherence in the *Letters* of Chion see Jackson forthcoming a.
29 As Morrison 2014a, 294–295 notes. See also Gösswein 1975, 91's summary of Bentley's argument that this lack of exposition, ironically, testifies to the letter's inauthenticity.
30 Gösswein 1975, 19 characterises this letter as 'einen Fürstenspiegel in nuce'.
31 Hanink 2010, 545; Nesselrath 2023, 142–145. See also Gösswein 1975, 25 and 91.
32 Poltera 2013, 157–159 argues for the Euripidean *Letters* as a successful narrative in this regard by contrast to the Platonic *Epistles*. Hanink 2010, 562 n. 81 also notes how this Pellaean story rewrites other anecdotes about Euripides' cruelty by showcasing his clemency.

Again, however, the *Letters* leave any interpretations frustratingly implicit. While the sequence of letters within the collection as a whole allows for such a coherent reading, the concern for reputation found in individual letters undercuts it. This is clear from the first mention of the young men of Pella in the opening letter of the collection (*Ep.* 1.2):

> περὶ δὲ τῶν Πελλαίων νεανίσκων καὶ πρότερον ἤδη ἐπεστείλαμέν σοι δεόμενοι, καὶ νῦν δεόμεθα σῶσαί τε αὐτοὺς καὶ ἀνεῖναι τῶν δεσμῶν· οὐδὲν γὰρ ἀδικεῖν ἐοίκασιν ἢ οὐδὲν βλάψειν ἀφεθέντες ἔτι. μέτριον δὲ καὶ τὸ χαρίσασθαι δεομένοις ἡμῖν καὶ τὸ ἐλεῆσαι δὲ τὸν πατέρα αὐτῶν, γέροντα (ὡς ἔστι πυνθάνεσθαι) τῶν εὐγενεστάτων ἐν Πέλλῃ καὶ κατὰ τἆλλα δοκίμων... ἀλλὰ μὴ φαυλότερος γένῃ περὶ ἡμᾶς ἢ ἐκεῖνος ὑπέλαβεν.

> I wrote to you previously about the young men of Pella to plead on their behalf, and now I am pleading that you spare them and release them from prison, for they seem to have done no wrong, or at any rate it seems that they will do no harm if set free. It is reasonable to grant this favour to me as I ask it of you and to take pity on their aged father, who (as one can find out) is one of the most noble men in Pella and distinguished in other respects... So do not act less nobly towards me than he supposed you would.

Euripides here appears to appeal to Archelaus' self-interest by encouraging him to behave as nobly as the young men's father might expect him to (ἀλλὰ μὴ φαυλότερος γένῃ περὶ ἡμᾶς ἢ ἐκεῖνος ὑπέλαβεν). Given that various epistolary treatises from antiquity stress the importance of adapting letters to the style and attitude of the addressee,[33] this might be seen as Euripides' attempt to persuade Archelaus in terms which draw upon the king's own concern for his reputation. But Euripides also stresses that the Pellaean men *seem* innocent, or at least harmless, rather than simply asserting their innocence (οὐδὲν γὰρ ἀδικεῖν ἐοίκασιν ἢ οὐδὲν βλάψειν ἀφεθέντες ἔτι).[34] While a rehabilitative reading of Euripides' actions necessitates reading the *Letters* as straightforwardly sincere, the emphasis upon Archelaus' reputation and the appearance as opposed to the reality of the young men's innocence opens up the possibility of a dissonant, less earnest interpretation.

These concerns for reputation and self-interest also recur in the next letter to deal with the Pellaean men's release (*Ep.* 3.1):

---

33 For example, Dem. *Eloc.* 234; pseudo-Dem. *proem*; Cic. *Fam.* 2.4.1, 4.13.1: summarized by Malherbe 1988, 13. See also the analysis of Trapp 2003, 40–42.
34 On the language of εἰκός and its ability to make visible issues of truth, falsehood, and fiction, see Wohl 2014, especially 143–146. See also Futre Pinheiro 2018 on verisimilitude in ancient rhetorical theory.

ἀφίκετο Ἀθήναζε πρὸς ἡμᾶς ὁ Πελλαῖος γέρων ἅμα τοῖς ἑαυτοῦ νεανίσκοις, καὶ ἐγένετο ἡ ὄψις, ὦ βέλτιστε βασιλεῦ, ἡδεῖα μὲν ἐμοὶ τῷ θεωμένῳ τε καὶ δι' ὃν ταῦτα ἐγένετο, καλὴ δὲ καὶ σοὶ ἀπόντι καὶ φέρουσα δόξαν πολλὴν καὶ ζῆλον παρὰ πᾶσι τοῖς τε ἐπιτηδείοις τοῖς ἐμοῖς καὶ Ἀθηναίων ὁπόσοι εἶδον· εἶδον δὲ πολλοί, καὶ οὐδεὶς ὅστις οὐκ ἠγάσθη τέ σου τῆς φιλανθρωπίας καὶ συνεύξατό σοι τὰ ἀγαθά.

The old man from Pella arrived at my house in Athens together with his sons, and the sight, my good king, was sweet both for me who saw it and was the cause of it, but also glorious for you in your absence, and it brought you much fame and admiration from all my friends and all the Athenians who saw it. Indeed many people saw it, and there was no-one who did not admire your humanity and did not pray for blessings for you.

Despite Archelaus' absence, Euripides stresses that his clemency towards the Pellaeans brought him extravagant praise from the Athenian crowd and enhanced his reputation amongst them. Descriptions for the benefit of an absent addressee are recognised in antiquity as a key function of epistolary writing,[35] one which, as Emilia Barbiero shows persuasively in this volume, overlaps neatly with ancient definitions of ekphrasis as descriptive language which makes unseen things seem clearly visible.[36] But the language of such theorisations emphasises ekphrasis' illusory qualities in ways which draw attention to the discrepancy between appearance and reality.[37] This is especially acute for epistolary texts, which always problematise the relationship between reality and representation by foregrounding the letter as an intermediary step between separated persons,[38] as the third Euripidean *Letter* makes clear. Here, Euripides undercuts any potential ekphrastic vividness and accentuates these discrepancies by emphasising both Archelaus' physical absence (σοὶ ἀπόντι) and the abstract benefits of his enhanced fame. As such, this continuing concern for reputation draws attention to the letter's artificiality as a representative artefact

---

35 For example, in the programmatic assertions that letters are half of a dialogue (Dem. *Eloc.* 223) and a substitute for a conversation or the presence of the addressee (Sen. *Ep. Mor.* 40.1; Pseudo-Libanius *Ep. Char.* 58), which stress the role of letters in minimising the distance between interlocutors and creating an illusion of presence. On the importance of absence as both a precondition and problem of epistolary conversation, see Trapp 2003, 39–40.
36 Most famously articulated at Theon *Prog.* 2.118.7–8: 'ekphrasis is descriptive speech, bringing what is portrayed clearly before the eyes.' (ἔκφρασις ἐστὶ λόγος περιηγηματικὸς ἐναργῶς ὑπ' ὄψιν ἄγων τὸ δηλούμενον). On ancient definitions of ekphrasis see Webb 2009.
37 Goldhill 2007, 3: 'rhetorical theory knows well that [ekphrasis'] descriptive power is a technique of illusion, semblance, of making to appear. This brings ekphrasis particularly close to the theatre — the space of seeing and illusion.' See also Chinn 2007, 268–269; Squire 2013, especially 97–104, and Barbiero (this volume).
38 On this see Altman 1982, especially the summary at 185–190.

capable of both manipulating and rewriting reality, which unsettles the foundations of the collection's apparent rehabilitative purpose.

These disjunctions come to a head in the fifth and final letter of the collection. While the previous two letters were addressed to Archelaus from Athens, here Euripides writes from the king's court in Macedon to a hitherto unmentioned Cephisophon, likely in Athens.[39] While the character does not appear elsewhere in the collection, this name appears in other biographical sources associated variously with a creative collaborator of Euripides, his favourite actor, or a rival who slept with his wife.[40] In an inversion of these traditions, Cephisophon here appears to be a confidant of Euripides who can be trusted to respond to the tragedian's critics back in Athens in one of the *Letters*' boldest strokes of biographical revisionism.[41] The longest letter of the collection, *Letter* 5 has often been seen as the climax of the work not just because it completes the playwright's transition to Macedon, but also because it reflects on his relationships with Archelaus and Sophocles, the addressees of the previous letters.[42] This allows for a neat circularity between the first and final letters of the collection to emerge, as while *Letter* 1 opens with Euripides refusing Archelaus' money, *Letter* 5 includes another example of this scene in order to reinforce that the tragedian did not move to Macedon for financial reasons.[43] As such, this closing letter reiterates the collection's central interest in rehabilitating Euripides' reputation from accusations of greed or sycophancy and testifies to the unity of the *Letters* as a whole.

And yet, while *Letter* 5 seems to tackle most directly the central mystery of why Euripides moved to Macedon, in practice it continues the collection's trend of refusing to offer a clear alternative to other biographical narratives even as it criticises them. This is clearest in Euripides' response to the rumours circulating in Athens about the reasons for his departure (*Ep.* 5.2):

---

39 *Letter* 5 does not specify Cephisophon's location, but given that the letter opens with Euripides' arrival in Macedon (καὶ ἀφικόμεθα εἰς Μακεδονίαν, ὦ βέλτιστε Κηφισοοφῶν, *Ep.* 5.1) and extensive instructions on how to respond to named critics of the playwright's move, it seems extremely unlikely Cephisophon would be anywhere else other than Athens.
40 Hanink 2010, 544–545.
41 Knöbl 2008, 235 describes it as 'a fine narrative *coup*.'
42 Gösswein 1975, 113–114; Hanink 2010, 551.
43 *Ep.* 5.4: 'You could even add further that a few days after I arrived in Macedon, when Archelaus offered me forty talents of silver and was annoyed at my declining it, I refused to take it.' (ἔτι δὲ δὴ καὶ προσθείης ὅτι, ἐπειδὴ τάχιστα ἀφικόμεθα εἰς Μακεδονίαν, ὀλίγαις ὕστερον ἡμέραις τεσσαράκοντα τάλαντα ἀργυρίου διδόντος Ἀρχελάου καὶ ἀγανακτοῦντος, ὅτι οὐ λαμβάνοιμεν, ἀντέσχομεν μὴ λαβεῖν).

περὶ δὲ ὧν ἐπέστειλας ἡμῖν σὺ μὲν εὖ ποιεῖς ἐπιστέλλων ἃ δοκεῖς ἡμῖν εἰδέναι διαφέρειν· ἴσθι μέντοι μηδὲν μᾶλλον ἡμῖν ὧν νῦν Ἀγάθων ἢ Μέσατος λέγει μέλον ἢ τῶν Ἀριστοφάνους φληναφημάτων οἶσθά ποτε μέλον. καὶ τούτοις γε ἂν ἀδικήσαις ἡμᾶς εἰς τὰ μάλιστα ἀποκρινάμενός ποτε, κἂν ὅλως μὴ παυομένους τῆς ἀναγωγίας αὐτοὺς ὁρᾷς. ἢν μέντοι τις τῶν ἀξίων περὶ Εὐριπίδου λέγειν τι ἢ ἀκούειν αἰτιᾶται ἡμᾶς τῆς πρὸς Ἀρχέλαον ὁδοῦ, ἃ μὲν τὸ πρόσθεν εἴπομεν περὶ τοῦ μὴ δεῖν εἰς Μακεδονίαν ἡμᾶς ἀποδημεῖν ἐπιστάμενος, ἃ δὲ μετὰ ταῦτα ἡμᾶς ἀπηνάγκασε βαδίσαι ἀγνοῶν, τοῦτον δὲ ἄξιον νόμιζε δηλοῦν αὐτῷ ἅπερ οἶσθα, ὦ Κηφισοφῶν· καὶ οὕτω πεπαύσεται ἀγνοῶν τὰς αἰτίας καὶ ἅμα, ὅπερ εἰκός ἐστι τὸν ἀγνοοῦντα πάσχειν, καταγινώσκων ἡμῶν ὡς φιλοχρημάτων γενομένων.

Concerning your letters to me, you do well to write what you think it interests me to know. But you should be clear that I have no more concern for what Agathon or Mesatus say than I had once, as you are aware, for the fooleries of Aristophanes. And you will do me a grave injustice if you reply to these men, even if you see that they let up not at all from their vulgarity. But if anyone worthy to speak or hear a word about Euripides should find fault with my journey to Archelaus, knowing what I said earlier about there being no necessity for me to go to Macedon but not knowing the subsequent circumstances that forced me to go, regard him as someone worthy to hear all you know, Cephisophon. And in this way he will cease to be ignorant of the causes and at the same time to condemn me—as is natural for one in ignorance to do—as greedy for gain.

This extract self-consciously places the *Letters* in opposition to other biographical narratives about Euripides, while simultaneously obscuring their own contribution to these traditions. Regardless of who the mentions of Agathon and Mesatus are understood to refer to,[44] the comparison with Aristophanes evokes the common story that Euripides was driven from Athens by the invective of comic poets,[45] even as Euripides' descriptions of such insults as φληναφήματα disclaim their legitimacy.[46] And yet, while Euripides gives Cephisophon permission to respond to these false rumours with the truth, *Letter* 5 never actually explains what the true story is.[47] Rather than naturalising the *Letters*' version of events, Euripides' insistence that Cephisophon has his permission to tell the truth without actually communicating what that truth is draws attention to this omission. This is made more pointed by the ending of the *Letters*, where Euripides

---

[44] On the possible identities of these figures, see Gösswein 1975, 117; Knöbl 2008, 239–240; Poltera 2013, 162. Nesselrath 2023, 142–145 suggests that this is a way of rejecting the suggestion of a love-affair between Euripides and his contemporary poet Agathon found elsewhere in the biographical tradition.
[45] Revermann 1999–2000; Hanink 2010, 551–552.
[46] While the noun φληνάφημα is rarely attested and only in postclassical texts, as Gösswein 1975, 118 notes, the verb φληναφάω appears in Aristophanes (*Eq.* 664, *Nu.* 1475), making its use here to criticise the comic playwright himself especially ironic. On this see Jouan/Auger 1983, 194.
[47] As noted by Hanink 2010, 546.

asks Cephisophon to write back while simultaneously ordering him not to share his true motivations for moving to Macedon with those he deems unworthy of hearing them (*Ep.* 5.6).[48] This refusal to offer a clear alternative despite their rehabilitative appearance reinforces the central paradox of the *Letters*, in that they seem to offer the tantalising conceit of hearing the truth directly in the playwright's own words, but they ultimately refuse to divulge this secret. If *Letter* 5 is meant to unify the collection and provide an appropriate climax to its implied positive rewriting of Euripides' biography, it leaves many key details tantalisingly unexplained.

This is not, however, purely aporetic. Ranja Knöbl has suggested that Euripides' cryptic remarks to Cephisophon allude to the tendency in biographical narratives 'to constantly create new versions and embellish existing stories. The reader is made to feel curiosity about unknown details, and then warned about the dangers of making assumptions and being ignorant.'[49] By attacking the biographical stories about Euripides already in circulation, the *Letters* attempt to invalidate their authority, even as their continual concern for reputation highlights the artificiality of the collection itself as a work of fiction. In this way the *Letters*' self-consciousness about their own inauthenticity not only undercuts the work's ostensible conceit to offer a genuine alternative to the Euripidean biographical tradition, but also draws attention to the potential fiction of biographical narratives more widely. Rather than simply putting forward an alternative rehabilitative narrative about Euripides' life, the *Letters* play more deviously with not just their own inauthenticity, but also the wider issues about truth and falsehood within the creative traditions of ancient biography.

2 Epistolary Exchange

But this is complicated by the epistolary format of the *Letters*. At first glance, the sheer prevalence of pseudonymous letter collections attributed to famous figures in circulation during the imperial period, when the *Letters* were likely

---

48 *Ep.* 5.6: 'You do well to write to me about these things when you think they are of importance to me. But just as you do well to write, so I shall say that you do me wrong if you reply on these matters to those who are not worthy' (σὺ μέντοι εὖ ποιεῖς περὶ τούτων ἡμῖν γράφων, ἐπειδήπερ οἴει ἡμῖν διαφέρειν· ἀλλ' ὥσπερ εὖ ποιεῖς γράφων, οὕτως ἀδικεῖν σε φήσαιμ' ἂν ἡμᾶς ἀντιλέγοντα ὑπὲρ αὐτῶν τοῖς οὐκ ἀξίοις).
49 Knöbl 2008, 231.

composed, downplays the significance of this choice.⁵⁰ Moreover, as a format which co-opts the authority of the poet's own voice, an epistolary structure allows the *Letters* to directly challenge the prevailing biographical traditions by offering at least the appearance of a more authoritative account endorsed by the tragedian himself.⁵¹ But not only is this format unique in the context of Euripidean biographical traditions, such epistolary authority is a double-edged sword. On the one hand, letters adopt at least a veneer of authenticity by writing in the voice of the famous figure they ventriloquise. On the other hand, however, in antiquity letters are repeatedly associated with deception, inauthenticity, and miscommunication, and letters' vulnerability to forgery is well-known in ancient sources.⁵² Consequently, rather than passively reflecting wider trends in imperial epistolography, the *Letters*' epistolary format adds further potency to their subversive approach to Euripidean biographical traditions and implicitly brings questions about authenticity and fiction to the forefront.

The *Letters*' exploitation of χάρις throughout the collection makes these issues explicit. Notoriously elusive and difficult to define, χάρις covers a wide spectrum of meanings, ranging from mutual gratitude, repayment of favours, erotic pleasure, and aesthetic beauty, all of which centre around its core connotation of reciprocity.⁵³ In the context of letters, however, χάρις makes visible the importance of exchange in both epistolary form and content. As a paradigmatic example, the treatise attributed to Demetrius on epistolary typologies discusses why χάρις is a suitable subject for certain types of letters (*Ep. Typ.* 3):⁵⁴

μεμπτικὸς δέ ἐστιν ὁ μὴ νομίζεσθαι βαρεῖν προσδεχόμενος. οἷον· εἰ μὴ παραδέδωκέ σοι μηδέπω ὁ καιρὸς ὧν εὖ πέπονθας ἐκτῖσαι χάριτας, οὐδὲ αὐτὸ τοῦτό γε καλῶς ἔχειν ὑπείληφα τὸ μὴ μνημονεύειν ὧν ἔπαθες.

---

50 Knöbl 2008, 190. Jouan/Auger 1983, 194 and Hanink 2010, 555–561 also draw parallels with other philosophical letters from this period. On imperial letter-collections more generally, see Rosenmeyer 2001, 255–337.
51 Knöbl 2008, 191. On the benefits of such pseudonymous collections in the imperial period more generally, see Hodkinson 2007.
52 Made clearest by Rosenmeyer 2001, who cites the example of Bellerophon from *Iliad* 6 as a key paradigm for the dangers of epistolary communication which resonates throughout ancient Greek literature. See also Steiner 1994.
53 The semantic range of χάρις is vast: MacLachlan 1993; Goldhill 1991, 128–166; Kurke 1991, 73–139, and Pontani 2013 offer useful overviews of the term in early Greek poetry with further bibliography. On erotic χάρις see Fisher 2013, on aesthetic χάρις with a particular focus on the imperial period see von Möllendorff 2006, 72–79.
54 Text and translation taken from Malherbe 1988.

> The blaming type [of letter] is the one that undertakes not to seem harsh. For example: 'Since you have not yet had time to express thanks for the favours you received, for that reason I thought it well not to mention what you had received.'

While somewhat petty, Pseudo-Demetrius' description highlights the network of reciprocal obligations invoked by χάρις which underpin epistolary communication. In this passage, letters both act as the vehicle for χάρις, in that they can fulfil these social debts or point out the failure of such reciprocity (ἐκτῖσαι χάριτας), and also come to embody it, since the letter itself symbolises the χάρις Pseudo-Demetrius expects from his recipient.[55] Similarly, the treatise attributed to Libanius describes χάρις as the key feature of letters which express thanks (εὐχαριστικὴ δι' ἧς χάριν γινώσκομέν τινι διά τι, *Ep. Char.* 10), which plays on the dual sense of χάρις as a stylistic attribute as well as the fundamental condition for epistolary communication.[56] While the connection between epistolary theory and genuine letters is notoriously complex, and it is far from clear how influential such treatises were on ancient letter-writers,[57] the theorists' focus on χάρις as a suitable subject for letters illuminates the reciprocity necessary to sustain an epistolary exchange.[58] If letters are indeed half of a dialogue, as various treatise-writers assert,[59] χάρις is the glue which maintains this illusion of conversation.

The Euripidean *Letters* repeatedly allude to the role of χάρις in epistolary communication, most visibly in the subplot relating to the young men of Pella. Here, Euripides' repeated pleas to Archelaus for the men's release implicitly evoke χάρις as a fundamental property of the relationship between poet and patron which underpins the collection. Although Euripides does initially describe the young men as seeming innocent, he also characterises Archelaus' release of the men as a favour to himself (μέτριον δὲ καὶ τὸ χαρίσασθαι δεομένοις ἡμῖν, *Ep.* 1.2), which frames their pardon as an interpersonal obligation rather

---

[55] On the narrative dynamics of unanswered letters, see König 2007, especially 267–270. I am especially grateful to Janja Soldo for her insight into the complex dynamics of χάρις here.
[56] The importance of χάρις as a stylistic feature of letters is also discussed in Dem. *Eloc.* 235: see also Gregory of Nazianzus *Ep.* 51.5.
[57] For an overview of epistolary handbooks from antiquity, see Malherbe 1988; Trapp 2003, 42–46; Poster 2007.
[58] Although Peirano Garrison 2021, 8 notes how writers of fictional letters such as Philostratus recognise and exploit χάρις through, for example, puns on χαῖρε as a traditional epistolary greeting (*Ep.* 14).
[59] Most famously at Dem. *Eloc.* 223, attributed to Artemon, the editor of Aristotle's *Letters*: Ἀρτέμων μὲν οὖν ὁ τὰς Ἀριστοτέλους ἀναγράψας ἐπιστολάς φησιν, ὅτι δεῖ ἐν τῷ αὐτῷ τρόπῳ διάλογόν τε γράφειν καὶ ἐπιστολάς· εἶναι γὰρ τὴν ἐπιστολὴν οἷον τὸ ἕτερον μέρος τοῦ διαλόγου.

than an act of mercy. This is reinforced in the third letter of the collection following the release of the Pellaeans (*Ep.* 3.2):

ἐγὼ δὲ πολλὰ μὲν καὶ ἕτερα εἰπεῖν ἔχω, οὐ βούλομαι δέ, ἐπιδεικνὺς ὅσῳ πλείονα ἐκ τούτου σεαυτὸν ὤνησας ἢ ἄλλον τινὰ ἀνθρώπων, δοκεῖν διὰ τοῦτο ἐλάττω σοι χάριν ἔχειν. ὁμολογῶ δὲ αὐτός τε εὖ τὰ μέγιστα πεπονθέναι καὶ πειράσεσθαι τοῦ καλοῦ τούτου ἔργου πολλὰ πάνυ καὶ μεγάλα παρασχεῖν σοι χαριστήρια, ὅτι οὔτε τὸν δείλαιον γέροντα ἐκεῖνον, ὅτε ἠτύχει, τῆς ἐφ' ἡμῖν οὔτε ἡμᾶς τῆς ἐπὶ σοὶ γενομένης ἐψεύσω ἐλπίδος.

I could tell you many other things, but I do not want, in demonstrating how much more benefit you did to yourself in this deed than to any other mortal, to seem to be less grateful to you for this reason. I admit that I myself have received the greatest benefit and will try to provide you with many great offerings of gratitude in return for this good deed, that you did not disappoint that poor old man in the hour of his misfortune of the hopes that he had placed in me, nor those that I placed in you.

This passage makes explicit the previously implicit power dynamics in these negotiations of favours and friendship.[60] On the one hand, Euripides insists that he will try to provide thanks-offerings (χαριστήρια) in order to provide evidence of his gratitude, which makes visible the system of patronage at play in this interaction.[61] On the other, however, Euripides emphasises that while Archelaus has done him a favour, his actions have primarily benefitted himself, although he also stresses that he is no less grateful to him as a result (οὐ βούλομαι δέ… δοκεῖν διὰ τοῦτο ἐλάττω σοι χάριν ἔχειν). This not only frames the letter itself as an embodiment of χάρις, but also links the content of the *Letters* and the network of social obligations which structures Euripides and Archelaus' relationship with the format of their epistolary dialogue.

This exchange of favours is developed further in the opening to the following letter, which acts as the prelude to Euripides' discussion of moral kingship (*Ep.* 4.1):

καὶ τὰ περὶ τοὺς Πελλαίους, ὦ βέλτιστε Ἀρχέλαε, καὶ πολλὰ ἄλλα πεπολίτευταί σοι καλῶς καὶ πρὸς ἐμὲ καὶ πρὸς ἑτέρους ἐπιεικεῖς τε καὶ σπουδῆς ἀξίους πολλούς, καὶ οὐχ ἧσσον αὐτά, εὖ ἴσθι, ὅσα πρὸς ἄλλους τινάς, ἢ ὅσα πρὸς ἡμᾶς ἰδίᾳ πέπρακταί σοι καλῶς, ἐπιμελές μοι εἰδέναι, οὐ φιλοπράγμονι ὄντι, ἀλλὰ χαίροντι ἐφ' οἷς εὐδοκιμοῦντα πυνθάνομαί σε, καὶ χάριν σοι οὐκ ἐλάττω ὑπὲρ αὐτῶν ἔχω.

---

60 Gösswein 1975, 18 goes so far as to label this as an example of the εὐχαριστική letter type, building on typologies from letter-writing manuals of antiquity.
61 Gösswein 1975, 102 discusses the exact form of Euripides' χαριστήρια, rather than seeing it as a metaphorical exchange.

> Both in the matter of the Pelleans, most excellent Archelaus, and in many other things you have acted well both in regard to me and to many others who were worthy of your efforts. Rest assured, I am not less concerned to learn about the actions performed for the benefit of others than those done for me personally. This concerns me not because I am a busybody, but because I take pleasure in the renown I perceive you enjoying, and I am no less grateful to you for these deeds.

Letter 4 stands in contrast to its predecessor, as while the third letter described the release of the Pellaeans and its immediate consequences, the following text uses this as the starting point for a more theoretical discussion of what makes a good ruler.[62] Again, Euripides emphasises his gratitude for Archelaus' benevolence even if it primarily benefits the king himself,[63] but followed as this is by Euripides' more abstract reflections on kingship, it is hard not to see this letter as a response to Archelaus' munificence.[64] In other words, if in the third letter Archelaus' benevolence was an act of χάρις towards Euripides, here Euripides repays the favour by offering advice on how the king can enhance his reputation.[65] As such, if the exchange of gifts between poet and patron is the dominant theme of the collection, as Jouan and Auger put it,[66] the *Letters* repeat this motif at a metaphorical level through the exchange of both favours and letters. The χάρις of epistolary exchange as dramatized throughout the *Letters* reinforces the impression of a reciprocal and mutually beneficial relationship between Archelaus and Euripides, and can be seen as an exemplary model of epistolary communication.

But even though the *Letters* repeatedly thematise ideas of exchange and dialogue, the very format of the collection stifles this. The *Letters* do not have any letters from Archelaus, only from Euripides, which makes the collection, in Ranja Knöbl's words, 'an unimpeded imaginary monologue by Euripides.'[67] As a result, any sense of exchange can only be perceived implicitly by a readerly desire to graft a coherent narrative onto the five separate letters of the collection.[68] As the idealised view amongst ancient theorists that a letter is half of a dialogue shows, letters are inherently a fragmentary format, which can only

---

62 See Hanink 2010, 552–553 on the sources and context of the fourth letter.
63 Knöbl 2008, 224–225.
64 The link between the two is noted by Gösswein 1975, 19.
65 Jouan/Auger 1983, 194.
66 Jouan/Auger 1983, 194: 'le motif dominant dans ces *Lettres* semble être celui de l'échange des dons entre Euripide et Archélaos.'
67 Knöbl 2008, 189.
68 For more on coherence and fragmentation in epistolary texts, see Jackson forthcoming a on the *Letters* of Chion within the wider context of ancient letter collections.

form a coherent conversation when ordered into a sequential narrative.[69] Here, however, the nature of the *Letters* means that while their content thematises the importance of reciprocity, their format thwarts this, and implicitly points out the pitfalls of epistolary exchange. This frustrated model of exchange, in which the *Letters* are both the medium of favours and yet in their very form make epistolary exchange impossible, culminates in the final letter of the collection (*Ep.* 5.1):

καὶ ἀφικόμεθα εἰς Μακεδονίαν, ὦ βέλτιστε Κηφισοφῶν... καὶ ἀπεδέξατο ἡμᾶς Ἀρχέλαος, ὡς εἰκός τε ἦν καὶ προσεδοκῶμεν ἡμεῖς, οὐ δωρεαῖς μόνον, ὧν οὐδὲν ἐχρῄζομεν ἡμεῖς, ἀλλὰ καὶ φιλοφροσύναις, ὧν οὐδ᾽ ἂν εὔξαιτό τις μείζους παρὰ βασιλέων. καὶ κατελάβομεν Κλείτωνα ἐρρωμένον, καὶ ἔστιν ἡμῖν σὺν ἐκείνῳ τὰ πολλὰ καί, ὅταν τύχῃ, σὺν Ἀρχελάῳ ἄμεμπτος ἡ διαγωγή· πρός τε τοῖς ἔργοις οὐδὲν κωλυόμεθα τοῖς τούτων γίγνεσθαι. ἀλλὰ καὶ πολὺς μὲν ἔγκειται ὁ Κλείτων, πολὺς δὲ ὁ Ἀρχέλαος, ἑκάστοτε φροντίζειν ἀεί τι καὶ ποιεῖν τῶν εἰωθότων ἀναγκάζοντες, ὥστ᾽ ἔμοιγε μισθὸν οὐκ ἀηδῆ μὲν οὖν, οὐ δὲ ἄπονον δοκεῖ Ἀρχέλαος ἀναπράσσεσθαι τῶν τε δωρεῶν, ὧν ἔδωκέ μοι εὐθέως ἀφικομένῳ, καὶ ὅτι ἑστιᾷ με λαμπρότερον ἢ ἐμοὶ φίλον ἦν ἑκάστης ἡμέρας.

I have arrived in Macedonia, my good Cephisophon...and Archelaus has received me, properly and as expected, not only with gifts, which I don't need, but also with kindnesses, greater than which one would not pray for from kings. I also found Cleiton in good health, and for the most part my time is spent unobjectionably with him and, whenever possible, with Archelaus, and I am in no way prevented from taking part in their works. But Cleiton is very pressuring, and so is Archelaus, and on every occasion they pressure me to think and compose some of my usual works. And so I think that Archelaus is extracting a payment from me — not unpleasant, to be sure, but not without toil — for the gifts he gave me on my arrival and for the fact he feasts me every day more splendidly than I like.

While Euripides' insistence that he has been received far more lavishly than he either wants or needs again refutes the accusations that he went to Macedon for financial gain, this contrasts with his subsequent claims of creative coercion. Writing to Cephisophon in Athens, Euripides complains that Archelaus and Cleiton are very pressuring (ἀλλὰ καὶ πολὺς μὲν ἔγκειται ὁ Κλείτων, πολὺς δὲ καὶ ὁ Ἀρχέλαος),[70] and are continually forcing him to compose his usual works (ποιεῖν τῶν εἰωθότων).[71] While Euripides claims that this work is not unpleasant (οὐκ ἀηδῆ), a double negative construction which emphasises the ambivalence

---

69 On the significance of editorial revision and ordering in epistolary collections, see Beard 2002; Gibson 2012; Morrison 2019.
70 See Knöbl 2008, 227–229 on the name and identity of Cleiton.
71 On this phrase see Gösswein 1975, 115–116.

of this characterisation,[72] the explicit description of this pressure as a payment (μισθόν) for Archelaus' generosity makes explicit the shift from the language of reciprocity which characterised earlier letters to the language of compulsion seen here.[73] The juxtaposition of *Letters* 4 and 5 makes this shift all the more stark, as while the preceding letter concluded with Euripides praising Archelaus for surrounding himself with poets, the realities of this arrangement as described in *Letter* 5 weaken this utopian ideal. While earlier letters continually idealised χάρις as a model of reciprocity, both in relationships and letters, *Letter* 5 undercuts this by dramatizing the failure of these models of exchange.[74] As such, this thematization of χάρις not only mirrors the collection's own conclusion and the collapse of the relationship between Euripides and Archelaus, but also highlights how self-consciously the *Letters* manipulate epistolary conventions. Rather than naturalising the *Letters* as genuine Euripidean texts, therefore, the collection's use of an epistolary format undercuts this veneer of authenticity and invites awareness of how this framework in fact enhances the work's fictional self-consciousness.

3 Sophocles

But the *Letters* are not unique, either as epistolary fictions or revisionist biographies. The Euripidean *Letters* have often been seen as in dialogue with the Platonic *Epistles* based on their shared narrative arc of the letter-writer advising a tyrant.[75] In particular, the opening of the Euripidean *Letters*, which portrays Euripides rejecting Archelaus' money as being more than he needs,[76] has been seen as a rebuttal of the first Platonic *Epistle*, where Plato rejects Dionysius II's

---

[72] A useful comparison here is Ach. Tat. *L&C* 1.19.1, where the narrator's description of Leucippe listening to his narratives not without pleasure (οὐκ ἀηδῶς) similarly draws attention to the possibility of a more lukewarm interpretation. On this see Whitmarsh 2020, 183–184.
[73] On ἔγκειται see Gösswein 1975, 115.
[74] This epistolary self-consciousness might also be alluded to in Euripides' comment that he found Cleiton ἐρρωμένον, in good health, which is also used as an epistolary sign-off. On this see Trapp 2003, 35.
[75] Holzberg 1994a, 14–15; Poltera 2013. For an opposing view, see Nesselrath 2023, 145–148. While both collections were likely referred to in antiquity as *Epistulae*, I here use *Epistles* to distinguish the Platonic collection from the Euripidean *Letters*.
[76] See also *Ep*. 5.1, where Euripides complains that Archelaus is giving him gifts he does not need (οὐ δωρεαῖς μόνον, ὧν οὐδὲν ἐχρῄζομεν ἡμεῖς).

money as insufficient (*Epistle* 1, 309b8–c2).⁷⁷ While the exact nature of the relationship between the two collections remains controversial,⁷⁸ arguments for a coherent philosophical stance in the *Letters* have proved tenacious. While Holzberg has gone so far as to suggest that the fifth Euripidean *Letter* corresponds to the seventh Platonic *Epistle*,⁷⁹ Jouan and Auger have seen parallels with philosophical motifs also found in the letter-collections of Cynics and Stoics,⁸⁰ and Knöbl has also identified Epicurean motifs in the *Letters*.⁸¹ This approach can be seen even in antiquity. As Johanna Hanink has argued, the transmission of the *Letters* alongside other pseudonymous collections attributed to philosophers both reflects Euripides' reputation as a 'philosopher of the stage' and also preserves it for later readers.⁸² Rather than singling out the *Letters* as unique for its epistolary format and biographical revisionism, these parallels both suggest a unifying purpose for the work and align it amongst the wider group of pseudonymous letter-collections attributed to philosophers.

This, however, is complicated by the prominence given to Sophocles within the *Letters*. If the *Letters* should be viewed as primarily about the ethically complex relationship between tyrant and advisor as in other philosophical letter collections, what role does Sophocles, the third most prominent character after Euripides and Archelaus, play? In a collection of only five letters, the inclusion of a letter addressed solely to Sophocles is especially notable not only as it is the only letter not to mention Archelaus in any way,⁸³ but also for how it disrupts the narrative coherence of the work. While the first and third letters follow the continuous narratives of the Pellaeans' false imprisonment and Archelaus and Euripides' relationship, the intervening letter to Sophocles contributes nothing to either narrative arc. Although this has led some scholars to question whether *Letter* 2 is in fact a later interpolation into the collection,⁸⁴ manuscript evidence suggests that the letter was perceived as integral to the whole work by some of

---

77 Poltera 2013, 157–159; Holzberg 1994a, 14: 'es liegt nahe zu vermuten, daß der unbekannte Autor der *Epistolai Euripidou* seinen Briefschreiber indirekt gegen den Platon der *Epistolai Platonos* polemisieren lassen wollte, und diese Vermutung wird durch eine Stelle in Platons Staat gestützt: Dort wird dem Euripides Tyrannenfreundschaft vorgeworfen (568a8–d3).'
78 Knöbl 2008, 227–229.
79 Holzberg 1994a, 14.
80 Jouan/Auger 1983, 194.
81 Knöbl 2008, in particular 198–199.
82 Hanink 2010, 555–561. See n. 7 above on the manuscript tradition of the *Letters*.
83 Hanink 2010, 545.
84 Gösswein 1975, 20–22. More recent scholarship, however, has argued for *Letter* 2's integral place within the collection: see Holzberg 1994a, 16; Poltera 2013, 163.

its earliest compilers. While some manuscripts contain only the first three letters of the collection, all extant copies of the *Letters* not only include the second letter, but maintain its place within the overall order of the collection.[85] This consistency of ordering suggests the disruption generated by *Letter 2* is not simply an accident of survival, but rather an intentional part of the collection, one which raises questions about exactly what the character of Sophocles contributes to the *Letters* as a whole.

Regardless of *Letter 2*'s structural integrity within the collection, its contents are still striking. In contrast to the political negotiations of the surrounding letters, Euripides writes in an intimate tone to express his joy that Sophocles has survived a recent shipwreck and promises to take care of his literary affairs as entrusted to him. This portrayal of the two tragedians not just as friends, but as literary executors represents a radical departure from the biographical tradition, which frames Euripides and Sophocles' relationship as at best a respectful rivalry and at worst outright antagonism.[86] As such, this letter might seem to be a straightforward inversion of the two tragedians' interactions as portrayed in other biographical sources,[87] but this is complicated by the fifth and final letter of the collection (*Letter* 5.5–6):

> καὶ μὴν εὐμετάβολόν γέ με οὔτε εἰς τὰ ἐπιτηδεύματα οὔτε εἰς ὑμᾶς τοὺς φίλους καὶ οὐχ ἧσσον εἰς τοὺς ἐχθροὺς σκοπῶν εἴποι τις ἄν, οἷς ἅπασιν ἐκ νέου μέχρι τοῦ νῦν τοῖς αὐτοῖς κέχρημαι πλὴν ἑνὸς ἀνδρός, Σοφοκλέους· πρὸς γὰρ δὴ τοῦτον μόνον ἴσασί με τάχα οὐχ ὁμοίως ἀεὶ τὴν γνώμην ἔχοντα. ὃν ἐγὼ ἐμίσησα μὲν οὐδέποτε, ἐθαύμασα δὲ ἀεί, ἔστερξα δὲ οὐχ ὁμοίως ἀεί, ἀλλὰ φιλοτιμότερον μέν τινα εἶναί ποτε δόξας ὑπεῖδον, βουληθέντα δὲ ἐκλύσασθαι τὰ νείκη προθυμότατα ὑπεδεξάμην. καὶ ἀλλήλους μέν, ἐξ ὅτου συνέβη, στέργομέν τε καὶ στέρξομεν· τοὺς δ' ἐμβάλλοντας ἡμῖν πολλάκις τὰς ὑπονοίας, ἵνα ἐκ τοῦ ἡμᾶς ἀπεχθάνεσθαι, τὸν ἕτερον θεραπεύοντες, αὐτοὶ πλεῖον ἔχωσι, διαβεβλήμεθα.

> The truth is that no-one who examined me could say that I was changeable either as regards my way of life or as regards you my friends and, to no lesser extent, my enemies. From my youth up until the present day I have regarded the same men as my friends and the same my enemies, with the sole exception of Sophocles. People know that in relation to him alone my attitude has been different. I never hated him, to be sure, but I never loved him as I do now. I thought he was a man too given to ambition and I was suspicious of him, but when he proposed to let go of our hostility I eagerly accepted. And since the

---

[85] Gösswein 1975, 18; Knöbl 2008, 200–201. While all manuscripts of the *Letters* are too late to prove conclusively the integrity of the collection in antiquity, their uniformity certainly does not support the alternative interpretation.
[86] Hanink 2010, 550–551 offers an overview of these traditions.
[87] Jouan/Auger 1983, 193–194, who also note that the two tragedians are framed elsewhere as the inverse of each other.

time of our reconciliation we have loved one another and will continue to do so. As for those who seek to sow suspicion between us so that, as a result of our falling out, they might serve one or the other of us and gain thereby, we have cast them off.

This brief but illuminating extract nuances the portrayal of Euripides and Sophocles' relationship seen in the second letter.[88] Set against the straightforwardly revisionist narrative of the earlier letter, Euripides' professed change of heart seems to acknowledge these divergent accounts of his and Sophocles' rivalry while also integrating them into the *Letters*' counterfactual narrative.[89] But the placement of this discussion at almost the very end of the final letter of the work emphasises the dissonance between these traditions rather than unifying them, and draws attention to Sophocles' key role in Euripides' life as portrayed in the *Letters*. Moreover, the claim that such accounts were spread by rivals looking to profit from their enmity 'implicitly accounts for — or at least renders plausible — all of these other stories'[90] and reinforces the supposed authenticity of the *Letters* against these other, allegedly false, narratives. As such, by characterising Sophocles as the sole exception to Euripides' otherwise consistent life, the *Letters* frame him as the key to the tensions between the *Letters*' version of Euripides and the version constructed in alternative biographical traditions.

And yet, in practice, this framework is more ambiguous than it appears at first glance. While the prominence of Sophocles in the *Letters*' version of Euripides' life implicitly reinforces the authenticity of the collection by depicting all other stories as false, once again the *Letters* do not offer a coherent alternative, but instead undercut their own foundations. The claim that Euripides' original antipathy towards Sophocles was based on the belief that he was too ambitious (ἀλλὰ φιλοτιμότερον μέν τινα εἶναί ποτε δόξας ὑπεῖδον) has been interpreted as further evidence of the *Letters*' moralistic undertones,[91] given the term's philosophical connotations in the imperial period in particular.[92] But a key trait of φιλοτιμία is its ambivalence, covering both productive competitiveness as well

---

[88] Gösswein 1975, 21 takes this so far as to suggest that the second letter might be a later addition to flesh out the relatively colourless portrayal of their relationship in *Letter 5*.
[89] As Hanink 2010, 551 suggests.
[90] Hanink 2010, 551. See also Morrison 2014a, 300: 'The fifth Euripidean letter sets up a different picture, but also leaves room to explain how such negative material might have arisen.'
[91] On φιλοτιμία and philosophy in the *Letters*, see Knöbl 2008, 236–238. Gösswein 1975, 128–129 notes that Sophocles' φιλοτιμία was a common theme in his biographies as a reflection of his civic dutifulness.
[92] On the philosophical significance of φιλοτιμία see Frazier 1988; Zadorojnyi 2006, 262. On imperial φιλοτιμία more generally see the essays in Roskam/De Pourcq/Van Der Stockt 2012.

as the negative consequences of excessive ambition.⁹³ This not only parallels ancient narratives about Sophocles and Euripides' friendship,⁹⁴ but also reiterates the ambiguity inherent in their relationship, even as the *Letters* superficially offers a less complex version of it. By setting themselves in contrast to the presupposed false narratives of the wider biographical tradition, the *Letters* make an implicit claim for their own legitimacy. Yet, in centring this claim around the most complex relationship of Euripides' biography, they invoke the spectre of their inauthenticity, since this innovative reworking of the two tragedians' relationship so flagrantly positions the *Letters* in opposition to prevailing traditions.

Against this, *Letter* 2 takes on a different tone (*Ep.* 2.1):

τὸ δὲ τοσούτου κακοῦ ἥκοντος περισῴζεσθαι σε καὶ τὸ τῶν συνόντων σοι φίλων μηδὲ θεραπόντων ἀποβαλεῖν μηδένα οὐκ ἄλλο τι ἔγωγε ἢ θεοῦ πρόνοιαν γενέσθαι πείθομαι. ἡ μέντοι περὶ τὰ δράματα συμφορά, ἥν τίς οὐχὶ κοινὴν ἁπάσης τῆς Ἑλλάδος νομίσειεν ἄν, δεινὴ μέν, ἀλλὰ περιόντος γε σοῦ ῥᾳδίως ἐπανορθωθήσεται.

The fact that when this calamity occurred you were saved and did not lose a single one of the friends or slaves who were with you, this I consider to be nothing other than divine providence. The misfortune regarding your plays, however – who would not consider it to be the common misfortune of Greece? – is terrible undoubtedly, but since you are alive it can easily be rectified.

While celebrating Sophocles' miraculous escape from a shipwreck, Euripides draws a contrast between the loss of his plays and the loss of his life, since, as he argues, the lost works can easily be replaced as long as the playwright is still alive.⁹⁵ This event is one of the *Letters*' most radical innovations, since this near-death experience is attested nowhere else,⁹⁶ but it also invites reflection on the purpose of the collection itself. While Euripides here insists that the lost Sophoclean texts can easily (ῥᾳδίως) be reproduced, the *Letters* themselves exploit precisely the absence of their purported author in order to create more works in

---

93 On the range of φιλοτιμία see the survey of De Pourcq/Roskam 2012.
94 As Hanink 2010, 551 demonstrates.
95 While most have taken Euripides' attempt at consolation here as sincere, as in Gösswein 1975, 94, the ascription of the survival of his slaves to divine providence might hint at Euripides' insincerity here, since the lives of slaves might well be considered less important than Sophocles' plays. Many thanks to Janja Soldo for bringing this point to my attention.
96 Although Knöbl 2008, 215–219 attempts to draw parallels with other narratives in the biographical tradition of both poets. See also Gösswein 1975, 26 on this motif in other poetic biographies. The motif of shipwreck can also have philosophical connotations, as in Seneca *Ep.* 87. I am grateful to Janja Soldo for pointing this parallel out to me.

his name. As in *Letter* 5, Sophocles becomes a catalyst for the collection's self-consciousness about its own inauthenticity, and invites reflection on the collection's inventions and interventions in Euripidean biographical traditions.[97] Just as the Platonic *Epistles* invoke questions about authenticity and authority due to their explicit divergence from and oppositional relationship with genuine Platonic writings,[98] the *Letters*' deliberately disjunctive portrayal of Sophocles makes visible the collection's inauthenticity in contrast to wider Euripidean biographical traditions.[99] As such, rather than seeing a direct relationship between the two collections, both works display a comparable self-consciousness about their own place within a wider literary and cultural context, one which makes issues of fiction unavoidable. This may even be visible in the anecdote from the *Vita Arati* attributing the authorship of the *Letters* to Sabirius Pollo. While this claim may reflect the work's creative contribution to biographical traditions, recognition of a genre of pseudonymous letter-collections, or a simple rejection of their authenticity, it may also respond to questions about authorship and authority raised within the *Letters* themselves. In other words, the *Letters*' inauthenticity is inherent to the collection, but the repeated exploitation and even thematization of this inauthenticity exaggerates rather than naturalises the work's status as fiction.

While much work has been done to break down the binary perception of ancient letters as either genuine or spurious, less work has been done on the wider consequences of this revision. As a collection which is both unquestionably fictional and yet rarely examined through this lens, the Euripidean *Letters* make visible the tensions inherent in classifying epistolary fiction. Their continual thematization of slander and simultaneous refusal to offer an alternative narrative, their dramatization of epistolary exchange and undermining of it, and their self-awareness about their own inauthenticity all reinforce the fiction of the work while also questioning exactly how to define it. Rather than just a by-product of a naturalised generic framework, the *Letters* continually raise the

---

[97] Knöbl 2008, 253: 'with...Sophocles' alleged shipwreck and loss of his play, neatly tucked into the main narrative of Euripides, the novel challenges stereotypes of biographical writing, literary history, and canonization.'
[98] Wohl 1998. See also Morrison 2013.
[99] As Gösswein 1975, 22 notes, *Letter* 2's position is so artificial it may in fact add to the authenticity of the collection, since its placement is so striking as to be inexplicable any other way ('vor allem aber machte es ihm nichts aus, den Zusammenhang zwischen dem ersten und dem dritten Brief zu unterbrechen, wenn nur der Fremdkörper eigener Manufaktur auf diese — etwas brutale — Weise so eng mit dem restlichen Corpus verklammert wurde, daß seine Authentizität garantiert sein mußte.').

question of their own inauthenticity in such a way as to make their own engagement with fiction an unavoidable part of reading the collection. In this way the *Letters* unsettle any assumptions inherent in the simplifying label of fictional letters, and invite both reflection on the tensions and rewards of the terminology as well as conscious and critical reflection of exactly how to define epistolary fiction.

Catharine Edwards
Greetings from the Margin: Ovid's *Epistulae ex Ponto*

Abstract: Ovid's *Epistulae ex Ponto*, particularly Book 1, the main focus of this discussion, repeatedly evoke the material experience of sending and receiving an individual letter, addressed to a particular addressee. The specificity of the addressees constitutes a strongly epistolary feature of these poems. Yet, the very characteristics which highlight the nature of the letter-poem as an individual material object, physically transmitted from author to addressee, underline the fictive nature of the versions which appear together in a single volume, the *liber* disseminated to Ovid's readers. All the same Ovid's repeated emphasis in the *Epistulae ex Ponto* on each individual missive making its lonely and perilous journey across land and sea, still serves to underline insistently the fragility of the poet's own material existence, far removed from Rome.

Keywords: epistolarity, naming, distance, materiality, reality effect

A battered, grubby papyrus package is delivered, sealed with wax, a name and direction written in ink, now somewhat smudged, on the exterior. It has been transported by land and sea over a great distance. The seal broken, its contents are eventually disclosed, a poem, slightly blotchy, in elegiac couplets, poignantly button-holing the package's addressee — or such is the reception scenario sketched for his individual poems on a number of occasions in Ovid's collection of *Epistulae ex Ponto*, 'Letters from Pontus', his final work.

For a long time, Ovid's exile poetry was read as non-fiction, corresponding to the 'real' circumstances of the poet's own beleaguered situation, relegated from Rome to Tomis in the province of Pontus, on the coast of the Black Sea. The poems were taken to offer insights into, for instance, the terrible weather conditions in the area, Ovid's experiments with writing poetry in Getic, his failing

---

With fond memories of the many stimulating discussions we had at the Fictionality in Ancient Epistolography conference in Cambridge in December 2019, from which I learned so much. Particular thanks go to Janja Soldo and Claire Rachel Jackson for organising the original event and for their thought-provoking comments on a draft of my paper.

literary powers and so on.[1] The last half century, however, has seen a cornucopia of more sophisticated analyses, drawing attention to the literary craft with which these works are composed and highlighting particularly the book structure of Ovid's poems from exile. Betty Rose Nagle analysed the relationship between the exile poetry and Ovid's first elegies, the *Amores*, while Patricia Rosenmeyer explored parallels between the *Heroides*, flagrantly fictive letters from mythical heroines, and, on the other hand, the *Tristia* and *Ex Ponto*. Other scholars, Harry Evans, Stephen Hinds, Gareth Williams, Jennifer Ingleheart notably, have foregrounded further fictive aspects of the collections. Notoriously in A. Fitton Brown's analysis (relying, perhaps unwisely, on the veracity of the Romanian tourist board's weather reports), the exile poems are entirely fictitious.[2] But even Williams finds in Ovid's deployment of, for instance, epic tropes to describe a battle, grounds for doubting that the battle took place at all.[3] Are these 'letters' (we shall consider in a moment just how letter-like they really are) perhaps no less fictional than, for instance, *Heroides* 1, the mythical Penelope's knowing and allusive 'letter' to her absent husband?[4] While the 'fictive' nature of the exilic collections has come under scrutiny, less attention, I think, has been paid to aspects of their specifically epistolary quality — though there are, of course, exceptions, notably Rosenmeyer (her focus is, however, particularly on the *Tristia*).[5] How far might the epistolary characteristics of these collections work to veil — or indeed to highlight — their fictive nature? Should we perhaps see the reception scenarios of the individual poetic *Epistulae ex Ponto* as one of their most ostentatiously fictive features?

My focus here will be on the *Epistulae ex Ponto*, which is explicitly identified by its *index* as a collection of letters, but it is worth noting that at least some of the poems in the *Tristia*, Ovid's first exilic collection, also show, at least intermittently, some letter-like features, even if there are significant points of contrast between the two collections. The opening of *Epistulae ex Ponto* Book 1 itself implies, as Michael Trapp notes, that the *Tristia*, too, are letters, though it is certainly the case that epistolary features are more evident in Book 5 of

---

[1] This tradition is discussed by Williams 1994, 3–4. Ovid refers to learning Getic at *Tr.* 3.14.48–52, 5.12.58; *Pont.* 4.13.18.
[2] Fitton Brown 1985.
[3] Williams 1994, 29, also stressing Ovid's use of *hyperbole* and literary cliché (cf. Williams 2002a, 235). His position is criticized by e.g. Tissol 2014, 16.
[4] On the epistolary character of *Heroides* 1, see particularly Kennedy 1984.
[5] Rosenmeyer 1997. Martelli's 2013 monograph on Ovid includes a chapter homing in on some key epistolary features of the *Epistulae ex Ponto*. See also the brief discussions of epistolary features in Claassen 1999, 114–119 and La Penna 2018, 370–371.

the *Tristia* than in earlier books, signalling a transition toward the epistolary form of the *Ex Ponto*.⁶ Including *Tristia* 5.13 in his anthology of letters, Trapp pertinently observes:

> Ovid's technique for establishing the epistolary credentials of his verse letters is broadly comparable to Horace's: he begins (less often ends) with allusive paraphrases of standard epistolary salutations, and in between he reproduces sporadically other epistolary elements.⁷

Still — and here there is an important contrast with the *Epistulae ex Ponto* — except in the case of Augustus (*Tristia* 2) and Ovid's wife (3.3, 5.2) and daughter (3.7), addressees, insofar as individual poems have a specific addressee, remain anonymous.⁸ This is an anonymity whose potency lies precisely in the status of the poem as a public rather than private communication (if a letter is physically delivered to its addressee, the absence of his or her name is far less significant).⁹

Not only are the addressees of the *Tristia*, in those instances where they seem to be specific individuals, generally anonymous, but Ovid makes almost no reference to the act of sending the individual poem as a personal communication, an inscribed text sent as a physical object to its individual addressee, another important point of contrast with the *Epistulae ex Ponto*. *Tristia* 5.2, addressing his wife, might constitute a partial exception:

> *ecquid ubi e Ponto noua uenit epistula, palles,*
> *et tibi sollicita soluitur illa manu?*

---

6 Davisson 1985, 238. Ovid's insistence on the similarity between *Tristia* and *Ex Ponto* (1.1.17) is disingenuous, as e.g. Hinds (2005, 225–226) notes.
7 Trapp 2003, 24–25. *Pont.* 4.13 is also included in his selection. On the epistolary character of 5.13, see also Davisson 1985.
8 Fear prevents him naming his friends (*Tr.* 3.4.63–74). Ovid claims to find this anonymity very irksome (*Tr.* 5.9.1–2, 25–34), as Oliensis 1997, 173 underlines.
9 See e.g. *Tr.* 4.5.9–10. Other poems which are presented as letters to specific individuals but with their names suppressed include, 1.5, 3.4.63–68, 3.5, 3.14, 5.9.33–34. Ovid sometimes claims he has offered clues from which the addressee's identity may be deduced (1.5.7), though this would not preclude multiple individuals from identifying themselves. On identification as a challenge to the reader, see Casali 1997, 82–84. He suggests (107) that 'all of the various enemies addressed in the *Tristia* and the *Epistulae ex Ponto* are fictitious characters' who, on some level, stand in for Augustus himself.

> What? When a fresh letter has come from Pontus, do you grow pale, do you open it with anxious hand?
>
> (*Tr.* 5.2.1–2)[10]

Yet rather than the letter's initial greeting, this is really a comment on the act of opening the letter.[11] *Tristia* 5.4 presents itself as a letter but a personified one, who reports on Ovid in the third person (a counterpart to the personified book of 3.1).[12]

> litore ab Euxino Nasonis epistula ueni,
> lassaque facta mari lassaque facta uia,
> qui mihi flens dixit 'tu, cui licet, aspice Romam…'
>
> From the Euxine shore have I come, a letter of Naso's, wearied by the sea, wearied by the road. Weeping he said to me, 'Do thou, who art allowed, look on Rome…'
>
> (*Tr.* 5.4.1–3)

The voice of the letter is distinct from the voice of the poet, its written quality elided. Epistolary features, then, are sometimes toyed with in the *Tristia*, but they appear much more prominently and consistently in the *Epistulae ex Ponto*. Especially pertinent in the latter collection is the strong sense that each poem is addressed to a particular, almost always named, individual and that it had its origin as an individual object sent physically from Tomis to Italy.

My focus here will be primarily on Book 1 of *Ex Ponto* (though I also want to highlight some other epistolary features which come to the fore later in the collection). Since Froesch's 1968 dissertation, if not before, the issue of book structure, as articulated largely through the identities of Ovid's addressees, has dominated scholarship on the *Ex Ponto*. This issue will not be a particular concern here, though I have been influenced by the productive way Laura Jansen (2012) relates the structure of the *Epistulae ex Ponto* to the material experience of reading the ancient book. I wish to consider rather the experience of reading the ancient letter as a material object and as an individual text and how this experience is evoked and manipulated in the poems.

Ex Ponto 1.1 begins with the word *Naso*, the author's name.[13] Indeed Ovid refers to himself by name on twenty-eight occasions in the *Ex Ponto* — more

---

10 Translations are from the Loeb edition of A.L. Wheeler.
11 Rosenmeyer 1997, 40–41 notes a suggestive parallel with the scenes of letter reception sketched in the *Heroides*.
12 On the personified book as a visitor to Rome, see Hinds 1985; Huskey 2006.
13 Though the individual poems also bear as titles their addressee's name in the dative, e.g. *Bruto*.

than in any of his other works.[14] This is, we should note, the only instance of a poetic book in Greek or Latin commencing with the author's name.[15] But such an opening is, of course, standard practice in prose epistolography. A Roman letter writer begins with his (or her) own name (thus *Cicero Attico salutem mittit*).[16] As Ellen Oliensis observes: 'To the recipient of a Latin letter, the use of the author's proper name in the initial "epistolary" formula signals at the outset the replacement of the absent author by the letter that bears his name.'[17] We might note a contrast in this respect between the *Epistulae ex Ponto* and the *Tristia* where Ovid is not named until the seventh poem, at 1.7.10 — and even then in words put in the mouth of another.[18]

The second word in 1.1, *Tomitanae*, indicates the place from which Ovid is writing. As Garth Tissol notes (*ad loc.*) 'the juxtaposition of *Naso* and *Tomitanae* is pointed, cruelly emphasising Ovid's long residency in Tomis'. This missive is addressed to Rome from the empire's margin. Line 2 further reinforces Ovid's geographical location: *hoc tibi de Getico litore mittit opus,* 'sends this work to you from the Getic shore'. The term *litus,* 'shore' — the very edge of the empire — recurs in both *Tristia* and *Ex Ponto* (these are *litterae de litore*).[19] The juxtaposition in 1.1.1 of the named author and the place from which he writes features repeatedly, we might note, in the opening lines of individual poems in the *Ex Ponto* (1.7, 2.2, 2.4, 2.6, 3.4, 3.5, 3.6, 4.9). This emphasis on locating the sender is also, of course, evident in the title of the collection, *Epistulae ex Ponto*.[20]

The opening couplet, as Tissol notes, evokes the opening of the first of the *Heroides,* Ovid's collection of fictional letters from mythical heroines, an early flag perhaps that we should be wary of reading this new collection of 'letters' at face value: *haec tua Penelope lento tibi mittit, Ulixe,* 'These words your Penelope sends to you, O Ulysses, slow of return that you are.' Penelope's letter to Ulysses (the first of the *Heroides*) urges her husband to come home to Ithaca. The message

---

14 See Gaertner 2005 *ad* 1.1.
15 Cf. 1.10. Tissol 2014, 20 observes: 'Unable to return to Rome himself, he makes his name a substitute for himself, as if to transform himself into his name'.
16 Though the formula may be abbreviated. See Cugusi 1983, 47–48.
17 Oliensis 1997, 185.
18 See Hardie 2002, 294: 'the name... is detached and displaced from its owner, spoken in quotation marks by another, far away from the real Ovid.' It is true, however, that Ovid repeatedly refers to his name as having the power to effect a presence for him back in Rome.
19 L. 16 Ovid refers to himself as ploughing a barren shore (*litus*); cf. *Tr.* 5.1.2: *hunc de Getico... Libellum / litore*; 5.4.1: *litore ab Euxino Nasonis epistula ueni*; *Pont.* 4.4.8: *naufragus in Getici litoris actus aquas.* For his location at the edge of the world, see also *Tr.* 4.9, 5.2.63.
20 As Gaertner 2005 *ad* 1.1.16–17 notes, *epistula* very likely alludes to the title of the collection.

is an ironic one, however, as (or so the acute reader may deduce) Ulysses himself is the visiting stranger freshly arrived in Ithaca to whom Penelope means to entrust her letter;[21] they will imminently be reunited after twenty years of separation. In the *Tristia* Ovid had already repeatedly compared himself to Ulysses, as he faced storms at sea, for instance, and resigned himself to protracted separation from his wife (she in turn is compared to Penelope).[22] But the contrasts between them are poignant ones. Ovid remains far from home and family with no prospect of return. Indeed, in *Tristia* 1.5, comparing himself at length to the *Odyssey*'s protagonist (57–80), he observes that he is more to be pitied than Ulysses, on the grounds not only that Ulysses was homeward-bound — but that his troubles, unlike Ovid's, were largely fictitious:

> *adde, quod illius pars maxima ficta laborum,*
> *ponitur in notris fabula nulla malis.*
>
> Moreover, the largest part of his labours is fiction; in my own no myth resides.
> (*Tr.* 1.5.79–80)

This apparent contrast is, however, somewhat destabilising in the context of a collection of poems which so insistently evokes 'fictional' parallels to convey the poet's situation.

Ovid's place of exile is, as Williams elegantly demonstrated in his 1994 monograph, fictionalised in numerous ways, evoking features of, for instance, the poetic underworld.[23] Winter is virtually unbroken, Ovid suggests (*Pont.* 1.2.23–24).[24] He refers to his location as Scythia; yet the small area around Tomis on the coast to the south of the Danube, though it was sometimes termed Scythia Minor, was quite separate from Scythia proper which extended far to the north and north east of the Danube.[25] Nevertheless it was a key function of letters to locate the sender; in Cicero's letter collections, it is particularly when Cicero is not in Rome that he indicates from where he is writing. The indication of place in the opening sentence is itself a strongly epistolary feature (even if the location given is in significant respects both imprecise and significantly fictionalised).

---

21 Kennedy 1984.
22 For comparisons with Ulysses, see e.g. *Tr.* 1.2.9, 3.11.61, 5.5.57–80, as well as *Pont.* 3.1.53, 4.10.9–34. Ovid's wife is compared at length to Penelope at e.g. *Tr.* 1.6.21–22. At *Tr.* 5.5.3–4, on the occasion of his wife's birthday, Ovid compares himself to Ulysses, celebrating albeit at a distance the birthday of Penelope.
23 Williams 1994, 8–11.
24 Helzle 2003, 77 offers a list of examples.
25 See e.g. 1.3.37 with Tissol 2014 *ad loc.*

The initial letter, then, foregrounds its epistolary character with the author's name and the identification of the place from which it is sent. It also names its addressee, with the second person address to Brutus (Brutus is again the addressee of 3.9, the final letter in book three, a poem generally regarded as the epilogue to the first three books).[26] Line 2's *mittit* is the conventional verb in an epistolary opening, though usually with *salutem* as object.[27] But the thing sent is in this case an *opus*, one composed of several *libelli* (books 1–3 of the collection), rather than *salus* 'health', as in the standard greeting — or indeed a single letter. Ovid assimilates this new work to his earlier writings, a little later describing it as a *liber* (1.1.28). Insofar as it is a material object, it takes the form of a substantial scroll (*uolumen*) with a *titulus* on the outside (Ovid comments on the difference between the *Tristia* and his new work, *rebus idem, titulo differt*, at *Pont.* 1.1.18).[28] And, despite the prominence of the author's name as the opening word of the collection, Ovid tells Brutus, if he has doubts, not to include Ovid's name on the cover of the published work (1.1.29–30).[29] Casting these poems from the outset (as far as the reader is concerned) as a single work rather than as a series of individual communications also serves to undermine the reality effect of the individual poems as letters.

In *Tristia* also, although Ovid's name, as we have seen, is not mentioned until the seventh poem of Book 1, Ovid himself has an important nominal presence. Ellen Oliensis and Philip Hardie both note the contrast in that earlier collection between Ovid himself, named frequently, and the poet's nameless friends.[30] 'The anonymity of Ovid's addressees is not only a feature but a theatrically pointed theme of the *Tristia*,' as Oliensis observes.[31] The *Epistulae ex Ponto* are, with regard to the poet's friends, very different; numerous other names are also in play alongside that of the author.[32] Ovid's characterisation of his addressees has, as I noted earlier, played a central role in debates among scholars

---

26 On 3.9 see Jansen 2012. She suggests we might also see *Pont.* 1.1 as a postscript to the *Tristia* (99).
27 Cugusi 1983, 47–48.
28 This *uolumen* too will no doubt be low-key in its appearance. See Williams 1992, 186 on the down-beat description of *Tristia* book 1 as a material object at *Tr.* 1.1.3–14.
29 As Martelli 2013, 192 notes, suggesting Augustus himself could consequently be cast as *auctor* of this work.
30 Oliensis 1997, 182; Hardie 2002, 294.
31 Oliensis 1997, 177.
32 For Oliensis 1997, 178: 'the naming of names does... suggest some degree of "normalisation" of life in Tomis'.

about the structure of the *Ex Ponto*.³³ Each letter (with one exception) has a named addressee (most of the addressees have more than one letter addressed to them; one, Cotta, has at least six).³⁴ Only one letter (3.6) is anonymous in this respect.³⁵ Indeed, at *Ex Ponto* 1.1.17–20 Ovid insists he will name his addressees whether they like it or not. Naming serves the purpose of celebrating some – but shaming others, such as Messalinus, the addressee of 1.7 and 2.2; Ovid characterises in some detail the nature of his relationship with each addressee.³⁶ This, too, is very much an epistolary marker. As Janet Altman observes, 'The *I* of epistolary discourse always situates himself vis-à-vis another; his locus, his "address" is always relative to that of his addressee.'³⁷ The specificity of the addressees constitutes a strongly epistolary feature of these poems.

Yet tensions are inevitably generated when an individual personal letter, a form of communication which normally privileges privacy (at least to a degree), as well as the specificity of the addressee, is published as part of a collection, as Martelli notes.³⁸ Ovid plays insistently with the fiction of the original letter's privacy.³⁹ Repetition, he suggests (3.9), is forgivable in a succession of letters to different individuals: 'Not to produce a book but to send a letter to each has been my care.' The aggregation of individual letters contributes to what La Penna terms 'lo scopo ossessivo dell' epistolario poetico' ('the obsessive scope of the poetic letters').⁴⁰ Once they are collected into a book their monotony, licensed though it is by the specificity of their addressees, becomes liable to criticism (3.9.2).⁴¹ To gather letters into a book is to create an *opus* which may be both more and less than the sum of its parts.⁴²

---

33 See e.g. Gaertner 2005, 2–7. The anonymous addressees of the *Tristia* are also individualised to a degree (Oliensis 1997, 177) but in the absence of names they do not themselves generate an explicit structure.
34 Some argue he is also the addressee of 3.8.
35 On the pointed anonymity of 3.6, see Casali 1997, 86–88.
36 Galasso 2009, 195; Formicola 2017, 28–34. Though disagreement remains over the identity of the addressee of 3.8 with some (e.g. Syme) arguing for Cotta Maximus and others (e.g. Luck, André, Formicola) for Fabius Maximus. Poems in the *Tristia* also gesture towards specific relationships, even where the addressee is not named (see n. 9 above).
37 Altman 1982, 119.
38 Martelli 2013, 188.
39 Martelli 2013, 189.
40 La Penna 2018, 293.
41 As Frampton 2019, 144 notes.
42 On the overriding preoccupation of critics with the structural shape of *Ex Ponto* 1–3, see Jansen 2012.

Having referred to his *opus* in *Pont.* 1.1, as noted above, in *Pont.* 1.2, Ovid shifts his concern from the book to the individual letter. This poem is addressed to Fabius Maximus. Its opening lines position the poem as an individual composition, which will be read as a separate work rather than as part of a book — at least this is the 'original' reception-scenario envisaged for the named addressee.[43] For while Ovid had conspicuously named himself in the opening word of the previous poem, *Pont.* 1.1, as well as specifying the location from which he wrote, in 1.2, having offered an elaborate greeting to his addressee, he remarks:

> *forsitan haec a quo mittatur epistula quaeras,*
> *quisque loquar tecum, certior esse uelis.*

> Perchance you may ask by whom this letter is sent and wish to be told who am I that talk with you.
> (*Pont.* 1.2.5–6)

Fabius Maximus, evidently ignorant of *Epistula ex Ponto* 1.1, which was not addressed to him (and is in any case composed — like any preface — in retrospect), is being prepared for the discovery of his correspondent's identity.[44]

Though this would be a significant breach of epistolary etiquette, Ovid even gestures towards the possibility of withholding his own name altogether:

> *uereor ne nomine lecto*
> *durus et auersa mente cetera legas.*

> I fear that when you read the name you will grow stern and read what remains with heart averse.
> (*Pont.* 1.2.7–8)

But here we encounter a textual problem. Following line 9, the pentameter which would have constituted line 10 is apparently missing.[45] Tissol, in his 2014 commentary, notes 'it is likely to have contained the poet's name'. This is also the view of Gaertner in his 2005 commentary. Yet not all scholars agree.[46] I am tempted to follow one of Peter Green's rather different suggestions for reconstruction, neither of which names the author. If Ovid's name did not occur in line 10 we might take the following lines to offer a succession of (not very difficult) clues

---

43 The first four lines play on the elements in his addressee's name.
44 On the intrinsically retrospective nature of *Pont.* 1.1 as preface, see Jansen 2012, 100–101.
45 Tarrant 1983, 263.
46 See e.g. Helzle 1988 *ad loc.* who accepts *audebo (et) propriis ingemuisse malis* (which appears in some mss.) and Green 2005.

to the poet's identity. Ovid alludes to his guilt and enumerates alarming features of his location (bows and arrows, armed horsemen circling, terrible weather). Eventually (129–136), with the repeated formula *ille ego sum*, a very specific personal connection is disclosed. That *formula* is, as Martelli notes, characteristic of the *sphragis*, most notably the lines appended posthumously to Virgil's *Aeneid*.[47] Yet here the formula introduces not the poet's achievements (as is conventional in the *sphragis* – and as happens indeed in *Tristia* 4.10, which opens with the phrase *ille ego fuerim*) but, as Martelli underlines, his role as passive recipient of his addressee's beneficence. Exile has significantly circumscribed the poet's agency.

Later in Book 1 Ovid teases another addressee with clues to the identity of the poem's sender (and once again the reader of the collection, equipped with superior knowledge, can savour the author's self-mystification). *Pont.* 1.7 opens as follows:

> *littera pro uerbis tibi, Messaline, salutem*
> * quam legis, a saeuis attulit usque Getis.*
> *indicat auctorem locus? an, nisi nomine lecto,*
> * haec me Nasonem scribere uerba latet?*
> *ecquis in extremo positus iacet orbe tuorum,*
> * me tamen excepto, qui precor esse tuus?*

> Letters, instead of spoken words, Messalinus, have brought you the greeting which you read all the way from the fierce Getae. Is the place a token of the author? Or unless you have read the name are you unaware that I who write these words am Naso? Does any one of your friends except myself – who pray that I am your friend – lie at the very edge of the world?

> (*Pont.* 1.7.1–6)

Invoking the face-to-face ritual of the *salutatio*, Ovid presents its epistolary counterpart, the long-distance offering of *salus* by letter,[48] as merely a pale imitation,[49] though he goes on to concede that he was not so assiduous as he might have been in offering greetings in person at Messalinus' door back in Rome

---

[47] Martelli 2013, 222–224.
[48] Though in prose *litterae* is the term regularly used to mean letter in the first century BCE, in the singular the word *littera* is unusual in this sense at this time (the singular is perhaps determined by metrical considerations here). Gaertner 2005 *ad loc.*
[49] Cf. the comparison Ovid draws between the exchange of letters and conversation with a friend at *Tristia* 5.13.27–30 (evoking Callim. *Ep.* 2 Pf.). See Trapp 2003 *ad loc.* (letter 10 in his collection).

(1.7.55).⁵⁰ The disclosure of the author's name is briefly deferred in this instance. Yet the letter's place of origin makes its author's identity unmistakable.⁵¹ Ovid scarcely needs to put his name on this poem; he is identified precisely by his place of exile. In this letter the chilly distance separating him from his addressee is to the fore, an instance of the letter not as a bridge between author and addressee but, in the terms of Altman's formulation, as an emblem of their separation.⁵²

Ovid characterises his relationships with his different addressees quite distinctly, as noted earlier. The third letter in Book 1, embracing the epistolary format in a more apparently straightforward manner, suggests a warmer connection to its addressee — but this is tinged with anxiety.

> *hanc tibi Naso tuus mittit, Rufine, salutem,*
>   *qui miser est, ulli si suus esse potest.*

> This greeting, Rufinus, your friend Naso sends you — if a wretched man can be anyone's friend.
>
> (*Pont.* 1.3.1–2)

To describe himself as *Naso tuus* is again to tweak epistolary convention, however. A letter to a close friend might well open with the formula: *Cicero Attico suo salutem mittit*; the possessive pronoun is applied to the addressee rather than the author. Here, Ovid at once qualifies the assumption of familiarity, casting himself in the role of hesitant client, as Sandra Citroni-Marchetti notes: 'The self-portrait of the poet as a friend degenerates towards his self-depiction as a client' ('l'autoraffigurazione del poeta come amico scade a raffigurazione di sè come cliente', 2000, 331). Ovid is afraid to offend powerful addressees. This approach will be echoed in 1.7.6 (in the lines considered above), where Ovid, addressing Messalinus, refers to himself as *me... qui precor esse tuus*.⁵³

---

50 The addressee is usually identified as M. Valerius Messalla Messalinus, cos 3 BCE (Syme 1978, 121–122) and the brother of Cotta Maximus. Ovid makes the same point in a later letter, 2.2, also addressed to Messalinus: *mittit... salute / quam solitus praesens est tibi ferre...*, later lamenting (121) 'I am separated from my country by the whole world's span'. Messalinus is generally seen as the addressee of *Tristia* 4.4, also.
51 A similar move is made at 3.5.1–4. Cf. as Rosenmeyer 1997, 35 notes, *Ep. Sapph.* 3–4.
52 Altman 1982, 15. Contrast e.g. 4.6 to Brutus, which begins with a reference to itself as a letter which is *ex illis locis* 'where you would not wish Naso to be'.
53 At 1.7.18 he expresses the fear that Messalinus will deny that Ovid is his: *nosque negas ulla parte fuisse tuos*.

In contrast to the opening of 1.1, where Ovid sent his *opus*, in 1.3 the object of the first verb *mittit* is the more conventional *salutem*.⁵⁴ 'The greeting is identified with the letter itself', as Tissol observes *ad loc.*, a move which is also made in numerous other poems.⁵⁵ Indeed the opening of 1.3 echoes *Tristia* 5.13, which begins:

> hanc tuus e Getico mittit tibi Naso salutem,
>   mittere si quisquam, quo caret ipse, potest

> This "Health" thy Naso sends thee from the Getic land, if anyone can send what he himself has not.

(*Tr.* 5.13.1–2)

'Health', abbreviating the standard greeting, serves here too as a metonym for the letter — yet in this context it has a bitterly poignant resonance, as Ovid underlines — repeatedly. *Pont.* 1.10 to Flaccus, for instance, begins in a very similar manner: 'Exiled Naso sends you a 'health', Flaccus, if one can send something that he himself lacks', going on to describe his own fragile state, a leitmotif of these poems.⁵⁶

Corresponding to the poet's poor physical state, the quality of his writing in his exile is insistently deprecated in the *Epistulae ex Ponto* (as in the *Tristia*).⁵⁷ Following 1.4 addressed to Ovid's wife (a poem which highlighted the physical transformation undergone by the poet and — he imagines — his wife also), the thread-bare nature of Ovid's writing features particularly in *Pont.* 1.5, addressed to Cotta Maximus. Ovid comments on his struggle to write poetry; his *ingenium* has undergone a deterioration parallel to that of his physical person, he insists in the opening lines of this poem (1.5.3).⁵⁸ No longer attentive to his art, he writes the first thing that comes into his head:

---

54 Indeed the verb *mittit* is itself often omitted in epistolary openings, as Dickey 2002, 36–37 notes. Prose letters regularly leave such salutations implicit (White 2010, 71).
55 *Pont.* 1.3.1, 1.7.1, 1.8.1, 1.10.1, 2.2.3, 3.2.1, 3.4.1, 3.5.5, 4.9.1, Cf. *Her.* 4.1, 13.1, 16.1, 18.1, 19.1, as well as the tortured missive of Byblis at *Met.* 9.530. In the *Tristia* only 5.13 begins thus.
56 Cf. 1.8, 4.9. Medical imagery is common in the exile poetry, e.g. *Pont.* 3.4. Indeed at 4.14.5 Ovid finally declares his own health *salus* is hateful to him. The emphasis on medicine in *Pont.* 1.10 addressed to Rufinus may incidentally be connected with the scientific interests of one Vibius Rufinus whose work was drawn on by the Elder Pliny (e.g. *NH* 1.14), as Gaertner 2005 *ad loc.* notes.
57 See Williams 1994, 50–59.
58 Williams 1994, 79–81 underlines the sophisticated Horatian references in play here, a feature which itself undercuts the allegation that Ovid's poetic powers are waning.

> *quod uenit ex facili, satis est componere nobis,*
> *et nimis intenti causa laboris abest.*
>
> Tis enough for me to compose what comes easily; I lack a reason for too earnest toil.
>
> (*Pont.* 1.5.59–60)

Williams highlights the metapoetic significance of Ovid's emphasis on his poems' lack of finish, both literal and metaphorical.⁵⁹ This work shall not be polished, Ovid declares in the opening poem of the *Tristia*, *nec fragili geminae poliantur pumice frontes*, 'Let no brittle pumice polish your two edges' (*Tr.* 1.1.11).⁶⁰ At *Pont.* 1.5.61, Ovid asks in similar terms, *cur ego sollicita poliam mea carmina cura?* 'Why should I refine my verse with anxious labour?' The Getae, he comments bitterly, are unlikely to complain about the quality of his writing — and he wonders if his poems will ever make it to Rome. Certainly Ovid is discussing his poetic compositions. Yet we might also see this emphasis on the carelessness of his current writing, his *scriptis mediocribus* (1.5.83), so lacking in refinement, as itself an epistolary marker. The Younger Pliny, for instance, characterises his letters programmatically as *paulo curatius scriptae* (1.1.1); letters, particularly letters to friends, should not seem carefully crafted.⁶¹

Letter 1.7 imagined Messalinus weighing up a communication which bore evidence of Pontus as its place of origin. The letter as a physical object is more explicitly evoked by several later poems in the collection. A missive from Ovid may be recognisable from its outward form, he suggests.

> *ecquid ab impressae cognoscis imagine cerae*
> *haec tibi Nasonem scribere uerba, Macer?*
> *auctorisque sui si non est anulus index,*
> *cognitane est nostra littera facta manu?*
>
> Does any inkling come to you, Macer, from the figure pressed upon the wax that Naso writes these words to you? If the ring be not an informant of its master, do you recognize the letters formed by my hand?
>
> (*Pont.* 2.10.1–4)

---

59 Williams 1992, 186.
60 Cf. 3.1.13. Unlike e.g. Catullus' refined *lepidum nouum libellum/ arido modo pumice expolitum*, 1.1–2.
61 As De Pretis 2003, 135 notes. On this phrase see also Barbiero's contribution to this volume. See Cic. *Fam.* 9.21.1, Sen. *Ep.* 75.1 (he wants his letters to be *inlaboratus ac facilis*). Gaertner 2006, 163–165 detects some prosaic and colloquial elements in the vocabulary of the exile poems, which we might see as in line with their epistolary character.

Macer is imagined with the unopened letter in his hand.[62] He notes the wax with which it is sealed, impressed with a distinctive mark.[63] He looks at the direction on the outside of the sealed letter, featuring his own name. He opens the letter and takes in a further sample of the author's handwriting.[64] The letter is visibly from Ovid.[65] Whether or not these poems were ever sent individually to their individual addressees, Ovid nevertheless invites his reader to imagine them thus transmitted.[66] Yet the very characteristics which highlight the nature of the letter-poem as an individual material object, physically transmitted from author to addressee, underline the fictive nature of the versions which appear together in a single volume, a *liber* which Brutus is charged (as we saw earlier) with disseminating to Ovid's readers.

Individual letters are generally time-sensitive acts of communication and the time taken for a letter to travel from writer to addressee is a recurrent concern in Roman letter-writing. While there is always a time-lag between composition and reception, that time-lag may vary hugely. Cicero's letters from, for instance, Antium to Rome might reach their addressees the same day they were

---

[62] On this letter, see Williams 1994, 42–48; La Penna 2018, 347–348. For a discussion of the external appearance of ancient letters as material objects, see Sarri 2017, 122–124.

[63] Cf. 3.7.6. We might recall here a ring referred to in the *Tristia* (1.7.9), worn by Ovid's (anonymous) addressee which is engraved with Ovid's own image. See Hardie 2002, 322. The process of sealing is also referred to at *Tr.* 5.4 where the letter describes Ovid: *flens quoque me scripsit, nec qua signabar, ad os est / ante, sed ad madidas gemma relata genas.* 'Weeping too he wrote me, and the gem with which I was sealed, he lifted first, not to his lips, but to his tear-drenched cheeks' (5–6).

[64] At *Tristia* 3.3.1–2, addressed to his wife, Ovid explains the unfamiliar handwriting on the grounds that, weakened by illness, he had to dictate this poem: *haec mea si casu miraris epistula quaere / alterius digitis scripta sit, aeger eram*. Cicero several times alludes to the recognisability of his own handwriting. Writing to Atticus or his brother Quintus, Cicero apologises if the letter is dictated (due to illness e.g. *Att.* 8.12.1) or when travelling (*Att.* 5.7.1) or very busy (*Att.* 2.23.1). Laziness (*pigritia*) is cited as an excuse in writing to Atticus only towards the end of his life (*Att.* 16.15.1).

[65] Elsewhere, Ovid emphasises rather the distinctiveness of his own literary style in identifying the author (*Pont.* 4.13.11–16). Williams 1994, 47 'recognition of the poet is attained through recognition of his verse, so that his verse becomes the *imago* of the poet's own self'. Hardie 2002, 318–25 explores the power of images to conjure up the absent in *Pont.* 2.10 and 2.8, which concerns images of the imperial family sent to Ovid by Maximus Cotta.

[66] Hardie 2002, 324 notes that the addressee of this letter, Macer, is also the addressee of *Am.* 2.18 in which Ovid described the project of the *Heroides*. The parallels between the opening of *Pont.* 2.8 and Sappho's epistle to Phaon (*Her.* 15.1–4) are notable — though the authorship of the latter poem remains debated.

sent.⁶⁷ Time, indeed, has a particular bearing in generic terms on the letter as a communication between different, sometimes distantly separate, locations, often functioning as a key index of separation. How long might letters take between Rome and Tomis? The personified letter of *Tristia* 5.4 describes itself (l. 2) as *lassaque facta mari lassaque facta uia*, 'wearied by the sea, wearied by the road'. Indeed, any letter must be transmitted by the same means Ovid himself used to travel to Tomis, a journey long enough — or so he claimed — for him to compose all of *Tristia* book 1.⁶⁸

A letter addressed to Sextus Pompeius (4.5), opens with an apostrophe to Ovid's own verse (*leues elegi*), as he imagines the journey to be traversed en route to Rome:

> *longa uia est, nec uos pedibus proceditis aequis,*
> *tectaque brumali sub niue terra latet.*
> *cum gelidam Thracen et opertum nubibus Haemum*
> *et maris Ionii transieritis aquas,*
> *luce minus decima dominam uenietis in urbem,*
> *ut festinatum non faciatis iter.*

Long is the way, nor do you advance with even steps, and a mantle of winter snow conceals the land. Crossing frozen Thrace with Haemus hidden in clouds and the waters of the Ionian sea, on the tenth day or before you will reach the imperial city though you make no hurried journey.

(*Pont.* 4.5.3–8).

The uneven steps are of course particularly characteristic of elegiac metre.⁶⁹ Ovid's choice to write in verse can thus be read as an impediment to his letter's progress.⁷⁰ As for the journey, this is, we should clearly infer, not ten days for the entire trajectory but rather for the transmission from Brundisium to Rome.⁷¹

---

67 In the *Tristia*, time generally stands still, suggests Hinds (Hinds 2005, 213–218, see e.g. *Tr.* 5.10); it continues to hang heavy in the *Epistulae ex Ponto*. Ovid notes at 4.10 that this is his sixth summer on the Cimmerian shore: *Cimmerio... litore*.
68 *Tristia* 1.11.1–2. See also 1.10. He describes travelling by sea (via the Adriatic) to Corinth, crossing the Isthmus and setting out again by sea (via the Hellespont) to Tempyra on the Thracian coast. From here, he describes travelling by land to Tomis. His journey through the Adriatic is described as taking place in December.
69 Cf. e.g. *Tristia* 3.1.11–12.
70 As Janja Soldo points out to me.
71 Though it is perhaps rash of historians such as Anne Kolb to use this figure as a reliable guide to standard journey time (Kolb 2000, 37; 323). Her main point of comparison is Horace *Satire* 1.5, itself Odyssean in inspiration (Gowers 2012 *ad loc.*).

Elsewhere, on more than one occasion, Ovid suggests the time between a letter being sent and a response being received might be as much as a whole year.

> *non ego cessaui, nec fecit inertia serum:*
> *ultima me uasti sustinet ora freti.*
> *dum uenit huc rumor properataque carmina fiunt*
> *factaque eunt ad uos, annus abisse potest,*

> I have not dallied, idleness has not made me slow; I am living on the most remote coast of the vast sea. While news is coming to me and hasty verse is being composed and when composed is travelling to you, a year may pass.
>
> (*Pont.* 3.4.57–60)

There is a poignant contrast between the hasty composition and the unbearably slow transmission of Ovid's work. Perhaps the bleakest evocation of the impact of distance on the speed of communication appears in his letter to Gallio (*Pont.* 4.11).[72] This letter of consolation to a friend who has lost his wife suggests that by the time Ovid's poem reaches him, the friend's grief will have been assuaged — by the passage of time.

> *dum tua peruenit, dum littera nostra recurrens*
> *tot maria ac terras permeat, annus abit.*

> While your letter has been on its way, while mine in answer is traversing so many lands and seas, a year has passed.
>
> (*Pont.* 4.11.15–16)

Gallio may even be married again, surmises Ovid. Green regards references to a year as exaggerated, commenting that *Pont.* 4.5 is 'considerably more realistic about travel time' (2005, 342) — though we might note that the total time for the transmission of the letter is not actually specified there. Yet in winter sea-borne transport may not have been possible at all.[73] Ovid describes the frozen waters at *Tr.* 3.10.25–39, noting at *Tr.* 3.12.31 that spring sees the opening of the shipping season, as the waters thaw.[74] Travel through the snowy uplands may also

---

[72] Discussed in Trapp 2003 (number 45 in his selection).
[73] The distance is so great, Ovid laments at one point (*Pont.* 1.5.71–6), he cannot conceive that his poems will ever reach Rome.
[74] Ovid describes the frozen landscape — including the frozen over Danube — at *Tr.* 3.10.

have been interrupted.[75] Evidence is very scarce for ancient journey times; some figures gleaned from the Theodosian code indicate a travel time from Ravenna (departing in early February) to Carthage of 349 days.[76] That year for a letter to travel from Tomis to Rome may not be so implausible. Certainly, Ovid's anxious reflection on the time taken for his individual letter-poems to reach their destination has a significant part to play in establishing the poems' epistolary character.

As in the letter to Gallio, Ovid several times suggests he is replying to the letters of others or that he has received individual responses to his own communications.[77] Letter 1.9 addressed to (Cotta) Maximus opens with a reference to a letter received from his addressee:

> *quae mihi e rapto tua uenit epistula Celso*
> *protinus est lacrimis umida facta meis;*
> *quodque nefas dictum, fieri nec posse putaui,*
> *inuitis oculis littera lecta tua est.*
>
> Your letter with its news of Celsus' death was at once wetted by my tears; and although it is an impious thing to say and, as I thought, impossible, a letter of yours was read with unwilling eyes.
>
> (*Pont.* 1.9.1–4)

The motif of the tear-stained letter is, of course, already familiar from Ovid's *Heroides*.[78] The poignantly dislocated word order of the first sentence of *Pont.* 1.9 aptly conveys the devastation of bereavement. Ovid surely implies here that he has received other — and far more welcome — letters from Cotta. A reference at 3.5 to the text of an oration given in the forum which Cotta Maximus has sent to Ovid also suggests a regular correspondence. At one point, indeed, in a letter to Severus (*Pont.* 4.2), Ovid casually reveals that not all his 'letters' are poems. Regretting that Severus has not yet been mentioned in his poetry (here *libellos*, l.3), he observes: 'Yet letters not in metre have never ceased to go on their mission

---

75 Duncan-Jones 1990, 7–29 on travel times quotes one month as the time for an imperial edict to travel from Illyricum, just across the Adriatic, to Rome — a far shorter journey. Herodian reports the Danube was frozen over in winter, *Roman history* 6.7.6–8.
76 Kolb 2000, 329.
77 E.g. 1.3, apparently a response to Rufinus' letter of consolation. He also refers to receiving letters at *Tristia* 5.11.1–2, 5.12.1–2 — and the disappointment of not receiving them at *Tristia* 4.7.3–10, 5.13.9–16.
78 This feature of Briseis' letter (*Heroides* 3) is discussed by Rosenmeyer 1997. The personified book of *Tristia* 3.1 describes itself as tear-stained (15–16); cf. *Tr.* 5.4.5–6. Tear-stains feature also in Cicero's letters from exile (e.g. *Att.* 3.15, *Fam.* 14.3). On elegy as the 'poetry of tears' see Hardie 2002, 63 n. 1.

between us', *orba tamen numeris cessauit epistula numquam/ire per alternas officiosa uices* (*Pont.* 4.2.5–6). As Martelli comments, 'With a characteristic twitch of the veil, Ovid dispels the illusion that these verse epistles are authentic, private communiqués whose publication is an incidental afterthought'.[79] We are to imagine a whole other body of epistolary exchanges in prose — a hidden counterpart to the far from intimate communications of the apparently epistolary poems. Thus teasingly highlighted, the 'fictional' nature of the poetic epistles again comes to the fore.

Ovid's emphasis in the early books of the *Tristia* on the physical form of his writings, each book a papyrus *uolumen*, already hints, as Stephanie Frampton has argued, at their vulnerability (in contrast to the lapidary inscriptions associated with the emperor).[80] Though they manage to reach Rome, his books, like the far distant author they represent, are battered and shabby, at the mercy of decay. His repeated emphasis in the *Epistulae ex Ponto* on the single epistolary poem as a material object, each individual missive making its lonely and perilous journey across land and sea, underlines still more insistently the fragility of the poet's own material existence, his distance from Rome. Authorial absence is the essential condition of these poems' epistolary form.[81] And yet these letters do make it through, offering a bridge, apparently tenuous and yet enduring, a vibrant connection to readers in Rome — and beyond — and a perpetual reminder of the fate of their author.

---

[79] Martelli 2013, 190. Later in this poem Ovid requests Severus send him his new poem.
[80] Frampton 2019, 147.
[81] Cf. on the *Heroides*, Oliensis 1997, 190: 'epistolary fiction... writes... absence into its form'.

___
Part II: **Editorial Fictions**

Michael Trapp
Just Some Notes for My Own Use: Arrian's ('Arrian's'?) Letter to Lucius Gellius

Abstract: This chapter re-examines the epistle to Lucius Gellius prefaced to Arrian's *Discourses of Epictetus* and problematises its status as a fictionalizing, fiction-generating and possibly also fictitious text. Naively understood as an honest account of the origins of the text it is attached to, it has generated diverse modern scholarly fictions of authorship that betray the interpretive agendas of their creators. If it is seen instead as a more calculating attempt to steer the reception of Arrian's text, the question arises whether the attempt is Arrian's own, or – like comparable accounts of philosophical authorship in the *Letters of the Socratics* – that of a later editorial/critical hand.

Keywords: 'diatribe', lecture notes, literary criticism, philosophical discourse, preface

Who is the real author of the work that the manuscript tradition presents to us as Books 1–4 of 'Arrian's *Discourses of Epictetus*' (ΑΡΡΙΑΝΟΥ ΤΩΝ ΕΠΙΚΤΗΤΟΥ ΔΙΑΤΡΙΒΩΝ Α — Δ)?[1] Is it the consular L. Flavius Arrianus, author of such other works as the *Anabasis of Alexander*, the *Indica* and the *Cynegetica*,[2] or the Phrygian ex-slave Epictetus, who taught philosophy at Nicopolis in Epirus from the early 90s until some time in the 130s CE?[3] For historians and critics of Imperial period philosophy, this is a weighty question, given the importance the contents of the *Discourses* have for our knowledge of both the substance of later Stoicism and the teaching styles of its practitioners. It is not without importance for students of Arrian either. Some words of guidance would be welcome, and, as if anticipating this very wish, the manuscripts provide them, in the form of a

---

I should like to record my thanks to the editors of this volume, both for helpful comments on a preliminary draft and for the opportunity to write out properly a set of thoughts I had been toying with for too long – I hadn't previously written this up in the way in which one might write up such things...

---

1 Bodleian Auct. T.4.13 (Gr. Misc. 251), *saec.* XI/XII, foll. 41r, 85v, 131v.
2 For Arrian, see Stadter 1980, with an outline of the life and works in Ch. 1 and Appendixes 1 (works) and 2 (chronology).
3 See Fuentez González 2000 for a comprehensive survey of life, works and bibliography.

letter, positioned somewhat unexpectedly in between a contents-list to the first Book and that Book's first discourse.[4] It reads as follows:

Ἀρριανὸς Λουκίῳ Γελλίῳ χαίρειν. οὔτε συνέγραψα ἐγὼ τοὺς Ἐπικτήτου λόγους οὕτως ὅπως ἄν τις συγγράψειε τὰ τοιαῦτα οὔτε ἐξήνεγκα εἰς ἀνθρώπους αὐτός, ὅς γε οὐδὲ συγγράψαι φημί. ὅσα δὲ ἤκουον αὐτοῦ λέγοντος, ταῦτα αὐτὰ ἐπειράθην αὐτοῖς ὀνόμασιν ὡς οἷόν τε ἦν γραψάμενος ὑπομνήματα εἰς ὕστερον ἐμαυτῷ διαφυλάξαι τῆς ἐκείνου διανοίας καὶ παρρησίας. ἔστι δὴ τοιαῦτα ὥσπερ εἰκὸς ὁποῖα ἄν τις αὐτόθεν ὁρμηθεὶς εἴποι πρὸς ἕτερον, οὐχ ὁποῖα ἄν ἐπὶ τῷ ὕστερον ἐντυγχάνειν τινὰς αὐτοῖς συγγράφοι. τοιαῦτα δ' ὄντα οὐκ οἶδα ὅπως οὔτε ἑκόντος ἐμοῦ οὔτε εἰδότος ἐξέπεσεν εἰς ἀνθρώπους. ἀλλ' ἐμοί γε οὐ πολὺς λόγος, εἰ οὐχ ἱκανὸς φανοῦμαι συγγράφειν, Ἐπικτήτῳ τε οὐδ' ὀλίγος, εἰ καταφρονήσει τις αὐτοῦ τῶν λόγων, ἐπεὶ καὶ λέγων αὐτοὺς οὐδενὸς ἄλλου δῆλος ἦν ἐφιέμενος ὅτι μὴ κινῆσαι τὰς γνώμας τῶν ἀκουόντων πρὸς τὰ βέλτιστα. εἰ μὲν δὴ τοῦτό γε αὐτὸ διαπράττοιντο οἱ λόγοι οὗτοι, ἔχοι<εν> ἄν οἶμαι ὅπερ χρὴ ἔχειν τοὺς τῶν φιλοσόφων λόγους· εἰ δὲ μή, ἀλλ' ἐκεῖνο ἴστωσαν οἱ ἐντυγχάνοντες ὅτι, αὐτὸς ὁπότε ἔλεγεν αὐτούς, ἀνάγκη ἦν τοῦτο πάσχειν τὸν ἀκροώμενον αὐτῶν ὅπερ ἐκεῖνος αὐτὸν παθεῖν ἠβούλετο. εἰ δ' οἱ λόγοι αὐτοὶ ἐφ' αὑτῶν τοῦτο οὐ διαπράττονται, τυχὸν μὲν ἐγὼ αἴτιος, τυχὸν δὲ καὶ ἀνάγκη οὕτως ἔχειν. ἔρρωσο.

Arrian to Lucius Gellius, greetings.
I did not write up Epictetus's discourses in the way in which someone might write up this sort of thing; nor was I myself responsible for releasing them to the world, seeing that, as I say, I didn't even write them up. Rather, I tried to set down everything that I used to hear him say, as far as possible in his very words, and to preserve this as a personal memoir of his thoughts and his straight talking for future reference. As you might expect, these are the kinds of thing one person might say to another on the spur of the moment, not the kinds of thing one might write up on the understanding that others would subsequently read them. Although that is all they are, they somehow or other spilled out into general circulation without my knowledge or consent. Well, it doesn't matter much to me if I'm going to look incompetent as a writer, and it doesn't matter in the least to Epictetus if people are going to think disparagingly of his words, since when he actually spoke them it was clear that his sole aim was to move his hearers' thoughts towards what is best. If these words now were to achieve just this effect, then I think they would have the quality that philosophers' words ought to have; but if not, then their readers should at least be aware that, when Epictetus himself spoke them, it was impossible for anyone hearing them not to feel what this man wanted him to feel. If the words on their own don't achieve this effect, then perhaps that's my fault, or perhaps it's inevitable.
Good health to you.

Arrian then, we are informed, attended Epictetus's classes,[5] and was impressed enough by both his teacher's thought and his frank speaking to make his own

---

[4] Bodleian Auct. T.4.13 (Gr. Misc. 251), fol. 2v, with the index to Book 1 on fol. 2r, and the text commencing on fol. 3r.

private notes for future reference, aiming for verbatim accuracy but aware that he didn't always attain it. At some later date, these private notes started to circulate more widely, even though Arrian himself had done nothing to make them available, and in the first instance wasn't even aware that there were copies in other people's possession. Learning of this development, Arrian wrote to a friend or peer by the name of Gellius to clarify the extent,[6] and the limitations, of his involvement in the process by which a wider public is now able to read what Epictetus once taught, and to assure him that what is being read is an only lightly mediated version of the inspiring philosopher's words, which may or may not succeed in reproducing the impact of the original.

The practical details implied in this account certainly check out well enough. Note-taking by students in philosophers' classes, and the publication of versions of those classes from the students' notes, are otherwise attested from the Imperial period, and shorthand systems existed to help with the note-taking, even if their flexibility and range of applications is open to discussion.[7] The mechanics of 'publication' in the ancient world, moreover — the multiplication of handwritten copies for more or less general circulation once an exemplar had somehow or another become available for copying — makes the story of unauthorized beginnings a perfectly possible one, which can also be paralleled from other ancient sources.[8] In other respects, however, the letter to Gellius raises more questions than it so blandly pretends to answer, when its relation to the main body of the *Dissertations* is brought under scrutiny, and the implications of this confrontation for the issue of authorship are probed. For discussion of the authorship of this particular text (the letter and the *Dissertations*) will turn out to raise larger questions to do with epistolary fiction and its relation to authorship and authority more generally, and the capacity of fictions of authorship to generate scholarly and critical fictions in their turn.

But to begin with the particular: in the first place, it is by no means clear that there is anything like a neat match between the kind of text suggested by the letter (Arrian's unvarnished lecture-notes) and what we find in the surviving

---

5 The fact that this refers to classes, rather than just casual 'listening', emerges from the combination of the verb (a quasi-technical term for studying with someone as pupil, LSJ ἀκούω II.4) with the imperfect tense, implying an extended process or repeated experience.
6 On Gellius, see further below.
7 Hartmann 1905, 259, 275 states the positive case; Stellwag 1933, 10 and Dobbin 1998, xx, following Radt 1990, 367 n. 3, urge that the manifest limitations in the systems attested are grounds for Epictetan authorship; cf. also Selle 2001, 271 with n. 9.
8 E.g. Galen *De libr. propr.* 9, 14 and 41–43; Cic. *Att.* 3.12.2 and 13.21; Quint. *Praef.* 7; Dio Chrys. *Or.* 42.4–5.

books of the *Dissertations*. It might not be a huge discrepancy in itself that the *Dissertations* intermittently include some narrative framing as well as direct quotation of Epictetus's utterances, but when this is taken together with other signs of calculated shaping and ordering, with the fluency of some of the longer stretches of Epictetus's sermonizing, and with the simple scale of the whole exercise — it originally ran to at least five books, and possibly eight, rather than the (already substantial) four that we now have — then a real gap opens between the relatively unprocessed personal notes that Arrian's words seem to envisage and the text as we now have it.[9] The presence of a few chapters of more miscellaneous notes in Book 3 (σποράδην τινά: 3.11 and 14) does little to bridge this gap.

There is moreover an unanswered question hanging over the status of the letter itself, and the process by which it came to be attached to the work it now introduces. Is it a 'real' letter — 'real' in the sense that this set of words was once committed to a physical medium like a sheet of papyrus or a wax tablet and transported across a distance to a Lucius Gellius — and only subsequently attached to a text of the *Dissertations*? And if so, when and by whom was this pairing effected? Or was it composed from the start as a prefatory or dedicatory letter, with the express purpose of introducing the *Dissertations*, as for instance Lucian's letter to Nigrinus introduces his dialogue of the same name, and so a letter in a secondary (or indeed fictitious) sense?

Criticism of the *Dissertations*, almost all of it coming from students of ancient philosophy, has generated an entertainingly diverse range of responses to such questions, in which the desire to understand the letter in as simple and straightforward a way as possible, and to avoid the imputation of any degree of calculation on Arrian's part, jostles with a readiness to come up with speculative hypotheses (i.e. fictions) to account for its presence and purpose. In very obvious ways, both the determination to read simply and the readiness to spin stories around the letter are in their turn motivated by a desire to minimize Arrian's authorial role in the production of the *Dissertations* and so to preserve them as genuine Epictetus.

For Helena Stellwag, in her doctoral dissertation of 1933,[10] the discrepancy between letter and main text was so glaring that they had simply to be dissoci-

---

9 Narrative framing: e.g. *Diss.* 1.11, 1.13–15, 2.4. Calculated shaping and ordering: De Lacy 1943; Wirth 1967, 161–186. Long stretches: e.g. 3.22, 3.24, 4.1, estimated by Selle 2001, 271 to take 45 minutes each to deliver. Original length: Book 5 cited in Gell. *NA* 19.1.14; eight books attested by Photius *Bibliotheca cod.* 58.
10 Stellwag 1933, 7–14.

ated from each other. Relying on the fact that ancient sources refer to Epictetus's discourses under a range of different potential titles — ὁμιλίαι, διαλέξεις and ἀπομνημονεύματα as well as διατριβαί[11] — and the statement in his *Suda* entry that he 'wrote much' (ἔγραψε πολλά), she hypothesized an original ancient collected edition of Epictetus, in which the *Dissertations* as we now have them (plus the now missing books), authored by Epictetus himself, were preceded by a separate work of Arrian's entitled *Recollections of Epictetus*; and she proposed that it was the *Recollections*, not the *Dissertations*, that Arrian was referring to in the letter.

Stellwag's solution implies a story about the textual transmission that is technically plausible,[12] and although it lacks any external support very neatly manages simultaneously to vindicate Arrian's good faith in the letter and to protect the Epictetan credentials of the *Discourses*. Robert Dobbin, in his translation and commentary on Book 1 for the Clarendon Later Ancient Philosophers series, attempts a similar trick, but with a differing inflection. While agreeing explicitly with Stellwag about the purely Epictetan origins of the *Discourses*, he does not follow her in dissociating the Gellius letter from them, and so needs an alternative way of dealing with the discrepancy between implied and actual contents. He finds it in the supposition that Arrian colluded with his former teacher in an effort to secure his work a wider circulation:

> I suspect that E[pictetus] is responsible for composing the *Discourses* as we have them, but that he tried to preserve the dramatic context from which they probably developed ... in

---

11 Cf. Fuentez Gonzalez 2000, 118–121.

12 The hypothesis would be that at some stage in the transmission prior to the making of the Bodleian manuscript, the pages of the earlier codex containing the *Recollections* became detached and lost, leaving only the prefatory letter behind; the case would be parallel to that of the transmission of the so-called '*collection philosophique*' attested now in its full form only by the contents list of Paris. gr. 1962, which at some point lost two of its five original constituent texts (Whittaker 1974; Trapp 1997, lvi–lvii). The odd positioning of the letter to Gellius in between the contents list to Book 1 of the *Dissertations* and the text of *Diss.* 1.1 shows that there has been at least some disturbance in the order of items in the manuscript tradition. Schenkl's comment (1916, 2) on the ease with which this state of affairs can be accounted for contains a neat, if unintended, acknowledgement, in his phrase *sibi finxerit*, that invention (fiction) is needed: one does indeed need to mould oneself the story that, in the Bodleian manuscript's exemplar or a still earlier ancestor, there will have been a title page to the whole collection of *Discourses*, and the prefatory letter will have come either immediately before or immediately after this, until a mechanical disordering of the opening pages of the codex removed the title page and muddled the order of those immediately surrounding it.

> a[n] ... effort to reach an audience beyond his immediate time and place. Arrian's foreword played its part in putting this slight deception across.¹³

Arrian is thus convicted of fictionalizing in his letter, but of fictionalizing so benignly and in such an admirable cause that his essential good faith is uncompromised.

Other scholars again have wanted no truck with even such a mild degree of deviousness and deception, preferring instead to see only candour and simple factual accuracy in Arrian's words. For Philip Stadter, seeking a comfortable resting-place between the over-stark extremes of purely Epictetan and purely Arrianic authorship,¹⁴ the words of the letter 'seem clear enough' and 'a simple explanation and justification of Arrian's manuscript', as an honest attempt to render the style as well as the contents of his teacher's discourses as accurately as possible, allowing for some selectivity, compression and reorganization, but no essential invention. In the same vein, Tony Long, in the most sensitive and stimulating recent treatment of Epictetus, advocates 'a purely factual reading of Arrian's prefatory letter', in which Arrian 'had no reason to declare his purpose as he did unless it reflected his acknowledgement that the speaker in the discourses is the real Epictetus.' For both Stadter and Long, in common with a number of older scholars, what above all guarantees the authentically Epictetan character of the *Discourses* is their style – the lively, 'diatribe' presentation, the demotic (*koinê*) vocabulary and morphology, and 'a strikingly urgent and vivid voice quite distinct from Arrian's authorial persona in his other works.' In Stadter's treatment, it is principally this decision to depart from normal linguistic propriety in order to preserve Epictetus's 'vivid vernacular', and so also the impact of his teaching, that Arrian is chiefly concerned to justify in the letter. For Long this style is (with something of a stretch) good reason 'for taking the gist of his record to be completely authentic to Epictetus's own style and language' – as if accurate stylistic mimicry necessarily brings with it fidelity of content as well.¹⁵

The status of the letter to Gellius and its relationship to the authorship of the *Dissertations* are thus envisaged in a number of different ways. In one version, the *Dissertations* are wholly the work of Epictetus, and the letter a truthful

---

13 Dobbin 1998, xxii.
14 Another recurring element in discussions of the issue – cf. Fuentes González 2000, 123: 'il semble raisonnable de chercher le juste milieu' – as if epistemological safety always lies in the avoidance of extremes.
15 There seems almost to be a (presumably unconscious?) echo here of Thuc. 1.22.1 – a famously slippery statement in its own right.

document; but because the truths told in the letter relate to another work entirely, it is wholly irrelevant to the *Dissertations*. In a second version, although the *Dissertations* are again wholly the work of Epictetus, the letter is the purveyor of a fiction, which supplies a false genealogy to the *Dissertations*; but the purpose of this falsehood is to ensure that an authentic version of Epictetus's words can bring its salutary truths to as wide a readership as possible. In a third version, a veracious letter reassures the apprehensive that involvement by Arrian in the production of the *Dissertations* — it is definitely his hand rather than Epictetus's that has committed them to written form — does not prevent them from preserving an essentially true reflection, in content as well as style, of the master's teaching.

The implications for these stories for the letter's generic status are for the most part less carefully considered. Stellwag and Long treat it by implication as a real (i.e. originally self-standing) epistle that has somehow or another become attached (whether legitimately or illegitimately) to our *Dissertations*, but do not see it as their business to enquire further about the process. Dobbin introduces it as a letter actually sent to Gellius, but subsequently describes it as a 'preface'.[16] Stadter, in the most scrupulous (and therefore also the most inventive) treatment, envisages a real letter 'prefixed' to the work but not therefore a 'literary preface'; he suggests that Gellius himself 'affixed' Arrian's missive to his own copy of the informal memoir that had slipped into circulation without authorization, and that our manuscript tradition must descend from this copy.[17]

The possibility that the letter to Gellius was from the start a fiction, a prefatory epistle composed expressly to accompany the *Dissertations*, rather than a sent missive only subsequently recruited to perform that role, and that it gives something other than a purely factual account of the genesis of the text, is thus only fleetingly, and confusedly, countenanced in the accounts surveyed so far.[18] The distinction of arguing for both possibilities belongs to Theo Wirth, in his two-part article of 1967, which is by far the most considered and plausible account of the issue so far. The relatively cursory dismissal of this substantial discussion by Stadter and Long, masked by a show of judicious consideration, is

---

16 Dobbin 1998, xx; xxii.
17 Stadter 1980, 28. One might wonder here about the practicalities of affixing a papyrus letter to a papyrus roll (as opposed to slipping extra unbound sheets into a codex).
18 The confused exception is Dobbin 1998, who compounds the confusion by twice referring to the role of the letter in securing the passage of the *Dissertations* into print (*sic*): xx; xxiii.

indeed the weakest point in both their treatments, and the clearest sign of their respective disciplinary biases.[19]

Wirth's analysis of the nature of the *Dissertations* themselves, and of the extent of Arrian's authorial activity, are not our main concern here, but deserve a brief summary. Contrary to the impression given by Stadter's and Long's disapproving reactions, he is far from arguing that Arrian presents a wholly fictional Epictetus. The Epictetus of the *Dissertations*, and the utterances credited to him, are indeed carefully crafted products in his account, in which individual exchanges, which Arrian cannot have known of from first-hand experience, are given a suspiciously neat and instructive shape, and may stitch together sequences of thought that were not so closely related by Epictetus himself; the supposedly distinctive, acerbic style and tone are as much the product of following well established traditions for the written representation of popular philosophical preaching ('diatribe') as of any close representation of the master's voice. Moreover, the whole project of recording Epictetus in this way is manifestly a part of Arrian's larger ambition to present himself as the Xenophon of the modern world, though one in which the influence of the *Memorabilia* as model is tempered by that of more recent exercises in presenting philosophical teachers, such as those inspired by Epictetus's own teacher, Musonius Rufus. Yet at the same time Wirth is happy to assert that Arrian's work is by no means pure invention, and indeed in some (even if not in all) of the collected pieces stays more faithful to the contents (even if not the exact wording) of Epictetus's thought than Xenophon did to Socrates's in his memoir. To a degree that Stadter and Long seem to have missed, his conclusion that 'the *Diatribes* should be cited under his [sc. Arrian's] name and not — as usually happens — under Epictetus's' should not in his view prevent them from being used as reliable evidence for Epictetus's teaching.[20]

---

[19] Baldly (and therefore unfairly) stated, Stadter the ancient historian does not particularly want a very philosophical Arrian (1980, 26–29), while Long the ancient philosopher does not want a text that he finds deeply rewarding philosophically to be the work of a moonlighting historian and huntsman (2002, 40–41). Dobbin, for his part, also dismisses Wirth, but without argument and relying on the authority of others (1998, xxi: 'Wirth's thesis has not been widely accepted').

[20] Wirth 1967, 149–161; quotation from 215 ('die Diatriben unter seinem und nicht — wie es meist geschieht — unter Epiktets Namen zitieren sollen'). If we are not simply to convict Stadter and Long of careless reading, some further explanation of the strength of their reaction seems called for: is it a combination of a reluctance to accuse Arrian in the letter to Gellius of (as they would see it) lying, with an anxiety that Wirth's analysis might be seen as licensing more sceptical readings than he himself is committed to?

More relevant to present purposes, however, is Wirth's discussion of the letter, in which he argues forcefully for the proposition that it was 'conceived right from the beginning for publication, and so a literary letter, with which Arrian dedicated the whole edition to Lucius Gellius.'[21] Step one in the argument to this conclusion is the assertion that even the simplest of readings of the letter has to concede that its apparent claims cannot be taken absolutely literally (can Arrian have recorded '*everything*' that he heard Epictetus say?). Step two is the observation that Arrian is known on other evidence as a careful composer of prefaces: witness both *Anabasis* 1.12.4–5 and the dedicatory epistle to one 'Massalenus' said by Simplicius originally to have been attached to the *Enchiridion*.[22] The third and most substantial step is to adduce a mass of comparative material to underline just how solidly packed with familiar introductory and commendatory gestures the letter to Gellius is. Arrian's words combine recommendation of the value of his subject matter (here are words that can really change you) with a becoming ('courtly') modesty about his own authorial powers, whilst at the same time implicitly, and ingratiatingly, 'apologizing' for the departure from conventional educated diction in the style. This manifest *captatio beneuolentiae* extends also to the suggestion that, far from thrusting his work on an unwilling world, Arrian has had his hand forced by someone else's *démarche*, much in the way that Ovid in *Tristia* 1.7.15–28, with a similarly studied vagueness about the actual circumstances, records how his own desire just to burn his inadequately polished interim draft of the *Metamorphoses* was frustrated by the existence of other, unofficial copies. We are thus in the same kind of territory as a poetic *recusatio*, or of Caesar's desire to portray his accounts of his campaigns as mere preliminary notebooks (*commentarii* = ὑπομνήματα).[23] At the same time, however, by underlining the effectiveness of Epictetus's words on his original audiences, Arrian also contrives to set his teacher in a distinguished tradition of inspiring philosophical preachers going all the way back to the Socrates of Plato's *Symposium* (215b and following) and Xenophon's *Memorabilia* (1.2.14),[24] and himself into the almost equally distinguished ranks of their chroniclers.

---

21 Wirth 1967, 153: 'von allem Anfang an auf die Veröffentlichung hin konzipiert, also ein literarischer Brief, mit dem Arrian die ganze Ausgabe Lucius Gellius widmet'; Wirth's analysis is usefully endorsed, but not much extended by Selle 2001, 270–272.
22 *Comm. in Epict. Ench.* praef. init. = Test. III Schenkl: ὡς αὐτὸς ἐν τῇ πρὸς Μασσαληνὸν ἐπιστολῇ ἔγραψεν ὁ Ἀρριανός, ᾧ καὶ τὸ σύνταγμα προσεφώνησεν, ὡς ἑαυτῷ μὲν φιλτάτῳ, μάλιστα δὲ τὸν Ἐπίκτητον τεθαυμακότι.
23 Cicero *Brutus* 262; *BG* 8 praef. 5 (Hirtius).
24 One might perhaps add here also *Apol.* 17b–18a, with its suggestion that a philosopher's idiosyncratic style is a guarantee of his sincerity.

Wirth's analysis is persuasive, and shows up the relative naivety of any attempt at a 'purely factual' reading of the letter as a 'simple explanation ... of Arrian's manuscript.' It can usefully be carried further, in several respects. In the first place, it can be underlined that the prefatory force of the letter extends beyond *captatio beneuolentiae* (through mock-modest self-deprecation and implicit apology for 'vulgar' style) to positive designs on readers' reception. As in a poetic *recusatio*, apparent apologies for incapacity not only alert the reader or listener to be on the lookout for the author's virtues, but also suggest where they are going to be found: in this case, in Arrian's skill in maintaining a style that, though 'low' on one set of criteria, is in fact entirely appropriate to the speaker and the subject matter of this particular work; and in his consequent ability, for all the modest disclaimer, in conveying the punch of a philosopher's teaching.

Wirth's observation that the letter sets Epictetus as inspiring teacher in a tradition running back via Musonius to the Socrateses of Plato and the other Socratics can also be extended. For, by phrasing its description in terms of a contrast between Epictetus's infallibly effective live discourse and a written equivalent that may fail to reproduce that effect, it also taps into a concern that I have argued elsewhere was widespread in the first and second centuries CE, about the ways in which the soul-therapy of philosophical discourse can be sabotaged by inappropriate concern for verbal style on the part of either preacher or audience or both.[25] It does so, moreover, in terms that recall a key point of reference for this area of concern in the classic repertoire, the discussion of written texts and live dialectical communication in Plato's *Phaedrus*, 274c–277a. The central contrast between the ability of Epictetus's spoken discourses to 'move his hearers' thoughts towards what is best' and the possibility of their written record achieving nothing of the kind matches Socrates's between dumb, inflexible written *logoi* and the capacity of live dialectic to 'sow seeds' in the soul (276d–277a). The depiction of the written notes of Epictetus's teaching as 'somehow or another spilling out into general circulation' and unable 'on their own' to achieve a useful effect parallels his description of 'a *logos* once written rolling around everywhere' and 'unable on its own to defend or help itself' (275e). And the modest characterisation of the original notes as merely ὑπομνήματα to preserve for the author's own subsequent recall echoes Socrates's description of the practitioner of writing 'storing up ὑπομνήματα for himself, for when he "reaches the threshold of old age"' (276d). There is once more here a

---

25 Trapp 2009; key texts in this connection include, besides *Discourses* 3.23.27–32, Musonius fr. 48–49; Seneca *Ep.* 108.5–7, and Plutarch *De aud.* 9.42c–e.

level of literary-critical reflectiveness and literary allusivity that seems hugely more appropriate to a dedicatory epistle than to an occasional letter to a friend.

All in all, therefore, a diagnosis of the letter to Gellius as a self-conscious literary preface rather than an originally sent missive only subsequently drafted into a prefatory role seems the most plausible. Critical fictions ('reconstructions') of the circumstances of sending, and the process(es) by which the letter changed function are thus disposed of, but only because replaced by others: the authorial fictions of a private letter, which the intending reader of the *Dissertations* is privileged to overhear, and of a fictitious account of the genesis of the text about to be read, intended to steer responses to it rather than to inform about any real events in its history.

Here we might rest, were it not for one further observation — an observation that might at first seem to offer a chance of reviving the idea of a 'real' letter, but which I shall go on to suggest points in yet another possible direction. The observation is this. For all the apparently calculatedly prefatory elements in the letter, it also creates a problem in the way it describes the 'publication' history of the record of Epictetus's discourses, a problem which could have been avoided with only a few further remarks. All would have been entirely straightforward and untroubling if the letter had informed its addressee (and its eavesdroppers) that its author was presenting him (and them) with a revised and corrected version of his student notes, to replace the imperfect versions that had escaped into circulation without his permission. But it does not; instead, it acknowledges that the notes are in circulation, and goes on to characterise and defend them as they are, without the least hint of revision or fresh addition. On the face of it, therefore, this is a comment on a (necessarily) separate book or books already in circulation, rather than an accompaniment attached to any fresh publication. And does this not, if pressed, take us back to a self-standing letter such as an Arrian might really have sent to a Lucius Gellius?

The conclusion is not however inevitable. Even staying within the terms of the discussion as we have already established them, the suggestion that the letter is separate from the text it introduces could perhaps be understood as contained within the over-arching fiction of the epistolary preface. Rather than appealing, as Wirth does, to a tactical vagueness on the author's part,[26] this would mean just accepting that, once one degree of imaginary separateness of preface from text is granted (as it is by granting that the preface 'is' a letter), then a further degree (in the fiction that the letter was 'sent' only after the notes were committed to writing and entered circulation) follows easily enough. But

---

26 Wirth 1967, 150; 154–155 (zu vage, Undeutlichkeit, Unbestimmtheit).

this too is not the only possible way of coming to terms with the oddity of a prefatory letter assuming the prior publication of the very text that follows it. We have so far left untouched the supposition that the letter to Gellius, whether a 'real' or a 'literary' letter, really is the work of Arrian. But what if that too is a fiction? What if we have to do with a pseudepigraphic composition, either penned expressly to accompany a new edition of the *Dissertations* (at whatever interval of time from the first, sponsored by Arrian himself), or separately composed and only attached to the collection subsequently, after a period of independent circulation?

It is at all events true that, whatever else, letters in general have form as a place for writers (and readers) to talk about their own and other people's writing, and that this affinity is exploited as enthusiastically in pseudepigraphic as it is in 'genuine' correspondence. Composing a letter in the persona of an admired author, or of one of their early readers, can be an excellent way of recommending thoughts, as if from a privileged vantage-point, about why that writer writes as s/he does — what they were really getting at or were motivated by, what they intended or hoped to achieve, what characteristics of their writing most deserve to be appreciated. It is also an opportunity to show off a cultivated acquaintance with the author's life and works, with the refreshing twist that well-known facts and phrases can be re-envisaged as events in prospect or in process, and as fresh invention not yet hardened into classic quotes. A set of examples that is particularly relevant to the case of Arrian is provided by the pseudepigraphic *Letters of the Socratics*: more precisely, by two of those attributed to Arrian's great hero, Xenophon (*Epistles* 15 and 18), and one which, although credited to him by some manuscripts and by Hercher, is in fact more likely to have been intended as the product of his fellow Socratic Aeschines (*Epistle* 22). The date of composition of these letters cannot be fixed with certainty, but the third century CE seems likely enough on stylistic grounds.[27]

Epistle 15 has its dramatic date in the middle part or later stages of the year 399 BCE. Though addressed to a pair of companions of Socrates (presumably, but not explicitly, Simmias and Cebes, as in *Ep.* 22), it also functions as a response to the preceding *Epistle* 14, in which not they but Aeschines has sent Xenophon an extended account of their mentor's trial, final conversations, death and burial. After some words of consolation, a report of the impression that the news of Socrates's execution has made in Sparta, and a promise to send

---

[27] Bolzan 2009, 9, citing Sykutris 1933, 118–121. In Sykutris's account, stylistic dating is supplemented by a hypothesis about the growth of the collection which sees the *Letters of Socrates* as a composition of the first century CE (109–111), followed only later by the *Letters of the Socratics*.

any help his friends may need, Xenophon thanks the friends collectively for supporting Aeschines and allowing him to correspond with him, and then announces that he too feels under an obligation to commemorate his master:

> I think however that I too should write up an account (συγγράφειν) of what the man once said and did, and that this would be my best way of defending him (ἀπολογία), for now and for the future, not by pleading his case in a court of law but by presenting the virtue he manifested over his whole life. And I declare that, if I wasn't delighted to write (γράφειν) this, I would be betraying our shared comradeship and, as he used to say, the truth itself. A work (σύγγραμμα) of Plato's along these lines has already come into my hands, with Socrates's name in it and the record of a weighty conversation (διάλεξις) with some other parties. I think I was in Megara when I read it ... For my part I have to say, not that I have never heard any such thing, but that I'm incapable of writing a memoir of it (ἀπομνημονεύειν): I'm not the poet that he is, even if he flatly denies any poetic activity (in a show of coquetry towards the pretty boys, he says that any 'poem' (ποίημα) is not by him but by a young and pretty Socrates). My best wishes for your health, my two most intimate friends.

The reader of this letter is thus privileged not only with a ringside view of the genesis of Xenophon's *Memorabilia* (*Apomnêmoneumata*), but also with some thoughts from the horse's mouth about how to place this text in relation to other Socratic writing: particularly Plato's more elaborate dialogues, but perhaps also Xenophon's own *Apology of Socrates*. We are invited to cast our imaginations back to a time when Plato was not yet the author of the collected *Dialogues*, each instantly recognizable by its title, but one of several experimenting commemorators of Socrates's conversations, and his denial of authorship, yet to be committed to writing in a letter to a Sicilian tyrant,[28] was hardly more than a chat-up line.

Epistle 18 moves the story on one more stage. Writing to the companions of Socrates in the plural this time rather than the dual, Xenophon can announce that he has finished a draft, and is beginning to show it around:

> I have composed some memoirs (ἀπομνημονεύματα) of Socrates. When I think they are completely ready (εὖ ἔχειν παντελῶς), I will send them to you as well: Aristippus and Phaedo [*sc.* when they visited Xenophon recently in Sparta] thought they were pretty well crafted (ἁρμόδιά τινα εἶναι). Say hello to Simon the cobbler for me and congratulate him for his continuing attention to Socrates's discourses and for not making his poverty or his profession an excuse for not philosophizing, as some others do who are averse to knowing and admiring rational discourses and their contents.

---

[28] *Ep.* 2.314c.

Here too, the glimpse of a Xenophon embedded in a circle of Socratic writers — Phaedo, Aristippus and Simon were all credited (by some at least) with Socratic dialogues[29] — who share drafts and encourage each other in their efforts, prompts (and/or reflects) thought about the relative merits of their products. It also continues the focus of the previous letter on one particular classic of the future at a time when, it is proposed, it was under way but not yet ready for release to a wider reading public. Unlike the Arrian of the letter to Gellius, this Xenophon aims all along for publication, rather than a record for his own private use; but if his interim drafts had 'slipped out' into more general circulation at this point, he too might have had to write, to some or all of his fellow Socratics, in explanation and excuse.

Four letters further on in the collection comes the disputed *Ep.* 22. While the facts that it is again addressed to Simmias and Cebes, and that it refers to the writer's own products as *apomnêmoneumata*, might seem to point once more to Xenophon, the opening reference to the writer's poverty ('although I do not own much, I have gained much from the care you friends have taken of me') does not seem to square so well, whence an alternative attribution to the notoriously austere and penurious Aeschines.[30] In either case, however, the reflections it contains on the writer's own compositions are full of interest. In terms of dramatic date, we seem to have moved on a few years from *Epistles* 15 and 18.

> As for my writings, I don't yet have anything in the sort of state that I'd be confident in showing to anyone else apart from me, as I was happy to tell you in conversation when you were there in the house where Euclides was lying sick. You know very well, my friends, that when a piece of writing has once become public it can't be taken back. Plato may be able to exercise great power with his works even in his absence, which is why he is now highly admired in Italy and throughout Sicily, but I can barely persuade even myself that this work of mine is worth anyone's serious attention. It isn't just that I'm anxious not to lose my own reputation as an intellectual; I have also to think of Socrates and make sure that he isn't put at risk by a botched account of his virtues from me in my memoir (ἀπομνημονεύματα). I think there's no difference between speaking ill of someone and being held not to have written worthily of one's subject's virtues. This then is the fear that now grips me, Simmias and Cebes, unless you are going to take some different view of the matter.

Plato is now an established author, with an international reputation; Dionysius I's invitation to his court in Syracuse (388 BCE) may not be so very far in the future. The reference to a meeting by Euclid's sick-bed, implying a recent visit to Megara by the writer of the letter, looks like an imaginative reshuffling of the

---

29 Diog. Laert. 2.9 (Phaedo), 2.13 (Simon), 2.83–85 (Aristippus).
30 Diog. Laert. 2.62.

dramatic setting of the *Theaetetus*.³¹ The game of compare and contrast (Plato with the other Socratics) is again being played, whether the comparand is Aeschines or Xenophon, but is now woven together not only with more explicit thoughts about the folly of premature publication, but also with reflections on an author's ability (or lack of it) to make an impression on his readership and on the sensitivity of the challenge to do justice to his distinguished subject. All of which nudges things still closer to the kinds of thought being broached in the letter to Gellius.

At the very least, then, it is clear in principle that pseudepigraphic letters can, among their many other modes and concerns, provide a very neat paratextual resource, in which reflections on the nature and origins of a celebrated work can be presented as the author's own declarations or requests, hesitant or confident as the case may be, from the very moment of its compilation or publication. The key question then becomes whether or not the letter to Gellius actually fits this model closely enough for it too to be declared pseudepigraphic. A good deal manifestly hangs on how, and how confidently, this question can be answered, in terms both of where the significant fictionalizing lies, and of the kinds of motive and interest that may be in play. A positive answer conjures up a reader of the *Discourses* who invents a fictitious version of Arrian in order to place him as an author (associated with the canonical commemorators of Socrates), and to underline the distinctive verbal style and communicative force of the work. A negative answer (reasserting Arrian's authorship) sends us back, as argued above, to authorial fictionalizing on Arrian's part, as he seeks on his own account to guide responses to his work, and to secure his and his subject's places in the annals of philosophical and authorial achievement.

On grounds of content alone, the epistle to Gellius would seem to fit the model of the *Letters of the Socratics* perfectly well. The level of generality, both as regards what this Arrian says about his own activity and as regards the more theoretical reflections on the challenges of recording a philosopher's words in writing, are such as to demand no very close knowledge of the finer details of his life and outlook. And the echoes of Plato and his Socrates that we have detected, though subtler and better integrated than those in Socratic *Epistles* 15, 18 and 22, are of a kind that demand only a good awareness of those texts, and their continuing resonance in relation to the image of Socrates and the issue of the effectiveness of philosophical discourse. As far as content goes, that is to

---

31 *Tht.* 142a–143c, where Euclides and Terpsion in Megara discuss the condition of the wounded and dying Theaetetus, who is on his way back from Corinth to Athens.

say, the letter could just as well be the work of an engaged and attentive reader of the *Dissertations of Epictetus*, keen to comment on them, as of their author.

But can we also provide a convincing story about the identity and motives of the pseudepigrapher who has now been conjured up? When and why will he have created his fiction? Here the grounds for scepticism may grow stronger. The idea of an originally free-floating epistle, detached from the *Dissertations* even though evidently commenting on them (as *Epp. Socrat.* 15 and 18 comment on Xenophon's *Memorabilia*), certainly seems implausible. Such compositions need company, in the form of a set of related items, and what set might an epistle of Arrian to Lucius Gellius belong to? The alternative suggestion, that the letter was expressly created to accompany a new 'edition' of the *Dissertations* therefore seems preferable. Given our ignorance of the detail of the textual history of the work before around 1100 CE (the date of the Bodleian manuscript), there is certainly a generous allowance of blank space into which this 'edition' could be inserted, but a date earlier on in that stretch, perhaps not long after Arrian's death in (?) the 160s CE,[32] would be appropriate to the letter's (Atticizing) stylistic polish and general conceptual and literary grip. Another potential stumbling-block however looms in the choice of the letter's addressee. For obvious enough reasons, pseudepigraphic letters attributed to great figures tend to select addressees who are also well-known, if only for their connection to the supposed letter writers (as Xenophon, and maybe Aeschines too, write to Simmias and Cebes). But how well-known was Lucius Gellius, either in his own right, or as a friend of Arrian's?

In point of fact, despite regular references in the literature to Gellius as 'otherwise unknown' (most recently on the part of Selle and Long),[33] an identification was made by Glenn Bowersock, as long ago as 1967, with a Corinthian aristocrat with the full name of L. Gellius Menander.[34] Although it was subsequently proposed by James Oliver that the identification should in fact be with L. Gellius Menander's son L. Gellius Iustus,[35] the element of uncertainty is if anything helpful, since it underlines the suggestion of a substantial family with considerable local prominence in the Province of Achaea, quite apart from the connection to Arrian. *Corinth* VIII.3.124 is an inscription set up by Menander and his son Iustus, perhaps accompanying a statue, in honour of a philosopher and Governor of Cappadocia who, although unnamed in the surviving portion of the

---

[32] Stadter 1980, 14–18.
[33] Selle 2001, 269; Long 2002, 39.
[34] Bowersock 1967, partly anticipated by Millar 1965, 142.
[35] Oliver 1970.

slab, can only be Arrian. The names L. Gellius Iustus and L. Gellius Menander recur on two further inscriptions, *CIL* III 7269 (139 CE) and an Isthmean victor list published by Biers and Geagan in *Hesperia* 39 (1970) 79–93 (127 CE), in configurations that imply a family tree containing two Menanders and two Iustuses, distributed over three generations.[36] This at least begins to look like enough of a profile for a pseudepigraphically inclined editor working in, say, Athens in the last quarter of the second century, not only to be aware of it himself, but also to be confident that his readers would be too.

Theoretical possibility should not however be mistaken for proof, so I shall not in conclusion press the fiction of a fictionalizing editor too hard. It is an intriguing possibility, but there are elements in the supporting argumentation that can all too easily be parried or even turned against it. For all the local prominence of his family, Lucius Gellius remains in a larger view a fairly obscure figure, and so perhaps an unlikely choice for a pseudepigrapher's pretended addressee. And because the hospitality of letters to literary and authorial chat is something that *pseudepigrapha* share with real letters, rather than inventing it for themselves, the presence of authorial chat in Arrian's letter to Gellius is as much an argument for its authenticity (at least as prefatory epistle) as it is for its bogusness.

In lieu of a confident verdict on its status we might then rest instead with the reflection that, whatever view one takes of it, the letter to Gellius has turned out on close consideration to be shot through and wound around with fiction, whether in its contents, its epistolarity, or the stories conjured up by critical analysis to account for its existence. Neither those stories nor argument over authenticity can be separated from diverging kinds of scholarly interest in the *Dissertations*, and disagreement over where to locate the rival candidates for authorship. Does this text belong in the canon under Arrian's or Epictetus's name? What grade or mode of philosophical discourse does it therefore embody? Is it philosophers or literary scholars who can more legitimately claim it as their territory? Is Arrian essentially a narrative and technical writer, low in authorial cunning, who can produce only an outsider's imitation of moral-reflective and protreptic discourse, but not create and shape it for himself, or do we need a more generous view of his capacities? Is Epictetus' a voice that we can hear directly in the written record, or is he as mediated through Arrian and his priorities as, say, Socrates is through Xenophon? Different preferences over these questions prompt differing views of the degree of fictionalizing in play

---

36 So at least Oliver 1970, summarised at 337.

and its location; but equally, more searching and open-minded consideration of the possibilities of fiction has the capacity to shift views on the larger questions.

Nothing here of course does any violence to expectations of epistolary genre. Letters quite in general invent (by positive construction or purposeful omission) and invite invention (from those eavesdropping on the one side of the conversation they are held to represent, and from believers and sceptics alike); Arrian's (or 'Arrian's') to Gellius (or 'Gellius') has found its own distinctive way of living up to the brief.

Serena Cammoranesi
Cicero's *Epistulae ad Familiares*: From Authentic Letters to Literary Artefact

Abstract: This chapter discusses Cicero's *Epistulae ad Familiares*, a collection posthumously put together and arranged by a number of editors at different stages, so as to produce a narrative of Cicero's life and *gesta* in the Civil War. Although the individual letters are authentic documents, written by Cicero for practical purposes, their arrangement in the collection produces narrative arcs and scenarios which diverge from historical reality or are altogether fictitious. By breaking linear chronology and organising the letters by addressee and theme, the editors have created self-enclosed plots, which interact with each other and collectively produce a complex and sophisticated narrative whole: a quasi-historical synthesis, comparable, to a certain extent, to the Greek pseudonymous letter collections, which fictionalise historical events and personages. Thus, authenticity and fictionality are intertwined and work together. The chapter illustrates this phenomenon by examining, as a case study, the two narrative threads created by the letters at the beginning of book 7: on one hand the separation and reunion of Cicero and Marius, on the other hand Pompey's downfall. These threads look both back and forward to other narrative clusters in the surrounding books, which also revolve around the themes of friendship and political failure, and thus help to create overarching patterns and bridge different parts of the collection.

Keywords: civil war, editor, exile, friendship, narrative

I am extremely grateful to my co-organisers of the workshop at Sidney Sussex, Claire Rachel Jackson and Janja Soldo, my respondent Emilia A. Barbiero, and all the other participants for their input and comments on the paper. Special thanks should go to Ruth Morello, Roy Gibson and Francesca Martelli for their valuable advice and the many discussions on Ciceronian letters. I also wish to thank the members of the Department of Classics, Ancient History, Archaeology and Egyptology at Manchester for their helpful contribution. Finally, I would like to extend my gratitude to the reviewers and the editorial committee at de Gruyter.

1 Introduction

Cicero's entire epistolary production has drawn scholarly interest since the early Modern Age and has been notoriously subject to several attempts at chronological re-ordering from its early printed editions.[1] This practice was no doubt encouraged by the letters' historical and biographical relevance, their authenticity and the anonymous identity of their editors. While Cicero's epistolary writings have all been liable to these concerns, the *Epistulae ad Familiares* stand out because of the evident mismatch between the ancient editorial design and the modern arrangement. These were real letters, written by Cicero and his correspondents for a practical purpose other than publication,[2] but were posthumously selected and arranged into the collection preserved in the manuscripts. Multiple anonymous editors conducted this operation at different stages between the first century BCE and the fourth century CE, and ultimately produced a narrative of Cicero's life and career with a focus on the Civil War.

This narrative arises from the interplay between the three main principles employed by the ancient editors in arranging the letters into the collection: non-linear chronology, correspondent and topic. The *Epistulae ad Familiares* have been organised in clusters of letters and books sharing themes and topics, and addressed to coherent groups of correspondents. These three principles work towards the creation of self-enclosed narratives both within and across books, which play on the letters' shared subject matter, themes, and lexicon, and together contribute to the creation of an overall Civil War narrative.[3]

The editorial principles employed to arrange Cicero's correspondence create a paradox. On the one hand, the letters comprising the collection are indeed authentic documents and the authoritativeness of the account relies on such authenticity. On the other hand, far from being an archival collection of historical documents, the epistles acquire a quasi-fictional status from and within their arrangement into the present collection; not only is the historical account heavily informed by the epistolary format and editorial choices in the selection and arrangement of the letters. In some cases, the narratives produced blur the boundaries between fictionality and historicity or are altogether fictional. As we

---

[1] Gibson 2013 offers a comprehensive and detailed overview of this phenomenon.
[2] In a letter to Atticus dating to 9th July 44 BCE Cicero voices his intention of editing some letters for publication (*Att.* 16.5.5). However, given the short period lapsed between this letter and Cicero's death, it seems unlikely that the orator managed to carry out this work (White 2010, 32–33, Cavarzere 2016, 32).
[3] See below for a fuller discussion with references.

shall see in the present chapter, an example of boundary-blurring is the story of separation and reunion between Cicero and M. Marius in book 7: the letters selected by the editors were written over a period of ten years and it is only because of their contiguity that a coherent plot is built on what would be mere conventions of letter-writing, such as separation, concern for a friend's health, wish to meet. Similarly, the editor has selected and arranged letters dating to the outbreak and early stages of the Civil War so as to enhance the myth of Caesar's swiftness and his depiction as an almost ghostly presence. While in books 5, 14, and 16, Cicero is continuously struggling to locate Caesar and predict his moves, the series of letters to Atticus dating from October to December 50 BCE (*Att.* 6.8–7.9) suggest that Cicero had, in fact, access to more information than the editor of the *Epistulae ad Familiares* leads us to believe.[4] In book 1 the boundaries are pushed even further towards fictionality: the series on Ptolemy's restoration to the throne of Egypt ends with Cicero implying that the task would be assigned to Lentulus Spinther, a suggested ending which does not match the historical events. The *Epistulae ad Familiares* have undergone an editorial process of transformation into a quasi-fictional historical narrative that Cicero did not himself plan or envisage. As such, this collection challenges any assumptions we may have about the opposition between fictionality and authenticity: the two categories do not work in opposition but are strictly intertwined. Although the subject matter is historical in nature and the letters are authentic, an editorial agenda is particularly obvious in the creation of narratives.

Building on recent scholarship on the literary aspects of the *Epistulae ad Familiares*, in this chapter I am investigating how fictionality and authenticity work together and build an epistolary historical narrative of Cicero's life and the Civil War. By focussing on the closing letters of book 6 and the first four letters of book 7, I will demonstrate that the editors have transformed authentic historical documents into the components of self-enclosed plots, which go beyond the boundaries of individual books and build towards an overall narrative across the sixteen books. The two narratives of *Fam.* 7.1–4, Marius' and Cicero's story of separation and reunion, and Pompey's downfall, are featured in a book mostly revolving around Caesar and his campaign in Gaul in 54–53 BCE. However, because of their themes and lexical elements they look back to book 6, which has a focus on Pompeian exiles and defeats, and bridge two major book clusters in the collection: books 4–6, recounting the Civil War from a Pompeian perspective, and books 7–9, focussing on the Caesarian side of the conflict. These are only a few examples of editorial narratives of friendship and failure,

---

4 See Fezzi 2019, 127–146 for a reconstruction of Caesar's movements up to the Rubicon.

in which fiction and authenticity, both in terms of authorship and historical truthfulness, are interwoven. As such, they show the need to move away from a strict opposition between the two categories and to suggest a framework to understand authentic letter collections that allows for both.

2 Arrangement, circulation and critical approaches to the *Epistulae ad Familiares*

The editorial history of the *Epistulae ad Familiares* helps us shed some light on the work's scope and fragmented structure, as well as the criteria behind its arrangement. Epistolary narratives are by default informed by the discrete nature of their basic components, i.e. the individual letters, and the meaning that lies in the intervals between them.[5] In the case of Cicero's *Epistulae ad Familiares*, the involvement of multiple editors across the centuries in shaping such narratives added to their inherent fragmented nature and overall complexity.

While there is no consensus regarding who first edited the collection, it is possible to reconstruct to some extent its publication and early circulation history.[6] The collection transmitted in the manuscripts is the result of an editorial process which went through multiple stages. From ancient evidence we know that the books comprising the *Epistulae ad Familiares* initially circulated independently, and the whole collection was put together at a later stage.[7] Cicero's correspondence was already known in the first century CE, as attested by Seneca the Elder.[8] By the second century CE, Gellius refers to single letters by the name

---

5 Altman 1982, 169–184.

6 It is generally agreed that Cicero did not edit and publish his letters himself and that the collection is posthumous (see discussions in Nicholson 1998, White 2010, and Cavarzere 2016). Two figures were likely involved in their initial editing and circulation: Atticus and Tiro. Both of them had certainly participated in the publishing of Cicero's works, when the latter was still alive, and might have had a role in the compilation and distribution of the individual books comprising the *Ad Familiares*. On the debate over Atticus see Phillips 1986; White 2010, 34, and Cavarzere 2016, 47. On Tiro as the editor see McDermott 1972; Shackleton Bailey 1977, 23–24; Nicholson 1998, 73–75; Cavarzere 2016, 56–57. Beard 2002, 131, calls for caution, even though she notices that Tiro is the only non-prominent correspondent of the *Ad familiares*. See also Martelli's forthcoming piece on book 16 as a paratextual mark of Tiro's editorial role.

7 Weyssenhoff 1966; Shackleton Bailey 1977 I, 23–24; Beard 2002, 116–118; White 2010, 31–34 and 174–175.

8 In *Suas.* 1.5, he quotes from *Fam.* 15.19 by naming its addressee: *in C. Cassi epistula quadam ad M. Ciceronem missa*, 'in a letter by C. Cassius to M. Cicero'.

of the correspondent and the first addressee of the book to which the letter belonged.[9] Strikingly, both the addressee of the epistles and the first correspondent of the book, in which the letter is found, match the collection that has been transmitted to us in the manuscripts. This would strongly suggest that single books had already been assembled by the second century CE and their internal organisation has retained some degree of stability throughout the centuries.[10] While it has been argued that the sixteen books of the *Epistulae ad Familiares* may have been arranged around the fourth or fifth century CE,[11] we have to wait until the ninth century before the collection as a whole is mentioned. The first references to the *Ad Familiares* as a 16-book collection appear in the catalogue of Lorsch and in the manuscript *Mediceus* 49.9 (M), both dating to the ninth century.[12]

From the 9th to the 14th century, the manuscript transmission of the *Ad Familiares* shows a high degree of stability. With a few exceptions, the two corpora circulating in antiquity (one containing books 1–8, the other books 9–16) have been passed down in the same order.[13] Nevertheless, modern editors have disregarded the manuscript structure and attempted various re-orderings according to chronology. In his 2013 article "Letters into Autobiography: The Generic Mobility of the Ancient Letter Collection", Gibson offers an overview of the editorial motivations behind these re-arrangements of Cicero's epistles from the sixteenth to the twenty-first century. While not all editors explicitly state their justification, the underlying motive is to effectively turn 'ancient collections into works of history and autobiography (where chronological ordering is a distinctive

---

[9] In his *Noctes Atticae*, Aulus Gellius mentions two letters belonging to the collection, namely *Fam.* 10.33 (Gell. *NA* 1.22.19: *ita enim scriptum est in libro epistularum M. Ciceronis ad L. Plancum et in epistula M. Asini Pollionis ad Ciceronem*, 'for it was thus written in the book of letters by M. Cicero to L. Plancus and in the letter by M. Asinius Pollio to Cicero') and *Fam.* 4.4 (Gell. *NA* 12.13.21: *in libro M. Tulli epistularum ad Seruium Sulpicium*, 'in the book of letters by M. Tullius to Servius Sulpicius').
[10] Cf. Martelli 2017, 2 n. 6.
[11] Weyssenhoff 1966, 10; Reynolds 1983, 138; Beard 2002, 117–118; Cavarzere 2016, 61. In the fourth century, Nonius, who explicitly mentions the book numbers for the *Ad Atticum*, refers to the single books or letters of the *Ad Familiares* by the name of the addressee and quotes mainly from book 15 (Weyssenhoff 1966, 51).
[12] Reynolds 1983, 138. It is worth noting that even after this point, the single books continue to be conventionally referred to by the name of the first addressee, not by number. Beard 2002, 117 notices that the manuscripts preserve both systems.
[13] For a detailed description of the manuscript tradition of the collection see Mendelssohn 1893, iii–xxvii.

generic marker in these genres in their modern forms)'.[14] The radical arrangement in a chronological line is increasingly a modern feature, in line with cultural contexts and assumptions about the function of letters.[15]

Gibson's work places itself in the context of the Ciceronian studies which followed Mary Beard's "Ciceronian correspondences: making a book out of letters": studies have since shifted from a modern historical-autobiographical approach to a literary one, with a corresponding move away from dependency on chronology.[16] Scholars started to examine the *Epistulae ad Familiares* as a coherent and unified collection and to appreciate the ancient editors' design. Three main principles of organisation have thus been identified in the collection: non-linear chronology, addressee and theme.[17] These three principles work in synergy to create narratives within and across books and paint a sophisticated and multi-faceted picture of the Civil War with a focus on friendship and political failure.[18]

While it has long been established that strict chronological order was not a concern for the ancient editors,[19] the collection displays an overall forward movement in the narrative from the peak of Cicero's career in the 60s BCE to his decline, alongside that of the Republic, in the 40s BCE. The years of the proconsulship are the focus of books 1–3. With books 4 to 6 we move to the next phase of Cicero's life, i.e. the Civil War, told from the perspective of the Pompeian side of the struggle: most of the correspondents in these books are ex-Pompeians in exile. In books 7 to 9 the events of the Civil War and those leading up to it are recounted with a focus on the Caesarian side. In this section we find a stronger focus on the causes of the war: we start from the Gallic Wars in 54 and 53 in book 7, we then move on to book 8 and the debate in 51 over the renewal of

---

14 Gibson 2013, 387–388; cf. Gibson 2012, 58. Such practice was partly validated by Nepos' claim that the *Ad Atticum* constituted a *historia contexta* of the late Republic, which 'cohere with modern use of the collection' (Gibson 2012, 57). But this collection is in fact an exception in the ancient epistolographical landscape, as strict chronology does not appear to be a principle of organisation in ancient letter collections (Gibson 2012, 57).
15 Gibson 2013, 387–389.
16 Beard's study was preceded by Leach's work on the letters of 46 (1999) and Hutchinson's 1998 book on the themes of the collection, both having a 'literary' focus. But it was Beard who first argued for an editorial design in the *Epistulae ad Familiares*.
17 For a full discussion of the letters' principles of organisation see Beard 2002, 129–130; White 2010, 31–62; Gibson 2012, 64–65.
18 Studies have been conducted on the structure of single books by Beard 2002; Grillo 2015 and 2016; Gunderson 2007 and 2016; Martelli 2017. In my larger project, I investigate the overall narrative.
19 White 2010, 56; Gibson 2012, 57.

Caesar's command in Gaul, and in book 9 we get to the years of Caesar's rule until his assassination.[20] The struggle against Antony and the post-Caesar phase of the war are the focus of books 10–12. The last four books, spanning from the 60s to the 40s, are addressed both to Cicero's colleagues and to members of his family, and offer revisions of events taking place in previous books. Despite the largely chronological advancement in the narrative, individual letters are often displaced from what would be a strict order of the letters by date.[21] The editors have deliberately created flashbacks and flash-forwards, which add to the narrative's sophistication and complexity. The second principle of organisation is correspondent: with a few exceptions, letters addressed to or written by the same figure tend to be clustered, a tendency which is also attested in the manuscript tradition. The third principle of arrangement is topic: groups of letters to or from the same correspondent tend to be focused on a specific event or issue.[22]

While these three principles work in synergy, topic seems to be the predominant one and often drives the letters' displacements in terms of chronology and correspondent. For example, *Fam.* 7.5, a letter of recommendation to Caesar, could have been included in book 13, alongside the other recommendation letters, but introduces Trebatius Testa, one of the main characters of book 7, and is therefore part of the 'Trebatius series'.[23] In fact, the letter gains significance in this position, since a major theme in that series is precisely the need for Trebatius to get close to Caesar. Similarly, book 4 is concerned with the pardon of Marcellus, who had strongly opposed Caesar and was sent into exile on Mytilene, but contains also Cicero's correspondence with Servius Sulpicius Rufus, Marcellus' consular colleague in 51. Notably, it is Sulpicius Rufus who reports the news of Marcellus' death (*Fam.* 4.12).

The selection and arrangement of letters by topic is reliant on the narratives contained in individual letters and the exploitation of repeated keywords within letter cycles and across the collection.[24] The major unifying themes of the *Epistulae ad Familiares* are Cicero's attempts to foster his friendship network during the

---

20 The Pompey and Caesar sections offer complementary perspectives on the same events. In this respect they resemble the diptych structure of the *Letters of Themistocles*, which can be divided into two series offering contrasting characterisations of the politician. See the discussion of Penwill 1978; Rosenmeyer 2001, 231–233; Morrison 2014b, 302.
21 White 2010, 56–61.
22 Both principles are discussed in the bibliography mentioned at n. 17 and 18.
23 Cf. Cavarzere 2016, 644: 'è [...] la lettera che serve da raccomandazione a Trebazio e costituisce dunque l'indispensabile premessa al carteggio con questo'.
24 These mechanisms, along with the significance of the letters' position within a series, have been explored in Grillo 2015 and 2016 on books 1 and 6, and Martelli 2017 on book 15.

challenging years of the Civil War and his political downfall. Such editorial narratives, which simultaneously exploit and enhance the thematic connections between the letters, are lost in a strict chronological re-ordering of the collection.[25] By arranging the letters according to these criteria, the editors created coherent narratives at all levels: letter cycles, books, book cycles, whole collection. The criteria used to structure individual books, when they first started to circulate, were later applied to the whole collection. It is from this series of self-enclosed plots that the overall narrative of the *Epistulae ad Familiares* arises.

3 Authenticity, history and fictionality

Although the letters are authentic and based on historical events, the editorial narratives are to some extent fictional. The editors' goal is to create their own versions of the Civil War and to offer both portrayals of its protagonists as well as insights into their public and private spheres. In this respect, the *Epistulae ad Familiares* are not far from ancient Greek pseudonymous letter collections described by Rosenmeyer in her *Ancient Epistolary Fictions*. Both are based on real figures and draw from historical events but fictionalise to some extent events and characters.[26] At the end of book 1, for example, Cicero suggests that Lentulus will be asked to restore Ptolemy to the throne of Egypt, a task which would be eventually carried out by Gabinius. Both types of letter collections fulfil the reader's interest in reading historical figures' words, whether they be genuine, as in the *Epistulae ad Familiares*, or not, as in the case of pseudonymous collections.[27] The story is created by editorial arrangement of the letters and narrated by the individual letter writers: this plurality of voices often results in contrasting accounts and views of the story and its protagonists.[28] One of the most striking examples is the assessment of Marcellus by Sulpicius and Cicero in book 4, where he is pictured as a defender of the State, in stark contrast to Caelius' doubts regarding the motives behind his opposition of Caesar in book 8. The similarities between the two subgenres raise questions regarding the opposition of authenticity and fictionality: for a better understanding of ancient epistolography, it is necessary to take both aspects into account.

---

25 Grillo 2016, 406–407; cf. Beard 2002, 127–130.
26 Rosenmeyer 2001, 193–199.
27 Rosenmeyer 2001, 197–198.
28 Rosenmeyer 2001, 201–203.

A further element to consider is the fragmented nature of epistolary collections. The narratives arising from series of letters and books are constructed as a linked succession of episodes and usually contain gaps and holes, which the reader needs to fill in.[29] In "Pamela and Plato: Ancient and Modern Epistolary Narratives", Morrison highlights how ancient letters have a 'greater tolerance for narrative gaps across a given collection as a whole'.[30] Similarly, when discussing pseudonymous letter collections, Rosenmeyer cautions against the urge to 'fit all the parts into a consistent and chronological smooth whole' and argues that epistolary fictions 'explore alternative modes of narration, which require the reader's active participation in reconstructing a plausible version of the story.'[31] While fragmentation is inherent in the genre, the composite nature of an epistolary collection made of real letters inevitably and deeply informs the narrative structure of the text.[32] Such a feature contributes to the complexity and multi-layered quality of the text: a reader is more explicitly required to piece together and interpret these episodes and gaps.[33] In *Fam.* 7.1–3 the reader is faced with this precise challenge: reconstruct the downfall of Pompey from a selection of letters and episodes operated by Cicero first (e.g. when he decided what episodes of the Civil War to include in *Fam.* 7.2) and the editors second (when selecting and arranging the epistles into this collection). The editor's arrangement has produced a fragmented narrative with varying degrees of authenticity and fictionality for the reader to explore and interpret.

So far, I have sketched out how the editors selected and arranged authentic letters by non-linear chronology, correspondent and topic to build a narrative of the life of Cicero at multiple levels throughout the sixteen books of the *Epistulae ad Familiares*: series of letters, books, series of books and collection. In the rest of this chapter, I will explore how layered narratives are constructed and connected across books. I will use book 7 as a case study, focussing on the first four letters, all of which are from Cicero to M. Marius. I will show that the opening

---

29 Beard 2002, 125 talks about 'epistolary narratives'.
30 Morrison 2014b, 308.
31 Rosenmeyer 2001, 229–230. On the same issue, but from a broader perspective, see Sharrock 2000: in her introduction to *Intratextuality: Greek and Roman Textual Relations*, Sharrock highlights the tension between the reader's inevitable designation of textual parts and the need to find unity in texts, and argues that the complexity of a text arises from the interactions among parts, gaps and the whole.
32 On fragmentation as a meaningful epistolary feature see Altman 1982, 169–184.
33 In addition to Altman (see previous note), see Fludernik 2007, 243, who argues that 'the structure of narrative that underlies the novel emerges from developments in episodic narrative that expand and eventually dissolve the patterns of episodic narrative'.

letter cycle, the 'Marius series' (*Fam.* 7.1–4), has several layers of narrativity and multiple narratives working together at the same level. I will also highlight how this series is thematically and lexically connected to book 6. Thus, I will explore how historical events and fictionality intersect in the narratives of the collection, and offer a reading that allows for both.

4 A closer look: fictionality in *Fam.* 6.21–7.4

The juncture between books 6 and 7 constitutes a turning point in the narrative structure of the *Epistulae ad Familiares*, as it marks the shift from the Pompeian to the Caesarian perspective.

Book 6 is mostly comprised of consolation letters and dates to the years 46–44 BCE, preceding Caesar's assassination: we are in the midst of the Civil War and at this stage Caesar is at the peak of his power. Most correspondents are Pompeians in exile, hoping to receive his pardon. The main themes are the death of the State, the correspondents' need to stay strong in the face of adversity, knowing that their conscience is clean, Cicero's foresight and loyal service to his friends in this time of hardship.[34]

In book 7, the narrative takes the reader through events already recounted or referred to in earlier books, but from a Caesarian perspective.[35] Notably, the transition from the 'Pompey narrative' to the 'Caesar narrative' does not match the book division, but carries from the end of book 6 to include the first three letters of book 7: in *Fam.* 7.1–3 Cicero offers a sketchy summary of Pompey's downfall. By connecting these two books, the editors enhance their dramatic quality and build a sophisticated overall narrative of failure, in which fiction and history coexist.[36]

The end of book 6 marks the defeat of the Pompeian side: their distance from power progressively widens and, as they suffer heavy military defeats, hopes for a positive resolution of the conflict fade. This is clear from the last two letters of the book. *Fam.* 6.21 to Toranius, dated to January 45, opens with a disheartened reflection on the war, which appears to be approaching its resolu-

---

34 Grillo 2016, 407–411.
35 This is one of the instances in which the principle of arrangement by correspondent prevails on linear chronology. Most letters in book 7 date earlier than those in book 6, but the editors have chosen to insert book 7 in the 'Caesar block' (books 7–9).
36 This is particularly striking if we consider that the individual books and the collection were arranged at different stages and that three centuries may have elapsed between them.

tion (*Fam.* 6.21.1).³⁷ The victory of the Caesarians seems inevitable and the losing side has to prepare for the consequences: the battle of Munda, which is only two months away, will mark their final defeat. Cicero himself admits that he has given up (*Fam.* 6.21.1):

> cum aliquid uidebatur caueri posse, tum id neglegi dolebam. nunc uero euersis omnibus rebus, cum consilio profici nihil possit, una ratio uidetur, quicquid euenerit, ferre moderate, praesertim cum omnium rerum mors sit extremum et mihi sim conscius me <et>, quoad licuerit, dignitati rei publicae consuluisse et hac <a>missa salutem retinere uoluisse.

> When it seemed that something could be saved, I was sorry for this opportunity to be neglected. But now that everything has been overthrown, that nothing can be achieved by deliberation, one seems to be the course of action: to endure with moderation whatever happens; especially since death is the end of all things and I know in myself that, as long as it was possible, I took care of the dignity of the State and, once it was lost, I preferred to preserve its safety.

By acknowledging that *consilium* is no longer of any use and endurance is the only possible way of conduct, Cicero marks his disillusionment and resignation to the new state of things, knowing that he has tried all he could to save the State. The only sensible thing to do now is to live a discreet life, out of the political spotlight. While the exhortation to stoically endure any misfortune is a topos in consolation letters, this acquires a greater significance from its position in the collection.³⁸ As we shall see shortly, *otium* and secluded living are also central themes of letter 7.1, which anticipates Cicero's predominant 'private' dimension in books 7 to 9.

Book 6 closes with *Fam.* 6.22, a gloomy epistle to Domitius Ahenobarbus, dated to May 46, shortly after the Pompeians' defeat at Thapsus on 6th April. The addressee is the son of Lucius Domitius Ahenobarbus, who had died at Pharsalus, and the nephew of Cato the Younger, who killed himself in Utica not long after the Battle of Thapsus.³⁹ In the opening of the epistle Cicero apologises for failing to write earlier, the reason being his inability to offer consolation (he lacks both

---

37 All texts and dates of Cicero's letters are from Shackleton Bailey's 1988 Teubner edition, unless otherwise stated.
38 Cf. Gildenhard 2018, 231, where he argues, with reference to *Fam.* 6.1, that 'Cicero here marries the Stoic maxims of self-sufficiency and contempt for the vicissitudes of fortune with civil ethics and a specific sense of political community'. In "A Republic in Letters: Epistolary Communities in Cicero's Correspondence, 49–44 BCE", Gildenhard explores the communities that Cicero builds both in and through his letters.
39 Cavarzere 2016, 630.

consilium and *consolatio*). He then goes on to voice his approval of Domitius' decision to withdraw from the war after Pharsalus (*Fam.* 6.22.1):

> [...] *nec quid tibi pollicerer ipse egens rebus omnibus nec quid suaderem, cum mihimet ipsi consilium deesset, nec quid consolationis adferrem in tantis malis reperiebam. haec quamquam nihilo meliora sunt nunc [etiam] atque etiam multo desperatiora, tamen inanis esse meas litteras quam nullas malui.* [...] *sed cum consili tui bene fortiterque suscepti eum tibi finem statueris quem ipsa Fortuna terminum nostrarum contentionum esse uoluisset* [...].

> [...] I had no promise to make, since I myself was in need of everything, no advice to give, since I was falling short of wisdom, no consolation to bring in such great misfortunes. Though the circumstances are now in no way improved and all the more desperate, yet I preferred to send you a pointless letter than none at all. [...] but since you set for yourself as a limit to the plan, which you had embarked on with honour and courage, the same that Fortune had determined as the end to our struggles [...].

Like in the previous letter, the Pompeians' situation appears hopeless and withdrawal seems the only possible solution. The disillusioned tone of the last two letters in book 6 is enhanced by Cicero's insistence on marking endpoints, a linguistic and thematic feature that the editors have carefully exploited. *Fam.* 6.21 opens with Cicero's reference to the *exitus huius calamitosissimi belli* ('the end of this most ruinous war'), which, as he acknowledges, might have already taken place (*iam...actum et confectum*). Further on, he reflects on how *omnium rerum mors sit extremum* ('death is the end of all things'). In *Fam.* 6.22, notably the last letter of the book, the *finis* which has been set by Domitius himself coincides with the *terminus* to the conflict decreed by Fortune. The design of book 6 reveals the editors' work: it is no chance that this book closes with the end of the war and the defeat of the Pompeian side. By selecting these two letters and placing them in this order, the editors have exploited and enhanced their literary quality to close the series of books devoted to Pompey and his supporters with a stress on their failure.[40]

This bleak ending is lost in a chronological ordering of the letters.[41] If we follow Shackleton Bailey's re-ordering, *Fam.* 6.22 (221 in his edition) precedes *Fam.* 6.21 (247) by over 20 letters. Furthermore, *Fam.* 6.20 (248), which would immediately follow *Fam.* 6.21 (247), does not show the same despair that we find in letters 21 and 22. In letter 20, Cicero first offers advice to Toranius on what is

---

[40] Grillo 2016, 416 notices a different aspect arising from this deliberate arrangement: 'Remarkably, after the whole collection has documented Cicero's solicitude and generosity toward friends in need, the editor reminds his readers that Cicero had promised he would do just that.'
[41] Cf. Grillo 2016, 406–407.

the best course to take (*Fam.* 6.20.1), he then continues by consoling him (*Fam.* 6.20.2) and closes with an exhortation to be strong and endure the circumstances, knowing that they were not at fault (*Fam.* 6.20.3). Despite the similar tone and themes, this letter would not give a closure as dramatic as that of *Fam.* 6.22. The explicit insistence on endpoints and on the end of the war is essential to marking the closure of the Pompeian block of the collection. Of course, we are far from the end of the civil conflict, and the editors play on these false endings: throughout the collection, the clock is re-set several times and narratives of failure take place over and over again.⁴² The conjunction between books 6 and 7 is one of these false endings: while the war between Caesar and Pompey seems to be over, in books 7–9 the narrative takes the reader again through the war, this time up to Caesar's rule and death. The juxtaposition of books 6 and 7, therefore, is essential to the editorial construction of a dramatic narrative of repeated failure and defeat across the collection.

In book 7 there is a shift in focus. The book is comprised of five blocks of letters: to M. Marius, C. Trebatius Testa, M. Fabius Gallus, Manius Curius and P. Volumnius Eutrapelus. Seventeen out of thirty-three letters are addressed to the jurist Trebatius Testa, adviser to both Caesar and Augustus,⁴³ and intermediary between Caesar and Cicero during the Civil War.⁴⁴ The first letter of the Trebatius series, *Fam.* 7.5, establishes Caesar as the pivot of the book, the background element connecting all the letter blocks, and indeed the next three books: the main themes are access to Caesar and distance from power in the aftermath of Pompey's defeat. Interestingly, the book opens with a series of letters to M. Marius, which sets the clock back from 46 to 55 BCE, and offers, along a narrative of friendship between Cicero and Marius, a fragmented summary of Pompey's (and Cicero's) downfall. The friendship plot is built on their separation: what moves the story forward is their wish to reunite.⁴⁵ Interwoven in this plot are the narrative about the Civil War and the years which precede it, as well as themes which recur throughout the collection: *otium* vs *negotium*, Cicero's reluctance to join the war, the shared miseries, concerns for the corre-

---

42 Book 3 brings the reader back from the end of Cicero's proconsulship (*Fam.* 2.19) to its early stages. After book 4, which dates to the years 49–45 BCE, the editors set the clock back by over 10 years in book 5 and tie the Civil War to Catiline's conspiracy. A similar move is made after book 7: book 8 constitutes a long flashback in which the causes of the Civil War are investigated. Finally, books 13–16 offer differing readings of events and the years covered in previous books.
43 Cavarzere 2016, 639–640.
44 Cf. Cic. *Att.* 7.17.3.
45 At least Cicero's wish, since he is the sole writer of these letters. Their friendship is framed from the beginning as *amor* (cf. *Fam.* 7.1 and 7.2).

spondent's ill-health. The narrative appears to be constructed as a series of snapshots of Cicero's and Marius' lives in these turbulent years, and closes with a long-sought reunion. These are letters written over ten years and would hardly constitute a plot if taken separately: their themes are by no means uncommon in epistolography, and only build a coherent, albeit fictional, narrative when placed next to each other. Along the friendship narrative, we find a gappy account of Pompey's decline, from the peak of his power to his final defeat.

This series shows how fictionality and history work in the *Ad Familiares* on two levels: at the collection level, since it connects books 6 and 7, and more broadly the 'Pompey narrative' and the 'Caesar narrative' through a fictional reunion plot; and at the book level, because its layered narratives reveal that the editors exploit narrativity to its fullest potential, by pushing the boundaries between history and fiction.

Despite the time gap, there is continuity between book 6 and *Fam.* 7.1, since a flashback brings us to the games given by Pompey to inaugurate his new Theatre and the Temple of Venus Victrix built inside. *Fam.* 7.1 is constructed on a double narrative: first, Cicero imagines how Marius has spent his days at Stabiae during the games, which he did not attend, then he proceeds to narrate the games themselves. These two narratives are strictly intertwined, since the 'imagined' narrative functions as the starting point for the 'real' narrative of the games.

In the opening paragraph, Cicero approves of his friend's decision not to go to the games, whether it be because of poor health or disdain of popular entertainment (*Fam.* 7.1.1).[46] He then offers his account of the games and imagines Marius' experience of *otium* and seclusion, creating his own fiction. From the very beginning, the letter's narrative is set up on the contrast between the crowd's low distractions and the wise man's calm contemplation and philosophical pursuits (*Fam.* 7.1.1–2):

> neque tamen dubito quin tu in illo cubiculo tuo, ex quo tibi Stabianum perforasti et patefecisti sinum, per eos dies matutina tempora lectiunculis consumpseris, cum illi interea, qui te istic reliquerunt, spectarent communis mimos semisomni. reliquas uero partis diei tu consumebas iis delectationibus, quas tibi ipse ad arbitrium tuum compararas; nobis autem er-

---

[46] Marius' illness is in fact immediately dismissed in the ironic opening which reveals the playful nature of the letter and their friendship (*Fam.* 7.1.1): *si te dolor aliqui corporis aut infirmitas ualetudinis tuae tenuit quo minus ad ludos uenires, fortunae magis tribuo quam sapientiae tuae*, 'If some pain in your body or your ill-health kept you from coming to the games, I credit Fortune more than your wisdom for this'. In the last letter addressed to Marius, Cicero addresses his friend's ill-health with a similar irony (*Fam.* 7.4). For more on this letter see Morello's chapter in this volume.

ant ea perpetienda, quae Sp. Maecius probauisset. [2] omnino, si quaeris, ludi apparatissimi, sed non tui stomachi; coniecturam enim facio de meo.

And yet I do not doubt that, in those days, you spent your mornings with/among light readings in that bedroom of yours, from which you made an opening and made the bay of Stabiae visible, while those who left you there, watched common pantomimes half-asleep. Indeed, you spent the rest of the day in those amusements, which you had devised to your own liking; instead, we had to suffer through what Sp. Maecius had judged good. [2] If you ask, the games were absolutely magnificent but not to your liking, for I can make this judgement by mine.

In this passage, Cicero contrasts the activities that Marius arranged for himself, i.e. enjoying the view and studying, and the seemingly spectacular games, which simultaneously took place in Rome. Both types of entertainment had been carefully devised, as the language too suggests (see the use of *comparas* and *apparatissimi*), but produced opposite outcomes.[47] The description of the audience, watching the shows *semisomni*, and the sentence opening the second paragraph encapsulate Cicero's opinion of the games and anticipate the following sections. Here, Cicero lists all the spectacles available to the people (pantomime, tragedy, gladiatorial games, hunting) and scatters his negative judgments of both the games and the audience, in a way that seems to prove Marius' point, but at the same time shows the games' grandeur (*Fam.* 7.1.2–3).[48] As Cicero himself acknowledges, these spectacles are no different than what they have both seen before (*Fam.* 7.1.3). The series of events culminates in paragraph 3, with the report of the last day of the games (*Fam.* 7.1.3):

extremus elephantorum dies fuit. in quo admiratio magna uulgi atque turbae, delectatio nulla exstitit; quin etiam misericordia quaedam consecuta est atque opinio eius modi, esse quandam illi beluae cum genere humano societatem.

The last day was that of the elephants. There was great astonishment among the crowd, but no amusement; in truth, it was even followed by a certain compassion and a belief that there was something in common between that beast and humankind.

---

[47] I owe this observation to Ruth Morello.
[48] To mention a few, the performance given by the actor Aesopus produced a sense of relief at his decision to retire (*Fam.* 7.1.2); the monumental tragedy productions had entertained the audience but would not have produce the same effect in Marius (*Fam.* 7.1.2); as for the hunting, a man of taste would not find them enjoyable (*Fam.* 7.1.3).

While initially the elephants raise amazement among the common people, soon Cicero's narrative comes to a bitter end, with the realisation that in fact that spectacle produced *misericordia* towards the animals rather than *delectatio*.

What initially appears to be a 'triumph' (the *ludi apparatissimi*) soon turns out to be the beginning of Pompey's downfall. The games did not have the effect hoped for, to the point that the writer claims (*Fam.* 7.1.3): *nam quid ego te athletas putem desiderare, qui gladiatores contempseris? in quibus ipse Pompeius confitetur se et operam et oleum perdidisse* ('or perhaps I should think that you miss the athletes, since you have scorned the gladiators? Pompey himself acknowledges that he has wasted time and oil with them'). Pompey himself acknowledges that the spectacles did not match his efforts and expectations. The games and this letter mark the beginning of his decline.[49]

But this letter is also significant because it opposes Marius' *otium* to Cicero's almost forced work in the forum (*Fam.* 7.1.4–5):

> *his ego tamen diebus ludis scaenicis, ne forte uidear tibi non modo beatus sed liber omnino fuisse, dirupi me paene in iudicio Galli Canini, familiaris tui. quod si tam facilem populum haberem quam Aesopus habuit, libenter me hercule artem desinerem tecumque et cum similibus nostri uiuerem. nam me cum antea taedebat, cum et aetas et ambitio me hortabatur, et licebat denique, quem nolebam, non defendere, tum uero hoc tempore uita nulla est. neque enim fructum ullum laboris exspecto et cogor non numquam homines non optime de me meritos rogatu eorum, qui bene meriti sunt defendere.*

> In these days, however, lest by chance it should seem to you that I have been not only fortunate but even free from work, I took a break from the spectacles, being utterly busy with the trial of your friend Gallus Caninus. And if I had a public as agreeable as Aesopus', I would gladly leave my occupation and live with you and those of our kind. For if it wearied me back when my young age and ambition incited me, and it was even possible for me not to defend someone I did not wish to take on, then at this time my life is of no value. For I am not expecting any fruit of my labours and I am sometimes compelled to defend men who are not deserving of me at the request of those who are much worthy.

The issue of *otium* (and its opposition to *negotium*) is central to the whole letter. In several instances, Cicero expresses his frustration at his dull occupations and wishes he could enjoy learned *otium* and study *humaniter uiuere*, like Marius himself (*Fam.* 7.1.4–5). On the contrary, the orator is in Rome, going to bad-taste spectacles and carrying out his *molestissimas occupationes* (*Fam.* 7.1.5). Notably,

---

49 Interestingly, Beard 2009, 28 notices that: 'As with the triumph itself, however, despite its lavishness (or perhaps, rather, because of it), Pompey's inaugural celebration prompted cynicism and disapproval as well as admiration. This was, no doubt, partly because Pompey's political pre-eminence had been eroded in the six years since his third triumph.'

here we learn that Cicero did not attend the games for their whole duration. The orator did not in fact attend the theatre spectacles for his own drama show – the trial of Caninius Gallus, which is interestingly described through the language of spectacles. What initially appeared to be a truthful account of the games reveals now its 'imagined' nature: because of the implication that Cicero did not witness the whole games, the reader is left wondering whether the narrative accurately reflects the events (Cicero's own judgment of them is real) or is constructed by Cicero just like the narrative of Marius' days at Stabiae. As the opening letter of the book, *Fam.* 7.1 is invested with a programmatic function: the editors have selected an epistle, in which Cicero plays with the boundaries between fictionality and accuracy, of what is real and what is imagined, of everyday life and spectacles, both in the narratives and the language.

The light and ironic tone gives away the playful quality of the letter from the very beginning. But in the closing paragraph this is pushed even further, as we learn the true nature of this epistle (*Fam.* 7.1.6):

> *haec ad te pluribus uerbis scripsi quam soleo, non oti abundantia sed amoris erga te, quod me quadam epistula subinuitaras, si memoria tenes, ut ad te aliquid eius modi scriberem, quo minus te praetermisisse ludos paeniteret. quod si adsecutus sum, gaudeo; sin minus, hoc me tamen consolor, quod posthac ad ludos uenies nosque uises neque in epistulis relinques meis spem aliquam delectationis tuae.*

> These things I wrote to you with more words than usual, not for abundance of leisurely time, but out of love for you, since you had invited me with one of your letters, if you remember, to write to you about something of this kind, so that you might regret less missing the games. And if I have accomplished this, I rejoice; if not, yet I find consolation in this, that in the future you will come to the games and see me, and you will leave to my letter any hope for your amusement.

The letter is a literary exercise requested by Marius himself.[50] Cicero has decided to comply to his friend's request on his own terms: he has built a literary *ludus*, from which he hopes Marius can derive some *delectatio*, on a double narrative regarding games, contemplative life and different notions of *otium*. Such construction suggests that both Cicero and the editors are well aware of the intrinsic predisposition of letters to the inclusion of narratives and capable of playing with this very notion.

It is strikingly ironic that after a book of consolation letters to Pompeians, marking the downfall of the Republic, this witty and playful flashback brings us back to Pompey's celebratory games. This is not the kind of triumph that we

---

[50] Shackleton Bailey 1977 I, 324; Cavarzere 2016, 646.

would expect at this point in the story, even more so since the second half of book 7 is about Caesar and the world after his victory. It is also significant that the addressee had already chosen the same private and secluded life that Cicero sees as the only possible way to live in *Fam.* 6.21. In letter 7.1 Cicero talks about *otium, amoenitas*, Marius' view of the bay of Stabiae, his *lectiunculae*. The letter to Marius was written 10 years before *Fam.* 6.21 and is very different in tone, but because of its position in the collection the references to leisure and spectacles echo and foreshadow the forced political inactivity of Cicero and his fellow Pompeians, producing that dramatic irony that pervades the collection. This becomes clearer as the book progresses. While in the first letters of book 7 we see Cicero in a 'public dimension' (he is in the theatre, in court, in the *forum*), the second half of the book, dating between 46 and 44 BCE, is concerned with his 'private life': he talks about philosophy writing, dinner parties, private discussions on financial matters. After Caesar's victory, his opponents have been relegated to leisure and have to find a new role and identity in Caesar's *res publica*.

The non-linear chronology is not destructive for the narrative, but a crucial component of the editors' strategy to heighten its dramatic quality: by placing *Fam.* 7.1 at this point, the editors create an ironic turn, which would be lost in a strict chronological order. This is, in fact, one of the earliest letters (number 24 in the Shackleton Bailey editions): if we were to read the collection in a chronological order, *Fam.* 7.1 would only be a witty letter on Pompey's games and Marius' wise decision to miss them. By arranging the letters in this order, and thus placing here a flashback to 55 BCE, the editors remind the reader what true celebration and leisure were like and introduce the main theme of the book, namely the inactivity to which many leading figures of the late Republic have been forced. Now, after Caesar's victory, what once was sought *otium* has turned into forced exclusion from *negotium*, in the best case, and exile, in the worst. Their inability to access the powerful players of the political game has relegated them to the role of mere spectators. With this design, the editors have decided to give prominence to the narrative of failure: by remembering the past, the reader is reminded, again, of what is now lost, a fact which is emphasised by the failure of Pompey's game, the starting point of his downfall.

Fam. 7.1 exemplifies how the editors exploit narratives within individual letters to build and connect larger narratives both within and across books. Here, the self-contained narrative of Pompey's games is connected both to the previous book and the following three letters: it opens a series of letters (*Fam.* 7.1–3) offering a sketchy summary of the general's downfall as well as the friendship plot involving Cicero and Marius (*Fam.* 7.1–4). The two plots will become more clearly connected as the series progresses. In letter 7.1 the correspondents' separation appears to be due only to Marius' ill-health: the epistle closes with Cicero urging Marius to look after his health so that they can meet in person (*Fam.* 7.1.6). Indeed, this is a recurrent theme throughout this series. But the editors have constructed this short narrative to show that it is rather the complex political situation that gets in the way of their reunion, as the two narratives become more and more entangled in letters 2 and 3.

In *Fam.* 7.2 the two friends' separation offers a frame to the main theme of the letter.[51] In this epistle, dating to 51, Cicero discusses the trial *de vi* against T. Munatius Plancus Bursa, who was responsible for the riots at Clodius' funeral in 52.[52] Cicero reports the events in a highly elliptic manner and builds the whole narrative around his experience and emotional response to the trial. This type of narrative is made possible by the *amor* between them, as Cicero himself frames their relationship at the very beginning (*Fam.* 7.2.1), as in the previous epistle.

The outcome of the trial is referred to obliquely at the beginning of the narrative (*Fam.* 7.2.2): *de Bursa te gaudere certo scio, sed nimis uerecunde mihi gratularis* ('I know for certain that you are rejoicing about Bursa, but you are too modest in congratulating me'). Although there is no clear mention of a trial, it seems clear from this opening remark that the events that Cicero is about to relate have a favourable conclusion. Cicero then urges Marius not to hold back and congratulate him, since Bursa's sentence brought to him more satisfaction than Clodius' own death.

The details and phases of the trial are not included.[53] The letter appears to be not an account of the trial, but rather Cicero's attempt to shape his own persona within the wider context of violence and civil unrest. Cicero first claims his higher moral ground and re-writes a past failure (*Fam.* 7.2.2): *primum enim iudicio malo quam gladio, deinde gloria potius amici quam calamitate* ('first I prefer to win at trial rather than by sword, then to rejoice for a friend's reputation rather than his ruin'). On the one hand, by prosecuting Bursa, Cicero distances himself

---

51 We have one reference at the beginning, where Cicero reassures Marius that he will take care of his *mandatum* in virtue of their *amor* (*Fam.* 7.2.1) and one at the end, where Cicero expresses his wish to see Marius soon (*Fam.* 7.2.4).
52 Shackleton Bailey 1977 I, 351–353, Cavarzere 2016, 654–655. The trial likely took place between 9th December 52, when Bursa's tribunate ended, and January 51. The letter is dated between January and early February 51.
53 The omission of details such as time and space coordinates is common in Cicero's epistolary narratives. Often an event is discussed over several letters, some of which were not included in the collection, or is known to the general public and addressee would be able to supply the missing information. This is one aspect of the issue of gaps and holes in letters and letter collections, which I discuss more extensively in my project on the *Epistulae ad Familiares*.

from those who regularly resorted to violence. On the other hand, Bursa's conviction for the violent riots he had caused at Clodius' funeral would have also vindicated Milo's own conviction for Clodius' death.[54]

Cicero then goes on to mention the highest obstacle to his victory, i.e. Pompey's support of Bursa (*Fam.* 7.2.2): *in primisque me delectauit tantum studium bonorum in me exstitisse contra incredibilem contentionem clarissimi et potentissimi uiri* ('first, I was pleased that such a great devotion of the *boni* towards me had stood against the extraordinary effort of a most famous and powerful man'). At this point in the narrative, Pompey still retains his power and prestige, as Cicero himself carefully emphasises, and Cicero needs all the support he can get from the boni to win. Interestingly, we do not get any detail on Pompey's intervention, which had wide resonance, since the *laudatio* on behalf of Bursa was against his own law.[55] The editors are marking yet another point of Pompey's downfall. This is all the more significant in light of the section that follows, where Cicero compares the Bursa trial to a greater plot devised by Clodius and his supporters (*Fam.* 7.2.3):

> *et ille, cum omnis res publica in meo capite discrimen esset habitura, magnum quiddam spectauit [...]. hic [...]me in quem inueheretur delegerat persuaseratque non nullis inuidis meis se in me emissarium semper fore.*
>
> But since the fate of the whole State was going to depend on my safety, he [i.e. Clodius] had a great spectacle before him [...]. This one instead [i.e. Bursa] [...] had chosen to attack me and had persuaded some men envious of me that he would always be their agent against me.

By evoking a new, albeit unsuccessful Clodius, Cicero frames the trial as an attack not only on him, but also on the State: the fate of the *res publica* and that of Cicero converge in the outcome of the trial. Despite this alliance of wretched men and the pressure exerted by Pompey, the judges courageously condemn Bursa (*Fam.* 7.2.3). By arranging the letters in this order, the editors are highlighting Pompey's trend of failure begun in letter 1 and culminating in letter 3.

Friendship and politics become more entangled, as the separation plot is linked yet again to the political context and Cicero being busy in the forum: the epistle closes with Cicero's wish to see Marius, despite the large number of high-

---

54 Shackleton Bailey 1977 I, 351; Cavarzere 2016, 654. Notably, Stone 1980, 109–111 suggests that the revised version of the *Pro Milone* started circulating in the aftermath of this trial. See also Steel 2005, 115–131 on Cicero's re-writing past failures.
55 Shackleton Bailey 1977 I, 351; Stone 1980, 108, who reports the episode of Cato blocking his hears; both refer to Plut. *Pomp.* 55, *Cat. Min.* 48, Dio 40.55.1; cf. Cavarzere 2016, 655.

profile trials taking place (*Fam.* 7.2.4).⁵⁶ A similar reason for their inability to meet had been given in the previous letter (*Fam.* 7.1.5: *si Romae esses, tamen neque nos lepore tuo neque te, si qui est in me, meo frui liceret propter molestissimas occupationes meas*, 'even if you were in Rome, it would not be possible for me to enjoy your wit nor for you enjoy mine, if there is any in me, because of my most troublesome business affairs'), along with Marius' poor health, and will be given in the following one. In the third epistle of the 'Marius series', a new element is added to the separation narrative: the Civil War and, in particular, Cicero's time in the Pompeian camp until Pharsalus. Their friendship constitutes the frame for the epistle, which opens with Cicero's last encounter with Marius on 12th May 49, before joining the war, and closes with his wish to see him (*Fam.* 7.3.6: *ego si quae uolo expediero, breui tempore te, ut spero, uidebo*, 'if I put the matters I want to settle in order, I hope I will see you shortly'). The correspondents' wish to meet was, of course, standard element in letter writing, and acquires a narrative significance because of the letters' arrangement in a larger separation plot.

Fam. 7.3 constitutes the final chapter of the Pompey narrative, as it marks the end of his power. In the letter, dated to the year 46, Cicero offers Marius and the reader a highly selective and fragmented summary of his experience of the war: from his reluctance to join Pompey, through the frictions in the Greek camp, to Pompey's victory at Dyrrachium, followed by his final defeat at Pharsalus and flight to Egypt, and Cicero's decision to return home despite the dangers. What is striking here is how Cicero describes Pompey's final defeat (*Fam.* 7.3.2–3):

> *ex eo tempore uir ille summus nullus imperator fuit. signa tirone et collecticio exercitu cum legionibus robustissimis contulit; uictus turpissime amissis etiam castris solus fugit.* [3] *hunc ego mihi belli finem feci.*
>
> From that moment the greatest man was no longer a general. He fought with a hastily-gathered army of new recruits against the strongest legions; he was defeated and fled alone most shamefully, after losing even his camp. [3] This was the end of the war for me.

At the end of his own narrative, the title character has lost his status as *imperator* and can only flee.

Cicero's stay in Brundisium and pardon are left out of the friendship narrative, which appears to end with Cicero and Marius' long-sought reunion in *Fam.* 7.4, a brief note from November 46.⁵⁷ Cicero has arrived at his Cuman villa, and

---

56 Gruen 1995, 348.
57 Shackleton Bailey 1977 II, 356.

is about to leave for Pompeii. He wishes that Marius is in good health and is able to meet him while he is still at Cumae. Cicero's words suggest that they will eventually meet (*Fam.* 7.4: *me hoc biduo aut triduo exspecta*, 'expect me in the next two or three days'), but their meeting is not confirmed in the following letters and the reader is left with an open ending.

5 Conclusion

The double narrative featured in *Fam.* 7.1–4 offers a perfect example of how fictionality and authenticity intersect in the *Epistulae ad Familiares*, and raises questions about any interpretative framework in which these two categories are mutually exclusive. The two storylines feed into each other, as Pompey's downfall from his games in 55 to Pharsalus is told within the frame of Cicero's letters to Marius, which build a fictional story of reunion. Both narratives are based on historical events and built off authentic letters, carefully selected and arranged. The editors have both exploited the fictional narratives contained in the single epistles (like Marius' day in *Fam.* 7.1) and thematic elements to create new ones. The story of separation and reunion is only visible to the reader because these four letters written over ten years have been placed in this order. It is in this context that formulas and expressions that are only epistolary standard practice (such as the wish to meet, or the care for the correspondent's health) gain a wider significance. Similarly, the summary of Pompey's fall and Cicero's picture of the world before the Civil War are all the more dramatic because of their position after book 6, which had closed on the Pompeians' final defeat.

These patterns are re-created at several levels throughout the *Epistulae ad Familiares*. As such, not only do they fall outside a binary opposition of fictionality and authenticity, but they also attest to the existence of alternative ways of doing and reading history. They reveal the centrality of the editorial agenda in shaping epistolary collections and raise questions on the criteria for selection of the material transmitted to us, as well as our interpretation of it.

Part III: **Pseudepigraphic Fictions**

Kathryn Tempest
The Latin Letters of Pseudo-Brutus (Cic. *Brut.* 1.16 and 1.17)

Abstract: This chapter looks at two letters attributed to Marcus Iunius Brutus (Cicero, *Ad M. Brutum* 1.16 and 1.17), the dubious authenticity of which has attracted much critical attention. Following a summary of earlier scholarship, the contribution steers the debate in a different direction by arguing that these letters are instead *pseudepigrapha*, fictional impersonations of Brutus, composed around the first century CE. To this end, it highlights the elements of the text which betray a learned and creative author: dexterous allusions and imitations of Ciceronian style; a deep knowledge and manipulation of Brutus' own writings and of a wide range of other sources about his person and philosophical ideas; echoes of the hostile biographical tradition developed against Brutus in later times; and self-conscious meta-literary games with the conventions of epistolarity.

Keywords: allusive dexterity, creative supplementation, historical fictions, literary fakes, pseudepigrapha

In letters 1.16 and 17 in the vulgate edition of Cicero's *Epistulae ad M. Brutum*,[1] Marcus Iunius Brutus — or an author pretending to be him — attacks Cicero's policy of supporting the young Octavian against Mark Antony in early 43 BCE. The first is addressed to Cicero personally, and it begins by taking aim at a letter Cicero had purportedly sent to Octavian, an extract of which had been sent to Brutus by their common friend T. Pomponius Atticus (1.16.1). But it soon develops into a wider ranging criticism of Cicero's policy and political conduct following the assassination of Caesar. The author's tone is abrupt and critical: the reader is meant to assume that Brutus wrote it in a fit of anger. In the letter that follows (1.17), we find many of the same criticisms, but this time they are repeated to Atticus, and they are embedded within a larger critique of Cicero's personality and his failings as a statesman. The key point in both letters is that Octavian is not a man to be trusted, and that Cicero's friendship with Caesar's heir is both deplorable and potentially dangerous — an opinion we know from

---

[1] I use Shackleton Bailey 1980 for the Latin texts of Cicero *Brut.* 1.16 and 1.17; translations are from Shackleton Bailey 2002.

other letters that the historical Brutus held.² Yet there are several features of these letters that have caused later readers to question their authenticity and attribution to Brutus. The only common consensus appears to be that the two letters should either stand or fall together.³

The present investigation of the letters attributed to Brutus will thus begin (1) with a summary of the key arguments for and against their authenticity, before suggesting we move beyond the standard debate by reading them as pseudonymous writings or *pseudepigrapha*⁴ (2). It will then consider the intellectual nature of the texts in relation to (3) their impersonation of Brutus and (4) the wider historical fiction they construct. To conclude (5) I draw all these threads together to argue that *Brut.* 1.16 and 1.17 offer evidence of their author's creativity and knowledge of the sources while representing a significant moment in the reception of the historical Brutus.

1 Authorship and authenticity

The modern scholarly debate surrounding the authenticity of *Brut.* 1.16 and 1.17 starts out with Karl Nipperdey, who was the first to declare the two letters as forgeries compared to the rest of the *Epistulae ad M. Brutum*, which he accepted as genuine.⁵ For Nipperdey, their tone, as well as the endless repetitions and deficient argumentation, set them apart from Brutus' other letters and marked them out as 'hohle Declamationen'. Rudolph Heine agreed and added that the two letters were rhetorical imitations which played on key ideas in Cicero's

---

2 See e.g., the letter from Brutus to Cicero at *Brut.* 1.6.3, as well as Cicero's defensive attitude towards his policy at *Brut.* 1.3.1.
3 The expression appears both at Shackleton Bailey 1980, 14 and Moles 1997, 149; cf. Heine 1875, 7: *hae epistulae ... eas unus iudico*. The only exception I have found to this consensus is that of Gudeman 1894, 148 who regards *Brut.* 1.16 as genuine and 1.17 as fake, but he does not give any reasons for the distinction he makes between them.
4 I use the two terms interchangeably in this chapter to designate the broader phenomenon (*pseudepigraphy*) and the common characteristics of such works, as well as the particular subset of *pseudepigrapha* to which pseudonymous works belong: that is, as works which purport to be and which survive under another name.
5 Nipperdey 1865, 71 n. 15. In the century before Nipperdey, doubts had been raised regarding the authenticity of the entire collection, but from the mid-1800s they were largely accepted as genuine; see e.g., the overviews in Heine 1875, 3–5 and Tyrell/Purser 1933, cxxv–cxxviii.

correspondence to Brutus,[6] while Ludwig Gurlitt complained that they were impossible to date, and he doubted that they could have belonged to the original collection.[7] In 1884, however, a more systematic and authoritative attack on their authenticity was penned by Otto Schmidt, whose objections to the letters were in turn adopted and expanded a century later by Shackleton Bailey in his Cambridge edition.[8]

One of Schmidt's minor points against the letters' authenticity was that, unlike some other letters in the collection, there is no signifier of date or location for *Brut.* 1.16 or 1.17, which makes them difficult to fit into the chronological sequence of the collection.[9] If we wish to posit Brutus in time and space, we must imagine him somewhere on the march, heading east along the via Egnatia from Dyrrachium, or perhaps in camp at Candavia, where we know he was based in the middle of May 43 BCE. Even though *Brut.* 1.16 is difficult to date with any certainty, the suggestion of May works for *Brut.* 1.17, since it refers to the bad health of Brutus' wife Porcia who died in early June 43 BCE.[10] Consequently, when Shackleton Bailey came to restate the case for their forgery, he did not take issue with the dating of the letters. But he did confirm the value of Schmidt's general observations regarding the letters' contents and style. For, as

---

[6] Heine 1875, 33–36. In particular, Heine draws attention to Cic. *Brut.* 1.3 and 1.15 to demonstrate the debt of the author — a '*rhetor quidam Ciceronem sermonem imitans*' (35) — to key sentiments found in the letters of Cicero.

[7] On the problem of chronology, see n. 10 below.

[8] Fuller overviews of the problems and the debate surrounding the two letters' authenticity — in large part responding to the criticisms of Schmidt 1884, 630–635 — can be found in Shackleton Bailey 1980, 10–13; Harvey 1991, 22–28; Gotter 1996, 286–288; Moles 1997, 148–161. In what follows, I only rehearse the information most useful for gaining an appreciation of the nature and context of the letters.

[9] Schmidt 1884, 630: this has been one of the least persuasive arguments against the letters' authenticity, in part because Schmidt does not build the case himself; instead, he refers to the arguments of Gurlitt (which I have not seen); the article of Schmidt is largely a review and expansion of Gurlitt's observations.

[10] Notwithstanding the problems of fitting these letters within the chronological sequence of the collection, suggested dates put them approximately in mid-July (*Brut.* 1.16) and May/June (*Brut.* 1.17): see Shackleton Bailey 1980, 11, 250–251; Moles 1997, 150–152; 2017, 239–241. The dating for *Brut.* 1.17 is supported by the *terminus ante quem* of Porcia's death in June, while Cicero's apparent complaint, to which Brutus responds, that he had not received congratulations following the defeat of Antony at Mutina, provides a *terminus post quem* of late April 43 BCE, when the news reached Rome (see Cic. *Fam.* 11.14.3). The letter *Brut.* 1.16 is vaguer; a reference to Antony being 'up in arms' (1.16.8: *in armis*) could refer to any time between December 44/January 43 (as suggested by Stockton 1971, 326 n. 69) and June (thus Gotter 1996, 288–289) or even July (as suggested by Moles and Shackleton Bailey, *op. cit.*).

Schmidt further pointed out, of all the letters attributed to Brutus, these two alone are written in the periodic style;[11] they contain a poverty of thought, he added, as well as the only use of the name Octavius for Octavian, compared to 'your Caesar' or just 'Caesar' in Brutus' other letters to Cicero.[12] As for the transmission of *Brut.* 1.16 and 1.17 in the manuscripts, Schmidt noted that the letters were not always included with the rest of the *Epistulae ad M. Brutum*; Bodleianus Canonicus Lat. 244 has them after the *Epistulae ad familiares*, while Bodleianus 197 only contains *Brut.* 1.16 between Cicero's *Somnium Scipionis* and an *ars metrica*.[13] The letters for Schmidt were thus best regarded as 'schmähbriefe gegen Octavian': that is, politically orientated letters of abuse against the young Caesar.[14] For Shackleton Bailey, however, they were nothing more than rhetorical exercises, the author of which had 'only a superficial knowledge of the sources.'[15]

Alongside these attacks on the authenticity of the two letters, there have been several attempts to reassert Brutus' authorship. For Tyrrell and Purser, the poverty of the author's thought appeared a mark of authenticity, not forgery; indeed, taking a dim view of Brutus as a 'narrow-minded, stiff, and ungracious' man, they argued 'when a feeble man gives way to irritability he is generally verbose.'[16] As for the author's use of 'Octavius', they contended it was not a mistake; instead, they suggested, Brutus did not accept the legitimacy of Octavian's adoption so that, when he did use 'Caesar', he was being sarcastic.[17] In an important chapter in 1997, John Moles added several other arguments as part of

---

11 Schmidt 1884, 632–633; for examples of long periods see e.g., *Brut.* 1.16.3, 5 as well as 1.17.1, 6.
12 For the use of 'Octavius', see *Brut.* 16.1, 2, 7, 8, 11 and 17.5–6. For Brutus' use of Caesar in other letters, see e.g., 1.4a.2, 3. Indeed, Schmidt 1884, 632 sees the use of 'Octavius' as a decisive factor in the case for forgery: 'man wird also ... in dem gebrauche des namens Octavius statt Caesar ein starkes moment für die fälschung erblicken müssen'. His argument is accepted by Shackleton Bailey 1980, 11, 251; Harvey 1991, 26–27; Beaujeu 1996, 253.
13 Schmidt 1884, 634. Those wanting to uphold the authenticity of the letters (e.g., Moles 1997, 149) can point out that the letters do still appear alongside genuine Ciceronian material; but see n. 19, below, for a further objection to Moles' reasoning.
14 Schmidt 1884, 634.
15 Shackleton Bailey 1980, 12.
16 Tyrrell/Purser 1933, 180. It is perhaps important to point out here that Tyrrell and Purser do not address their criticisms to the work of Schmidt directly; instead, they respond to points raised by the scholarship on which Schmidt had in turn built his case: namely, Meyer 1881, Ruete 1883, and especially Gurlitt 1883.
17 Tyrrell/Purser 1933, 181; cf. Moles 1997, 153–154.

his case for accepting them as genuine.[18] On matters of transmission, he pointed out that, despite their displacement in two minor manuscripts, *Brut.* 1.16 and 1.17 had always appeared alongside genuine Ciceronian material, such as the letters to Atticus or Quintus.[19] With regards to the dating of the letters, he believed that the consensus around their belonging to the early summer of 43 BCE only contributed to the likelihood of Brutus' authorship, because 'the later the letters, the better the political analysis' — and this pair, in Moles' verdict, shows Brutus to have had more political acumen than is normally assumed.[20] He also found fault with arguments against the style of the letters since such responses are largely subjective and do not produce conclusive responses: 'scholars of wonderful Latinity (Gelzer, Syme) have accepted the letters;' he added, 'scholars of wonderful Latinity (Schmidt, Shackleton Bailey) have rejected them'. To support the attribution of these letters to Brutus, however, he further adduced Eric Laughton's study on participles to show how Brutus' own use of this Latin verb form tends to increase with the intensity of his thought: *Brut.* 1.16, he argued, is representative of this trend, since it contains an unusually high number of participles: twenty in total, over just five pages of Latin text.[21] Meanwhile, like Tyrell and Purser, he considered Brutus' use of Octavius sarcastic, but he added that the consistency of Brutus' rejection of Octavian's status in this and other letters was another mark of their authenticity.[22]

Despite these efforts, however, neither the believers in the letters' authenticity or the rejectionists have so far scored enough points to win a consensus. This is not surprising, since slight variances in epistolary style, tone and practice can hardly prove that a letter was or was not written by Brutus; after all, even contemporary readers could not always agree on a letter's authorship

---

18 As Moles points out, many of his ideas stem from the arguments found against Shackleton Bailey in discussions by Miriam Griffin, Elizabeth Rawson, and David Stockton; see Moles 1997, 148.
19 One might object that Cicero's *pridie quam in exilium iret*, which is certainly not authentic, has been transmitted in excellent MSS (such as the Paris 7794), alongside the genuine speeches of Cicero; for a survey of the manuscripts for *pridie*, see Corbeill 2020, 18–19.
20 Moles 1997, 150–152; quotation from 151.
21 Moles 1997, 152–153; he is referring to Laughton 1964, 154–156. On the use of participles as a potential mark of inauthenticity, however, see Harvey 1991, 25–26. As Harvey points out, the use of the future participle at *Brut.* 1.17.2 is more characteristic of Latin in the imperial era, where its use was common; it is not usually found in late Republican Latin. For the argument that the author imitates Brutus' style, see also Calboli 2015, 252.
22 Tyrrell/Purser 1933, 181; cf. Moles 1997, 153–154.

when its contents did not conform to their impression of its writer.[23] But the following passage, in which Brutus reports Cicero's attack on Casca for his share in the assassination of Caesar, has posed perhaps the most serious obstacle for those who wish to defend it as the genuine handiwork of Brutus, since its statements appear to fly in the face of historical reality:

> *nescio quid scribam tibi nisi unum: pueri et cupiditatem et licentiam potius esse irritatam quam repressam a Cicerone, tantumque eum tribuere huic indulgentiae ut se maledictis non abstineat iis quidem quae in ipsum dupliciter recidunt, quod et pluris occidit uno seque prius oportet fateatur sicarium quam obiciat Cascae quod obicit et imitetur in Casca Bestiam. an quia non omnibus horis iactamus Idus Martias similiter atque ille Nonas Decembris suas in ore habet, eo meliore condicione Cicero pulcherrimum factum uituperabit quam Bestia et Clodius reprehendere illius consulatum soliti sunt? Sustinuisse mihi gloriatur bellum Antoni togatus Cicero noster!*
>
> (Cic. *Brut.* 1.17.1–2)

> I don't know how to put it to you, except simply to say that that boy's [Octavian's] ambition and lawlessness have been stimulated rather than checked by Cicero; and that he goes so far in this indulgence as not to refrain from offensive expressions which recoil upon himself in two ways. For he [Cicero] took more than one life, and he must confess himself an assassin before he says what he says against Casca ... Because we are not bragging every hour about the Ides of March like Cicero with his everlasting Nones of December, is he in any better position to revile a splendid action than Bestia and Clodius when they used to attack his consulship? Our Cicero in his gown boasts to me that he has taken the brunt of Antony's war.

Counter to the claims in this letter, Cicero's support for the assassination of Caesar is well-documented: in the months after the Ides, he hailed the conspirators as *heroes*, *tyrannoctoni*, and *liberatores*, while elsewhere he celebrated their great and glorious deed (*pulcherrimum factum*).[24] Adding to Schmidt's concerns about the letters' authenticity, then, Shackleton Bailey rightly objected to Brutus' report that Cicero had called Casca a cut-throat killer (*sicarius*), for this was the very word, in the plural, that Mark Antony and others were using to generate

---

[23] An interesting parallel is the letter of Brutus discussed at Cic. *Brut.* 2.5, which was declared a forgery by the senate, although Cicero insinuates that he regarded it as genuine; for further discussion of Cicero's reaction to this letter see Ortmann 1988, 288–290.

[24] See e.g., *heroes* at 14.4.2; *tyrannoctoni* at Cic. *Att.* 14.15, 14.6.2; *liberatores* at Cic. *Att.* 14.12.2; for their great and glorious deed, see Cic. *Att.* 14.11.1 πράξεως καλῆς; cf. Cic. *Phil.* 2.114: *pulcherrimi facti*. It is perhaps worth noting a similar use of the superlative adjective at Tac. *Ann.* 1.8, *cum occisus dictator Caesar aliis pessimum, aliis pulcherrimum facinus uideretur*.

hostility against the self-acclaimed liberators;²⁵ thus, it would have been inappropriate, not to mention inconsistent, for Cicero to have described Casca in this manner.²⁶

In the same way, Cicero cannot be accused of reviling the conspirators' actions. For as Shackleton Bailey pointed out, both the phrases *sicarii* and *pulcherrimum factum* originated in, and were probably appropriated from, a letter written by Cicero to Cassius, in which he warned of Mark Antony's attempts to malign the liberators:

> *auget tuus amicus furorem in dies. primum in statua quam posuit in rostris inscripsit 'parenti optime merito,' ut non modo **sicarii** sed iam etiam parricidae iudicemini. quid dico 'iudicemini'? iudicemur potius. uestri enim **pulcherrimi facti** ille furiosus me principem dicit fuisse.*
> (Cic. *Fam.* 12.3.1)

> Your friend [Antony] gets crazier every day. To begin with he has inscribed the statue which he set up on the Rostra 'To father and benefactor' — so that you are now set down, not only as assassins but as parricides to boot! I say 'you' but ought rather say 'we,' for the madman declares that I was the leader in your noble enterprise.

For Shackleton Bailey, this recycling of Ciceronian words and phrases was a tell-tale sign of the forger's incompetence: 'nothing else in the document is quite so damning as this', he claimed, arguing that by his clumsy use of sources the author had effectively 'given himself away'.²⁷ He also found suspicious the references to Cicero's boastfulness, which he suggested were more compatible with the later critical tradition surrounding Cicero than the contemporary opinion of him in 43 BCE.²⁸ Yet, in condemning the two letters as rhetorical exercises

---

25 On the use of *sicarius/sicarii* see also Cic. *Phil.* 2.31 with discussion by Shackleton Bailey 1980, 12.
26 Moles 1997, 157 replied that Casca was the only conspirator left in Rome in the early summer 43 BCE, and he imagined a scenario in which Cicero might have bad-mouthed him to ingratiate himself with Octavian. In his exact words: 'Cicero the chameleon might have found it politic so to blacken one of the assassins'. But his objection on this point is not convincing, not least because it fails to address the wider issue of forgery with which Shackleton Bailey was concerned; nor, as Shackleton Bailey observed, is there any evidence of a fallout between Cicero and Casca.
27 Shackleton Bailey 1980, 12.
28 Although Cicero's attempts to champion his consulship certainly drew scorn from some of his contemporaries, Shackleton Bailey 1980, 13 found it 'highly improbable that in 43 Cicero was trying his friends' patience in this fashion'; Moles 1997, 158 points out that there is an example of Cicero's boastfulness at *Philippics* 2.28 (among others in his *De Officiis*), where Cicero explicitly calls the assassination of Caesar an achievement similar to his own actions in suppressing the Catiline Conspiracy: *cum rem gessisset consimilem rebus eis quas ipse gesseram.*

'of little historical importance', the whole tenor of Shackleton Bailey's attack on their authenticity was simultaneously an attack on what he elsewhere termed the 'sorry genre' of spurious works.[29] In spite of his astute observations, then, there is good cause to question Shackleton Bailey's hasty dismissal of the letters' literary merit. For a more positive approach to the phenomenon of *pseudepigrapha*, which mainly surfaced in the last decade, offers a new means of interpreting the letters and helps support the idea that they belong in a later period, probably the first century CE, under the authorship of a pseudo-Brutus.[30] Indeed, as I argue, far from being failed forgeries, the letters demonstrate the author's mastery of the sources pertaining to the real Brutus and his historical setting.

2 *Brut.* 1.16 and 1.17 as literary fakes

Pseudonymous writings or *pseudepigrapha*, as Irene Peirano forcefully demonstrated in her defence of the Roman fake, have received a bad press in traditional scholarship.[31] The term *pseudepigrapha* itself is ambiguous and applies both to works that have been mistakenly attributed to a particular author as well as those published under a pseudonym. As such, they have often been banished

---

Moles thinks this passage 'will have irked Brutus' and thus motivated the attack here, yet the context of the passage in the *Philippics* precludes such a reading: in this passage, Cicero is answering Mark Antony's accusation that he was involved in or had even spurred on the conspiracy. As proof of this claim, Mark Antony alleged that Brutus had congratulated Cicero on the recovery of freedom in the immediate aftermath of Caesar's murder. Yet, to obviate this charge, Cicero praises the patriotism of the Liberators; his mention of their similar achievements is thus best read as a carefully formulated hypothesis to offer an alternative explanation: namely, that Brutus was declaring himself a rival to Cicero in glory: *me potissimum testatus est se aemulum mearum laudum exstitisse*. It is unlikely to have 'irked' Brutus. Cf. Keeline 2018, 193 who also dismisses Moles' argument in favour of the idea that we see the later critical tradition speaking in *Brut.* 1.17. Keeline's argument is based on the double coincidence of *togatus* and *gloriatur* at *Brut.* 1.17.2: *sustinuisse mihi* **gloriatur** *bellum Antoni* **togatus** *Cicero noster* and the pseudo-Sallustian address to Cicero at [Sall.] *in Tull.* 6: *quasi uero* **togatus** *et non armatus ea, quae* **gloriaris**, *confeceris*.

29 Shackleton Bailey 1980, 10: 'of little historical importance'; on the 'sorry genre' of spurious works, see Shackleton Bailey 2002, 339 (referring to the pseudo-Ciceronian letter to Octavian).
30 To avoid confusion, in what follows I shall refer to the author of the letters as 'Pseudo-Brutus' but I shall use 'Brutus' when referring to the voice of the letter-writer. I will refer to the author as masculine for the sole reason that this gender is consistent with that of the assumed persona of Brutus.
31 Peirano 2012; for her reflections on the term *pseudepigraphon*, see esp. 1–7.

from the canon as 'unwanted imposters', as Shackleton Bailey came close to suggesting for *Brut.* 1.16 and 1.17, or potentially rehabilitated as authentic, as Moles aimed to achieve.[32] Yet, as Peirano argued, a third interpretative framework exists for the type of *pseudepigrapa* which 'self-consciously purport either to be the work of the author to whom they are attributed or to be written at a different time from that in which they were composed'. The former she calls 'impersonations', which either rework lines that are autobiographical in content or else impose onto the authorial persona certain attributes from the master-author's texts; the latter she terms 'chronological or historical fictions' since they profess to be addressed to famous personalities composed on a specific historical occasion.[33] The letters *Brut.* 1.16 and 1.17, as we shall see, fit perfectly with these ideas of the literary 'fake'.

Indeed, building on Peirano's theoretical reflections about *pseudepigrapha* and combining them with Shackleton Bailey's objections to the letters of Brutus, this is precisely the case sketched out by Thomas Keeline in his study of Cicero's early reception.[34] Instead of clumsy errors on the part of an incompetent forger, he proposed that the appearances of both *sicarius* and *pulcherrimum factum* in *Brut.* 1.17.1–2 form part of an 'intertextual declamatory aesthetic' — that is, the kind of playful reuse of Ciceronian words and phrases which would appeal to an appreciative and knowing readership. According to this line of thinking, 'the authors positively *want* their allusions to be recognized'[35] and their reworking of Ciceronian source material to criticize Cicero is typical of such compositions. As the products of the rhetorical classroom, Keeline concluded, they tell us much about the 'ideas about Cicero that were drummed into the heads of young Romans in their school days' and, by extension, they offer a direct insight into the early cultural memory of Cicero.[36]

But we can go further: for *Brut* 1.16 and 17 explore the authorial persona of Brutus, as well as the Ciceronian tradition, while simultaneously probing the

---

32 See Peirano 2012, 8; for the contrasting approaches of Shackleton Bailey and Moles, see section I, above.
33 On 'fakes' as either 'impersonations' or 'chronological fictions', see Peirano 2012, 3.
34 Keeline 2018, 188–195; discussion of *Brut.* 1.17.1–2 is at 191–194. I had already prepared a draft of this paper when Keeline's book was published. Yet, although some of his observations anticipate the main thrust of my argument, as will become clear we differ in the way we approach these texts in terms of their 'characters': whereas Keeline uses the key observations of Shackleton Bailey to argue for their pseudepigraphic status and the reception history of Cicero, in this chapter I examine the construction of Brutus' authorial persona.
35 Keeline 2018, 194.
36 Keeline 2018, 194–195.

complex dynamics of their relationship in the period after the Ides. In so doing, the author responds to the rhetorical practice of 'creative supplementation' which treats authors and their lives as 'textual entities whose gaps can be productively filled with new texts'.[37] In the case of Cicero, it is well known that his role in the political crisis of the late Republic, as well as his importance in the rhetorical schools, stimulated the production of such *pseudepigrapha*: as in the letters under consideration here, his character and actions continued to fascinate.[38] But Brutus too enjoyed a vibrant afterlife in the early Roman Empire. Seneca the Younger's *De Beneficiis* offers good evidence of how Brutus' moral dilemma and decision to assassinate Caesar might have captured the attention of declaimers, when he mentions propositions such as 'should Marcus Brutus have accepted the gift of his life from the divine Caesar' and 'what reasoning did Brutus employ in killing Caesar?'[39] Meanwhile Brutus' speeches, letters, treatises, and even his coins continued to circulate and be interpreted;[40] the words and ideals of Brutus thus lived on, and they offered material that could be used in the construction of his epistolary persona.

However, before we consider the larger question of the impersonation of Brutus in the letters, it is important to make some general reflections on their status as pseudonymous texts. For the argument that *Brut.* 1.16 and 1.17 are the handiwork of a pseudo-Brutus faces a formidable methodological challenge: that is, because the authors of pseudepigraphic works employ the tropes and concerns of authentic material to achieve an air of verisimilitude, how each reader

---

[37] Peirano 2012, 10.
[38] For other extant examples of pseudepigraphic writings focused on the character of Cicero, see the *epistula ad Octauianum*, with discussion by Van der Velden 2020 and the *Pridie quam in exilium iret*, discussed by Corbeill 2020; for the importance of Cicero in the pseudepigraphic tradition generally, see Peirano 2012, 231–232 and Keeline 2018, 147–151; on the speeches of Cicero in Lucan as literary fakes, see La Bua 2020, esp. 84–86.
[39] Sen. *Ben.* 2.20.
[40] Fragments and testimonia for Brutus' speeches can be found in Malcovati, *ORF* 158, pp. 460–468; cf. Manuwald 2019, 202–231. There is evidence for several books of letters of Brutus that were published and circulating in antiquity, most of which we have lost; see especially Nonius Marcellus, whose references and citations from the letters are usefully gathered in Watt 1958, 152–175. Of his philosophical works, there are references to *de Virtute* at Cic. *Fin.* 1.3.8, *Tusc.* 5.1 and 30; cf. Sen. *Cons. Helv.* 9.4. A treatise *Peri Kathēkontos* is mentioned by Charisius 83; Priscian *Inst. gramm.* 6.7; Sen. *Ep.* 95.45. We also know of *De Patientia*, a small fragment of which is quoted by Diomedes, in Keil, *GL* I, 383, 8. For Brutus' famous coin celebrating the Ides of March, see Cass. Dio. 47.25.3; even though the coin may not have been in circulation at the time Cassius Dio was writing, Rowan 2013, 29–30 suggests there was a memory or archive of coin types, or that it may have been known through other texts.

judges that content will very often be determined by their own preconceptions about the material's authenticity.[41] There is a certain danger, then, of falling into a circular argument.

To illustrate this interpretative difficulty, let us begin with the opening paragraph of *Brut.* 1.16, written by 'Brutus' to Cicero, which runs as follows:

> *particulam litterarum tuarum, quas misisti Octauio, legi missam ab Attico mihi. studium tuum curaque de salute mea nulla me noua uoluptate adfecit. non solum etiam usitatum sed etiam cottidianum est aliquid audire de te quod pro nostra dignitate fideliter atque honorifice dixeris aut feceris. at dolore quantum maximum capere animo possum eadem illa pars epistulae scripta ad Octauium de nobis adfecit. sic enim illi gratias agis de re publica, tam suppliciter ac demise — quid scribam?*
>
> (1.16.1)

> I have read a small part of your letter to Octavius, sent to me by Atticus. Your devoted concern for my welfare gave me no novel pleasure accustomed as I am (indeed it happens every day) to hear of some loyal and complimentary action or words of yours in support of our public standing. But that same extract from your letter to Octavius, in which you write about us gave me all the distress of which my mind is capable. You thank him on public grounds in such a fashion, so imploringly and humbly — I hardly know what to write.

A believer of the letter's authenticity might see in these lines a perfectly reasonable opening statement: Brutus introduces the cause of his anger immediately before elaborating further on his dissatisfaction in Cicero's policy. But a sceptic might see something else going on. The word order and emphatic position of *particulam litterarum tuarum* recalls the opening of one of Cicero's own letters to Brutus — his rebuke upon having received an insultingly short missive at *Brut.* 1.14, which starts with the similarly abrupt formula *breues litterae tuae*. The author's insistence that he is only replying to a part of a letter (cf. *eadem illa pars epistulae*) focuses our attention on the source of this information: Atticus himself, whose replies are famously erased from the Ciceronian corpus. The piece thus fills a gap in the terse, triangular relationship between Cicero, Atticus and Brutus, with Atticus meddling behind the scenes. However, in so doing, these lines also appear to make a self-referential gesture to their own status as a letter constructed out of other correspondence (*quas misisti Octauio, legi missam ab Attico mihi*); this impression of meta-literariness is further reinforced by the

---

41 Compare the following observation of Grafton 1990: 'The forger needs to give his work an air of conviction and reality, a sense of authenticity' (50). As Grafton also points out (see esp. 19–22), the very features which can guarantee authenticity, such as an author's style, are the same as those used to implicate texts as forgeries, since they are exactly what forgers would mimic.

authorial *aporia, quid scribam* — 'what am I to say?' — a clear marker of the text's rhetorical style, as 'Brutus' confronts the challenge awaiting him.

Such a reader might start to wonder whether they are in fact reading the words of a pseudonymous author. And indeed, their suspicions would grow stronger as the same paragraph continues by demonstrating a debt to the Ciceronian material on which it is based:

> *pudet condicionis ac fortunae, sed tamen scribendum est — commendas nostrum salute illi (quae morte qua non perniciosior?) ut prorsus prae te feras non sublatam dominationem sed dominum commutatum esse. uerba tua recognosce et aude negare seruientis aduersus regem istas esse preces.*
>
> (1.16.1)

> I am ashamed of the situation, of what Fortune has done to us, but write I must. You commend our welfare to him. Better any death than such welfare! It is a downright declaration that there has been no abolition of despotism, only a change of despot. Read over your words again and then dare to deny that these are the pleadings of a subject to his king.

Dominus and its cognates are not uncommon in Cicero's references to Caesar's regime.[42] But what is more striking here is the chiastic arrangement of *non sublatam dominationem sed dominum commutatum esse,* for it is a construction we see in a variety of guises in Cicero's letters. As he wrote to Cassius in the May of 44 BCE, 'we are free of the despot but not the despotism' (*Fam.* 12.1.1, *non regno sed rege liberati uidemur*), or to Atticus, twice in April of the same year, 'the tyranny is alive, the tyrant has fallen' (*Att.* 14.9.2, *uiuit tyrannis, tyrannus occidit*) and 'although the tyrant has been removed, I see the tyranny remain' (*Att.* 14.14.2, *sublato tyranno tyrannida manere uideo*). Once again, it looks like Cicero's own ideas are being used to attack him and that the reader is meant to observe and admire the author's allusive dexterity.[43] From this perspective, the subsequent call to Cicero to recognize his own words (*uerba tua recognosce*) reads as a nod to the intrusion of its Ciceronian model.

Of course, if we were to accept the letter as sincere, the stark imperative might be read as a wakeup call to Cicero — and perhaps an effective one at that: after all, Cicero had launched a bitter attack against Mark Antony and his ambi-

---

42 See e.g., Cic. *Fam.* 4.8.2: *hoc dominatu*; 9.7.1: *qui nunc dominantur*; 12.3.1: *dominum ferre non potuimus*; cf. the letter written by Cassius to Cicero at *Fam.* 15.19.4.

43 It is, of course, possible that Brutus — and not an impersonator of Brutus — used Cicero's own words to attack him. But note here that when the real Brutus does potentially echo Cicero, as at *Brut.* 1.4a.3, he uses *regnum* and *tyrannus*, not *dominus*.

tions to rise to the position of Caesar's power in 44 BCE, only to support the aspirations of Octavian who was openly declaring to aspire to his father's position. Yet, studies of epistolary fictions, and especially pseudepigraphic texts, have also shown that such compositions frequently refer to the act of writing, reading, or sending a letter. As Patricia Rosenmeyer has explained, although the letter form generally invites reflections on its production and reception, in the case of fictional letters 'it is an ongoing attempt to give the fiction at least the veneer of genuineness'.[44] The very features which lay claim to a text's authenticity thus also paradoxically support its identification as inauthentic.

This point returns us neatly to the problem of circular argumentation identified above. The interpretation presented here is that, by using the imperative *uerba tua recognosce*, 'Brutus' posits his letter in the chain of his ongoing correspondence with Cicero, calling to mind the different policies the two men pursued in the period after the Ides. Not only does this contribute to the hyper self-referentiality established by the opening paragraph; it serves to establish the letter's historical setting and invites the reader into the literary game. Yet the only real way to test the hypothesis is, first, to identify multiple instances of direct or indirect borrowings from other sources, and then to isolate as unusual any that appear unnecessary to the setting of the letters or inconsistent with their putative authorship by Brutus.

A useful example to illustrate this methodology appears in *Brut.* 1.16. For, just as we have seen how the author uses notable aspects of the Ciceronian source material in his own composition — from the periodic style of his Latin, to select words, phrases and sentiments that betray a knowledge of Cicero's works — so the evidence of Cicero can be detected behind the author's presentation of Octavian, who is continuously evoked in terms that recall Antony's contemptuous description of him as 'a boy who owes everything to his name' (as reported at Cic. *Phil.* 13.24, *puer, qui omnia nomini debes*).[45] Thus, 'Brutus' writes that Octavian is 'scarcely yet a grown man' (*Brut.* 1.16.3, *uix etiam nunc uiri*), and asks 'this very boy, who is apparently incited by Caesar's name against Caesar's killers — what will he not give ... in return for our support, for the power which I suppose will indeed be his' (*Brut.* 1.16.5, *hic ipse puer, quem Caesaris nomen incitare uidetur in Caesaris interfectores, quanti aestimet ... posse nobis auctoribus*

---

44 Rosenmeyer 2001, 204.
45 See also Suet. *Aug.* 12.1: *quasi alii se puerum iactassent.* Cicero rarely uses *puer* to describe Octavian (for an exception, see *Brut.* 1.15.7); elsewhere, he tends to use *adulescens* (see e.g., Cic. *Phil.* 3.3: *C. Caesar adulescens*), or *iuuenis*, e.g., at Cic. *Att.* 10.12a.4, 14.17a.2, 16.14.2.

tantum quantum profecto poterit).⁴⁶ Yet this last line also appears out of context to the letter's historical setting. We might question whether the real Brutus, who was raising and equipping a strong army to fight Octavian, would have been so ready to admit the inevitability of his enemy's success; this is a point of view that can only otherwise be detected in the writings after Actium.⁴⁷ Rather, the author appears to have drawn on material from Cicero's *Philippics* to lend expression to Brutus' frustration at the *puer* Octavian and his use of the *nomen Caesaris*, in much the same way that *sicarius* and *pulcherrimum factum* were recycled to chastise Cicero at *Brut.* 1.17.1.

As I elaborate in sections 3–4, however, this kind of intellectual engagement extends far beyond the works of Cicero: the polemic of the letters, as well as their philosophical and political arguments, show a thorough familiarity with the sources for Brutus' life and legacy. Even if it remains impossible to admit of absolute proof, in what follows I hope to dispel doubt and demonstrate the depth and breadth of the material, as well as the artistry involved, in pseudo-Brutus' handling of his *persona* and the fictional setting of the letters. Indeed, the most compelling supportive evidence for this point of view is to be found in the range of material that is common to the letters and the tradition surrounding Brutus.

3 Impersonating Brutus

Although very little of Brutus' published works survive for us to perform the same kind of intertextual treasure hunt that we can for Cicero, still we can see that key aspects from Brutus' biography and reception history are reflected in these two letters. Thus, if we look back at the opening paragraph of *Brut.* 1.16.1 (cited in full, above), where Brutus admits he despairs of the situation and of fortune (*pudet condicionis ac fortunae*), the line introduces a train of thought repeated at *Brut.* 1.17.5, where 'Brutus' is made to say: 'I no longer attach any value to those arts in which I know Cicero is so well versed' (*ego uero iam iis artibus nihil tribuo quibus Ciceronem scio instructissimum esse*).⁴⁸ Yet this rejection

---

46 See also *Brut.* 1.16.6 where 'Brutus' criticises those who 'fear the name of a boy' (*timeat in puero nomen*) more than they desire the recovery of freedom.
47 On the perceived inevitability of Octavian's rise to power, see e.g., Pandey 2018, 35–82, where she traces the history of the idea through the literary reactions to the *sidus Iulium*.
48 As the context of this sentence makes clear, *iis artibus* at *Brut.* 1.17.5 refers to philosophy; cf. Shackleton Bailey 1980, 13. On philosophy as one of the *artes*, see e.g., Cic. *Fam.* 4.4.4, where

of his philosophical studies is not consistent with the image the real Brutus aimed to project. Rather it seems that the author had in mind Brutus' famous last words, as recorded in the hostile tradition surrounding him — a quotation from an unknown tragedy in which Hercules proclaims, 'O wretched virtue, you were but a word, and yet I practised you as a deed; only now, does it seem, you were a slave to fortune' (Cass. Dio 47.49.2, ὦ τλῆμον ἀρετή, λόγος ἄρ' ἦσθ', ἐγὼ δέ σε / ὡς ἔργον ἤσκουν· σὺ δ' ἄρ' ἐδούλευες τύχῃ).[49]

We shall return to how the author introduces material from the biographical tradition below (4). But first it is interesting to examine how the author develops the philosophical aspect of Brutus' character elsewhere in the letters. For the real Brutus had left behind a remarkable intellectual legacy as a freedom-fighter and activist against one-man rule. In his pamphlets *De Dictatura Pompei* and *Pro T. Annio Milo*, both published in 52 BCE, Brutus had argued that servitude was intolerable and that murder in defence of one's country was justifiable. One of the only fragments to survive records his expressed opinion on that point: 'it is better to rule no man than to be the slave of any: for one may live honorably without the former, while the latter is no way of living' (*praestat enim nemini imperare quam alicui seruire: sine illo enim uiuere honeste licet, cum hoc uiuendi nulla condicio est*).[50] Likewise, his coins, circulated first in the 50s and then between 43 and 42 BCE, had carried the message that Brutus was devoted above all to the *libertas* of the Roman people — a principle he enacted when he 'liberated' Rome from the tyranny of Caesar.[51]

It is not surprising, then, that *Brut.* 1.16 and 1.17 should refer to Brutus' devotion to *libertas* and his opposition to *seruitium*.[52] This theme is already present

---

Cicero tells us that he enjoyed all the liberal arts from his earliest years, but philosophy most of all: *a prima aetate me omnis ars et doctrina liberalis, et maxime philosophia delectauit*. Philosophy is included within a discussion of the arts at *Tusc.* 1.4 ff.

49 For the fragment, see *TGF* 374; Florus 2.17.11 has Brutus utter very similar words with his dying breath whereas Plut. *Brut.* 52.4–6 has Brutus celebrate the reputation for virtue he leaves behind, and he only blames fortune for his country's sake. On the alternative endings for Brutus' life, see Tempest 2017, 208–210. On the hostile tradition surrounding Brutus and Cassius generally, see Rawson 1986; on the hostility directed specifically against Brutus in the period after his death, see Tempest 2023.

50 Malcovati *ORF* 158.16 (trans. Manuwald).

51 For the coins see e.g., Crawford *RRC* 433/1 (*Libertas* and Lucius Junius Brutus, 54 BCE); *RRC* 433/2 (Lucius Junius Brutus and Servilius Ahala, 54 BCE); *RRC* 508/3 (celebrating the Ides of March).

52 At *Brut.* 1.16.2, 'Brutus' refers to himself and the rest of the conspirators as *liberatores orbis terrarum*, while at 1.16.9 he tells Cicero that his actions and thoughts eternally pertain *ad liberandos ciuis meos*.

in the rest of the collection: as at *Brut.* 1.10.4, when Cicero tells Brutus he has liberated the *res publica* once before (*rem publicam ... liberauisti*) and urges him to return to Italy with his army to save it for a second time: 'Hope of liberty', he adds, 'lies nowhere but in your and his [Cassius'] headquarters' (1.10.5, *spes libertatis nusquam nisi in uestrorum castrorum principiis est*).[53] Yet in objecting to Cicero's request for Octavian to assure the safety of Brutus and Cassius, *Brut.* 1.16 turns on the conditions of slavery in a manner that is more evocative of Brutus' own words on the matter: 'why did we rejoice at his [Caesar's] death', he asks, 'if we were going to be slaves just the same after he was dead and gone?' (1.16.5 *cuius interitu quid gauisi sumus si mortuo eo nihilo minus seruituri eramus?*). It is this idea which is picked up and expanded in his firm rejection of slavery in the paragraph that follows:

> *an tu Romae habitare, id putas incolumem esse? res non locus, oportet praestet istuc mihi; neque incolumis Caesare uiuo fui, nisi postea quam illud consciui facinus, neque usquam exsul esse possum, dum seruire et pati contumelias peius odero malis omnibus aliis.*
>
> (1.16.6)

> Or do you think to live in Rome is to be a citizen? That is a matter of condition, not of place. I had no citizenship in Caesar's lifetime until after I resolved upon that deed, nor can I be in exile anywhere so long as I hate to be a slave and suffer indignities more than all other evils.

If we think that this last line — *seruire et pati contumelias peius odero malis omnibus aliis* — echoes the general sentiment of Brutus' speech against Pompey, cited above — *alicui seruire ... hoc uiuendi nulla condicio est* — the larger context in which it is couched seems to nod to another source of inspiration: Brutus' *De Virtute*, composed in the mid-forties BCE.[54] Indeed, a strong link to

---

[53] Compare *Brut.* 1.11.2, where Brutus compliments Cicero on defending *libertas* in the service of the *res publica* (*animo gloriaque libertatem nostram defendis et dignitate*) and several references in *Brut.* 1.15 where Cicero lambasts Brutus' decisions after the Ides and credits himself and Octavian with the attempted restoration of liberty: e.g., 1.15.4: *erexerat enim se ciuitas in retinenda libertata consentiens*; 1.15.5: *excessistis urbe ea quam liberaratis*; 1.15.6: *consilia inire coepi Brutina plane ... rei publicae liberandae*; 1.15.7: *ut enim primum libertatem reuocare coepimus.* Likewise, at 1.15.2, Cicero reminds Brutus that he had 'lifted the yoke of servitude' (*seruitutem a tuis ciuibus depulisti*).

[54] Hendrickson 1939 identifies this treatise with the letter Brutus sent from Asia to Cicero while the latter was awaiting Caesar's pardon in Brundisium (48–47 BCE); this letter is referenced at Cic. *Brut.* 11, which would mean the treatise was written before 46 BCE; cf. Cic. *Fin.* 1.8 (published in 45 BCE). In any case, the letter of Seneca *Ad Heluiam matrem*, which provides our

this text appears in the statement that 'Brutus' cannot be in exile anywhere (*neque usquam exsul esse possum*) provided he remains true to his principles; for the idea that Brutus was an exile in 43 BCE is incompatible with the contemporary evidence that suggests he could have returned to Italy in the summer of that year.[55] Yet the real Brutus had reflected on the status of being 'an exile' in *De Virtute*. As Seneca the Younger reported to his mother Helvia, when trying to reassure her that he was not personally suffering in his own period of banishment: 'Marcus Brutus thinks that this is enough – the fact that those who go into exile may take along with them their virtues' (Sen. *Cons. Helv.* 8.1, *M. Brutus satis hoc putat, quod licet in exilium euntibus uirtutes suas secum ferre*).

As the rest of Seneca's work makes clear, however, Brutus was not talking about himself; rather he was reflecting on the fate of Marcus Marcellus who had withdrawn to the island of Mytilene at the outbreak of the civil war between Pompey and Caesar. Brutus had visited him there on his own return to Rome, yet the meeting had prompted Brutus to reconsider his own position under Caesar, when he pondered that returning to Rome under the latter's dictatorship was akin to going into exile:

> *Brutus in eo libro, quem de uirtute composuit, ait se Marcellum uidisse Mytilenis exulantem et quantum modo natura hominis pateretur, beatissime uiuentem neque umquam cupidiorem bonarum artium quam illo tempore. itaque adicit uisum sibi se magis in exilium ire, qui sine illo rediturus esset, quam illum in exilio relinqui.*
>
> (Sen. *Cons. Helv.* 9.4, trans. Basore)

> Brutus, in the book he wrote on virtue, says that he saw Marcellus in exile at Mytilene, living as happily as the limitations of human nature permit, and that he had never been more interested in liberal studies than he was at that time. And so he adds that, when he was about to return to Rome without him, he felt that he was going into exile instead of leaving him behind in exile.

The reflections of 'Brutus' in *Brut.* 1.16 – that citizenship is a 'matter of condition, not of place' (1.16.6: *res non locus*) – thus hark back to the idea expressed

---

firmest evidence for Brutus' *De Virtute*, puts the dramatic setting on Brutus' return to Rome after Pharsalus, thus providing a *terminus post quem* of 48 BCE.

55 On 25th July 43 BCE, for example, Brutus' mother Servilia hosted a meeting at her home to seek advice on whether Brutus should be encouraged to return to Rome; see Cic. *Brut.* 1.18.2; *Att.* 15.11.1–2. It was not until the *lex Pedia* was passed on 19th August that Brutus and the other conspirators were officially incriminated; until then, Brutus continued to style himself as a proconsul on his coins, and there is no reason to doubt he viewed himself as such. For the designation 'PR (O) COS' on the coins of Brutus in the first half of 43 BCE, see *RRC* 501,1; 502,1; 502,4; 502,3; 503,1. Discussion in Laignoux 2012, 787.

in *De Virtute*, that no man can be an exile if he is in possession of his virtues. Moreover, when 'Brutus' returns to this argument later in the same letter, his insistence that 'wherever I can live as a free man there for me shall be Rome' (1.16.8: *mihique esse iudicabo Romam ubicumque liberum esse licebit*) appears to make a further allusion to the consolations of Brutus, quoted by Seneca, that 'to the wise man every place is his country' (Sen. *Cons. Helv.* 9.7: *omnem locum sapienti uiro patriam esse*).

It is in this philosophical twist, however, that we can detect a further handle on the sources pertaining to Brutus. For, in the following passage of the letter, as he continues his reflections on citizenship and exile, Brutus emerges as a man who steadfastly (*constans*) holds to his principles: his happiness (*mihi quidem ita beatus esse uidebor*) is associated with decisive action (*consilium*), while he expresses a determination to rise above the vicissitudes of human experience (*neglegere humana*):

> *mihi quidem ita beatus esse uidebor, si modo constanter ac perpetuo placebit hoc consilium, ut relatam putem gratiam pietati meae. quid enim est melius quam memoria recte factorum et libertate contentum neglegere humana?*
>
> (1.16.8)
>
> I shall think myself so happy, if only I cling steadfastly to this intention, that I shall consider my patriotism as well rewarded. For what is better than to be indifferent to the vicissitudes of life, content with freedom and the memory of deeds well done?

Here, the mention of Brutus' happiness not only recalls his observation in *De Virtute* that Marcellus was living happily in exile (Sen. *Cons. Helv.* 9.4, *beatissime uiuentem*); it also communicates a more generalised Stoic world view that is not incompatible with later assessments of Brutus' philosophical identity.[56] For, although the real Brutus professed allegiance to the principles of the Old Academy, the idea that he was a Stoic, or that he sometimes adopted a position which came close to Stoicism, was one that particularly followed Brutus in the later tradition surrounding him.[57] As the passage continues, then, it is intriguing to observe how the Stoic position of Brutus becomes further exaggerated as he presents himself as indifferent to fortune:

---

56 See Prost 2001, 265–269.
57 Moles 1987, 64 lists some of the ways in which later literature tended to conflate Brutus' philosophy with the principles of Stoicism. But the idea that Brutus actually leaned towards Stoicism has been excellently dismantled by Sedley 1997, who stresses Brutus' philosophical attachment to the Old Academy. For more on Brutus' Antiocheanism, see Lévy 2012, 300–303.

> sed certe non succumbam succumbentibus nec uincar ab iis qui se uinci uolunt, experiarque et temptabo omnia neque desistam abstrahere a seruitio ciuitatem nostro. si secuta fuerit quae debet fortuna, gaudebimus omnes; si minus, ego tandem gaudebo.
>
> (1.16.9)

> But assuredly I shall not submit to the submissive or be defeated by the defeatists. I shall try every expedient and never abandon my efforts to draw our society away from thraldom. If deserved good fortune follow from the enterprise, we shall all be glad. If not *I* shall still be glad.

In other words: whereas others may rejoice only if fortune favours them, 'Brutus' will feel *gaudium* — or what the old Stoics termed *chara*, an elation of the spirit — regardless of the outcome. What is constant here is his determination to defend Rome from tyranny and his application of philosophical principles to political action (*abstrahere a seruitio ciuitatem nostro*). We may question the Stoic doctrine in which this intention is embedded, but the passage is certainly revealing of the reputation of Brutus. Indeed, a striking similarity can be detected between the lines of 'Brutus' in this letter and Valerius Maximus' account that, as he went into his last battle at Philippi, the real Brutus had declared: 'Confidently I go into battle, for today either all will be well or I shall not be caring' (Val. Max. 6.4.5, *'fidenter' inquit 'in aciem descendo: hodie enim aut recte erit nihil curabo'*). In both passages, the confidence and steadfastness of Brutus is the same, only the author of *Brut.* 1.16 has couched the expression in terms of Stoic sentiment.

This emphasis on Brutus' philosophical identity is part of what Carlos Lévy has called a 'mirror game' in the letters, one in which Brutus and Cicero 'show up the other less for what he thinks than for what he does not want to be.'[58] In this larger context, 'Brutus' also writes to Atticus of Cicero's fear of things a real philosopher should not fear:

> nimium timemus mortem et exsilium et paupertatem. haec mihi uidentur Ciceroni ultima esse in malis.
>
> (1.17.4)

> We dread death and banishment and poverty too much. For Cicero I think they are the ultimate evils.

---

58 Lévy 2012, 301. For Lévy the question of authenticity is not an issue; as he points out, if they are not genuine: 'the forgery is ancient and thus at least revealing of the reputation of the two writers in their own times or soon after'.

In a pattern with which we are by now familiar, Cicero's own words are used against him: thus, in the fourth book of the *Tusculan Disputations*, when Cicero blames men who feel fear, he especially targets those who are afraid of 'poverty, infamy and death' (Cic. *Tusc.* 4.46: *qui paupertatem, qui ignominiam qui mortem timent*). We might also detect a nod to the broader discussion of Cicero's *De Finibus* lurking behind the criticism. For there too, in a work which seeks to define what nature regards as supremely desirable, and what she avoids as the ultimate evil, we find a similar reproach against the Epicurean who has been 'schooled to make light of death, of exile, even of pain itself' (*Fin.* 2.56: *erit enim instructus ad mortem contemnendam, ad exilium, ad ipsum etiam dolorem*). While this last point on its own cannot be taken to prove the work of a pseudonymous writer, since the real Brutus too could have made such a play on Cicero's philosophical convictions, when we examine the broader tissue of intertextual allusions, the inclusion of Cicero's philosophical texts is significant for demonstrating the wide range of sources to which *Brut.* 1.16 and 1.17 allude.

4 Recreating the past

The voice and manners of 'Brutus' are only a part of the historical fiction that the author seeks to create in the letters; for, elsewhere, his personality is developed with reference to details of Brutus' biography, especially his family life, and the general circumstances of 43–42 BCE. These features all help in the re-creation of the historical setting and the ambiance in which the texts were purportedly written.[59] But they often appear dropped in gratuitously, without any real need for them in the surrounding context. What is more, as in the case of Brutus' final words (discussed above), the resemblances between the contents of *Brut.* 1.16 and 1.17 and the later, often hostile, tradition surrounding Brutus are suggestive of a pseudonymous hand.

Take, for example, the following objection against the increasing power of Octavian at *Brut.* 1.16:

---

[59] On this aspect of the literary fake, especially the ideas of historical setting and ambience as crucial elements of the fiction, see Peirano 2012, 205–208; as Peirano is careful to note, issues of authorship (i.e. impersonation) and chronology (i.e. historical fictions) are closely related, for the 'authorial impersonation is always to some extent a historical fiction' (206).

> *sed mihi prius omnia di deaeque eripuerint quam illud iudicium quo non modo heredi eius quem occidi non concesserim quod in illo non tuli sed ne patri quidem meo, si reuiuiscat, ut patiente me plus legibus ac senatu possit.*
>
> (1.16.5)

But may the gods and goddesses take away everything I have sooner than my determination that nobody shall have more power than the Senate and the laws with my consent. What I did not tolerate in the case of the man I killed, I shall not concede to his heir, I should not concede it to my own father if he came back to life.

Brutus' argument is clear enough: he refuses to concede to Octavian the power he denied to Caesar. But the subordinate point that he would refuse to allow his own father to rise above the Senate and laws is both irrelevant to the larger discussion and ultimately meaningless, as his father had long since deceased. So why does 'Brutus' mention it here? One explanation is that the death of Brutus' father at Mutina in 77 BCE was a topic of some notoriety, primarily because it was a famous example of Pompey the Great's early cruelty and misconduct.[60] The incidental nature of this remark thus points to a process of engagement with the source material that extends beyond the construction of an authorial persona. For, as Peirano explains, common phrases or ideas could also be used as cues to create fictional scenarios. This approach was common in the rhetorical schools, she adds: '[b]ecause so many exercises were based on mythological or historical scenarios, practitioners were asked to display knowledge of the literary texts that dealt with those stories.'[61] Taking this idea further, we might think of these allusions as a sort of 'checklist' of material used both to demonstrate the author's knowledge of the wider tradition surrounding Brutus and to amuse the reader by the specificity with which it is applied.

That the reader of such texts was expected to benefit intellectually from the recognition of allusions can be seen from the playful allusions of the *Historia Augusta* or the patchwork creations of the Vergilian *Centos*.[62] The same can be

---

60 On the death of Brutus's father, see Plut. *Pomp.* 16.2–5; Livy *Per.* 92; App. *B. Ciu.* 2.16.111; Oros. 5.22.17. Consequently, M. Iunius Brutus the elder became an obvious exemplum of Pompey's cruelty (see, e.g., Val. Max. 6.2.8) and other rhetorical treatments of this period, such as the *Oratio ad Caesarem senem*. For discussion of the use of Brutus in the pseudo-Sallustian *Oratio*, cf. Hinard 1985, 53 and Santangelo 2012, 45.
61 Peirano 2012, 19.
62 I draw inspiration here from Rohrbacher 2016, whose work on the *Historia Augusta* starts from the premise that the author is a creative inventor for whom allusions and the identification of allusions form the work's *raison d'être*. See also McGill 2005 who underscores the rich and creative ways that the Virgilian *centos* rework lines taken from Virgil's poetry to create an exciting reading experience.

said of *pseudepigrapha*: readers were regarded as potential collaborators and not the victims of historical fictions,[63] while the texts serve for us as valuable witnesses to the reception history of their subjects.[64] It is in this context that Brutus' refusal to tolerate any man's ambitions for sole power, *ne patri quidem meo, si reuiuiscat*, performs a double service; for the implied threat against his own father's life also recalls Brutus' reputation in antiquity as a parricide, the man who had killed the *parens patriae*.[65] As we saw above, Cicero had warned of Mark Antony's damaging rhetoric as early as 44 BCE, in a letter in which he described how an inscribed statue base of Caesar set up the liberators *non modo sicarii sed iam etiam parricidae* (*Fam.* 12.13.1); he also repeated the claim in his *Second Philippic* as he challenged Mark Antony on his stance towards Brutus and Cassius, with whom he had earlier agreed an amnesty for the death of Caesar.[66] But the representation of the murder as *parricidium* was particularly prominent in later writings; the Tiberian historian Valerius Maximus, for example, is perfectly consistent in his usage of the term to designate both the assassination of Caesar generally and Brutus specifically.[67] Indeed, in Tacitus' account of the trial of Cremutius Cordus in 25 CE, he makes it clear that the label *parricidae* was a current, and fairly recent, charge at the time of the events he describes.[68] The erroneous threat against his father in *Brut.* 1.16 thus betrays a side to Brutus' character that is more consistent with the hostile tradition surrounding him and which would have appealed to later reader of the letters; it fits less comfortably

---

[63] The idea that 'fiction' was an accepted mode of reading in which the reader becomes a participant is taken up and expanded by Peirano 2012, 28; 208.

[64] While both Rohrbacher 2016 and McGill 2005 emphasise the clear connection between allusions and reception studies, this aspect is developed most explicitly in relation to *pseudepigrapha* by Keeline 2018, 147–195.

[65] Caesar is represented as the *parens patriae* on coinage in the period either prior to or immediately after his death; see e.g., *RRC* 480/10 and *RRC* 480/19, with discussion by Weinstock 1971, 200–205; Crawford 1974, 494–495; Stevenson 2015, 139–152; Woytek 2003, 427.

[66] Cic. *Phil.* 2.31; for further discussion of this passage in the context of Mark Antony's rhetoric of 43–42 BCE, see Tatum 2020, 196–199.

[67] On the murder of Caesar as *parricidium*, see Val. Max. 1.6.13, 4.5.6; on Brutus as a parricide, see Val. Max. 1.5.7, 6.4.5; the term is also used of Cassius at Val. Max 1.8.8, 6.8.4; cf. Bloomer 1992, 210–211, 222–223.

[68] In this passage, Tacitus has Cremutius defend himself against the charge of praising the liberators by invoking earlier writers' praise of them. One example is Livy: 'this very Cassius, this same Brutus, he nowhere describes as brigands and traitors, terms now applied to them, but repeatedly as illustrious men' (Tac. *Ann.* 4.34, *hunc ipsum Cassium, hunc Brutum nusquam latrones et parricidas, quae nunc uocabula imponuntur, saepe ut insignis uiros nominat*).

with the historical Brutus' efforts to portray himself as a clement and merciful commander.[69]

A similarly out of place remark appears in the next paragraph as 'Brutus' continues his objections against Octavian's rise to power and argues that 'in Greece when tyrants are suppressed their children suffer the same penalty' (1.16.6, *cum in Graecis ciuitatibus liberi tyrannorum oppressis illis eodem supplicio adficiantur*). But this recourse to Greek custom is not an example the real Brutus is likely to have used in the summer of 43 BCE. For on 30th May 43 BCE Brutus' brother-in-law Lepidus sent a letter to the Senate announcing his defection to Mark Antony, a measure that Brutus knew would have consequences on the lives of Lepidus' family, including Brutus' half-sister, Junia Secunda, and her sons. And he was especially frustrated at Cicero who proposed stern measures against Lepidus, whom he declared a public enemy and whose penalty he thought should be extended to Lepidus' children; 'that is an ancient rule found in all communities,' Cicero argued. 'Even Themistocles' children lived in poverty' (*Brut.* 1.15.11: *id et antiquum est et omnium ciuitatum, si quidem etiam Themistocli liberi eguerunt.*). Far from the real Brutus arguing that Octavian should have been punished as Caesar's heir and the son of a tyrant, it is more likely that the author of *Brut.* 1.16 had Cicero's words in mind when he needed to present the case of 'Brutus' against Cicero's support of Octavian.

Finally, there is a group of throw-away allusions in *Brut.* 1.17 which cumulatively serve to complete the sketch of Brutus' life circumstances in 44–43 BCE. First, at 1.17.3 'Brutus' drops in mention of Flavius, who had unsuccessfully called on Atticus to start a fundraising campaign for Brutus' cause; once again the allusion is shoehorned into an unnecessary clause in which 'Brutus' uses the example to illustrate Atticus' refusal to take sides in disputes. The context here is the same as that of Cornelius Nepos, who records that Atticus declined Flavius' request on the grounds that he had always kept himself aloof from such schemes, preferring to support friends instead of factions (Nep. *Att.* 8.4). Next there is the comment that Cicero has been flattered and duped by Octavian, who calls Cicero father (1.17.5: *patrem appellet Octauius Ciceronem*) — a line of thought that may reflect a latent anti-Ciceronian tradition.[70] And, thirdly, at

---

[69] On Brutus' *clementia*, see Cic. *Brut.* 2.5.5, 1.2a.2, 1.15.10; in the later, favourable, tradition to Brutus represented by Plutarch, the Greek term *praotés* is often used e.g., at Plut. *Brut.* 6.10, 18.4.5, 26.6, 29.3, 32, 45.4–5.

[70] Compare Plutarch's statement that 'the young man [Octavian] carried his court to him so far as actually to call him father' (Plut. *Cic.* 45.1: οὕτω γὰρ ὑπῄει τὸ μειράκιον αὐτόν, ὥστε καὶ πατέρα προσαγορεύειν). However, for the sake of transparency, we should note that Plutarch seems to have had Brutus' letter in mind when he composed the *Life of Cicero*, and so, although

Brut. 1.17.7, 'Brutus' both thanks Atticus for showing concern over Porcia's health, while expressing his own anxieties about Atticus' choice of a future husband for his daughter Attica. Yet I do wonder about this: references to family members were a typical way of closing letters between close friends, and so they make sense in their epistolary setting. The reference to Porcia is particularly appropriate since we know from Cicero's letter of consolation that she died soon after the dramatic date of *Brut.* 1.17.[71] But Attica was born in 51 BCE, which makes her only eight years old at the time of the letter. Such an early engagement was not impossible, of course, but it could be another playful allusion: for just six years later, in 37 BCE, she married Marcus Vipsanius Agrippa, a life-long friend and supporter of Octavian. One might feel justified in doubting whether Atticus — the famously impartial political player — had already set such a premium on the outcome of the war that he had sought a marriage alliance with Octavian's side. Either way, however, if this marriage is what the author had in mind, it could explain why 'Brutus' would like to have been consulted.

To return to my idea, mentioned above, that we might think of such allusions as a sort of 'checklist' for inclusion in a work pertaining to represent the 'real' Brutus, we can start to appreciate how the author has exploited the markers of the letter form, as well as the biographical tradition surrounding Brutus. But there is one more consideration that I would like to raise before I conclude. For, in asserting the authenticity of these letters, Moles argued that the writer is evidently angry, and that the historical Brutus was known to have a temper, even if he only lost it occasionally.[72] Yet the only evidence for Brutus' anger can be found in the later tradition represented by Plutarch. On the contrary, a close reading of the extant letters between Cicero and Brutus, as well as the reflections

---

it looks like an allusion to a well-known charge against Brutus, there is no firm evidence for the appearance of this claim prior to *Brut.* 1.17. As Lintott 2013, 66 *ad loc.* notes, however, there is no reason to doubt that Cicero was so addressed by Octavian. Even though Lintott doubts the authenticity of the letter, he adds that the letter might still express the genuine feelings of Brutus' camp. If so, the line might be representative of a wider anti-Ciceronian feeling which is why I have included it here.

[71] Cicero's letter of consolation is *Brut.* 1.9; on the dramatic date of *Brut.* 1.17, see n. 10 above. The death of Porcia was a popular story among later writers; according to some sources she took her own life (allegedly by swallowing hot coals). On balance, it seems more plausible that she had a disease prior to that, even if she did give up the fight for her life. See Val. Max. 4.6.5; Plut. *Brut.* 53.5; App. *B. Ciu.* 4.136; Cass. Dio 47.79.3. For an overview and discussion of the evidence, see Treggiari 2019, 208–209.

[72] Moles 1997, 149 only cites Plutarch's biography as evidence of this temper, e.g. at Plut. *Brut.* 34.3 and 45.9; he does not consider representations of Brutus in contemporary sources.

of Brutus' temperament in Cicero's *Epistulae ad Atticum*, suggest that he rarely if ever indulged his temper, either in person or in writing.

Two examples will prove illustrative. The first is a letter Cicero wrote to Atticus justifying his abandoned attempt to sail to Greece in summer 44 BCE (Cic. *Att.* 16.7). Cicero's trip had come at a bad time for Brutus' and Cassius' cause; had he been present at Rome, Cicero could have represented their interests in the ongoing struggle against Mark Antony. Even Atticus had accused Cicero of forsaking his country and showing a lack of resolve (16.7.3); 'The most hurtful thing comes at the end.' Cicero added on replying to Atticus' letter: 'Our Brutus holds his tongue'. That is to say, he does not venture to admonish a man of my age' (16.7.5: *extremum illud uel molestissimum:* '*nam Brutus noster silet,*' *hoc est, non audet hominem id aetatis monere*). For Brutus was particularly upset that Cicero had missed an important meeting of the Senate on 1st August.[73] Indeed, when Cicero subsequently met Brutus at Velia, these words came back to him: 'Heavens, how delighted he was at my return or rather my turning back! Everything he had kept back came pouring out. It made me remember your words, "as for our friend Brutus, he holds his tongue"' (16.7.5: *quam ualde ille reditu uel potius reuersione mea laetatus effudit illa omnia quae tacuerat! ut recordarer illud tuum 'nam Brutus noster silet.'*). Far from reproaching Cicero in anger, Brutus had used Atticus to intervene on his behalf, and he had treated Cicero with respect.[74]

The second example belongs to the period when Brutus was angry with Cicero following the *hostis* declaration against Lepidus and its consequences for Brutus' family. Yet we can observe Brutus once more 'holding his tongue' and maintaining his silence in the form of a short letter: 'Does Brutus write me only three lines in times like these?' Cicero complains, 'Better nothing at all' (1.14.1, *tribusne uersiculis his temporibus Brutus ad me? nihil scripsisses potius*). At that point, any trace of Brutus' letters drops out of the extant correspondence, and we are left only with Cicero's change of heart at 1.18.13, where he tells Brutus he is working assiduously on behalf of Junia's children. Yet the short missive fits a pattern of reluctance on Brutus' part to express his anger: in his dealings with Cicero, Brutus' frustration with his senior seems to have manifested itself through a form of moody silence.

---

[73] The precise nature of the matter under discussion is not made clear, but it was probably related to the allocation of provincial commands and the insulting grain commission attached to Brutus and Cassius; see Tempest 2017, 139–140 with further bibliography.

[74] Respect and expressions of friendship also feature strongly in the two letters of Brutus, long believed to be genuine, in which he does venture to disagree with Cicero, Cic. *Brut.* 1.4 and 1.4a.

As the author had perhaps alluded to at the beginning of *Brut.* 1.16.1, conjuring up emotions for Brutus was not an easy task: 'what am I to write', *quid scribam*? he had asked. On the other hand, at 1.17.3, he explains to Atticus why he is taking the unusual step of breaking his customary silence: 'Since I have not been permitted to hold my tongue, you will have to read what cannot but be disagreeable to you' (*quoniam mihi tacere non licuit, leges quae tibi necesse est molesta esse*). Far from proving the authenticity of the letter, as Moles suggested, the acknowledgement that 'Brutus' has been forced to speak out of character explains a jarring discrepancy between the tone of *Brut.* 1.16 and 17 and Brutus' genuine letters to Cicero.[75] Either because Pseudo-Brutus needed to explain this difference to a reader familiar with the wider corpus of the *Epistulae ad Brutum* and *ad Atticum*, or because he was drawing on later representations of Brutus as a volatile man, the references to Brutus' lack of temper in *Brut.* 1.16 and 1.17 offer further evidence of the allusive play at work in the creation of Brutus' *persona*.

5 Conclusion

The search for certainty in cases of disputed authorship is often frustrated by the lack of evidence required to make a final verdict. And, as we have seen in the specific case of *Brut.* 1.16 and 1.17, scholars have not reached, nor are they likely to form, a consensus on the matters of style, chronology and transmission that would normally be required in the identification of spurious works. Yet we can, at least, attempt to build a fuller picture of the letters' provenance by finding multiple instances of statements that appear out of context or historically implausible and by scrutinising verbal parallels or allusions that appear within them. Thus, when Shackleton Bailey set out to demonstrate that the Latin letters of Brutus were forgeries, he largely focused on the 'tracks' in *Brut.* 1.17, which revealed the author's reuse of Cicero's own words;[76] Keeline, too, focused his attention on the strong intertextual allusions between *Brut.* 1.17 and Cicero's writings to argue that the letters were *pseudepigrapha*. In revising Shackleton Bailey's observations, he thus made a strong case for appreciating the compe-

---

75 Heine 1875, 34–35 compares *Brut.* 1.16 and 1.17 to *Brut.* 1.4 (a genuine letter from Brutus to Cicero written at about the same time) to illustrate the striking difference in tone. He concludes that they cannot all be written by the same man: *uides igitur, opinor, epistulae I,4 sermonem tantopere discrepare ab epistularum I,16 and I,17 sermone, ut ab eodem uiro eodem fere tempore de eisdem fere rebus scriptae esse non possint* (35).
76 By contrast Shackleton Bailey 1980, 14 noted that *Brut.* 1.16 'offers no such handles'.

tence of the author as a writer of declamatory exercises: 'whatever one thinks of their literary or artistic abilities,' he added, 'their allusive practices deserve to be recognized on their own merits'.[77] This chapter, however, has gone one step further. By examining the allusions to the ideas of Brutus that were still in circulation after his death, as well as the larger biographical tradition surrounding him, I have suggested that *Brut.* 1.16 too exhibits characteristic features of the pseudepigraphic enterprise. What is more, in the construction of Brutus' epistolary persona and the recreation of his past, both letters reveal the breadth of material the author had at his disposal.

Naturally, we have seen points of contact with the contemporary sources pertaining to this period. These range from Cicero's authentic letters to Brutus, as well as to other correspondents such as Cassius and Atticus in the *Epistulae ad Familiares* and *ad Atticum*; they also extend to Cicero's *Philippics*, and his philosophical ideas in *Tusculanae Disputationes* and *De Finibus*. Yet, in the construction of Brutus' authorial persona, we have also seen the resonance of ideas between *Brut.* 1.16 and 1.17 and the fragments of the real Brutus' (otherwise lost) works, especially his *De Virtute*, as represented by Seneca the Elder. But in the development of these ideas, the attribution of a more Stoic voice than might be expected of the historical Brutus was suggestive of the later tradition surrounding him; likewise, the sentiments of 'Brutus' in the letters were evocative of his posthumous reputation as an assassin and parricide, and as a man who rejected his philosophical principles at the end. In so doing, the author gave voice to a side of Brutus' personality that was only represented in the sources which were hostile to him; the real Brutus was far more concerned to advertise his *clementia* and regard for the laws and Senate. In another striking difference, the picture of Brutus that emerges from the evidence of those who knew him is that of an enigmatic and shadowy figure; he was a man who maintained a respectful silence in anger as opposed to giving way to rage. The same cannot be said of the authorial voice behind *Brut* 1.16 and 1.17.

The suggestion that the author was working with later material also appears plausible when we consider his handling of the biographical tradition surrounding Brutus, and especially the stories that were popular among late-republican and early imperial authors such as Cornelius Nepos and Valerius Maximus, and which we subsequently find in Plutarch too. Details from Brutus' childhood, such as the death of his father, are seemingly 'dropped in', as are references to Porcia's bad health, Atticus' refusal to spearhead a collection to fund Brutus' campaigns, and Brutus' final words before Philippi and his death. Some allusions are less

---

77 Keeline 2018, 189–190.

secure, as for example the detail that Octavian called Cicero 'father', or the reference to a future husband for Atticus' daughter. But I have included them in the discussion anyway, in the belief that their relevance is reinforced by the presence of more obvious allusions, and that together they form a much larger allusive web than has hitherto been appreciated.

To conclude, however, it is not enough simply to state that *Brut.* 1.16 and 1.17 are the products of a later author. We must also consider the literary culture to which they belonged, as well as their likely aim, audience, and date of composition.[78] To this end, we may note that several collections of Brutus' letters circulated in the first-century CE, and they initially appear to have done so independently of Cicero's correspondence to Brutus;[79] indeed, a useful *terminus ante quem* for *Brut.* 1.16 and 1.17 is provided by Plutarch who made use of them in his biography of Brutus, written in the early years of the second century CE.[80] There is good evidence to suggest that Cicero's *Epistulae ad Atticum* and *ad Familiares* were also published around the same time as the letters of Brutus, and by the 60s CE at the latest — even if some authors, like Cornelius Nepos, had earlier and privileged access to private collections.[81] Given the continued interest in historical personalities and hypothetical situations as a source for rhetorical elaboration in the early imperial age, especially when it came to conflicting or contrasting characters, the declamatory classroom provides one potential arena for the composition of letters such as *Brut.* 1.16 and 1.17.[82]

Yet, as Peirano has argued, even labels such as declamatory and fictitious can appear reductive because they appear in opposition to 'authentic'.[83] Instead, she has suggested we read such texts as creative and highly self-conscious

---

78 Compare the criteria for the verification of literary fakes set out by Syme 1972: namely, what was its aim? For whom or what kind of reader was it intended? When was it composed?
79 Tacitus knew of a collection of Brutus' letters to Cicero (see Tac. *Dial.* 18.5), while Plutarch exploited some of these letters (including *Brut.* 1.16 and 17) in his *Life of Brutus*, see n. 80 below.
80 On Plutarch's use of Brutus' letters, see Pelling 1979, 87. As Pelling has also pointed out, Plutarch appears to have used them exclusively, while there is no evidence that he knew of Cicero's letters to Brutus (see ibid., 87 n. 93). This suggests that the letters of Brutus initially circulated in a separate tradition to the Ciceronian correspondence; see Harvey 1991, 28. For the date of Plutarch's *Brutus*, see Moles 2017, 19–26 who narrows it down to 105–116 CE.
81 On the publication of Cicero's letters, see the useful overview by Setaioli 1976; Beard 2002, 116–119; and White 2010, esp. 174–175 with further bibliography. Cornelius Nepos notes his privileged access to the letters at Nep. *Att.* 16.3.
82 Thus Harvey 1991, 28 and Keeline 2018, 188–195 who posit them alongside works such as the pseudo-Ciceronian *Epistula ad Octauianum* and the pseudo-Sallustian *In Ciceronem*.
83 Peirano 2012, 207.

responses to the literary and recent past.[84] That is to say: such texts were performance pieces that take us to the heart of how audiences in the early imperial period responded to their history. In this intellectual climate, personalities such as Cato, Cicero and Brutus became the object of literary evaluation, criticism, or admiration as the memory of the Republic impressed itself on imperial literature.[85] The availability of Cicero's published letters for this period, coupled with the creation of public libraries, were doubtless important factors that encouraged the production of pseudonymous works.[86] What is more, the impersonation of such figures and the recreation of their circumstances — the mingling of history and fiction so characteristic of literary fakes — tended to coalesce in genres that naturally invited aspects of role play. Through the format of the imaginary letter, then, 'Brutus' could be reimagined and (re)performed in an age still deeply interested in the crises that followed the assassination of Caesar. And, although it was possible to find admirers of Brutus in this period, it is perhaps not surprising that the authorial persona of *Brut.* 1.16 and 1.17 cuts an unsympathetic figure: as our ancient sources reveal, and as Pseudo-Brutus was well aware, Brutus was and has remained a controversial character.

---

84 Peirano 2012, 242–243.
85 For the significance of the Republican past for later generations, see Gowing 2005 and Gallia 2012. MacMullen 1966, 1–45 offers a comprehensive overview of the interest attached to Cato and Brutus; cf. Fehrle 1983 and, more recently, Gäth 2011 (on Cato); on the reception of Brutus see Clarke 1981, esp. 79–84 and Tempest 2017, 211–231; 2023. On Cicero's reception in the early imperial period, see Keeline 2018.
86 On the importance of libraries, see Syme 1958a, 47.

Janja Soldo
Fictionality and Pseudepigraphy in the Apocryphal Letter Exchange between Seneca and Paul

Abstract: This chapter is dedicated to the only self-standing pseudepigraphic collection of letters extant in Latin: the apocryphal correspondence between Seneca and St. Paul. Rather than taking the obvious shortcomings and implausibilities of the collection as signs of authorial inefficiency, the article considers them as self-conscious signals of the text's fictionality. The pseudepigrapher borrows elements from Seneca's *Epistulae Morales* and expands them with imaginary scenarios of his own (a meeting of Seneca and Lucilius, a narration of Seneca's altering attitude towards Nero), so as to adapt them to his fictional world. The meta-textual discussions of the rules and practice of epistolography in these letters, as well as the emphasis on the theme of reading, are further markers of fictionality and make the collection assume at times the form of a manual of letter-writing.

Keywords: pseudepigraphy, Seneca *Epistulae Morales*, Seneca and Paul, reading, epistolary handbook

In one of the most famous passages on ancient letter-writing, *De Elocutione* 227, Demetrius suggests that

> the letter should be strong on characterization, like the dialogue; everyone in writing a letter more or less composes an image of his own soul. One can indeed see the writer's character in any other kind of writing too, but in none so clearly as in the letter.[1]

The passage is embedded in a discussion of the stylistic aspects of letter-writing which emphasises that a letter ought to be written in a personal tone and plain style. In the quote above, Demetrius temporarily breaks free from purely stylistic observations and reflects on the content and the purpose of letters: they give

---

I am indebted to Claire Rachel Jackson for her thought-provoking comments on several drafts of my paper.

---

1 Translation: Trapp 2003.

direct access to the letter writer's inner life (their soul) and ought to reveal their character. Thus, letters promise intimacy and authenticity.

But things are not that simple. Those who look for the truth and nothing but the truth in letters stand to be disappointed: not even a letter delivers complete authenticity because, as Patricia Rosenmeyer so convincingly demonstrated, 'the letter is a construction, not a reflection, of reality'.[2] No matter how authentic or unmediated a letter might look it always contains an element of make-believe; letter writers always write with an eye to how they present themselves and always create their own personas in their letters, whether consciously or not[3].[4] Demetrius' decision to describe the letter as an *eikon*, an image of the soul, already points us in the direction of Rosenmeyer's conclusion: the letter is, after all, only a representation of one's soul. Reading a letter requires constant switching between taking it at face value and regarding certain elements as fictional, in turn applying belief and suspending disbelief.

Authenticity is an even thornier issue in pseudepigraphic letters (letters that profess to have been written by, or that have been falsely attributed to, a certain author). These letters are actually a figment of the forger's imagination but try very hard to look real by imitating the style and thought of the writers they pretend to be and by incorporating more or less obvious allusions to the author's original work.[5] There is a big gap between the fictionality and purported authenticity of pseudepigraphic letter collections, much bigger than in other letter collections. The letter genre's claim to intimacy and authenticity makes it relatively easy to forge an individual letter or a whole letter collection. Who knows for sure with whom an author corresponded, how many letters they produced in their life-time, or what really went on in a private correspondence? Slipping in one letter or more into an already existing exchange or claiming that one has discovered a hitherto unknown correspondence are relatively straightforward acts of fraud. The forger or pseudepigrapher only needs some imagination, a good knowledge of the biography of the person(s) they want to impersonate and an eye for the particularities of their style. The inclusion of references to historical events or specific places also helps create the illusion of authenticity. Apart from that, plausibility is key in the creation of a pseudepigraphy: the reader must never doubt the letter's authenticity because the work — who writes to

---

[2] Rosenmeyer 2001, 5.
[3] Rosenmeyer 2001, esp. 3–11.
[4] Compare the contribution by Morello which uncovers fictionalising elements even in Cicero's letters, cherished for their authenticity and value as historical documents.
[5] On pseudepigraphic letter collections, see also Tempest's contribution to this volume.

whom about what — is entirely plausible (even though it is worth pointing out that plausibility is a construct: different cultures have different conceptions of what is considered plausible).[6]

While there is an abundance of pseudepigraphic letter collections in Greek,[7] there is only one such collection written in Latin: the apocryphal exchange between Seneca and the apostle Paul. And it is a rather odd pseudepigraphy at that, as we will see below. Long deemed an authentic testimony to the philosopher's and the convert's friendship and evidence of Seneca's interest in, and intellectual closeness to, Christianity, the collection was exposed as a fake by Erasmus of Rotterdam. Today, it is widely regarded as spurious and commonly dated to the 4th century, even though it is debated whether the exchange is the abridged version of an earlier (and better) Greek original and whether certain letters are later additions.[8] The circumstances in which the exchange was created are unclear but Claude Barlow, who edited the collection in 1938, has, quite convincingly, suggested that it is essentially a school exercise, arguing that the letters show a great interest in stylistic matters and exhibit a good knowledge of epistolary tropes and etiquette. Moreover, the exercises in rhetorical schools provided a natural breeding ground for pseudepigrapha as they trained students in imitation and innovation.[9]

Scholars have not always treated the short collection, which consists of only 14 letters (eight by "Seneca" and six by "Paul") and which does not follow a strict chronological order, kindly. Erasmus' verdict that *his epistolis non uideo quid fingi possit frigidius aut ineptius* (*Ep.* 2092) still reverberates through scholarship, with many arguing that the exchange is devoid of content and that it trivializes Seneca's Stoicism and Paul's Christian beliefs, highlighting its inconsistencies and anachronisms, and emphasizing the forger's linguistic and stylistic shortcomings.[10] Indeed, the letters are oddly trivial, providing little information and displaying almost no philosophical or theological expertise. They tell a story of the developing friendship between the philosopher and the apostle but their friendship is often expressed through rhetorical clichés and formulaic assurances. Because of its lacklustre style and absence of an overarching topic

---

6 See Schmitz 2000; Peirano 2012; Tempest in this volume.
7 See Gibson/Morrison forthcoming.
8 Ramelli 2013 argues that the collection might have been composed in Greek before 180 CE and that *Ep.* 11 and 14 were created by a different pseudepigrapher.
9 Peirano 2012, 13–19.
10 Particularly harsh is Fürst 1998; 2006; he also gives a good overview of the relevant judgements made by scholarship; see also Frenschkowski 2009.

and narrative, the collection raises questions about its purpose or message.¹¹ The most convincing explanation is that the anonymous author wanted to make his readers believe that a friendship between Seneca and Paul existed and that it manifested itself in their letters.¹²

The strangest feature of the text, which distinguishes it from most other examples of the genre, is that it is so *bad* at pretending to be *real*, which puts it at odds with the basic purpose of pseudepigraphy. This basic failure of the text raises questions about its plausibility, one of the key elements of pseudepigraphic writing (see above).¹³ While the collection's premise — that the prolific letter writers and teachers of morality Seneca and Paul exchanged letters with each other — is entirely plausible, its shortcomings make it implausible: the collection does not imitate Seneca's style as convincingly as one might expect from a forgery and even contains some rather bad Latin in Paul's letters;¹⁴ moreover, it rarely mentions or alludes to Seneca's and Paul's philosophical and religious works and beliefs. It is quite easy to figure out that the collection cannot have been written by Seneca or by Paul.

But rather than regarding the collection's obvious inauthenticity as a failure,¹⁵ I propose to read it as the pseudepigrapher's way of signposting the collection's fictionality.¹⁶ The letters, I argue, break the illusion of the pseudepigraphy and signal to the reader that they are fictional.¹⁷ By pointing to its own fictionality, the collection self-consciously reflects that it supplements and expands the text on which it is based, in this particular case Seneca's *Epistulae Morales*.¹⁸ Like many other fakes, it engages creatively with a well-known text and fills in the gaps (Peirano 2012, 10). But the exchange between Seneca and Paul goes even further than that: it acts as a commentary on epistolary writing in general and on pseudepigraphic letter writing in particular.

---

11 The different views are neatly summarised in Fürst 2006; see also the overview in Bocciolini Palagi 1985.
12 See also Fürst 2006's discussion of the purpose of the collection.
13 See Fuhrer forthcoming for a sensitive discussion of the text's plausibility.
14 Though Ramelli 2013 argues that "Paul's" deficiencies in Latin are part of the fiction because the apostle thought in Greek.
15 Fürst 2006 even went so far as to claim that the inconsistencies and the forger's clumsiness amount to a disgrace ('Desavouierung der Fiktion', 10).
16 Compare Peirano 2012, 3 on the self-conscious efforts of fakes to hint at their own forgery.
17 Thus, they strike the 'fictionality pact' between author and reader 'in which the requirement of factual reporting was suspended' (Ehrman 2013, 133).
18 My contribution focuses on the collection's relationship to the *Epistulae Morales*, not to Paul's letters because it seems to engage with Seneca's *Letters* in a more striking fashion. For the pseudepigraphy's allusion to the apostle's letters see e.g. Krauter 2009; Ramelli 2014.

I shall analyse two elements of the collection that lay bare its fictionality:
1. the text's relationship to Seneca's *Epistulae Morales*: the pseudepigraphic collection adopts certain elements of the historical Seneca's letters in order to create a plausible setting and narrative. However, the *anonymus* changes signi-ficant features of the master text and tries to fill some of its gaps, thus making their own innovative contribution to the *Epistulae Morales* and presenting the pseudepigraphy as a continuation of them.
2. the meta-discourse on letter-writing and reading: the *anonymus* shows an extraordinary interest in the technical aspects of letter-writing, signalling that the collection is as much about providing the reader with an epistolary manual as it is about the friendship between the philosopher and the apostle. The collection repeatedly highlights Seneca's and Paul's interest in reading each other's works, presenting them not so much as real, historical persons but as literary characters who do not really know each other but have only read about each other.

1 The apocryphal exchange and Seneca's *Epistulae Morales*

In the first letter of the exchange, "Seneca" fills in "Paul" about a meeting that took place the day before:[19]

> *Credo tibi, Paule, nuntiatum quid heri cum Lucilio nostro de apocrifis et aliis rebus habuerimus. Erant enim quidam disciplinarum tuarum comites mecum. Nam in hortos Sallustianos secesseramus, quo loco occasione nostri alio tendentes hi de quibus dixi uisis nobis adiuncti sunt. Certe quod tui praesentiam optauimus, et hoc scias uolo: libello tuo lecto, id est de pluribus aliquas litteras quas ad aliquam ciuitatem seu caput prouinciae direxisti mira exhortatione uitam moralem continentes, usquequaque refecti sumus. Quos sensus non puto ex te dictos, sed per te, certe aliquando ex te et per te. Tanta enim maiestas earum est rerum tantaque generositate clarent, ut uix suffecturas putem aetates hominum quae his institui perficique possint. Bene te ualere, frater, cupio.*

> I believe that you have been informed, Paul, of the discussion which my friend Lucilius and I held yesterday concerning the apocrypha and other matters: for some of the followers of your teachings were with me. We had retired to the gardens of Sallust, and it was

---

[19] In order to distinguish between the historical and the pseudepigraphic Senecas, Pauls and Neros, I shall use quotation marks when I discuss the Seneca, Paul and Nero of the apocryphal exchange, no quotation marks when I refer to the historical Seneca, Paul and Nero.

our good fortune that these disciples whom I have mentioned saw us there and joined us, although they were on their way elsewhere. You may be sure that we wished that you, too, had been present, and I also want you to know this: when we had read one of your treatises, that is to say one of the many letters of wondrous exhortation to an upright life which you have sent to some city or to the capital of a province, we were completely reinvigorated. These thoughts, I believe, were expressed not by you, but through you; though sometimes they were expressed both by you and through you; for they are so lofty and brilliant with noble sentiments that in my opinion whole generations of men could hardly be enough to become established and perfected in these matters. I wish you good health, brother.[20]

The short note makes clear straightaway that the pseudepigrapher was more concerned with the letter form than with content. Instead of letting the reader in on the secrets (*apocrifi*) that "Seneca" discussed with "Paul's" friends, the pseudepigrapher presents a polite little letter whose main function is to establish the idea that Seneca and Paul knew each other and were on friendly terms with each other. The mention of the *apocrifi* almost teases the reader whose curiosity about these mysterious insights is disappointed. His preoccupation with the formal aspects of letter writing shines through in his knowledge and mastery of epistolary etiquette, such as his emphasis on friendship — declared by Demetrius as the main purpose of epistolography (*Eloc.* 232) — and having "Seneca" express the wish that "Paul" were present to engage in conversation with him, a trope of ancient letter writing. The *anonymus* also conforms to the idea that a letter ought to be short, perhaps the one epistolary feature that all ancient letter writing experts can agree on (cf. e.g. Demetr. *Eloc.* 228; Julius Victor *Ars Rhetorica* 27: *in familiaribus litteris primo breuitas obseruanda*). He implicitly explains the reason for the letter's brevity by having "Seneca" mention that "Paul's" friends have already reported on their meeting; hence, it suffices for the letter to provide only a very brief description of the events and to explain the circumstances in which "Seneca" found himself. While the strange emptiness of the first letter might be disappointing to readers yearning to find out more about "Seneca's" thoughts and insights, the exchange of polite pleasantries does make sense within the narrative of the letter exchange: there is no need for "Seneca" to explain to "Paul" what he already knows.

What makes this letter interesting for my argument is the setting that "Seneca" describes. Through the details of "Seneca's" meeting with "Paul's" friends, the pseudepigrapher sets out the text's relationship to Seneca's *Epistulae Morales* by paying tribute to them and by adapting some of their main features to the

---

[20] All translations of the apocryphal exchange are taken from Barlow 1938.

world imagined in the pseudepigraphy. The inclusion of Lucilius, the addressee of *De Prouidentia*, *Naturales Quaestiones* and, most significantly, the *Epistles*, demonstrates the *anonymus*' familiarity with Seneca's writings. While the extent and depth of his knowledge is debatable,[21] the author of the exchange certainly knew at least the letters well enough to know that Lucilius plays a key role in the *Epistulae Morales*.[22] The possessive pronoun *noster* in *cum Lucilio nostro* is not just meant to designate "Lucilius" as a friend of both "Seneca's" and "Paul's", as Fürst 2006, 45 points out, but might be an allusion to Seneca's habit of adding *noster* to the names of friends, Stoics and important Romans, such as Vergil (a habit that is so prominent that even someone without intimate knowledge of the collection will notice it).[23] The letter's scenario bears a striking resemblance to Seneca's *Ep.* 64 in which he meets up with some friends and reads a book by Quintus Sextius the Elder with them, accompanied by lively conversation.[24] The letter opens with the astonishing remark that Lucilius had been together with Seneca the day before (64.1: *fuisti here nobiscum*) which, as Seneca hastens to add, is not meant literally but metaphorically: for Lucilius is always with him (*mecum enim semper es*). It is almost as if the pseudepigrapher had taken the passage literally by having "Seneca" and "Lucilius" meet up with each other. This is how far the parallels to Seneca's *Letters* go, let us now turn to the differences and the pseudepigrapher's innovation.

The collection immediately and strikingly reworks a key feature of the *Epistulae Morales*, even as its inclusion might seem subtle or banal: that is, the pseudepigrapher's decision to eliminate the physical distance between "Seneca" and "Lucilius" and to make them appear together. This poses a significant change from the *Epistulae Morales* in the course of which it transpires that Lucilius has taken up a procuratorship in Sicily and that he is far away from Seneca, whose exact whereabouts are never revealed (more on that below). While Seneca repeatedly laments his separation from Lucilius and wishes that he could be together with him in person,[25] his wish is never fulfilled. Regrettable

---

21 Since the apocryphal exchange is almost devoid of explicit allusions to Seneca's works it is difficult to judge how well the pseudepigrapher knew them. Smolak 2010's close reading of the exchange argues that the *anonymus* has read the *Epistulae Morales*.
22 Krauter 2009, 767–768 doubts that the pseudepigrapher imitates the *Epistulae Morales* by referring to Lucilius, but interprets it as a form of name-dropping: by mentioning Lucilius' name, the anonymus gestures to his audience's familiarity with Seneca's letter collection.
23 See, for example, *Ep.* 20.9 and 21.5 with Soldo 2021 *ad loc.* and Mollea 2019, 328.
24 Davies 2014, 88–90 argues that Seneca in this letter 'models reading for the reader, revealing the types of things he valued in a text, which in turn show the type of texts he valued'.
25 Cf. e.g. *Ep.* 49.1–2.

though the distance may be, it does keep the letter collection going: for, the distance between them is a central conceit of the letter collection as it necessitates a written exchange. The fact that sender and addressee are apart from each other is the very reason for the collection's existence. In the fictional world of the apocryphal exchange, the meeting must have taken place before or after Seneca has written the *Epistulae Morales*; most likely before as Seneca clearly writes his letters in old age and as it is unlikely that he lived much longer after finishing them.[26] By imagining that "Seneca" and "Lucilius" are together in Rome, the pseudepigrapher does two things to the fictional conceit of the *Epistulae Morales*: he takes away the need for "Seneca" and "Lucilius" to exchange letters and thus frees "Seneca" to address "Paul" instead, and he develops the narrative of Seneca's letter collection further by filling the gaping hole of Lucilius' absence and thus imagining a time and place in which they are (finally) together. For anyone familiar with the *Epistulae Morales*, the pseudepigraphy poses a very interesting question: *what if* Seneca and Lucilius met before or after writing all these letters?[27] What would their relationship be like without having to rely on written means of communications, what would they do together, what would they talk about? But the pseudepigrapher is not interested in sharing details of such a scenario and merely takes it for granted that Seneca meeting up with Lucilius is a plausible backdrop for depicting the friendship that actually matters to him, namely the friendship between the philosopher and the apostle.

The fact that "Seneca" is in Rome is another feature in which the pseudepigraphy diverges from the *Epistulae Morales*. As mentioned above, Seneca very rarely specifies in his letters *where* he writes; the most famous exceptions are *Ep.* 53, written after a visit to the bay of Naples and a bout of heavy seasickness, and *Ep.* 56 in which he describes the cacophonous sounds of the baths reaching his accommodation above them.[28] Surprisingly, Rome is mostly absent from his letters, as Catharine Edwards has shown.[29] For the purpose of the pseudepigraphy, however, trying to make us believe that Seneca and Paul could have met and could have even been friends, Rome is a sensible choice. The anonymous author seems to know very well that Seneca's and Paul's biographies overlapped, that they both lived in Rome and that they could have

---

[26] Seneca portrays himself as an old man close to death, see e.g. *Ep.* 12 and 29 with Soldo 2021, xix–xx; xxviii–xxix. He probably wrote the *Epistulae Morales* between 62 and 65 CE, shortly before his forced suicide.
[27] On other what if-scenarios in the exchange see Fuhrer forthcoming.
[28] On these letters and their geography see the commentary by Berno 2006.
[29] Edwards 2018.

potentially known each other.³⁰ The restrictions of the letter format, however, mean that "Seneca" and "Paul" never meet in the course of their letters, as that would render the letters themselves obsolete.

Not only is the "Seneca" of the pseudepigraphy in Rome, his exact location is also revealed: the *horti Sallustiani*. As other contributors to this volume have observed, references to and descriptions of specific places play an important role in letters; they can make a letter look more 'real', functioning as markers of a letter's authenticity, or, in turn, less 'real', hinting at a letter's fictionality.³¹ As for our letter collection, the pseudepigrapher certainly meant to add credibility to his letter by referring to the Gardens of Sallust. The mention of a specific place makes the letter more detailed and allows the reader to imagine the scene more easily. But there might be more to it: the reference to the Gardens of Sallust, which became the property of the Imperial household after Sallust's death (Tacitus describes how Nero walks through them in *Ann.* 13.47),³² provides a framework for the text's depiction of "Seneca's" relationship to "Nero" and subtly prepares the reader for one of the main plot lines of the apocryphal exchange: "Seneca's" and "Paul's" interactions with the Emperor and their struggle to communicate with him correctly.

With bravado, the pseudepigrapher tackles the most intriguing gap left behind by the *Epistulae Morales*: the conspicuous absence of the Emperor. Seneca's letter collection not once refers to him by his name nor does it contain any (overtly) political comments or gossip. However, some remarks can be read as cryptic allusions to, and sharp criticism of, Nero.³³ Needless to say, Seneca's veiled criticism requires a good deal of patience from his reader as well as an ability to read between the lines, and only a reader with intimate knowledge of the letters will be able to decode his hidden messages. Thus, it is thrilling when "Seneca" more or less openly mentions "Nero" and when he adds the insight that is so desperately missing in the historical Seneca's letters. The pseudepigrapher might not have excelled in imitating the style of the *Epistulae Morales* but he did very well to notice Nero's absence and to add his own view on Seneca's relationship to his student; his imagination adds insight and detail to the parts where the *Epistulae* remain silent.

---

30 Hine 2017 sketches out the biographical similarities between Seneca and Paul.
31 As Bocciolini Palagi 1985, 74–75 points out, meeting outdoors for a philosophical conversation is a literary topos and draws parallels to Cicero's dialogues.
32 On the passage see also Barlow 1938, 83.
33 Cf. e.g. *Ep.* 7.5; 14.3; 15.7; 21.5; 115.12–13; see Soldo 2021 *ad loc.*

References to "Nero", and his wife "Poppaea Sabina", run through the entire apocryphal exchange between "Seneca" and "Paul", amounting to a narrative that gives the otherwise disparate collection some cohesion.[34] The "Nero" 'plot' traces the significant change in how "Seneca" and "Paul" view the Emperor and depicts their growing disapproval and fear of him, similar to the pseudepigraphic topos of a philosopher writing to a tyrant, as for instance in Plato's *Letters*.[35] At first, both the apostle and the philosopher are full of praise for the Emperor: in *Ep.* 2, "Paul's" first letter in the exchange, "Paul" admiringly refers to "Seneca" as *magister tanti principis* (the teacher of so great a ruler) and thus not only flatters his addressee but the Emperor as well. "Seneca" portrays "Nero" as a reasonable person who shows great interest in, and openness about, Christianity (*Ep.* 7):

> *Et ne quid tibi, frater, subripiam aut conscientiae meae debeam, confiteor Augustum sensibus tuis motum. Cui perlecto uirtutis in te exordio, ista uox fuit: mirari eum posse ut qui non legitime imbutus sit taliter sentiat.*
>
> And in order that I may not keep anything secret from you, brother, or have a guilty conscience, I confess that Augustus was affected by your sentiments. When my treatise on the virtue that is in you was read to him, this was his reply, that he was amazed that one whose education had not been regular could have such ideas.

The contrast with "Poppaea Sabina's" angry reaction to "Paul's" conversion to Christianity, which "Seneca" addresses in *Ep.* 5 (*indignatio dominae, quod a ritu et secta ueteri recesseris et aliorsum conuerteris*, 'the displeasure of our empress because you have withdrawn from your old rite and creed and are turning elsewhere'), shines an even more positive light on the Emperor's magnanimity. When "Paul" cautiously admonishes "Seneca" not to divulge any more information about his religious views to the Emperor out of fear of "Poppaea Sabina's" anger and influence over him (*Ep.* 8), the exchange suddenly turns to strong criticism of "Nero". Thus, *Ep.* 9 contains an astonishing remark:

> *Scio te non tam tui causa commotum litteris quas ad te de editione epistularum tuarum Caesari feci quam natura rerum, quae ita mentes hominum ab omnibus artibus et moribus rectis reuocat, ut non hodie admirer, quippe ut is qui multis documentis hoc iam notissimum habeam.*
>
> I know that it was not so much for your own sake that you were disturbed when I wrote you that I had read my letters to Caesar as because of the nature of things, which sum-

---

34 See also Jackson's contribution to this volume which discusses a plot spanning multiple letters and making the Euripidean letter collection more cohesive.

35 I am grateful to Claire Rachel Jackson for pointing me in the direction of the Platonic letters.

mons the minds of men away from all upright pursuits and practices — so that I am not astonished in the present instance, particularly because I have learned this well from many sure proofs.

Though presented as a general comment on human nature, the observation on humans' propensity to do what is morally wrong is a thinly veiled criticism of "Nero". "Seneca" even draws on his own bad experiences with the Emperor, revealing that he has many pieces of evidence (*multis documentis*) that prove "Nero's" immorality and, ultimately, untrustworthiness.[36] "Seneca's" sudden change of heart is somewhat clumsy and does not sufficiently explain how the Emperor's loyal admirer, who trusted him enough to discuss "Paul's" religious beliefs with him, turns into a sharp critic and why he indirectly admits his failure as a teacher, not having succeeded in convincing his student to lead a moral life.[37]

The strongest criticism of "Nero" appears in letter 11, in which "Seneca" laments the anti-Christian and anti-Jewish resentments in Rome:

Aue, mi Paule carissime. Putasne me haut contristari et non luctuosum esse quod de innocentia uestra subinde supplicium sumatur? Dehinc quod tam duros tamque obnoxios uos reatui omnis populus iudicet, putans a uobis effici quicquid in urbe contrarium fit? Sed feramus aequo animo et utamor foro quod sors concessit, donec inuicta felicitas finem malis imponat. Tulit et priscorum aetas Macedonem, Philippi filium, Cyros Darium Dionysium, nostra quoque Gaium Caesarem, quibus quicquid libuit licuit. Incendium urbs Romana manifeste saepe unde patiatur constat. Sed si effari humilitas humana potuisset quid causae sit et impune in his tenebris loqui liceret, iam omnes omnia uiderent. Christiani et Iudaei quasi machinatores incendii — pro! — supplicio adfecti fieri solent. Grassator iste quisquis est, cui uoluptas carnificina est et mendacium uelamentum, tempori suo destinatus est, et ut optimus quisque unum pro multis datum est caput, ita et hic deuotus pro omnibus igni cremabitur. Centum triginta duae domus, insulae quattuor milia sex diebus arsere; septimus pausam dedit. Bene te ualere, frater, opto.
Data V Kal. Apr. Frugi et Basso consulibus

---

36 As Claire Rachel Jackson points out to me, this detail bears striking similarity with Petronius who, according to Tac. *Ann.* 16.19, detailed Nero's debauchery in his will and embarrassed him even after his death.

37 *Ep.* 14 even goes so far as to say that "Seneca" had little influence over the Emperor and his friends and that his pedagogical efforts were in vain: *...sophiam, quam propemodum adeptus regi temporali eiusque domesticis atque fidis amicis insinuabis, quibus aspera et incapabilis erit persuasio, cum plerique illorum minime flectuntur insinuationibus tuis*, '...wisdom which you have almost achieved and which you will present to the temporal king and to the members of his household and to his trusted friends, whom you will find it difficult or nearly impossible to persuade, since many of them are not at all influenced by your presentations'.

> Greetings, my beloved Paul. Do you think I am not saddened and grieved because you innocent people are repeatedly punished? Or because the whole populace believes you so implacable and so liable to guilt, thinking that every misfortune in the city is brought about by you? But let us endure it calmly and take advantage of whatever opportunity fortune allots to us, until happiness all-victorious gives us release from our troubles. Earlier ages endured the Macedonian, the son of Philip, the Cyruses, Darius, Dionysius; our own age put up with Gaius Caesar; all of them were free to do whatever they pleased. The source of the frequent fires which the city of Rome suffers is sufficiently clear. But if lowly people had been allowed to tell the reason and if it were permitted to speak safely in these times of ill-fortune, everyone would now understand everything. Christians and Jews, charged with responsibility for the fire — alas! — are being put to death, as is usually the case. That ruffian, whoever he is, whose pleasure is murdering and whose refuge is lying, is marked for his time of reckoning, and just as one good man gave his life for many, so he shall be sacrificed for all and burned by fire. One hundred and thirty-two private houses and four thousand apartment-houses burned in six days; the seventh day they gave respite. I hope that you are in good health, brother. Written March 28 in the consulship of Frugi and Bassus.

While the letter does not explicitly use Nero's name it does make abundantly clear that "Seneca" believes that his former student is behind the fire that wrecked Rome in 64 CE: "Seneca's" admission that it is 'obvious' (*constat*) where the fire originated comes right after a historical comparison that lists unrestrained rulers and ends with Caligula (*Gaium Caesarem*), Nero's pre-predecessor and notoriously bad Emperor. The letter also alleges that "Nero" used Christians and Jews as scapegoats. In his portrayal of "Nero" as an arsonist and merciless persecutor of Christians, the pseudepigrapher echoes rumours that had sprung up immediately after the fire of 64.[38] After Nero's death, his reputation underwent a rapid decline and he was seen as a cruel tyrant and bad Emperor.[39]

Unlike Fürst who argues that the pseudepigraphy's contradictory views on the Emperor are a sign of the author's artistic shortcomings,[40] I argue that "Nero's" portrayal is not inconsistent but that it undergoes change in the collection and that his development from friend to foe fits in very well within the fictional setting of the exchange. From "Paul's" view, it does make sense to be apprehensive about the Imperial family as he is part of a threatened religious minority. "Seneca", on the other hand, has to express a more positive view of the Emperor, given that the letters emphasise his role as "Nero's" teacher. "Seneca's" growing concern over his pupil's character and behaviour may appear rather abrupt-

---

38 E.g., Ps.-Sen. *Oct.* 831; Plin. *NH* 17.5; Tac. *Ann.* 15.44.2.
39 On Nero's portrayal as *malus princeps* see Cordes 2017; Malik 2020; Schulz 2019.
40 Fürst 1998 and 2006. Less scathing is the verdict of Bocciolini Palagi 1985 who refers to "Nero's" depiction in the exchange as ambivalent.

ly in the exchange but mirrors the historical Seneca's estrangement from Nero. The "Nero" 'plot' fast forwards the reader through the relationship between the real Seneca and the real Nero that went from initial optimism to distrust, led to Seneca's withdrawal and involvement in the Pisonian conspiracy and, finally, to his forced suicide. With his forgery, the *anonymus* aims to give his readers an (allegedly) personal insight into the deteriorating relationship that cannot be found anywhere else. The "Nero" 'plot' also mirrors the later historiographical assessment of Nero which regarded the first five years of his reign as a success before it turned into a disaster.[41]

Just as suddenly as the pseudepigraphy turned to sharp criticism of "Nero" the discourse disappears and the letters return to assurances of "Seneca's" and "Paul's" mutual friendship and to their discussions of epistolary etiquette.

2 Meta-epistolary discourse: writing and reading in the apocryphal exchange

The collection shows great interest in letter-writing and in reading, which in particular has not received enough attention from scholars. My discussion of *Ep.* 1 (see above) has already shown the *anonymus*' mastery of epistolary *topoi* when his "Seneca" emphasises his friendship to "Paul" and expresses his desire to meet him in person. A similar sentiment is expressed in one of "Paul's" letters in which he reciprocates the longing for an in-person encounter and writes that his friend's letters conjure up his presence (*Ep.* 4): ...*Quotienscumque litteras tuas audio, praesentiam tui cogito nec aliud existimo quam omni tempore te nobiscum esse* ...('As often as I hear your letters, I think that you are present and I imagine nothing else than that you are continually with us').[42] They also discuss technical aspects of letter-writing, as can be found in epistolary handbooks, giving the impression that the collection might double as a manual that is intended for an audience beyond the apostle and the philosopher:[43] in *Ep.* 2, "Paul" — rather unnecessarily — explains to "Seneca" how to choose the right messenger to deliver a letter (*Scis enim quando et per quem et quo tempore et cui quid dari committique debeat*, 'You know when and by whom and at what time

---

41 Bocciolini Palagi 1985, 42.
42 Cf. e.g. Sen. *Ep.* 32.1: *uerba dare non potes: tecum sum.*
43 On the difficult relationship between letter-writing handbooks and letter-writing see Claire Rachel Jackson's contribution to this volume.

and to whom a thing should be given or intrusted'); the same letter also alludes to one of the elementary rules of letter-writing, namely to adapt the letter's style to the recipient's social status and level of education (*personae qualitatem respicio*, 'I pay attention to a person' status', see e.g. Dem. *Eloc.* 234; Cic. *Fam.* 2.4.1); *Ep.* 6 addresses the status of privacy, or lack thereof, in letter-writing as it hints at its potential interception (*De his quae scripsistis* (i.e. Seneca and Lucilius) *non licet harundine et atramento eloqui*, 'I may not speak with pen and ink concerning what you have written to me'). Two further aspects of letter-writing, the correct address and the dating of a letter, play a prominent role in the second half of the exchange: whenever "Paul" addresses "Seneca" he puts his own name after his addressee's, a habit that became popular in the second century CE (one of several anachronisms that makes out the collection as a fake). In letter 10, "Paul" even suggests that his name should take up the last position in the letter, as a sign of his humility and respect for "Seneca" to which "Seneca" replies in letter 12 that the apostle is worthy of the first position in the letter, i.e. the position occupied by the addressee's name. The dating of letters is not discussed explicitly but it is conspicuous that *Ep.* 10–14 all end with a precise date, specifying the day and the consuls. Some of these dates are incorrect (*Ep.* 10 and 11), some mention the *consules suffecti*, probably as a means of experimenting with different ways of dating a letter (*Ep.* 13 and 14; see Fürst 2006, 61), and one date disturbs the strict chronology of the exchange (*Ep.* 12), all of which are signs that the dates serve no other purpose than to demonstrate to the reader how to date a letter. They allow the readers to see the rules of letter-writing applied in practice.

The letters have a curious interest in reading and present "Seneca" and "Paul" as readers of each other's works, so much so, I argue, that the metadiscourse on reading in *Ep.* 1, 3 and 7 reveals their own fictionality. The exchange suggests that the philosopher and the apostle only know each other through reading their works and that their friendship is exclusively based on written communication: they have never, and will never, meet in person, only in their works. "Seneca" and "Paul" are not presented as figures made of bone and flesh but as authors whose inner lives are only accessible through their writings. In this regard, the apocryphal exchange bears great resemblance to the *Epistulae Morales* in which, as Mark Davies has shown, Seneca builds a relationship 'with his reader (that) is consciously mediated by texts'.[44] The letter collection shows a remarkable preoccupation with reading: what one ought to

---

[44] Davies 2014, 75.

read, how one ought to read, with whom one ought to read.⁴⁵ Seneca's fixation on reading finds its way into the pseudepigrapic exchange, albeit in a more pragmatic form and without the philosophical and pedagogical implications that it has in the *Epistles*.

The collection's focus on reading becomes apparent already in the first letter (quoted in full above) in which "Seneca" reveals that he read one of "Paul's" letters together with his friends: *libello tuo lecto, id est de pluribus aliquas litteras quas ad aliquam ciuitatem seu caput prouinciae direxisti mira exhortatione uitam moralem continentes* ('when we had read one of your treatises, that is to say one of the many letters of wondrous exhortation to an upright life which you have sent to some city or to the capital of a province').⁴⁶ It is plausible that the moral exhortations of "Paul's" letter would arouse the philosopher's interest, but perhaps less plausible that he believes "Paul" to be God's mouthpiece (*Quos sensus non puto ex te dictos, sed per te, certe aliquando ex te et per te*, 'These thoughts, I believe, were expressed not by you, but through you; though sometimes they were expressed both by you and through you'). What is remarkable about the gathering in the Gardens of Sallust is that "Seneca" gains access to "Paul's" beliefs and thoughts only through his writing, not through conversations with his friends who might provide information that cannot be found in his letters. This jars somewhat with the expressed desire to meet him in person; a meeting or a conversation does not seem to add any further insight or any further guidance towards a moral life, and the letter even seems to suggest that (*Tanta enim maiestas earum est rerum tantaque generositate clarent, ut uix suffecturas putem aetates hominum quae his institui perficique possint*, 'for they are so lofty and brilliant with noble sentiments that in my opinion whole generations of men could hardly be enough to become established and perfected in these matters'). The "Seneca" of the apocryphal exchange is happy enough to *read* what "Paul" has to say, both in the letters addressed to various cities and in the letters addressed to him (and Lucilius). The Seneca of the *Epistulae Morales*, however, repeatedly emphasises that moral instruction which is mediated through writing can never fully replace or even come close to the effect of direct instruction and learning from a teacher's behaviour and everyday life

---

45 Davies 2014, 73: 'Seneca appears conscious of how he would like to be read and he seeks to shape this by advising his reader on how to read philosophical works. He situates himself in a constellation of philosophical writers: his relationship to previous writers is variously imagined, and the reader is invited to relate to Seneca in similar ways'.
46 The communal reading is reminiscent of the scenario in Sen. *Ep.* 64; see the discussion above.

(e.g. *Ep.* 6.6; 75.2). Here, the pseudepigraphy diverges again from its master text. Given that "Seneca" and "Paul" never meet in the duration of their letter exchange, the collection's emphasis on exhortation through reading takes on an even greater importance. Moreover, it justifies the whole pseudepigraphic enterprise: if the pseudepigrapher had believed letters to be inferior to direct communication and in-person meetings, he would not have chosen the letter format for his work. Obviously, readers of the pseudepigraphy attached cultural value to it since they regarded it as worthy of being preserved and read.

More curious is "Seneca's" desire to read his own and "Paul's" works to the Emperor, at best a willing or indifferent listener, at worst a danger to their lives. *Ep.* 3 imagines a scenario in which the philosopher would read his own books to "Nero" and discuss them with "Paul":

> *Quaedam uolumina ordinaui et diuisionibus suis statum eis dedi. Ea quoque Caesari legere sum destinatus. Si modo fors prospere annuerit, ut nouas aures adferat, eris forsitan et tu praesens; sin, alias reddam tibi diem, ut hoc opus inuicem inspiciamus. Et possem non (prius) edere ei eam scripturam, nisi prius tecum conferrem, si modo impune hoc fieri potuisset; hoc ut scires, non te praeteriri. Vale, Paule carissime.*

> I have arranged some of my works and set them in order according to their proper divisions. I also intend to read them to Caesar. If only fate is kind enough to cause him to show renewed interest, perhaps you will be there also; if not, I will at some other time set a day on which we may examine this work together. I could not show him this writing without first conferring with you, if only it were possible to do so without getting into trouble, so that you may be sure of this, that you are not being forgotten. Farewell, dearest Paul.

The letter casts "Seneca" in the role of a writer, busy finishing and editing his books which are neither named nor specified otherwise, and "Paul" in the role of a reader, thus establishing a balance between them: "Seneca" is familiar with some of "Paul's" letters and "Paul" is asked to read "Seneca's" books. The letter even goes so far as to suggest that "Seneca" cannot finish his books without the apostle's advice, certainly a flattering gesture. Equally flattering is the idea that "Paul" should be present when "Seneca" reads from his work in the Emperor's presence, attributing him the same importance and status as the Emperor.

Whatever the intention is behind inviting "Paul" to his audience with the Emperor, "Seneca" certainly did not expect to improve his style through "Paul's" feedback as the following letter addressed to "Paul" and "Theophilus" (*Ep.* 7) makes clear:

> *Profiteor bene me acceptum lectione litterarum tuarum quas Galatis Corinthiis Achaeis misisti, et ita inuicem uiuamus, ut etiam cum honore diuino eas exhibes. Spiritus enim*

sanctus in te et super excelsos sublimi ore satis uenerabiles sensus exprimit. Vellem itaque, cum res eximias proferas, ut maiestati earum cultus sermonis non desit. Et ne quid tibi, frater, subripiam aut conscientiae meae debeam, confiteor Augustum sensibus tuis motum. Cui perlecto uirtutis in te exordio, ista uox fuit: mirari eum posse ut qui non legitime imbutus sit taliter sentiat. Cui ego respondi solere deos ore innocentium effari, haut eorum qui praeuaricare doctrina sua quid possint. Et dato ei exemplo Vatieni hominis rusticuli, cui uiri duo adpararuerunt in agro Reatino, qui postea Castor et Pollux sunt nominati, satis instructus uidetur. Vale.

I admit that I enjoyed reading your letters to the Galatians, to the Corinthians and to the Achaeans, and may our relations be like that religious awe which you manifest in these letters. For the holy spirit that is in you, surpassing the highest, with lofty speech utters thoughts worthy of reverence. Therefore I wish, since you have such excellent matters to propose, that refinement of language might not be lacking to the majesty of your theme. And in order that I may not keep anything secret from you, brother, or have a guilty conscience, I confess that the Augustus was affected by your sentiments. When my treatise on the virtue that is in you was read to him, this was his reply, that he was amazed that one whose education had not been regular could have such ideas. I answered him that the gods are accustomed to speak through the mouths of the innocent and not of those who are enabled by their learning to distort anything. When I gave him the example of Vatienus, a farmer, to whom appeared in the territory of Reate two men who later were found to be Castor and Pollux, he seemed thoroughly enlightened. Farewell.

"Paul's" vocabulary and overly plain style become a constant topic in the exchange. While the first letter first praised the loftiness (*maiestas*) of his writings the exchange soon admonishes him to improve his style (see above in *Ep.* 7). The gentle advice quickly turns to criticism and admonition as "Seneca's" *Ep.* 9 accompanies a thesaurus (*librum de uerborum copia*) which ought to provide stylistic help, and *Ep.* 13 outright asks "Paul" to pay more attention to using correct grammar.

3 One more observation (in lieu of a conclusion)

I have argued that the apocryphal exchange between "Seneca" and "Paul" marks its fictionality through allusions to Seneca's *Epistulae Morales* and through its meta-epistolary discourse. Both of these elements concern the content of the collection. But even before we have read any of the letters we can tell that they are not authentic because of one formal feature: the fact that the collection contains both sides of the exchange. Fictional and pseudepigraphic collections are the only ancient letter collections that systematically include replies from others and that provide us with rare evidence of complete letter exchanges.⁴⁷ We can only speculate as to why these collections tend to be complete but there seems to be a deep seated desire and curiosity in readers to get to know the whole story. The only way to satisfy them is to create a letter exchange that shows both sides, and to include both letters and replies. The pseudepigrapher satisfies this curiosity by presenting the collection as a to and fro which includes a reply to every letter (except *Ep.* 11 and 12 which are both addressed to Paul) and thus develops a narrative (however weak the narrative is at times). The inclusion of both sides of the letter exchange makes the pseudepigraphy markedly different from Seneca's *Epistulae Morales* which do not include his addressee's replies. Even though Lucilius' imaginary replies are crucial for understanding the *Epistulae Morales*, he takes on the role of the passive recipient of increasingly long letters and remains a rather colourless character throughout the collection. The exclusion of his letters from the exchange (if they ever existed) is to blame for that. The exchange between "Seneca" and "Paul", on the other hand, presents a more equal, more dynamic and less restrictive relationship in which both sides see eye to eye.

But even a complete letter exchange that gives us both sides of the epistolary dialogue, fills in so many gaps, further develops the narrative of its foundational text and creates a new story, still manages to leave us with many more questions and new gaps that someone else will need to fill.

---

47 Aelian's letter collection, for example, opens with some individual letters that receive no reply (*Ep.* 1–6) but regularly includes responses from there on (*Ep.* 7–8; 11–12; 13–16). In a similar vein, Ovid's *Heroides* start off as a one-sided collection, focusing on the female letter writers who long for their far away husbands or accuse their partners of abandoning them. But with letter 16, the letters morph into a two-sided collection where the women's letters are followed by the men's replies.

Part IV: **Ekphrastic Fictions**

Ruth Morello
Fictions in the Real World: Language and Reality in Cicero's Letters

Abstract: This paper explores the contributions of imagery, temporal ambiguity, and intertextuality in creating fictionalising colour in Cicero's *Ad Familiares*. An opening study of 'epistolary' fictionality in Ovid's *Tristia* 4.2 lays groundwork for subsequent discussions of fictionalising scenarios in Cicero's *Ad Fam.* 7.1 and *Ad Fam.* 9.2, of Caelius's theatrical imagery in his persona as Cicero's political 'futurologist' in Book 8, and finally of the ancient editor's use of thematic sequences that extend across whole books to amplify the fictionalising qualities of individual letters. The outcome of the creative manipulations of perceived reality in Cicero's letters is an ambiguous, potentially fictionalising (but not necessarily *fictional*) space for epistolographical communication. In that space, life itself is represented as a staged performance, in which the most 'fictional' material paradoxically expresses the 'real' world of the writer himself.

Keywords: intertextuality, temporality, spectacle, theatricality, humour

> *The future is there...looking back at us. Trying to make sense of the fiction we will have become.*
>
> William Gibson, *Pattern Recognition*

In *Tristia* 4.2, after two or three miserable years by the Black Sea, Ovid imagines triumphal celebrations in Rome for Tiberius' German campaigns.[1] The triumph

---

I am grateful to audiences in Cambridge and Leeds for their responses to earlier versions of this paper, and to Olivia Elder and Serena Cammoranesi for illuminating discussions of fictionalising spaces in letters. Owen Hodkinson has generously shared unpublished work on metafiction in fictional letter collections that has especially influenced my view of how the inherent metafictionality of some epistolary tropes supports fictionalising modes in authentic letters and letter collections.

1 On *Tr.* 4.2, see Feldherr 2010, 160–167; Beard 2004; Oliensis 2004, 308–313; Hardie 2002, 309; Heyworth 1995, 145–148. The real thing may, of course, never take place, and even has an inherent fictionality: see, e.g., Beard 2004, 117: 'the triumph is now largely celebrated by *not being celebrated*.' On the multiple roles of the poet (as audience for the report of the triumph, as spectator, as narrator and as captive), see Feldherr 2010, 165–166. Other imaginary recreations of public events may be found at Ovid *Pont.* 2.1, 4.5 and 4.9.

https://doi.org/10.1515/9783111308128-009

is 'fake news', the poet's own imaginative creation, for which he is both author and audience:

> *at mihi **fingendo** tantum longeque remotis*
> *auribus hic fructus percipiendus erit.*
> (*Tr.* 4.2.67–68)
>
> But as for me, this reward must be enjoyed **in imagination** only and with ears exiled far away.

In a scene set just before the triumphal parade itself, tenses and moods are manipulated to create a plausible, but fabricated, event. The opening 'now already' (***iam** fera ...Germania*) quickly dissolves into hypothetical subjunctives: garlands are *perhaps* up on the Palatine (*uelentur fortasse*), preliminary sacrifices *may be* underway and the imperial family are *probably* about to make their offerings to the gods.[2] The city audience's experience of the celebration (19–26) lies in the future (*poterit spectare, leget, uidebit, cernet, quaeret, referet*), when Caesar himself (as addressee, internal observer and star of his own triumph) will ride to the Capitol (47–56). Nothing in this scene is 'real', and the elegy rehearses the kind of thing that happens on such occasions, but the poet still anticipates that this fantasy triumph will one day be authenticated by some anonymous traveller's report of the event (4.2.69–72).[3] *Tr.* 4.2 is, one might say, a deliberately invented rumour that plays upon the lengthy gaps in ancient epistolary communication that allowed space for letters to transmit error and speculation, as well as factual news.[4] It also exploits the epistolary trope that a letter writer can 'see' what is happening at the other end of the correspondence (4.2.57–64).[5]

---

[2] Cf. Lee 2008 on Tibullus' use of subjunctives to create an alternative subjective narrative mode of imagination and wishfulness that is in tension with an external narrative of reality; cf. Miller 1999.

[3] On *Tr.* 4.2 as Ovid's 'failed fantasy', see Kennedy 2016, 52.

[4] Rumours can form a rich seam of potentially fictional epistolary content. E.g. in *Fam.* 8.1, a letter stuffed with rumours of all kinds, the most striking of which is one about Cicero's death that Caelius (knowing its falseness) plays up for comic effect: the *subrostrani* who have manufactured and spread the rumour of Cicero's death are staged here as narrators of the fiction that his personal narrative has ended — a humorous touch to open a book of spirited letters to the still living Cicero. On the rumours about Caesar's campaign in Gaul in this same letter, and on Caelius' particular skill in distinguishing fact from rumour, see Cammoranesi 2022, 106–109.

[5] E.g. Sen. *Ep.* 55.11: *uideo te, mi Lucili; cum maxime audio. adeo tecum sum, ut dubitem, an incipiam non epistulas, sed codicillos tibi scribere* 'I see you, my dear Lucilius, and at this very moment I hear you; I am with you to such an extent that I hesitate whether I should not begin to write you notes instead of letters.'

The poem's fictionalising power is fuelled partly by the hypothetical subjunctives and the future tenses, but also by the interplay between different time streams. These include the imagined present, as the triumphal celebrations begin at Rome, and the anticipated future confirmation that the fictional triumph was real — and as Ovid described it — after all. There is also an implicit awareness of a further layer of the literary (and inherently fictional) past, when Ovid ascribes eyewitness commentary to self-proclaimed 'experts' in the imaginary crowd (4.2.37–46).[6] These mendacious man-splainers come straight from Ovid's own *Ars Amatoria* 1.217–238, where a young man in a triumphal crowd learns to impress a girl with feigned knowledge (*quae nescieris, ut bene nota refer*, 'and whatever you don't know, speak it as if you knew it well').[7] The deliberate over-confidence of the present indicative verbs that Ovid puts in the mouths of these viewers highlights the poem's crucial paradox: Ovid's invented (and characteristically unreliable) eyewitnesses are the most avowedly fictional element in the whole piece, and yet their commentary on the imaginary procession is implicitly the 'truth' that will one day be reported to the exiled poet. Ultimately, our twice-met know-it-all is the inventive poet himself whose exilic poem embroiders upon exiguous, potentially inaccurate information,[8] and spins 'truth-like' inventions that he paradoxically marks as the real thing (*uera... spectacula*, 4.2.65) to be viewed by the crowd that is there on the day (*praesens*).[9]

Cicero's correspondence might seem very different from such Ovidian inventions, stocked as it is with authoritative reports of senatorial decisions to restore foreign kings, accounts of the private conversations of eminent men, outlines of literary work planned or completed, news and instructions of all kinds, or requests for dinner or a hot bath at the end of a journey — real life, in other words, captured in documentary form, and claiming evidentiary truthful-

---

6 This invented commentary is itself framed by future tenses: 'some of the people *will inquire* the causes, the objects, the names, and others will answer, though they know all too little' (*quamuis nouerit illa parum*, 4.2.26).
7 Cf. *A.A.* 1.227–8: *ille uel ille, duces; et erunt quae nomina dicas, si poteris, uere, si minus, apta tamen* ('that man, or that one, they are leaders: there'll be names you can give them — the right ones, if you can, but if not, at least well-chosen ones'). Beard 2004, 125 discusses Ovid's pastiche of earlier triumph poems, including the opening of *Georgics* 3, *Amores* 1.2.34, and Propertius 3.4.14, and notes that Ovid 'has rubbed our noses in the idea of the triumph not *in* but *as* poetry.'
8 'The common rejoicing is unknown to me (*nos... fallunt*)... and nothing but a slight rumour comes this far.' See Kennedy 2016, 53.
9 The slippage between the viewer in *Tr.* 4.2 and the poet himself is suggested also by the reference to Ovid's former presence at imperial triumphs (*paruaque cuius eram pars ego nuper eques*, *Tr.* 4.2.16).

ness.¹⁰ As personal testimony to past events, such letters seemingly share historiography's relationship with authenticating evidence (including reliable corroborating witnesses); they are implicitly records of autopsy, rooted in factuality.¹¹

Nevertheless, a letter's documentary status need not preclude fictionalising 'epistoliterary' discourse;¹² Books 7 and 9 of the *Ad Familiares* collection are especially hospitable to creative fictionalising games in letters that (like Ovid's quasi-epistolary poem from exile) conjure up an imaginary future or a life elsewhere. Cicero's more self-consciously 'literary' letters, in particular, apply fictionalising colour to lived experience, sometimes precisely in order to highlight the implausibility of real life. The letters of the mid-40s BCE, in particular, explore a contemporary reality that seems so unlikely or absurd an outcome of the writer's earlier career that it begins to seem inherently *un*-real. Their jarring contrasts between past and present call into question the authenticity of the letter-writing self and dramatise the writer's increasingly tortured and unstable persona – a phenomenon enhanced by Cicero's habit of clothing absurd or painful aspects of his life in the colours of the dramatic stage (both tragic and comedic).

Furthermore, the ancient editor's arrangement enhances these Ciceronian effects across the collection. It is fanciful, perhaps, to read books 7 and 9 as an Odyssean 'other worlds' section of the collection, a correlate in prose to those quasi-autobiographical books at the heart of the *Odyssey* in which the lost Odysseus explores the most highly fictionalised spaces of the epic, in the long attempt to achieve his *nostos* and restore himself to his past life and persona. Nevertheless, Cicero's ancient editor has built his selection in these books around fantasies of our hero's ideal and/or past life, highlighting the perceived mismatch between his true self and the circumstances in which he finds himself.¹³ He has done so by creatively exploiting the quasi-fictional colour applied to the letters by Cicero and his correspondents themselves.

---

10 This sort of material seems even more characteristic of the *Ad Atticum* corpus, where the 'fictionalising' strategies I discuss in the *Ad Familiares* are relatively sparingly used. Cf. Nepos' famous characterization of the letters to Atticus as a worthy substitute for a *historia contexta* (*Att.* 16.3–4). Nevertheless, see Cappello 2016, 471 for Cicero's articulation of "Atticus" as himself a quasi-fictional creation.
11 On historiography's dependence upon a third level of referentiality in addition to the familiar binary of story / discourse, see Cohn 2000.
12 See Henderson 2004, 4.
13 During this period, Cicero is himself struck by Atticus' characterization of Caesar's entourage as a *nekuia* – a term that itself suggests the Odyssean possibilities of the life they must live during the period of Caesar's pre-eminence. See *Att.* 9.10.7 (with Shackleton Bailey *ad loc.*), 9.11.2 and 9.18.2.

This paper presents a set of interlocking arguments about the mechanisms and effects of fictionalising colour in Ciceronian epistolography.[14] In what follows, I devote each of the first two sections to close reading of a single letter (*Fam.* 7.1 and 9.26, respectively) in which the interplay of different temporal streams — and different literary genres — becomes a mechanism for bathing Cicero's 'authentic' correspondence in fictional colour. In both these letters, the focus is especially on the spaces and activities of *otium*, both public and private — specifically the bedroom of a quiet intellectual (contrasted with the new Theatre of Pompey during its founder's quasi-triumphal shows), and the dining room of one of Rome's prominent aesthetes; both letters play upon life as itself a 'performance'. A third section moves away from close reading of single letters to more general reflections on Caelius' lightly fictionalising use of the imagery of public theatre to enhance his work as Cicero's political 'futurologist' in *Fam.* Book 8. An extended conclusion steps back to consider the wider effects achieved by temporal and generic dynamics in the letters, and explores the degree to which the ancient editorial arrangement amplifies the fictionalising qualities of the letters in the thematic sequences that extend across whole books. As we shall see, the outcome of the creative and imaginative manipulations of perceived reality in Cicero's letters is an ambiguous, potentially fictionalising (but not necessarily *fictional* space) for epistolographical communication, in which epistolary accounts of real events are overlaid with fictionalising (often dramatic) colour that conveys a different stratum of reality: a truth, as the letter writer sees it, about his own subjective experience.

1 *Fam.* 7.1: imagined idyll as richer reality

In *Fam.* 7.1 Cicero imagines Marius' days of contented *otium* at home on the bay of Naples, contrasting this fictionalised idyll with two concurrent 'real' narratives: the scenes of the urban festival that marked the opening of Pompey's theatre in 55 BCE, and the courtroom business that forced Cicero himself to miss

---

[14] I use the term 'fictionalising' throughout this paper in a non-technical sense, to explore the ways in which Cicero and his correspondents use quasi-fictional colour to convey their own perceptions of their lives and circumstances. In doing so, I shall explore e.g. intertextuality and epistolary conventions as themselves generative of fictionalising colour. On fictionality broadly defined as 'the conventions and practices one associates with creative writing — such as structure, poetic or literary descriptions of people and places, ordering of events to create certain effects — rather than simply things that are 'made up', see Gudmundsdóttir 2003, 4.

some of the theatrical shows that his letter describes.[15] Like Ovid's triumph, Cicero's version of Marius' seaside existence draws upon his friend's usual practices:

> neque tamen dubito, quin tu in illo **cubiculo tuo**, ex quo tibi Stabianum perforasti et patefecisti Misenum, per eos dies matutina tempora lectiunculis consumpseris, cum illi interea, qui te istic reliquerunt, spectarent communis mimos semisomni. reliquas uero partes diei **tu** consumebas iis delectationibus, quas tibi ipse ad arbitrium tuum compararas; **nobis** autem erant ea perpetienda, quae Sp. Maecius probauisset.
>
> (Fam. 7.1.1)

> And after all, I don't doubt that throughout the period of the show you have spent your morning hours on little readings **in that private chamber of yours** with its window that you let into the wall to overlook the bay of Stabiae. Meanwhile those who left you there were watching the public pantomimes half-asleep. As for the rest of the day, **you** have been spending it in such diversions as you have provided to suit your own taste while **we** have had to endure what Sp. Maecius presumably thought proper.

Multiple binary contrasts differentiate the semi-somnolent state of the audience at the communal *ludi* from Marius' refreshing solitary contemplation, awake and relaxed beside a deliberately designed window in his private chamber that looks over the bay (a kind of stage set?). The division of Marius' day into morning and afternoon entertainment mirrors within a domestic space the schedule of a day at the *ludi*. However, unlike the crowd at the games, who must endure the programmer's artistic choices right to the bitter end (***perpetienda quae Sp. Maecius probauisset***), Marius can select the texts he wants to hear, and exclude others – such as Cicero's speeches – that will bring no pleasure (7.1.3).[16]

Cicero's fantasy of Marius' quiet day at home is made richer by empathic recreation of the lived experience of the scene's internal creator, Marius himself. Marius is both stage-designer (*perforasti*; *patefecisti*) and artistic director of a sequence of pleasures arranged and scheduled exactly to his own taste (*iis delectationibus, quas tibi **ipse ad arbitrium tuum compararas***);[17] the city audience can

---

15 Shackleton Bailey 1965, 59–60 nominates 7.1 as a likely candidate for the self-edited letter collection Cicero had in mind because of its self-consciously literary qualities. Morello 2013 defends it against Stockton's suggestion that it is not a 'real' letter. See also Cammoranesi's discussion in this volume.

16 Wiseman 2015, 88. In the context of this letter, a Ciceronian speech belongs to the 'real' present of Cicero's *negotium*, and is, therefore, rightly excluded from the idealised entertainment space at Marius' villa (that later represents Cicero's dreams for future *otium*).

17 The relatively ordinary verb *comparo* suggests (as one would expect in a literary or artistic context) his control of his own composition and artistic production: cf. *Orat.* 208: *orationem generis eius quod esset ad delectationem* **comparatum**.

feel only *admiratio*, at best, in the face of the grand entertainments on offer, but Marius ensures for himself true *delectatio*[18] as a lively and alert cultural connoisseur. One might say that as an artist in entertainment scheduling, Marius is here conceived of in fictionalising terms as master of his own 'possible worlds'.[19]

This is a fiction of minimalist simplicity, in which the drastically streamlined imaginary scene on the Bay of Naples eclipses the grandeur of the real events at Rome. Paradoxically, the real shows are depicted as themselves consisting of *failed* fictions: the excessive visual scale of the dramatic performances (i.e. the fictions on stage) detracted from everyone's enjoyment.[20] Pompey himself (named only as yet another disappointed spectator) regarded the athletics events, too, as a waste of oil and effort (7.1.3). Staged animal hunts similarly foundered by preferring impressive scale to artistry: the slaughter of elephants, in particular, no doubt intended to impress at least partly because of the size of the victims, aroused pity for the touching 'humanity' of these sympathetic beasts.[21]

Despite his focus on the scale of the shows, Cicero entirely ignores the visual impact of the new theatre complex, and partially occludes the achievements — and even the great man himself — that it commemorates.[22] Pompey's military successes in the East are represented only symbolically within the fictions of the

---

18 The show as inherently an object of admiration: *quae ceteri mirantur; quae sine causa mirantur alii* (7.1.1); contrast between mass admiration and true personal pleasure in the more extravagant aspects of the shows: *quid enim delectationis habent… quae popularem admirationem habuerunt, delectationem tibi nullam attulissent* (7.1.2); cf. the animal shows (*admiratio magna… delectatio nulla,* 7.1.3); Marius' activities as inherently rich in pleasure: *his delectationibus* (7.1.1); Cicero's letters themselves as providing *spem aliquam delectationis tuae* (7.1.6). Note also the contrast between the tepid *lepor* at the games (7.1.2) and the innate *lepor* of Marius' persona (7.1.5).
19 On possible worlds, see Doležel 1998; Ronen 1994.
20 For quasi-triumphal shows clogged with props and military tableaux, cf. Horace *Epist.* 2.1.187–93; *Aen.* 2.765: *crateresque auro solidi*; cf. Goldberg 1997, 167.
21 Cicero himself has form for playing theatrical 'size and numbers' pranks on this addressee: in *Qfr.* 2.9.5 he recalls a litter journey with Marius from Naples to Baiae in the same year as Pompey's games. As Cicero tells it, he had provided a 'super-litter' (an 8-man 'palanquin' borrowed from a friend who had spent time in the East), and an equally exotic armed escort: not just *milites* with good Roman *gladii* or *pila* to protect them from bandits, but 100 *machaerophoroi* ('machete infantry'). Marius opened the curtains of the litter and nearly died of fright at the unexpected sight of these troops, Cicero fell about laughing — and that moment became part of their shared history.
22 Cf. Catullus 55, another piece in which the writer locates himself at (among other city spots) Pompey's theatre complex, thinking about an absent friend, whose current activities he can only imagine. On the absence of Caesars and Pompeys from this poem, and from Cat. 10, see Damon 2021, 22–23. On Pompey's theatre, cf. Pliny *NH* 36.24; Val. Max. 2.6.

shows. The dramas (updated productions of early Latin tragedies — the *Clytaemnestra* and the *Trojan Horse*) create a new, fictionalised, version of Pompey's triumph(s), in which 600 mules and 3000 bowls serve both as stage props and as quasi-triumphal paraphernalia celebrating Pompey's 'epic' victories and his return from heroic regions in the east.[23] Historical reality is fictionalised on stage by being costumed in the trappings of the Trojan campaign, and Cicero's very selectivity in highlighting this phenomenon is itself a fictionalising strategy.

The figures of three hired 'performers' (two of them celebrities) complement and extend the binary contrasts between Rome and Marius' villa: Protogenes, Marius' reader at the villa, Aesopus, the aging celebrity actor at the theatre, and finally Cicero himself, whose oratorical/forensic output is treated with humorous or weary self-deprecation in both seaside and urban scenes. In this letter that is so much about a better life 'elsewhere', these figures — each representing a different version of 'elsewhere' — focus the reader's attention upon the issue of good choice in life. On the one hand, Marius lives better (virtually alone in front of ideal scenery) as he listens to a single skilled reader, Protogenes, than the whole crowd at the theatre — provided that Protogenes reads something other than Cicero's speeches (7.1.3). On the other, Aesopus' experience at the shows becomes the model for Cicero's professional frustration (7.1.4). Cicero tells Marius that Aesopus' voice gave out at a crucial moment: the actor should have known better than to attempt another grand performance, and the audience would willingly have seen him retire once more (*ut ei **desinere** per omnes homines liceret*, 7.2).[24] At the same time Cicero was straining himself (*dirupi me paene*, 7.4) — and far from free (*ne forte uidear... liber omnino fuisse*, 7.4) — in the defence of Gallus Caninius.[25] This miserable commission prompts dreams of his own honourable retirement (*quod si tam facilem populum haberem, quam*

---

[23] On the shows as re-stagings of Pompey's triple triumph of 61 BCE ('a theatricalized representation of a theatricalized event'), see Erasmo 2020.

[24] Aesopus, one of the letter's key practitioners in bringing the staged fictional world to life, is paradoxically obliged to take the Jupiter stone oath forswearing deceptiveness, thereby according a kind of authenticity to his performance; it seems no accidental irony that Cicero describes Aesopus' voice failing just as he begins the oath: *si sciens fallo*. For a less fictionalised epistolary account of such shows, including an unfavourable review of a well-known actor, cf. e.g. *Att.* 4.15.6.

[25] Like Ovid in *Tr.* 4.2, then, Cicero the fictionalising reporter was not actually present for at least part of the shows he describes. He specifies that although he was present for the beast hunts — *haec spectauimus* — he missed at least some of the *ludi scaenici* (7.1.3–4). He mentions his own feelings about the performance of Aesopus and seems to be reporting on the tragic productions as an eyewitness, so the shows he missed may have been the Oscan and Greek plays.

*Aesopus habuit, libenter mehercule artem **desinerem** tecumque et cum similibus uiuerem*, 7.1.4). Here the public celebrations of 55 BCE are not primarily the grand culmination of Pompey's latest success; instead, they are the trigger for reflections on careers past the point of their maturity, and on the better choices that could be made in *otium*.

These games, unlike Tiberius' triumph in *Tr.* 4.2, are not fictitious. Nevertheless, Cicero's letter exploits Pompey's quasi-triumphal show as scaffolding upon which to build a world of fictions that are layered upon one another to create a deeply satisfying (if carefully contrived) texture of experience and longing.[26] Each of the concurrent narratives contains a strong message about the importance of timely and well-considered retirement. *Fam.* 7.1 is a letter about the value of the imagined and the fictionalised in structuring and enriching human experience — and above all about the deliberate, craftsmanlike construction of pleasure within a good life. The letter's final sections reveal that this imagined alternative reality is also the letter writer's design for his own (still imaginary) future when he will be truly 'free' to choose and design a life that satisfies.[27]

2 *Fam.* 9.26: fictionality and generic colour

By the end of Book 9, Cicero is indeed living a life of literary *otium*, but it is not like that of Marius, and it is not spent (as Cicero had wished in 7.1) *cum similibus*.[28] Indeed, *Fam.* 9.26 presents a Cicero who is not even *like himself* in any respect except in his sociable wit. As the letter opens, Cicero reclines at dinner at the house of Volumnius Eutrapelus. The scene seems firmly anchored in reality: we know the time of writing (*hora nona*), the venue (*apud Volumnium Eutrapelum*), and the names of respectable and trustworthy witnesses (Atticus and Verrius recline on either side of Cicero). Nevertheless, the reader is about to be drawn into a fictionalising maze, in which the writer's sense of his own inauthenticity is implicitly conveyed in deft switches of mode and genre. Once again, this letter

---

[26] On 7.1 as itself a *ludus*, see Cammoranesi 2022, 31–32.
[27] Cicero himself is not yet in *otium* ('I have written thus to you at greater length than usual out of the abundance not of my leisure, but of my love for you') but approves of the life he imagines Marius enjoying: *teque et istam rationem oti tui et laudo uehementer et probo*. Cf. Cicero's image of Varro (*Fam.* 9.1, 9.5) as one who has chosen a better life of literary productivity (see Leach 1999, 166).
[28] Cf. Cammoranesi 2022, 53.

raises broader philosophical questions about what kind of life one ought to lead in circumstances like those of 46 BCE, a period when the reality of life for Cicero seemed inherently implausible – even *un*-real.

The moment of the letter's first composition is captured in a pleasantly mind-bending double layer of epistolary past tenses – the pluperfect (*accubueram*, literally 'I had lain down') and the perfect (*exaraui*, 'I scratched out'):[29]

> *accubueram hora nona, cum ad te harum exemplum in codicillis exaraui.*
>
> I am scribbling the lines of which you are reading a copy on my tablets after taking my place at dinner at two-thirty of the afternoon.

The characteristic epistolary past of Latin letters (masked in English translation) neatly encapsulates a relationship between event time, production time (i.e. the writer's present), and reader time that differs from our modern practice (we tend to privilege the present tense of the writer at the time of writing). It is a time machine in which the Roman epistolary artist may lift the reader back into the moment when these events were happening in the breathless present, while also acknowledging clearly that at the time of the letter's arrival they are already long past.[30]

Here the normal epistolary past is revivified by a parallel slippage between the *exemplum* ('draft copy)[31] scratched out at dinner *then* and the letter in the addressee's hands *now*. The materiality of the tablets (*codicilli*) and of the process of 'ploughing a furrow' (*exaraui*) through the wax seems yet another anchor to 'reality' in this scene, as we watch Cicero begin to stage his experience for the reader. Paradoxically, the result is that the distinction between production time and reader time is both enhanced and collapsed. As modern readers, we are simultaneously in Cicero's writing time on a dining couch, as he jots down the preliminary draft, and in the reading time of Papirius, as he holds *this* letter (*harum*) – the finished product, reshaped and recorded on a different

---

[29] Cicero is not alone in conducting correspondence while at dinner – this was Caesar's habit too (Plutarch *Caes.* 63.7).

[30] On the importance of 'the disparity between two or more moments' for the creation of meaning in epistolary texts, see Altman 1982, 129–130; such moments include 'the actual time that an act described is performed, the moment when it is written down, the respective times that the letter is mailed, received, read and reread.' On the epistolary past, see Mellet 1988, 189–206.

[31] See Shackleton Bailey *ad loc.* on *exemplum*.

medium.³² What you see at the beginning of the letter is not quite what you get in the finished version. The visible presence of the writer *as he writes* enhances the letter's self-consciousness,³³ while the exercise in 'seeing double', as regards the materiality of the letter, conspires with the temporal *trompe l'oeuil* of the epistolary past tense to boost the fictionality (even meta-fictionality)³⁴ of the letter's opening. 'Looking at Cicero' will become a central motif of the letter, and in the same way as the letter is simultaneously an image of its first drafting on tablets and a finished product on paper (to be read by others in new settings), the man will be simultaneously the man he was and something very different as beheld by others in new circumstances. As a reader proceeds through the letter, s/he may increasingly re-interpret the epistolary past tense, in hindsight, as an appropriately destabilising introduction to the letter's temporal and material uncertainties. Our experience of the story world, one might say, makes us reconsider the frame.³⁵

These games with tenses and reality are in themselves a playfully fictionalising touch, but the teasing of readers' expectations continues further in this letter. Since earlier letters in Book 9 dwell extensively upon Cicero's new practice of bartering rhetorical instruction for fine dinners, the ancient editor of Book 9 has primed the book's linear reader for heightened curiosity about what

---

32 To paraphrase Mordine 2010, 530 on Ovid's *Tristia* 1.1, 'we readers are encouraged to imaginatively *create* this [letter], a [letter] very unlike the one we hold in our hands. We are both witnessing and sharing in the creation of fiction.'

33 We find a close parallel for *Fam.* 9.26 in the opening of *Att.* 12.1: *undecimo die postquam a te discesseram hoc litterularum exaraui egrediens e uilla ante lucem* ('ten days after saying goodbye to you I am scribbling this note as I leave the villa before daybreak'). However, the short letter that follows, although performative in the sense that it parades interruptions and restarts ('just as I was folding up this letter, a ...courier arrived with a letter from you', 12.1.2), does not build upon fictionalising possibilities as 9.26 does. Cicero's 'scratchings' in *Att.* 12.1 seem to be the letter itself, rather than a preliminary draft, and he writes about planned actions and appointments in the next few days, rather than stopping time to stage a tableau in the domestic setting.

34 As we shall see, Cicero gives multiple cues in the letter that guide a reader's response to the events it describes — a strategy made more 'metafictional' by the fictionalising colour overlaid upon the description of events. It is the layers of light touch fictionality and metafictionality that create the atmosphere of the letter and its impact upon the reader, even though metafictionality might normally seem unlikely in a letter that is not itself fictional.

35 A process that Hodkinson (unpublished) sees as a characteristic epistolary phenomenon in fictional letters. Perhaps a sophisticated reader's awareness of fictional letters (e.g. in comedy) can open up space for Cicero and other writers of 'authentic' letters to apply light touches of fictionalising colour in their epistles.

happens at such occasions: here, at last, we are brought into the dining room with Cicero, and might expect to find details of food or conversation.

We are to be disappointed. The letter presents a meditative tableau rather than a developing dramatic scene — the ancient equivalent of an enigmatic Instagram selfie of Cicero, tablets in hand.[36] The writer remains thoughtfully detached and psychologically alone, despite the proximity of his closest friend; he simultaneously observes himself in the scene, and offers himself for astonished contemplation by the reader.[37] At the same time, he reaches outside the frame of the dinner scene to initiate a quasi-philosophical 'consultation' of his addressee:

> *miraris tam exhilaratam esse seruitutem nostrum? quid ergo faciam? te consulo, qui philosophum audis. angar? excruciemne me? quid assequar? deinde quem ad finem? uiuas, inquis, in litteris. an quidquam me aliud agere censes? aut possem uiuere, nisi in litteris uiuerem? sed est earum etiam, non satietas, sed quidam modus.*

> Does it surprise you that we have become such a merry lot of slaves? Well, what am I to do? I ask *you*, since you are going to philosophy lectures. Am I to torture and torment myself? What should I gain? And how long should I keep it up? You may advise me to spend my life in literary work. Do you suppose that I do anything else? Or that I could live at all, if not in literary work? But even in those pursuits there is, I won't say a saturation-point, but a certain limit.

The real topic of this letter (as of *Fam.* 7.1) is the broader question about the best way to live. Here more specifically it asks how a profoundly unhappy man may yet be lively and sociable, and also explores the degree to which there is a 'life' within the confines of one's own literary productions.

The initial styling of the letter as a philosophical dialogue — a genre at home in convivial settings since well before Plato's *Symposium* — establishes a fictive frame and generic colour. For Cicero, literary activity itself is a pursuit that can satisfy and that is at least commensurate with the writer's true tempe-

---

36 On Cicero 'staging himself' as the 'self-observing guest', cf. Leach 1999, 152; this, too, is a mode that is inherently available in the epistolary form, in which the narrator of the letter's contents is also involved in the action he describes, and commenting on it — as Hodkinson (unpublished) notes — with varying distance or irony. Leach also notes that 'nothing here concerns food', an omission of 'real' detail from this letter that is reminiscent of the omission of details about the new theatre in *Fam.* 7.1.

37 One might apply here Feldherr's observation (Feldherr 2010, 162) about the visual aspects of Ovid's poetry: 'obviously, a text's power to evoke the visual is one of its supreme fictions.' Cicero's successful conversion of an account of an event into a relatively static tableau here is itself a fictionalising manoeuvre.

rament; he explicitly distinguishes social dining (a practice reserved for times when he has reached satiety in *literary* consumption) [38] from his intellectual work. Nevertheless, the description of the party is itself a markedly literary exploration of his own experience; it cycles rapidly through different shades of generic colour, some only fleetingly perceptible, but all contributing to a cumulative sense of unreality, as Cicero evokes elegy, tragedy and even comedy in search of a recognizably 'Ciceronian' persona.

Cicero's surreal situation is vividly encapsulated by the presence of a surprise celebrity guest: the host's freedwoman, the demi-mondaine Cytheris — professional actress, mistress of both Antony and Brutus, and perhaps also the model for Gallus' elegiac beloved, Lycoris.[39] Her presence briefly bathes Cicero and his best friend in the generic colours of elegy or of sympotic lyric — a generic 'lighting filter', to extend my anachronistic Instagram metaphor. She prompts the letter's central reflections upon the incongruity of Cicero's participation in what turns out to be a glamorously sexualised society dinner — an odd setting for a mournfully disappointed sixty-year-old orator, particularly one whose lifelong indifference to sex makes elegy an unlikely habitat for him.[40] If a letter allows the writer to create 'fictions of the self', Cicero here constructs himself as not only 'out of character' but even implicitly 'out of genre' — itself a fictionalising move that confers new meaning upon the idea of living a life *in litteris*.[41]

Cicero's internal reflections on the dissonance between his real self and his quasi-elegiac setting prompt readers to measure the distance between the Cicero *they* know and the figure on the dinner couch at Volumnius' house.[42] This emphasis on the eye of the beholder activates yet another new generic colour, as Cicero briefly applies a tragic 'filter' to reconfigure himself as a ruined hero:

---

38 *Fam.* 9.26.1.
39 On Cytheris' presence in the homosocial context of this dinner party, see Keith 2011.
40 It seems not accidental that the editor has positioned this reflection only four letters after *Fam.* 9.22, on the importance of frankness and un-selfconscious use of plain speech in matters of sexual terminology (9.22).
41 On the performance of the Ciceronian self, see Leach 1999. On the epistolary self, see also Curry 2018, Riggsby 1995. Cicero's interest in these letters in constructing or maintaining a recognisable persona for himself has much in common with the attempts of pseudepigraphic letters to achieve plausibility.
42 On 'the interaction of present and former Ciceros' in the letters of Book 9, see Leach 1999, 155. On a comparable encouragement to the triumphal spectators in *Tr.* 4.2 to look for changes in the demeanour and appearance of formerly proud kings in the procession, see Feldherr 2010, 16. The poet's grief for his own past persona is a key motif already in *Tr.* 4.1.99–102; see Oliensis 2004, 309–310.

> audi reliqua. infra Eutrapelum Cytheris accubuit. 'in eo igitur' inquis 'conuiuio Cicero ille' quem aspectabant, cuius ob os Grai ora obuertebant sua?
>
> (Fam. 9.26.2)

> Well, to the rest of my tale. Cytheris lay down next to Eutrapelus. 'So?' I hear you say, 'Cicero at such a party, "He the admired, upon whose countenance the Greeks all turned their eyes"?[43]

This quotation, variously ascribed to Accius' *Eurysaces* or Ennius' *Telamo*, is a favourite of Cicero's at this period; he recycles it (less than a year after *Fam.* 9.26's composition) in *Tusc.* 3.29, as part of an attack on Epicurean instructions to turn to pleasure in times of suffering, drawing a similar contrast between the hero grieving for his noble past and the pleasure-laden environment around him.[44] Here in 9.26 it acts as a distancing mechanism, embedding into the sexually charged environment of Volumnius' dinner party *a* Cicero, no longer the grand Roman consular of old, but now re-staged as the fallen Telamon of tragedy. It presents us with the hermeneutic challenge of 'reading' the new Cicero, in an epistolary palimpsest that overlays the fictionalising shadow of a disgraced hero in a tragic scene upon an embarrassingly real contemporary Roman gathering. This palimpsestic quality is itself a further enhancement of the competing layers of time in the instance of the epistolary past with which the letter opened; in Cicero's picture of himself as Telamon, too, we witness a lost heroic past of tragedy, Cicero's own lost republican past, and the challenges of the constrained present.[45]

The dramatic quotation boosts the sense of a staged tableau in this letter,[46] and expresses the writer's experience in a mythological register that is in itself

---

[43] For a fuller quotation preserved by Varro, see *LL* 6.60: *hicine est Telamo ille, modo quem gloria ad caelum extulit, / quem aspectabant, cuius ob os Grai ora obuertebant sua*? For Ciceronian use of dramatic material as a mechanism of time-bending self-representation, see also *Pro Sestio* 120f., with Leach 2000, 388 on the *ludi Apollinares* of 57 BCE: 'there now stands before us, on stage, as it were, a restored Cicero playing the role of Aesopus, who at the time of Cicero's exile had been playing a role to be identified with the voice and feelings of the Roman people towards Cicero....[Aesopus'] artistry crossed the lines of fiction and reality.'

[44] See most recently Čulík-Baird 2022, 149–150.

[45] For the fictionalising potential in Cicero's introduction of a hero of myth, cf. Waugh 1984, 112: 'ostentatious use of literary and mythic allusion reinforces the notion of fictionality, and the reader's awareness of the construction of alternative worlds.' On Ovid's assumption of an 'Odysseus' persona in his exilic verse epistles (a useful parallel to Cicero's move in 9.26), see Ingleheart 2006. On the practice of 'recasting Greek myth to define the present' cf. Feldherr 2010, 167.

[46] One might compare Emily Dickinson's high degree of audience consciousness in her letters: see, for example, Messmer 2001, 11 on Dickinson's 'histrionic self-constructions.'

imbued with fantasy and fiction.⁴⁷ Cicero delivers an epistolary rendition of what Brook has called the 'symbiotic relationship ... between the non-fictional world of politics and the fictional world of the stage.'⁴⁸ The tragic quotation both masks the real Cicero, and simultaneously discloses a subjective psychological truth about Cicero's incredulous sense of displacement and failure in a world in which grand historical events have produced a tragically absurd dinner scene that the reader may find equally hard to believe.

This is a human and subjective narrative of courage in adversity. The letter's intertextual cleverness is itself an instantiation of the sole aspect of Cicero's characteristic *persona* to which he still lays claim: his ebullient wit, which allows him to 'transform lament into belly laughs' (*gemitum in risus maximos transfero*).⁴⁹ The letter's design aligns with Cicero's own rhetorical model of personal narrative in which the crucial element is a vivacity (*festiuitas*) constructed of 'fluctuations of fortune, contrast of characters, severity, gentleness, hope, fear, suspicion, desire, dissimulation, delusion, pity' (*Inv.* 1.27). This text's multiple generic signposts progressively influence 'the reader's conception of the kind of story or text he is encountering', and open up new interpretive possibilities as we become aware both of the self-conscious fictionalising touches and of the subjective truth to which they point.⁵⁰ Cicero's selection of generic colours (philosophical dialogue, elegy/lyric, tragedy, and — above all — the overall comedic effect achieved by this generic *mélange*) lightly suggests the range of fictionalities that the reader is invited to detect and enjoy. The shifting generic colour helps to focus our minds upon the writer's subjective view of his own

---

47 Cf. the (non-fictional) letters of Julie de Lespinasse and of Dorothy Osborne in the early modern period, in which 'the border between fiction and non-fiction may be fuzzy' (Camiciotti 2014, 27); Osborne, in particular, had a habit of conceptualising her own experience in terms of the figures of French romances (see Ottway 1996, 152). Quintilian would later class the myths of tragedy and epic as the material most obviously 'removed not only from truth but even from the appearance of truth' (*Inst.* 2.4.2). See Reinhardt/Winterbottom 2006, 78–79. Quintilian's tripartite division of narrative types offers two poetic narratives (the first associated with tragedy or epic, and the second with comedy) and one 'historical' narrative. On a 'sliding scale of fictiveness' envisaged by ancient theoreticians, see Feeney 1993, 232.
48 Brook 2016, 51. Cf. Connolly 2007, 198–236. A comparable strategy dominates the remarkable recommendation letter to Caesar on behalf of Precilius (*Fam.* 13.15). This self-consciously unconventional recommendation (*genere nouo sum litterarum ad te usus*, 13.15.3), interweaves lines from Homer with the 'real' past conversations between Cicero and Precilius's father.
49 Wit and laughter is not only marked by Cicero elsewhere as a characteristically epistolary mode (*Fam.* 2.4.1), but it is also already thematically embedded in Book 9 as a hallmark of his true self (see below on *Fam.* 9.16.4).
50 Bruner 1986, 7.

situation, and demonstrates the power of what Bruner calls 'psychological genre.' Ultimately, the 'reality' of Cicero's draft notes in wax (anchored to the real scene of a Roman dining room) gives way to the fictions and metaphors of Cicero's 'real' experience of generic rootlessness.

As Orlemanski observes, the conventions of genre 'are an important mid-level category for mediating between particular literary texts and the vast and protean discursive mode of fictionality.'[51] *Fam.* 9.26 is a *tour de force*, in which literary and philosophical genres act as signatures and levers of fictionality. Indeed, its fictionality is almost over-determined: the sense of unreality (even of the surreal) is heightened by the sparkling cycle of genre markers, by the distancing mechanism of the epistolary past (itself revivified and revealed as an important mechanism of fiction-creation in this highly fictionalised context), and by the further distancing mechanism of Cicero's 'staging' of his own persona.[52]

3 The fictional future: sight, spectacle and epistolary autopsy

This paper's two close readings have explored fictionalising representations of events and experiences based in *otium*, that the writer describes predominantly in past or present tenses. Nevertheless, the imagined future has a crucial role as the *telos* of many of Cicero's fictions. The invented scene at Marius' villa in *Fam.* 7.1, for example, only gradually reveals itself as the template for an idyllic future that Cicero imagines for himself in his retirement.[53] As Altman notes, 'preoccupation with the future is intrinsic to the epistolary form, where each letter arrests the writer in a present whose future is unknown.'[54] Several letter types dwell more consciously upon the future, including dinner invitations, letters of recommendation, requests for new socks or for hot water at a journey's end, and even declarations of love. The epistolary future in these instances is still only an 'invented' scenario, conjured up by hopeful — even manipulative — correspondents,

---

51 Orlemanski 2019, 158.
52 In its mix of fact and fictive overlay, this letter is a good example of what Orlemanski 2019, 161 calls 'referential dappling.'
53 On the future as 'the primary direction of care' in Ricoeur's three dimensions of time (future, past and present), see Ricoeur 1980, 181.
54 Altman 1987, 127.

but the letter itself is a mechanism to engineer that future.[55] In Altman's words, epistolary narrative 'is particularly adapted to the schemer or calculator figure, who plots future events and analyzes past ones.'

There is no dearth of scheming, calculating, plotting and analysing in Ciceronian letters, which are often keenly interested in political prediction, in particular. During Cicero's absence in Cilicia, for example, he asks Caelius Rufus to keep him up to speed on the political situation in Rome. The resulting exchanges vividly illustrate the two correspondents' shared interest in an epistolary 'futurology', and the fictionalising techniques that may be applied to produce a usable advance narrative of impending events.

Caelius' initial approach was to delegate much of the factual reporting to an assistant (8.1.1), whose output is characterised as *commentarii rerum urbanarum* (8.1.2), a *mélange* of 'decrees, edicts, gossip and rumours' with seemingly little fictionalising emplotment. Cicero robustly dismisses this material (*Fam.* 2.8– 16) — any correspondent could produce such stuff — but demands instead that Caelius exercise his creative flair for envisioning the future, thereby feeding Cicero's political imagination:

> qua re ego **nec praeterita nec praesentia** abs te sed, ut ab homine longe in posterum prospiciente, **futura** exspecto, ut ex tuis litteris, cum formam rei publicae uiderim, quale aedificium futurum sit scire possim.
>
> (*Fam.* 2.8.1)

> So I do not expect things past or present from your pen. What I want from so far-sighted a fellow as yourself is the future. From your letters, having seen, as it were, an architect's drawing of the political situation, I shall hope to know what kind of building is to come.

Cicero employs a visual language (*uiderim*) of architectural design to express his correspondent's endeavour to conceptualise a reality that is yet to be constructed — a familiar image from elsewhere in his letters. We have already seen Marius' architectural renovation of his bedroom window as a crucial symbol in a fictionalising scenario, but Cicero uses a more technical image of the professional builder or architect in his famous exhortation to Varro in *Fam.* 9.2.5 that

---

55 This volume's editors remind me that such future-oriented letters entail some temporal complexity for later readers. A love letter, for example, implies a writer who is still hoping for a positive outcome at the time of writing; subsequent readers, separated in time from the writer, see the letter as a closed text that captures both the wooing and its outcome as past events. A dinner invitation is a completed action in itself, but the dinner is still in the future for both writer and addressee; for the modern reader, however, the planned dinner is only another 'past future', in Koselleck's phrase.

they should both offer their services *non modo ut architectos, uerum etiam ut fabros, ad aedificandam rem publicam.*[56]

As Book 8 develops, Caelius rises to Cicero's challenge and envisions a convincing emplotted future. He eschews the quasi-technical architectural metaphor that Cicero favours, but invokes a more clearly fictionalising language of sight and spectacle, drawn from semantic fields associated with *otium* and particularly with the inherently fiction-soaked world of the theatre. As an epistolary futurologist, he models possible narratives on the basis of carefully selected clues in the world around him, making liberal use also of rumour and intelligent conjecture (both potentially strongly fictionalised, if not actually fictional).[57] His political forecasting uses the language of sight to express both his 'view' at the time and his *fore*sight of the future.[58]

No surprise, of course, that savvy political anticipation is described as prognostic fore**sight** (*prouidentia*),[59] but in this fictionalising futurological context, in which history is being imaginatively anticipated, it may not be too fanciful to reconceive this 'sight' as a different kind of autopsy. Caelius as futurologist can use the epistolary genre to create a new reality that would be unavailable to him in the more rigorous context of historiography, where 'autopsy' signifies an eyewitness account of verifiable past events. Here Caelius

---

56 '…if anyone wants to employ us [i.e. Cicero and Varro], not merely as master-builders, but even as masons, to build up the Republic…' Even if all this means is that they both write a 'politeia', such work in itself creates a quasi-fictional parallel world as a practical blueprint for a future restoration and renovation of political structures. Cf. Cicero's criticism of Cato's naïveté in behaving as if the real Roman political sphere matched up to his ideals: *dicit enim tamquam in Platonis* πολιτείᾳ, *non tamquam in Romuli faece, sententiam* ('he speaks in the Senate as though he were living in Plato's *Republic* instead of Romulus' cesspool,' *Att.* 2.1.8). Here the psychological distance between Cato's political 'fiction' and Cicero's reality is vividly marked by the contrast between πολιτείᾳ and *faece*; the Greek title emphasises the written constructedness of Cato's ideal world — intellectually and linguistically 'somewhere else' from the reality of the city.
57 Studies of organizational foresight and strategic futurology have described these phenomena as 'modal narratives' that focus on 'what might have been or what might yet be.' See e.g. Booth/Clark et al. 2009, 118.
58 E.g. *ut* **uideo**, *causa haec integra in proximum annum transferetur et, quantum* **diuino**, *relinquendum tibi erit qui prouinciam optineat* (*Fam.* 8.9.2); *Curionem* **uideo** *se dupliciter iactaturum…* (*Fam.* 8.10); *in hac discordia* **uideo** *Cn. Pompeium senatum quique res iudicant secum habiturum…* (*Fam.* 8.14.3); *de summa republica saepe tibi scripsi, me ad annum pacem non* **uidere**… (*Fam.* 8.14.2).
59 Cf *Fam.* 2.8.2: *neque enim fuit quod tu plus prouidere posses quam quiuis nostrum in primisque ego* ('there has been nothing which you could foresee any better than the rest of us— myself especially').

uses the language of sight — applied to imaginative autopsy of the future — to support the creation of his own epistolary authority as a commentator.[60]

Fam. 8.14 (dating from August 50 BCE) yields a typical instance of predictive spectacle in Caelius' letters, as he uses the language of sight to remind his addressee of previous confident predictions of war (*Fam.* 8.14.2: *de summa republica saepe tibi scripsi, me ad annum pacem non **uidere***). However, he frames this same letter with metaphors of theatrical 'spectacle.' He begins by consoling Cicero for missing the recent 'spectacle' of events in Rome (in this instance elections), and he ends by promising even better 'spectacle' to come when war finally breaks out: 'Fortune is preparing a mighty and fascinating show for your benefit (*magnum et iucundum tibi fortuna **spectaculum** parabat*, *Fam.* 8.14.4).[61] All of this naturally reflects the theatricality of much of public behaviour in Rome, and both Caelius and Cicero demonstrate how a Roman *letter* could reflect and transmit theatricality to those absent citizens who were unable to witness the 'show' in person.[62] Such a letter is both an authentic reflection of urban reality and a fictionalising reproduction of its performativeness. Like the audience in *Fam.* 7.1, the citizens of Rome are in the hands of a theatrical impresario — in this case *Fortuna* herself who is designing the future show while Caelius writes (the epistolary imperfect *parabat* is crucial here).

The language of spectacle in this context may remind a modern reader of well-bred British war heroes in John Buchan's Hannay novels who describe even the most brutal military action as a 'show', casually contrasting images from middle-class domestic leisure with war's 'theatrical' horrors.[63] The lightness and

---

60 See also Cammoranesi 2022, 114. Cf. Cicero's own 'divinations' and the extended play upon his augural expertise as a metaphor for his political perceptiveness in *Fam.* 6.6, to Caecina.
61 *hoc tibi non inuideo, caruisse te pulcherrimo **spectaculo**,* (*Fam.* 8.4.1); ***spectaculo** carere* (*Fam.* 8.14.1); ***scaena** rei totius haec* (*Fam.* 8.11.3). Ciceronian examples of the application of theatrical language to political commentary may be found outside the *Ad Fam.* collection (e.g. *Att.* 1.18.2: *introitus fuit fabulae Clodianae*), but such language is employed in an especially sustained manner by Caelius in the letters assembled in Book 8.
62 On the theatricality of Roman culture, see e.g. Hölkeskamp 2011, 162, who grounds his own deliberate use of metaphors of performance in the Roman culture's 'imperative of immediacy, an intensified degree of visibility, personal presence, public performance and sheer physicality that determined the whole scale of practices and patterns of behaviour.' This immediacy demands that a writer enhance a letter's generic duty to create a sense of the addressee's personal presence.
63 'There was no prouder man on earth than Richard Hannay [*i.e. the speaker here*] when he took his Lennox Highlanders over the parapets on that glorious and bloody 25th day of September. Loos was **no picnic**, and we had some ugly bits of scrapping before that, but the worst bit of the campaign I had seen was **a tea party to the show** I had been in with Bullivant before the war started.' (John Buchan, *Greenmantle*)

seeming frivolity of such language is not innocent in Buchan, of course, whose self-consciously gentlemanly characters use the quasi-fictionalising language of theatre as a coping mechanism, highlighting the incongruity of their own presence at hellish scenes of war. The irony implicit in the narrative of the Caelius letters, by contrast, is that although Book 8's predictions of war (and of Caesarian success) do come true, it will be the subsequent peacetime depicted in Books 7 and (especially) 9 that Cicero will perceive as an 'unreal' world of enforced *otium* with himself as one of its most incongruous prisoners.

4 Temporal games, epistolary fictionalising, and the architecture of the collections

Complex temporal effects are available, as we have seen, when a letter writer creates counterfactual or alternative time streams to convey what he imagines *might/must* have occurred in the past, what he wishes were true (or what might be occurring elsewhere) in the present, or what he anticipates may occur in the future. Fictionalising strategies of all kinds fuel these experiments in subjective reality, as the writer invents and imagines other times, other places and other realities. *Fam.* 7.1, for example, fictionalises multiple temporalities: in the 'alternative' or 'parallel' narratives of this letter, we have already noted the contrast between the fictionalised simplicity of Marius' environment and the visual overload of the scenes in Pompey's theatre. The official shows are also focussed upon a set of fictional worlds (enacted in games and theatrical shows) in which a real audience was trapped during those lazy days in the Campus Martius. The real past – and much of the real present – are converted into absences and symbols: the real-world booty that marks Pompey's military success is heaped up as an ineffective theatrical prop, and Cicero's letter draws out themes of failure and hubristic display from the allegorical representation of mythical conquests at Troy.[64] Nevertheless, the most compellingly 'real' of all the letter's fictions is the wholly imagined scene around the addressee at the seaside; as in *Tr.* 4.2, an epistolary surmise about the addressee's imagined world is more

---

64 We might compare the impact of the triumphal parade in *Tr.* 4.2.27–46, as described by the unreliable eyewitness. Although the show is impressive, the captured leaders are not known by name and can be described only generically (*dux fuerat belli; hic; ille ferox; perfidus hic*).

vividly foregrounded than the writer's eyewitness account of his own lived experience — textuality takes precedence over reality.[65]

A letter is inherently a technology that both captures and tries to communicate across different times and different places; it represents what is happening in the writer's time and place for the benefit of a distant addressee, but also often attempts to envisage the scene at the other end. The resulting marriage of reportage and fictionality gives rich opportunity for creative play, as the case studies in this chapter demonstrate. At its most basic, an epistolary meditation upon 'your time/place' and 'my time/place' embeds fictionality within that binary of the epistolary dialogue (I report my reality, but imagine and invent yours). However, *Fam.* 7.1 and 9.26 both, in different ways, go beyond that binary infrastructure and further multiply the number of alternative, concurrent or metaphorical times and places in order to generate the letter's message, using familiar literary devices in new ways within a specifically epistolary context. The intertextuality of 9.26, for example, builds a collage of several times, places and genres, juxtaposing fictions with verifiable 'historical' scenes to represent Cicero's subjective experience. When Cicero overlays a Telamon from the fictional past upon a Cicero we see in the 'real' present, the readers see more clearly how different *this* Cicero is from past versions; the micro-shifts of generic colour push us to look afresh at the interplay between character and context, and between reality and fiction. This epistolary collage melds genre, memory, and reportage, with destabilising effects; the letter that is initially rooted in the humdrum present reality of Cicero's *codicilli* before dinner in Rome develops into an 'auto-fiction' in which our hero is trapped in a 'nowhere world' that feels utterly unreal to him. Paradoxically, it is the fictional and imagined elements of the text that most vividly convey the author's lived experience.[66]

Similarly, multiple concurrent scenes are stitched together in *Fam.* 7.1 as the initial epistolary binary (us in Rome, you at the villa) gives way to a more complex and fragmented account of competing realities in Rome. The imagined scene at Marius' villa remains stable and consistent, but Cicero builds another collage, this time composed of alternative scenes in Rome: the wild-beast hunts Cicero witnessed, the *ludi scaenici* that he missed, and his performance in court on behalf of Caninius that called him away from them. As these scenes proliferate,

---

65 Cf. Feldherr 2010, 161 on the battle in Ovid's poetic accounts of imperial victory celebration between reality and textuality.
66 Rimell aptly quotes Saïd ('the exile's new world...is unnatural, and its unreality resembles fiction') in her discussion of Ovid's unreal Tomitan landscape, concluding that 'this fictionality is itself, potentially, an expression of actual experience.' See Rimell 2015, 279; Saïd 2000, 18.

the viewer/reader is asked to spot significant similarities (e.g. a recurring 'performer' figure, each instance of which echoes all the others) or differences (e.g. between the 'scene' before Marius and the 'scene' in the theatre before the bored crowd). We are also invited to notice the performative fictionalised dimension of the 'historical' events that have prompted the production of the shows, as Pompey's conquests are reflected in those of Agamemnon, and the real booty of the mid first century piled up as stage props in the drama of mythical Greek *nostos* on the stage.

In Cicero's correspondence with Caelius at the end of the 50s BCE, at least two temporal layers are in play, particularly from the reader's perspective. As Caelius predicts the imminent outbreak of war, the modern reader of the letters (encouraged by the editor's design, which makes the most of the image of Caelius as a true prophet) sees *at the same time* both the time immediately before the war began and the time afterwards.[67] We see what Reinhart Koselleck has termed a 'past future', seen from the uncertain and open perspective of the letter writer and his addressee, but also the outcome in hindsight. The letter as a genre allows for 'sight' of the future, or — as in 7.1 (or *Tristia* 4.2) — of an alternative concurrent present, while the epistolary collection implicitly compares the writer's vision with the verifiable historical outcome.

So far, I have focussed on fictional aspects of individual letters or small groups of letters. However, the 'collage' effects in individual letters are infinitely multiplied and enhanced by the unknown editor's design for the collection as a whole. The editor as an implied narrator selects and arranges the letters in a way that emplots factual or documentary material within implicit narratives, and makes new sense of historical 'realities.'[68] In this way letter collections preserve the openness and uncertainty of the original writer's perspective, from which the future is unknown and can be only imagined, while simultaneously suggesting a structure and irony that are visible to later readers.[69]

In many instances, the thematic architecture of a single book enriches and contextualises the most fictionalised elements of individual letters. Even Caelius'

---

[67] The effect on our perception of the present (as experienced by Cicero and Caelius) is considerable. We might compare Morson's observation on the effects of foreshadowing: 'when foreshadowing is used, the sense of many possible futures, which in life we experience at every present moment, is revealed as an illusion.' Morson 1998, 601.

[68] Cammoranesi 2022, 28.

[69] See Morson's contrast between the 'texture of daily life', in which 'the weight of chance and choice may lead to many different outcomes', and the inherent artificiality of even the most realistic narrative (which is predicated upon structure and closure) illuminates the dual effect of epistolary collections (Morson 1998, 599–600).

characteristic deployment of the language of spectacle is enhanced by the proximity of his attempts to persuade Cicero to supply exotic animals for the arena. This young aedile, with his foresight and his creative vision, is imaginatively anticipating a 'show' to come that will have been especially designed to grip his addressee's attention, while routinely pestering that same addressee to guarantee the supply chain for the showstopping Cilician panthers in his own aedilician games (8.2.2; 8.4.5; 8.6.5; 8.9.3).[70]

My two case studies, *Fam.* 7.1 and 9.26, are thematically well rooted in their books, which repeatedly reflect upon various aspects of *otium*, such as jokes, dinners, literary composition, villa decoration, or the unwelcome *otium* imposed by illness. Both books share an interest in the interplay between *otium* and political realities, and it seems not coincidental that the editor has built them out of so many letters that explore quasi-philosophical responses to enforced or unsatisfying *otium*, allowing Cicero to explore the right way to live both in the present and (implicitly or explicitly) in the future, even when facing times of politically-enforced misery and constraint.[71]

Themes of jokes and dinners begin to appear in Book 7. In a letter of November 54, Cicero claims that he rarely dines out (7.16.2; cf. 7.9.3). Thereafter, however, dinners become a recurrent — and increasingly performative — motif in this book (especially in the letters to Papirius),[72] as Cicero plays himself as a quasi-comic figure who opens his own 'School for Caesarian Orators' in return

---

70 This itself prompts an instance of humorous epistolary fictionalisation. Caelius' persistent nagging elicits from Cicero an epistolary animal fable about his feline constituents (the only disgruntled citizens of his province): 'about the panthers, the usual hunters are doing their best on my instructions. But the creatures are in remarkably short supply, and those we have are said to be complaining bitterly because they are the only beings in my province who have to fear designs against their safety. Accordingly they are reported to have decided to leave this province and go to Caria' (*Fam.* 2.11.2). For animals 'moving out' cf. *Att.* 14.9.1. On the animal fable as one of the most clearly marked fictional utterances from early Greek society, see Bowie 1993, 3; on the fictional communications in animal fables as an *imago quaedam uitae hominum*, cf. Isidore of Seville 1.40.
71 Cf. De Giorgio 2015, 178–180, who analyses Cicero's famous list of Greek *theseis* on tyranny for oral declamatory practice in *Att.* 9.4 as a quasi-fictionalised means of temporarily detaching from the subjective self and from its reality; De Giorgio argues that the theses (expressed in self-consciously distancing Greek) allow Cicero to compensate for the 'worn-out' written (specifically epistolary) mechanisms for evaluating and coping with the current political situation. Cf. Gunderson 2003, 105–106. These *theseis* are also, as de Giorgio points out, represented as vital in the development of a thoughtful *persona* in the political emergency of the early 40s.
72 E.g. in 7.20 Cicero has borrowed a book 'On Eating Too Much'; in 7.26 he has indigestion and diarrhoea from eating too much of some fibrous vegetable dishes at an augural banquet; in 7.22 we find a less food-focussed drinking session with Trebatius.

for lessons in gourmet eating at the tables of Caesar's friends. *Fam.* 7.33 (addressed, perhaps not altogether coincidentally, to the Volumnius with whom he dines in *Fam.* 9.26) picks up a recurrent and cumulative motif of human life as a performance. Here Cicero acknowledges that as regards Caesar he has been playing a part — one that he would like to abandon from now on (*Fam.* 7.33.2: *deponere illam iam personam*), in favour of a hidden life in *otium* with likeminded literary types. This echoes not only Cicero's rueful picture of himself as constrained to play the hired celebrity performer in 7.1, but also Trebatius' role (humorously captured in one of the book's central correspondences) as the quasi-comedic lawyer in Caesar's entourage in Gaul and in Britain.[73]

Reflections upon *otium* in these books often revolve around the question of what is real and what is not. We see in *Fam.* 7.1 the beginnings of Cicero's paradoxical reflections upon unsatisfying and 'unreal' reality, on the one hand, and a more nourishing and emotionally substantial literary idyll (itself also a product of Cicero's imagination), to which one might reasonably retreat when powerful individuals control the real world. *Fam.* 7.1 (although set before Caesar's dictatorship) also lays groundwork for a theme of empty, unsatisfying activity in the city that will develop into the stifling atmosphere of Book 9.[74] Book 9 intensifies the motifs of unreality, dwelling repeatedly upon fictions — even fakes — of all kinds, interwoven with reflections upon how Cicero can express his 'real' self.

Humour as both survival mechanism and distinctive marker of the true Cicero becomes increasingly prominent, culminating in the dinner scene of *Fam.* 9.26. Paradoxically, the most authoritative authentication of the true Cicero in these books comes from the same quarter as the power that has distorted every other aspect of his life and persona. It is Caesar himself who is figured as true connoisseur of 'authentic' Cicero: 9.16.4 tells us about Caesar's request that Cicero's humorous remarks be reported to him as part of the daily news briefing, and his accurate discernment in rejecting any that have been falsely ascribed to Cicero.[75] The 'golden threads' of Book 9 are Cicero's inability to tolerate the *otium* forced upon him by Caesar's political dominance,[76] and his attempts to cling to some version of a 'real' self. The correspondence with Varro earlier in Book 9 already explores related issues about the 'fit' between persona and setting, and

---

[73] 7.33 also echoes 7.1 also in telling its addressee that he missed nothing (in this case by missing Cicero's demonstration performances in rhetoric), and likewise gradually explores Cicero's longing to spend leisure time with his addressee in some more bearable future.
[74] See Cammoranesi 2022, 53.
[75] Cf. *Fam.* 15.21 on Trebonius' compilation of Ciceronian witticisms.
[76] As Cammoranesi 2022 points out, Books 7–9 are dominated by Caesarian narrative.

the degree to which the letters' protagonists can remain recognizable as their old selves; 9.1, for example, presents an fable of Cicero's reconciliation with his books (i.e. a return to an old self), while in 9.2 and 9.3 Cicero writes of his misgivings about a proposed trip to the resort of Baiae, which might shock or surprise their critics.[77] The dinner scene of *Fam.* 9.26, then, is but the culmination of an extended set of epistolary reflections in this book upon (among many other things) the authenticity of the Ciceronian self and the degree to which the great man seeks to portray himself as taking on a lightly fictionalised set of alternative personae.

Fictionalising material has a natural place, then, even in 'authentic' correspondence, and is even at home in letters on political, professional, and historical topics. Fictionalisation is a personal coping mechanism for a letter writer; in crisis it becomes a means of expressing (emotional and non-factual) truths about painful subjective experience, but it can be employed to ease even mildly uncomfortable social interactions. Fictionalising strategies express the management of self and of subjective experiences, and they help a letter writer explore quasi-philosophical choices about how to live. Epistolary fictionalisation is also itself a political strategy in the broadest sense; it is applied and explored especially at moments when Cicero most feels the constraints imposed by the great generals, including, initially, Pompey, whose success (and the ensuing celebrations described in 7.1) shut down personal agency in the Roman populace. It reflects Cicero's career in Caesar-management, too, from the weary acquiescence of his defence of Caninius during the days of Caesar's alliance with Pompey, to the retreat into literary work and the uncharacteristic gourmandise of 46–45 BCE. The Ciceronian letters I have discussed do not fabricate the events they describe. Nevertheless, in their constructions of alternate, parallel and imagined worlds, they make dazzlingly creative use of even familiar techniques of literary intertextuality, or of epistolary tropes and conventions, drawing attention to their own inventiveness to explore the writerly process of interpreting and improving subjective experience.

---

77 See Leach 1999.

Emilia A. Barbiero
Let's Get Real: Ekphrasis, Reality and Fiction in Pliny's *Epistles*

Abstract: Does Pliny's *Epistles* contain real correspondence actually sent to and received by the author's friends, or are its texts fictional, originating not 'in the mail' but as literary exercises cast in epistolary form? My paper considers this much-debated question from a new angle, arguing that it is a generic problem contemplated by the text itself. I show that the *Epistles* self-consciously inhabits an ontological space between document and literature which it explores through the use of ekphrasis. This rhetorical device is an 'almost *but not quite*' means of producing sight: its fundamental fictiveness undercuts the reality of the vision generated through *enargeia*. Such ambiguity of a trope that is at once very real in effect and *not-real* in its mimesis of perception gestures towards the status of Pliny's letters as similarly suspended between the real and the fake, ultimately acknowledging this epistolary collection's novel 'in-between-ness'.

Keywords: ekphrasis, *enargeia*, *mimesis*, Pliny the Younger, rhetoric

1 Introduction

> The boundary between document and literature is inevitably a contested one; and private letters, published or unpublished, are always a challenge to it.[1]

Much ink has been spilled in debating the authenticity of Pliny's *Epistles*. Does this corpus contain real correspondence actually sent to and received by the author's friends, or are its texts fictional, originating as literary exercises cast in epistolary form?[2] The long-standing *quaestio* remains *uexata*. In what Whitton has called a 'critical cold war' between Pliny's literary and historical readers,[3]

I am grateful to David Levene and Claire Rachel Jackson for their comments on earlier versions of this paper.

1 Beard 2002, 124.
2 For a review of the critical debate (genuine *vs* literary), see Gamberini 1983, 122–136 and, more recently, Whitton 2019, 37–50 especially nn. 87, 88 and 89, as well as Gibson's contribution to this volume.
3 Whitton 2019, 37.

no consensus has been reached and interest in the matter has waned, with scholarship moving on to different avenues of inquiry.[4] And yet something remains to be said about this old question. My paper reconsiders the *Epistles*' historicity *vs* its existence as a literary artifact from a new angle. In what follows, I show that rather than a sterile controversy invented by modern scholarship, the matter of real or fake is a generic problem contemplated by the text itself.[5] For Pliny's letters self-consciously inhabit an ambiguous ontological space — the 'contested boundary' between document and literature identified in the quote with which this chapter begins.

The collection's equivocal status is acknowledged in its very first text, a letter addressed to Septicius Clarus (Plin. *Ep.* 1.1):

Frequenter hortatus es ut epistulas, si quas paulo curatius scripsissem, colligerem publicaremque. Collegi non seruato temporis ordine (neque enim historiam componebam), sed ut quaeque in manus uenerat. Superest ut nec te consilii nec me paeniteat obsequii. Ita enim fiet, ut eas quae adhuc neglectae iacent requiram et si quas addidero non supprimam. Vale.[6]

You have often urged me to collect and publish my letters, if there were any I had written a little more artfully. I've collected these without keeping to their chronological order (after all, I wasn't writing history), but as each had come into my hand. It remains for you not to regret your advice and for me not to regret following it. And so it will be — that I'll

---

[4] Intertextuality and the letters' arrangement (including the sequence of the books' publication) represent the two major trends in Plinian studies over the past decade or so. For the former, see especially Marchesi 2008 and Whitton 2019. For the latter, see Gibson/Morello 2012 and Marchesi 2015b. There has also been critical interest in how the *Epistles* serves as a means of elite self-presentation and self-fashioning: see Hoffner 1999 and Henderson 2002.

[5] Similarly, Whitton 2019, 47: 'If modern readers struggle to agree how far the *Epistles* represents real, historical, naïve, lightly edited correspondence, how far an artistic, literary, learned work of Alexandrian proportions, that reflects an equivocation essential to the collection itself'. And yet for Whitton, this equivocation operates on the level of the individual readers — and thus individual readings — 'of many hues': 'There are the epistoliteralists of antiquity, willing to swallow the confessional conceit (or suspend disbelief), read the letters at face value, and admire the author's splendid figure; perhaps that included readers towards the lower-brow end of the spectrum. Others can remove the first layers of the artichoke, observing and savouring the artistry of these sketches, of the prose, of the *imitatio*. (That need not preclude compliant suspension of disbelief.) For those able and willing to peel further still, succulent rewards in the shape of minute formal and intertextual *doctrina* await.' My own reading of the *Epistles*' equivocation has a different focus, looking as it does not to reveal the plurality of possible responses to the collection but rather to show how the text works out its own ambiguity.

[6] The text is from Mynors' OCT. All translations are my own.

search out those [letters] still lying around overlooked and I won't keep back any that I'll write in future. Goodbye.

Whether Clarus ever really urged Pliny to publish his correspondence or not, we have no reason to doubt this letter's central claim — *viz.* that like most Romans of his class, Pliny was a prolific letter-writer. The text's final line seems in fact to refer to a collection yet in progress[7] and to an active epistolary life which kept Pliny's circle up to date and survives for us as a unique store of information about the world of the early empire. Between notes about nothing at all besides the frequency of correspondence (e.g. Plin. *Ep.* 1.11), discussions of intimate family matters (e.g. Plin. *Ep.* 8.10–11 on Calpurnia's miscarriage) and letters filled with historical accounts and political commentary crucial to our understanding of the period (e.g. the Vesuvius letters, or those about Regulus), the richly varied miscellany of correspondence in the *Epistles*' 9 books[8] paints a portrait of an ancient life lived whose veracity is held up by its consistency: Pliny's oeuvre transmits to us an image of the author that, while dynamic in reflecting changes of its author's mindset and general disposition,[9] exists as a coherent presentation of self which goes undisrupted by the sorts of contradictions that we find in Cicero's letters, for example.[10] By reading the *Epistles*, we get to 'meet' Pliny and experience slices of his life — or at least the side of his persona and the episodes of his existence that he has selected for us.

And herein lies the trouble, a conundrum of epistolary literature which the *Epistles* itself lays bare in *Ep.* 1.1 by the characterization of the letters to follow it

---

[7] Whether Pliny's comment can tell us anything about the order of the *Epistles*' composition and publication is controversial. Had Pliny already written Books 2–9 upon the release of Book 1, or did he perhaps intend to? Put a different way, does 1.1 introduce the entire collection, or just Book 1? Sherwin-White 1966, 86 is skeptical that the letter can be taken to imply anything beyond the publication of Books 1 and 2, but the question of whether Pliny's collection represents a unified literary programme conceptualized as such *ab ouo*, or something that came together gradually as Pliny wrote and sent letters to his friends, is far from certain. The matter has been most recently taken up by Bodel 2015.

[8] Although technically Pliny's oeuvre as we have it contains 10 books of letters, *Epistles* 10 (the correspondence between Pliny and Trajan) appears to have been appended to the nine-book collection in late antiquity and was likely not edited by Pliny. See, recently, Whitton 2019, 413–415.

[9] Thus, for instance, Gibson 2015 argues that the trajectory of the entire collection amounts to a 'broad thematic movement' from light to dark which stands for Pliny's increasing pessimism brought on by the presence of the emperor Trajan at Rome.

[10] E.g. Cicero's flipflopping about his career-making nemesis Catiline, whom he considers defending in the earliest preserved letter to Atticus (Cic. *Att.* 1.2) dating to 65 BCE.

as *epistulae paulo curatius scriptae*.¹¹ This expression has generated controversy, raising doubts about whether the collection is an innocent assemblage of outgoing mail or something more literary and thus more deliberate. What exactly does *curatius* mean in this context? Were some of Pliny's letters actually 'more artfully composed' than other, more mundane messages so as to justify their inclusion in a publication, or is Pliny hinting at literary composition? Or does *cura* perhaps refer to content rather than style, underscoring the attention paid to the image conveyed by each text selected for publication? Further questions arise if we consider this assertion alongside the accompanying claim of the collection's random arrangement. Pliny declares that he has assembled his correspondence in no particular order at all, slotting in his letters as he dug each out from a box of old mail, as it were. In short, *Epistles* 1.1 alleges a discrepancy between the work's constituent parts and its whole: although it demonstrates literary finesse on the micro level, the macro level of Pliny's text was apparently created randomly (*collegi ... ut quaeque in manus uenerat*).¹² Only adding to the confusion is this letter's final line which claims that Pliny's future correspondence will be included in the book(s) indiscriminately: *et si quas addidero non supprimam*. Will all of these missives be *curatius scriptae*, then, or not? And since included upon composition and not recovered later, will these texts appear in chronological order?

The opening letter to Clarus is thus anything but *clarus*,¹³ painting as it does a deliberately paradoxical picture of the *Epistles*' creation that leaves us wondering about both its individual parts and its collective whole. And it is precisely in this way that the text is programmatic: by claiming for the material it prefaces both the nonchalance of raw, private documentation and the artistry of an edited collection, *Epistles* 1.1 teases us with the equivocal status of a corpus that is self-consciously suspended between the authentic and the fictional. For Pliny's oeuvre, crafted from real parts, is just that — his letters about real people, real events and real places are the sort that Romans wrote to and received

---

11 Pliny uses the phrase elsewhere, too; see Sherwin-White 1966, 85.
12 And, indeed, we now know that the ordering of the 246 epistles to come is anything but random. Criticism of the last decade has shown that Pliny's *Epistles* is modeled on the Augustan poetry book, containing meaningful paths of reading which go both forwards and backwards and which cut through individual books as well as through the collection as a whole. For the recent work on the arrangement of and reading sequences in Pliny's *Epistles*, see n. 4. In what follows, I suggest yet more 'paths of reading' through the ekphrastic letters in Books 1, 2, 5 and 8.
13 On the significance of the *Epistles*' book-ending by letters to addressees called Clarus (Plin. *Ep.* 1.1) and Fuscus (Plin. *Ep.* 9.40), see Barchiesi 2005, 330–331.

from each other regularly; the *Epistles'* literary whole comes together as a tessellation of authentic bits that were the basic medium of social intercourse. This dual designation, which is, crucially, authorial,[14] innovates within the genre of epistolography that in Pliny's time had been previously published in one form and in the other *but never* (as far as we know!) *in both at once*. Fictional letter collections composed in verse and carefully arranged had been published by Ovid, Horace and, most recently, Statius.[15] And even if Cicero's correspondence stood as the non-authorial assemblage of private letters *par excellence*,[16] we hear that compilations of real missives by major figures like Brutus (Plin. *HN* 33.39) and Caesar (Suet. *Iul.* 56.5–7) circulated, too. There was, of course, an established Greek tradition of fictional epistolography in prose, and an emerging one in Latin attested to by Seneca's philosophical essays presented in letter form. So Pliny's *Epistles* — casual correspondence between friends compiled by the author himself into a finely wrought work — does something entirely new, combining these existing paradigms in a literary experiment[17] that blurs the line between document and literature. In other words, the missive to Clarus invites us to ask precisely what we *have* been asking, namely whether what we are reading is real or fake, documents or literature. And nor is it the only text in Pliny's collection to extend this invitation.

This chapter demonstrates that one (more) way the *Epistles* explores its double ontological status is through the use of ekphrasis, a mode of rhetorical discourse that seeks by vivid description (a force called *enargeia*) to make one's

---

14 This is not to say that *author*-ity is a necessary precondition of such artful arrangement; an editor can create literature out of someone else's letters (or poems, etc.). See Beard 2002 on the arrangement of Cicero's corpus and, in particular, of *Fam.* 16.

15 Ovid's *Epistulae Ex Ponto* is an especially important influence. As Syme 1985, 176 first perceived, Pliny's declaration in 1.1 about the collection's haphazard arrangement invites comparison with a similar claim in Ov. *Pont.* 3.9.53–4: *postmodo collectas utcumque sine ordine iunxi: / hoc opus electum ne mihi forte putes.*

16 The bibliography on Pliny's allusions to and relationship with Cicero's epistolary corpus is vast; see especially Marchesi 2008, 207–240 on how the epistolographer confronts his 'Ciceronian anxiety'.

17 So Marchesi 2008, 7: '...while traditional unwritten norms for what an epistle should look like did exist [in the tradition of Roman epistolography], and Pliny conformed to them, the "epistolary paradigm" Pliny had inherited left ample margins for independent experimentation with the architecture of the collection, and he certainly took advantage of them'. Marchesi's introduction (1–11) explores Pliny's generic innovation with a special focus on the *Epistles'* poetic nature and strong tendency to literary allusion, which is the topic of her monograph.

audience or reader 'see' something[18] that is not actually here or even something that does not exist — whether it be a place, a person, an event or an object.[19] It is no revelation that the rhetorically trained Pliny inserts ekphraseis into various letters throughout his 9-book collection; the villa letters, *Epistles* 2.17 and 5.6, have attracted critical attention on this score,[20] but there are yet others that make us 'see' — and not only. I will have something to add to the conversation by pointing out that ekphrastic discourse is introduced as a major theme of the *Epistles* in the triplet prefacing the collection, as well as by demonstrating the synaesthetic quality of Pliny's ekphraseis. But my main *telos* consists in unpacking how this mode of description works as a two-way street. While ekphrasis is employed in the *Epistles* to enhance the reality of the letter form by conjuring within a genre that is itself capable of conjuring, it is also used to subvert its own *effet de réel*.[21] Pliny accomplishes this by capitalizing on the unreality of ekphrasis as an 'almost *but not quite*' means of producing sight: as rhetorical theory on ekphrasis repeatedly reminds us, the vividness of the experience this device offers to the listener or reader is undercut by its fundamental fictiveness. Ekphrasis, that is, remains aware of the fact that what it conjures is just pretend. Such ambiguity of a trope that is at once very real in effect and *not-real* in its mimesis of perception gestures towards the status of Pliny's letters as similarly suspended between the real and the fake, ultimately acknowledging this epistolary collection's novel 'in-between-ness'.

---

18 In strictly theoretical terms, ekphrasis is a means of *subiectio sub oculis*. Cf. e.g. Quint. *Inst.* 9.1.45.
19 Ekphrasis has garnered much attention in recent decades; see, e.g., Fowler 1991; Graf 1995; Elsner 2002; Goldhill 2007; Squire 2009; Webb 2009. This discourse has focused in particular on textual descriptions of works of art. But as Webb has shown, the emphasis in ancient discussions of ekphrasis is not on its subject matter — which is, further, by no means limited to art, but its effect (*enargeia*).
20 *In primis* Chinn 2007, but see further below. There is a substantial bibliography on the villa letters which have generated interest from perspectives literary, social and archaeological; the discourse is summarized by Gibson/Morello 2012 (see Appendix 3), to which should be now added Whitton 2013, 218–255 and Whitton 2015a.
21 A term coined by Barthes 1968 to describe the sense of continuity between text and reality created by the accumulation of details in a narrative. Exactly like ekphrasis, such realism in a text makes the narrative subject 'real' to the reader. It is used specifically of *Epistles* 5.6 by Chinn 2007, 270.

2 PART I: The Real Real

While ekphraseis appear in a wide variety of genres, the device especially suits and is analogous to the epistolary medium which likewise works as a textual means of creating presence *in absentia*. Letters exist precisely to rectify (but also, occasionally, to create)[22] an absence between correspondents, and were envisioned in antiquity as capable of actually evoking the persona (*parousia*) of their author, transacting a kind of imaginary teleportation.[23] Epistolary discourse, aptly called *sermo absentium* ('the speech of those absent') in ancient epistolary theory, can bring the absent author 'here' — to wherever his letter is received and, crucially, read out, since the use of the epistolary motif on the dramatic stage suggests that recitation was particularly key to this quasi-magical experience.[24] But letters are also occasionally depicted as performing the opposite movement. Instead of transporting its author, an epistle may serve to transport the addressee back towards its (the letter's) own point of origin in what we might call a 'postcard effect': just like the modern postcard sent from a beautiful or exotic destination, some ancient letters invite their addressees to visit another place (or time),[25] if only for a brief moment.[26] This can be accomplished through a type of ekphrasis known as the *laus locorum* or the *descriptio regionum*[27] (ἔκφρασις τόπων in Greek), which entails a detailed portrayal of a place through words so as to make one's audience, whether it is reading or listening to the description, feel as if it were there. Take, for instance, what Ps. Longinus says of one such ἔκφρασις τόπων in Herodotus Book 9 which depicts the journey from Elephantine to Meroe ([Longinus], *Subl.* 26.2):

---

[22] On this point, see Hodkinson 2007.
[23] For this evocative power of epistolary discourse, see Thraede 1970.
[24] In this context, letters stand for the script and are read out to conjure up absent characters who by that very act of recitation 'appear'; thus, for instance, in the opening scene of Plautus' *Pseudolus*, a *meretrix* is made to 'appear' through her letter. See further Barbiero 2023.
[25] Second Sophistic and Late Antique epistolographers seek by their fictive letters to turn back time and conjure up the bygone world of classical Athens. See Höschele 2012 and Barbiero 2018.
[26] For example, Seneca uses the *laus locorum* to invite his addressee Lucilius to 'be' with him in various places — at Baiae, at the baths and at various country estates; see Sen. *Ep.* 51, 55, 56 and 86.
[27] Cf. Quint. *Inst.* 4.3.12–14.

ὁρᾷς, ὦ ἑταῖρε, ὡς παραλαβὼν σου τὴν ψυχὴν διὰ τῶν τόπων ἄγει τὴν ἀκοὴν ὄψιν ποιῶν;

Do you see, my friend, how he [Herodotus], seizing on your soul leads it through those places, making hearing into sight?

Several missives in Pliny's collection employ the *laus locorum* to stunning effect, and these will be our focus throughout the following pages.[28] Among them is the final text of Book 4, a letter that neatly showcases the 'postcard effect' by literally enacting its addressee's visit to the locale it depicts.

In *Epistles* 4.30, Pliny writes of a spring in his hometown of Comum which fills up and is drained from a grotto three times a day.[29] Addressed to Licinius Sura, a man renowned for his deep learning,[30] the text seeks an explanation for this peculiar phenomenon (Plin. *Ep.* 4.30.1–3):

> *Attuli tibi ex patria mea pro munusculo quaestionem altissima ista eruditione dignissimam. Fons oritur in monte, per saxa decurrit, excipitur cenatiuncula manu facta; ibi paulum retentus in Larium lacum decidit. Huius mira natura: ter in die statis auctibus ac diminutionibus crescit decrescitque. Cernitur id palam et cum summa uoluptate deprenditur.*

> Instead of a gift, I've brought along from my hometown an investigation most worthy of your learning. A spring rises up in a mountain, runs down over the rocks and is caught up in a little grotto made by hand; once it has been held there for a little while it falls down into the Larian Lake. Here's what's marvelous about it: three times a day it swells and empties with regular increases and decreases [of water]. This is easy to see and a delight to watch.

The spring is described in typical ekphrastic detail which encompasses not only visual features of the subject but also movement and its development through time. Together with the missive's primary addressee, we are urged to 'see' the water as it performs its unusual trick from where it leaves the ground, flowing thence down the mountainside, first into the *cenatiuncula* and then the Larian Lake. But we do not just 'witness' this watery curiosity, for the ekphrastic effect goes beyond sight. Pliny capitalizes on the epistolary medium's transportive faculties to invite Sura (and us) to not just 'see' but actually '*be*' at the spring and

---

28 Pliny's ekpkrastic practice is not limited to the *laus locorum*. See the extended ekphrasis of a Corinthian bronze statue of an elderly man in Plin. *Ep.* 3.6. The description of this statue is seminal in the discussion of Henderson 2002.
29 This spring still exists and can be found on the grounds of the so-called Villa Pliniana in Como. See Sherwin-White 1966, 310.
30 For more on Licinius Sura, to whom *Epistles* 7.27 is also addressed, see Sherwin-White 1966, 309–310.

to engage in a series of activities while there. Here is the continuation of the passage quoted above (Plin. *Ep.* 4.30.3–4):

> Iuxta recumbis et uesceris, atque etiam ex ipso fonte (nam est frigidissimus) potas; interim ille certis dimensisque momentis uel subtrahitur uel adsurgit. Anulum seu quid aliud ponis in sicco, adluitur sensim ac nouissime operitur, detegitur rursus paulatimque deseritur. Si diutius obserues, utrumque iterum ac tertio uideas.

> You lie down nearby to eat, and you even drink from the very spring (the water is most cool); in the meantime, it ebbs and rises at regular and measurable intervals. You place a ring or whatever else where it is dry; gradually the water washes against it until at long last it is covered, and then again, bit by bit, it is uncovered and given up. If you should watch it a little longer, you would see each process happen again and then a third time.

Epistles 4.30 carries out the addressee's transportation by incorporating him into the ekphrasis, using verbs in the second person so as to allow Sura to literally experience the spring. That is, 4.30's addressee is sucked into the text's ekphrastic narrative by reading it. Once 'at Comum', Licinius Sura is made to observe the spring's miraculous ebb and flow, conducting a mini experiment while he enjoys a picnic which includes drinking the spring's cool water. The subject of description/observation (or: observation *within* the description) — a pool of water — implicitly 'mirrors' the effect: by 'gazing' at the water described by Pliny in this self-reflexive and self-reflective ekphrasis, Licinius Sura sees himself 'in' it although he is not *really* there.

I will return to the reflective property of water later on in this chapter, for we 'see' bodies of water described in ekphraseis elsewhere in the collection, and this is no coincidence: Pliny uses the quintessentially mimetic (and therefore deceptive) element to underline the fictionality of ekphrasis, the very trope through which water is described.[31] For now, let us focus on the fact that *Epistles* 4.30's ekphrasis about the spring at Comum is *real*-ized within the letter containing it: the reader who through 'enargetic' description becomes a seer goes one step further into what amounts to a perceptual mimesis to materialize (or should we say 'textualize'?) inside the ekphrasis itself, morphing into an actor

---

31 We find water working as a metaliterary emblem elsewhere in ancient literature, too. The sea and sea-voyaging, for example, function as symbols of epic poetry from the Hellenistic period onwards. See Harrison 2007. In what follows I consider specifically how Pliny makes use of the potential for literary self-reflection offered by water's reflective properties, to which we might compare (e.g.) the mirroring pond in the Echo and Narcissus myth in *Metamorphoses* 3: like the figure of Echo, the body of water reifies Ovid's intertextual strategy (i.e. his echoing/mirroring of other texts) inside the text. See Gildenhard/Zissos 2000.

who can see, touch and taste. By casting its reader into the very scene it conjures up through his (the reader's) own act of reading, letter 4.30's ekphrasis models the correct response to its vivid description and illustrates its own all-encompassing quality. In short, the missive shows us how through its simulation of reality, ekphrasis (and epistolary ekphrasis *in particular*) is capable of transporting us elsewhere.

But does Sura's ekphrastic experience at the spring actually replace a visit? Has the addressee 'seen' enough to explain this curiosity? *Epistles* 4.30 both asks this question and leaves it unresolved, manifesting a hesitation between ekphrastic realism and fictionality that we will explore at length in *Epistles* 5.6. In letter 4.30, Pliny follows his all-encompassing description of the spring with a number of perfectly plausible explanations for its strange behaviour (the distension of unseen air, a sort of tide, the presence of a reservoir etc.; Plin. *Ep.* 4.30.7–10), inviting Sura to choose one and thereby effectively answering his (Pliny's) own query. What, then, is the purpose of the ekphrasis to begin with, if not to allow Sura to come up with his own explanation by 'seeing' the watery phenomenon himself? Or perhaps ekphrastic description is *not* vivid enough for its reader to discern the trick's *causa* (after all, ekphrastic seeing isn't *really* sight), a possibility suggested in the text's final line where Pliny not only raises the prospect of ekphrastic failure (can we detect some sarcasm in *potes enim*?) but, further, disclaims responsibility for Sura's knowledge of the spring altogether (Plin. *Ep.* 4.30.11):

> *Scrutare tu causas (potes enim), quae tantum miraculum efficiunt: mihi abunde est, si satis expressi quod efficitur. Vale.*

> You, now, investigate the forces behind such a miraculous phenomenon (certainly you're able to do so): it's more than enough for me if I've accurately described what happens. Goodbye.

The immersive and yet fundamentally fictional literary experience that letter 4.30 animates occurs throughout Pliny's *Epistles*. Ekphrasis features prominently in the oeuvre, both thematically and quantitatively: letters 2.17 and 5.6, which contain lengthy ekphraseis of (two of) Pliny's vacation villas, are the fourth longest and longest missives in the entire collection, respectively; ekphrasis is employed to portray the terrifying setting of both Pompeii letters (surely highlights of the collection as much for ancient readers as they are for us) and, as I argue below, operates as a prominent motif in Book 8, where through ekphrastic description we 'see' a spring at the river Clitumnus, the destruction wrought by flooding around Rome and a remarkable lake on a property at Ameria. Ekphrasis' importance to the collection *tout court* is also suggested by its introduction in *Epistles* 1.3 to Caninius Rufus. Letter 1.3 is the final text in an opening triplet that introduces Pliny's oeuvre but also contemplates its genesis by thematizing publication and the editorial toils involved — what Ilaria Marchesi has seen as a 'response to the cultural expectations that Pliny's readership might perceive as imposed by the act of publishing one's own work'.[32] Put another way, all three of the *Epistles'* opening texts are concerned with justifying Pliny's literary programme which entails (the novelty of) an author making literature out of his own private correspondence. But before seeking to discern what ekphrastic description is doing in this programmatic miniseries, let us continue reading the letters that compose it in order (as Pliny intended!), for *Epistles* 1.3 'says' much more about the matter at hand in conversation with its neighbours in the text.

We have already observed that letter 1.1 to Septicius Clarus engages with (the problem of) the collection's equivocal status; the following missive, addressed to Arrianus Maturus, does, too, if in a slightly different vein. *Epistles* 1.2 accompanies the draft of a speech Pliny has recently composed and seeks the addressee's comments. It describes the work to be edited as one of considerable artistry. Pliny tells us that in composing the speech he imitated the style of Demosthenes, Calvus and Cicero, and apparently quite successfully, since the piece has already earned the approbation of various other peers. And yet this oeuvre is absent, its elegance left to the reader's imagination while the 'cursory' note about it is included in the published collection. Like its textual predecessor, *Epistles* 1.2 juxtaposes casual writing and literary finesse, apparently switching in the former for the latter although once again it is a sleight of hand. Pliny's collection is in fact replete with the sort of refinement that 1.2 ascribes to the author's speech — including 1.2 itself. In talking *about* style, that is, Pliny employs it, using in his epistle the very same kind of *figurae orationis* (Plin. *Ep.* 1.2.2) which it (the letter) tells Arrianus to expect in the attached oration.[33] Letter 1.2 is also fundamentally literary in its dense allusivity: the text quotes Virgil and echoes Quintilian as well as various texts of Cicero, standing as a fine *exemplum* of Plinian *imitatio* in a letter precisely about literary *imitatio*.[34]

---

32 Marchesi 2015a, 228.
33 To name but a few such devices, the text employs synkrisis (*Demosthenen semper tuum, Caluum nuper meum*), a tricolon of sorts (the naming of Demosthenes, Calvus and, slightly later, Cicero as Pliny's literary models in the speech), alliteration and homoioteleuton (*uim tantorum uirorum*), parenthesis (*uereor ne improbe dicam*) and repetition (*blandiuntur ... blandiantur*). For Pliny's remarks on style, see Gamberini 1983, 37–40.
34 Whitton 2019, 487 calls the text a 'performative meditation on *imitatio*'. He gives a full analysis on pp. 61–67.

In this way, *Epistles* 1.2 asks the same question as 1.1, although it is phrased in slightly different terms, namely: can a casual letter about a piece of literature itself count as a piece of literature? In and by its very literary fabric, letter 1.2 answers its own question, and its textual neighbour 1.3 continues the demonstration. Here is the text, in full (Plin. *Ep.* 1.3):

> *Quid agit Comum, tuae meaeque deliciae? Quid suburbanum amoenissimum, quid illa porticus uerna semper, quid platanon opacissimus, quid euripus uiridis et gemmeus, quid subiectus et seruiens lacus, quid illa mollis et tamen solida gestatio, quid balineum illud quod plurimus sol implet et circumit, quid triclinia illa popularia illa paucorum, quid cubicula diurna nocturna? Possident te et per uices partiuntur? An, ut solebas, intentione rei familiaris obeundae crebris excursionibus auocaris? Si possident, felix beatusque es; si minus, 'unus e multis'. Quin tu (tempus enim) humiles et sordidas curas aliis mandas, et ipse te in alto isto pinguique secessu studiis adseris? Hoc sit negotium tuum hoc otium; hic labor haec quies; in his uigilia, in his etiam somnus reponatur. Effinge aliquid et excude, quod sit perpetuo tuum. Nam reliqua rerum tuarum post te alium atque alium dominum sortientur, hoc numquam tuum desinet esse si semel coeperit. Scio quem animum, quod horter ingenium; tu modo enitere ut tibi ipse sis tanti, quanti uideberis aliis si tibi fueris. Vale.*

What's up with Comum, your favourite and mine? And what about your most delightful estate and its eternally spring-like portico? What about its shadiest grove of plane trees, its canal green and sparkling, and the nearby lake which affords a pleasant view? What about the promenade, soft and yet firm? How about that bath — the one much sun fills and surrounds, and the dining rooms — those for the many and those for the few, and what of the bedrooms for both day and night? Do these places possess you and share in your presence in turns? Or are you, as usual, called away by frequent errands for the purpose of attending to family matters? If they possess you, you are blessed; if not, 'welcome to the club'. But really, why don't you hand the minor and lowly stuff over to other people and plant yourself in your deep and rich retreat for studies? It's about time. Let this be your business and your pleasure, this your toil and your rest; for these pursuits ought to be reserved both your waking hours and your sleep. Make something, hammer it out — something yours for all time. For everything else you have will fall to some other owner's lot after you, but this will never cease to be yours once it comes into being. I know what mind and spirit I'm urging on; you just *try*, so that you may be worth to yourself as much as you will be worth to others — once you shall be so in your own eyes. Goodbye.

As has been recognized, the missive to Caninius Rufus introduces villa description as a major trope of the *Epistles* and identifies the vacation home as an ideal space for literary production.[35] But there is clearly something programmatic about 1.3, too. If 1.2 continues to tease us with the collection's ambiguous status

---

35 On the villa in Pliny's *Epistles* as a 'factory of literature', see Hoffer 1999, 29–44 whose discussion focuses specifically on letter 1.3. Hoffer calls this missive a 'miniature version' of the longer villa letters to come (33).

between raw documentation and literature by swapping in a finely wrought letter *about* a finely wrought speech for the speech itself, 1.3 concretely stands in for that absent piece of oratory to which 1.2 claims to be attached by showcasing a rhetorical technique that will figure so prominently over the following books — ekphrasis. In fact, since letter 1.2 never tells us what sort of speech Pliny is sending to Maturus, we might well assume on the basis of the *Epistles*' arrangement that is it an epideictic *laudatio loci*.³⁶ For our purposes, the letter matters in particular for what it 'says' about this discursive mode, posing questions to the addressee about his villa at Comum that solicit the kind of involvement *real*-ized by letter 4.30 but which also simultaneously illustrate the rhetorical trope at hand. So, for instance, via Pliny's requests to read about these places and things in a return missive, we are granted a glimpse of Caninius' *euripus uiridis et gemmeus*, invited to witness the warmth of his *porticus* where it is always spring and to feel with our feet the property's *gestatio* whose ground is at once soft and solid. It is worth noting, too, that the architectural features of Caninius Rufus' villa which Pliny asks about are the very same spots the author will 'show' us later in the collection;³⁷ that is, Pliny asks his addressee for precisely the sort of epistles he himself will write (has written?) about his own vacation properties/literary retreats in 2.17 and 5.6. And indeed, just like his famous villa letters, whose synaesthetic texture we will soon discover, 1.3 is richly engaging in its evocation of not only sight but also sensations like temperature and texture, seeking in this multisensory way to simulate the reader's presence 'there' — which is, after all, a crucial part of letter 1.3's *raison d'être*, for this text that urges its addressee to quit his everyday life and retire to Comum *does just that*, transporting Caninus Rufus (and us) to the lovely villa there.

Like 4.30, letter 1.3 engenders a vividly immersive involvement with the text which seeks to simulate the reader's presence in the scene evoked. Rhetorical theory recognizes this mesmeric, all-encompassing quality of ekphrastic discourse. And although the *Progymnasmata* refer specifically to ekphrasis' power to make the listener/reader see the subject of description, they do not exclude the arousal of other senses,³⁸ characterizing the device as a force that acts on its listener or reader telepathically via a quasi-physical impact.³⁹ Consider the fa-

---

36 Sherwin-White 1966, 86 assumes the speech to be the *De Heluiti Ultione*, but the text seems to be hinting otherwise.
37 Noted by Sherwin-White 1966, 91–92.
38 See Webb 2009, 22.
39 So Plutarch reports that Xenocrates advocated putting ear guards on the young, since the ears are the main point of entry for both virtue and vice (Plut. *Mor.* 38b).

mous definition offered by Ps. Longinus, who claims that ekphrasis 'not only persuades the listener, but even enslaves him' (οὐ πείθει τὸν ἀκροατὴν μόνον, ἀλλὰ καὶ δουλοῦται, [Longinus], *Subl.* 15.9), or Quintilian's comment that ekphrasis is capable of 'penetrating the mind' (*in adfectus... penetrat*, Quint. *Inst.* 8.3.67). Furnishing much more than a simple description, ekphrasis creates an experience. As Ruth Webb puts it:

> The difference [between ekphrasis and description] is more than a technical distinction between 'showing' and 'telling'. Instead, it lies in the way each mode of discourse is received by the listener: *enargeia* derives from the innermost recesses of the speaker's mind and works its way inside the listener to produce its intense effect.[40]

It should be no wonder if letter 4.30 strikes us as a narrative re-enactment of precisely this dynamic; Chinn has shown Pliny's engagement with the rhetorical theory on ekphrasis in letter 5.6, and the same is true of 1.3, albeit on a smaller scale. For when Pliny asks Caninius of the places he has just ('enargetically') described (*Possident te et per uices partiuntur?*) his words are suggestive of ekphrasis' unique ability to overpower and take possession of the audience's mind and thereby underscore the impact of this very missive which 'transports' Caninius to Comum through a mini tour of its various parts. 1.3's addressee is thus 'seized' by the ekphrasis of his own villa and transported there in as much as the imaginative engagement it engenders sweeps him in. Pliny's ekphrastic *pièces de résistance*, letters 2.17 and 5.6, showcase this dynamic more extensively than any other texts in the collection. But let it be said that letter 1.3 tries out their ekphrastic *modus operandi* first, tracing their rudiments and foregrounding their effect more closely than criticism has realized.

Having been prepared for (literary) travel by 1.3, we are properly taken away on all-out tours of Pliny's own vacation properties in the villa letters. These texts show us each house room by room (we 'see' all the spaces asked about in the missive to Caninius Rufus and more) as well as the surrounding gardens. While it has long been perceived that these missives bring the subjects of their description *sub oculis*, it remains to be said that by lingering over minute details they create stunningly lifelike impressions of the properties that go beyond sight to affect the reader's other senses. Consider, for instance, the following excerpt from 2.17, a description of Pliny's villa in the *ager Laurens* addressed to Gallus (Plin. *Ep.* 2.17.13–19):

---

[40] Webb 2009, 99.

Let's Get Real: Ekphrasis, Reality and Fiction in Pliny's *Epistles* — **221**

Est et alia turris; in hac cubiculum, in quo sol nascitur conditurque; lata post apotheca et horreum, sub hoc triclinium, quod turbati maris non nisi fragorem et sonum patitur, eumque iam languidum ac desinentem; hortum et gestationem uidet, qua hortus includitur. Gestatio buxo aut rore marino, ubi deficit buxus, ambitur; nam buxus, qua parte defenditur tectis, abunde uiret; aperto caelo apertoque uento et quamquam longinqua aspergine maris inarescit. Adiacet gestationi interiore circumitu uinea tenera et umbrosa, nudisque etiam pedibus mollis et cedens. Hortum morus et ficus frequens uestit, quarum arborum illa uel maxime ferax terra est, malignior ceteris. Hac non deteriore quam maris facie cenatio remota a mari fruitur, cingitur diaetis duabus a tergo, quarum fenestris subiacet uestibulum uillae et hortus alius pinguis et rusticus. Hinc cryptoporticus prope publici operis extenditur. Vtrimque fenestrae, a mari plures, ab horto singulae sed alternis pauciores. Hae cum serenus dies et immotus, omnes, cum hinc uel inde uentis inquietus, qua uenti quiescunt sine iniuria patent. Ante cryptoporticum xystus uiolis odoratus. Teporem solis infusi repercussu cryptoporticus auget, quae ut tenet solem sic aquilonem inhibet summouetque, quantumque caloris ante tantum retro frigoris; similiter africum sistit, atque ita diuersissimos uentos alium alio latere frangit et finit. Haec iucunditas eius hieme, maior aestate. Nam ante meridiem xystum, post meridiem gestationis hortique proximam partem umbra sua temperat, quae, ut dies creuit decreuitue, modo breuior modo longior hac uel illa cadit. Ipsa uero cryptoporticus tum maxime caret sole, cum ardentissimus culmini eius insistit. Ad hoc patentibus fenestris fauonios accipit transmittitque nec umquam aere pigro et manente ingrauescit.

There is also another storey; in this there is a bedroom in which the sun rises and sets, and behind a large wine cellar and store-room. Underneath is a dining room which does not suffer the stormy sea except for the noise of its breaking, and even this is faint and dying out. It looks out on the garden and promenade which is surrounded by the garden. The promenade is encircled by a boxwood hedge or by rosemary where the boxwood does not grow; for the boxwood, where it is protected by buildings, grows abundantly but is dried up by open sky and open wind as well as by the sea spray, even if at a distance. A tender and plentiful vine pergola lies adjacent to the interior of the promenade, [where the ground is] soft and yielding even to the unshod foot. The garden is dense with mulberry and fig trees which that soil is most productive of, but it is more hostile to others. On this side, the dining room removed from the sea enjoys a view not inferior to that of the sea itself. It is surrounded from the back by two rooms from the windows of which lies a view of the entrance to the house and another rich, if more natural, garden. From here, a covered portico stretches out, almost as large as a public building. On each side are windows, more facing the sea; on the garden side there are fewer, one for every two. When the day is peaceful and windless these are all opened; when the day is restless because of winds [coming] from this side or that, the windows on the side where the winds are calm are opened without harm. In front is a covered portico fragrant with violets. The covered portico intensifies the warmth of the beating sun by reflection, and as it retains the sun it restrains and breaks off the north wind. For this reason, it has as much warmth in front as coolness behind. So, too, does it check the south-west wind and thus it breaks and cuts off a variety of winds by one or another of its sides. This is its allure in winter which is even greater in summer: for by its shade the gallery is kept cool before midday and after midday the nearest part of the promenade and the garden. As the day waxes and wanes, its shade falls now shorter and now longer on this side and on that. In fact, it is then that the covered portico has the least sunshine, when the sun, burning most brightly, beats down on its roof. For this reason it receives and ushers through the west winds when its windows are open and nor does it ever grow oppressive with stuffy and stale air.

As we tour this part of the estate, all but one of our five senses are aroused. We feel the sun's warmth and the coolness of the shade in different parts of the house throughout various times of day as well as in different seasons of the year, and experience the winds (north, west and south-west, high and low) through windows that afford marvelous views of the Mediterranean Sea as well as of the garden on the other side. From the sitting room we can *just* hear the sea's roar, and if we get close to the rosemary planted in the place of boxwood, we will get sprinkled by it, too. We even smell the flowers planted on the open colonnade and test the texture of the alley round the promenade with our bare feet. When we cannot only see but also hear, feel and smell the Laurentine villa, we find ourselves very much 'there'. Thus the invitation to Gallus to come to Pliny's property with which 2.17 ends (Plin. *Ep.* 2.17.29) turns out to have been already fulfilled, since a 'visit' has been occurring all the while, enacted by Pliny's lengthy description of his villa in all its spaces and the sensations these offer to guests.

The brief glimpse of Caninius Rufus' estate in a few lines of letter 1.3 is much expanded upon in 2.17. But Pliny does not exhaust his capacity for description in what is only the second book of his collection. 1083 vivid words on his Laurentine villa turn out to be only 'the winter warm-up act for the summer paradise',[41] massively outdone by 1520 words about the Tuscan estate in *Epistles* 5.6 which is the longest text in Pliny's collection by far.[42] 5.6 contains all that 2.17 does, only much more of it: the addressee, Domitius Apollinaris, is treated to a barrage of details on (*inter alia*) the country surrounding the property and the texture of its soil, the area's climate and prevalent breezes in different parts of the year, the many different rooms of the villa and their feel (shady and breezy, bright and hot) and the noises (or lack thereof) in various parts of the house — all conveyed by 'enargetic' description that re-enacts the experience of actually touring Pliny's estate. For instance, we are invited into a seaside dining

---

41 Whitton 2015a, 133.
42 I owe these word counts to Whitton 2015a, who makes some fascinating observations on the 'architexture' (i.e. the interaction of textual and physical architecture) of *Epistles* 2, including how letter 2.17's length and position prepares us for and relates to the structural weight of its partner 5.6. So Whitton points out that whereas 2.17 is the 41st letter in the *Epistles*, standing two-fifths of the way from 1.1 to 5.6, 5.6 is n. 101 and itself comes two-fifths of the way through the collection as a whole (132–3).

room and a nearby portico flanked by a cabana of sorts in the following paragraph whose multisensory portrayal entails details on what we 'see', 'feel' and 'hear' in these spots (Plin. *Ep.* 5.6.19–21):

> *A capite porticus triclinium excurrit; ualuis xystum desinentem et protinus pratum multumque ruris uidet, fenestris hac latus xysti et quod prosilit uillae, hac adiacentis hippodromi nemus comasque prospectat. Contra mediam fere porticum diaeta paulum recedit, cingit areolam, quae quattuor platanis inumbratur. Inter has marmoreo labro aqua exundat circumiectasque platanos et subiecta platanis leni aspergine fouet. Est in hac diaeta dormitorium cubiculum quod diem clamorem sonum excludit, iunctaque ei cotidiana amicorumque cenatio: areolam illam, porticus illam, eademque omnia quae porticus adspicit.*

> From the head of the portico extends a dining room; this looks through its doors upon the end of the terrace and then, in a continuous sight, a meadow and much of the countryside beyond it. Through its windows here it gazes upon the side of the terrace and part of the villa that sticks out, whereas there [it gazes upon] the grove and trees of the adjacent riding grounds. Almost opposite to the middle of the portico a room recedes a little and surrounds a small courtyard which is shaded by four plane trees. Between these, water flows from a marble basin and with its gentle spray it supports the surrounding plane trees and the ground lying beneath them. In this room there is a bedroom which shuts out the day, the commotion, the noise, and next to it is an everyday dining room for friends; this looks upon that small courtyard, that portico and all which is visible from the portico.

And just as it takes the ekphrastic mode one step further (Domitius Apollinaris' visit to Tuscany 'lasts' much longer and is more in depth than any other such epistolary voyage in the *Epistles*), 5.6 demonstrates acute self-awareness of its 'postcard effect', emphasizing the conjuring trick it realizes by equating the act of reading a text about the seaside retreat with visiting it[43] (Plin. *Ep.* 5.6.41):

> *Vitassem iam dudum ne uiderer argutior, nisi proposuissem omnes angulos tecum epistula circumire. Neque enim uerebar ne laboriosum esset legenti tibi, quod uisenti non fuisset, praesertim cum interquiescere, si liberet, depositaque epistula quasi residere saepius posses.*

> I would have long since avoided seeming excessively wordy if I had not intended for this letter to take you around into every corner. Nor was I worried that it would be boring for you to read about a place that it would not have been boring for you to visit — especially since you would be able to pause and rest (so to speak) by putting down the letter as often as you liked.

---

43 Whereas Chinn 2007, 268–272 considers this conceptual 'blurring' of the acts of reading and seeing/visiting as part of a larger theoretical discourse on ekphrastic description in letter 5.6, Gibson/Morello 2012, 214–216 discern a metatextual dynamic at work, whereby the villa's characteristics embody those of Pliny's epistolary project.

As it is for Pliny's reader, so, too, for us should it by now be abundantly clear that the *Epistles* offers us much more than a one-dimensional portrait of its author's life and experiences. Enriching the epistolary medium's conjuring ability through ekphrasis, Pliny urges his readers into a truly sensuous engagement with the content of select epistles which mimic the perception of his personal reality. Enraptured, enslaved, possessed (or however you want to put it) by this discursive mode that is rendered especially vivid by its synaesthetic quality, the reader's 'here and now' is temporarily eclipsed and replaced with a visit to the *ager Laurens*, to Comum or to the river Clitumnus, as the case may be. The next natural step is to ask *why*. What is Pliny's objective in granting so prominent a place in his literary project to the so-called *effet de réel*, a realization of the epistolary content that invites us to temporarily inhabit the lived experience depicted in the *Epistles* and make it our own? An intimate look into the author's everyday life is of course fundamental to any collection of private correspondence; but by casting his readers *into* some of those missives, Pliny makes the lifelike snapshot of his life come to life, literally. As we marvel at the curious waterworks at the spring in Comum or share in the author's terror at the strange cloud enveloping the Bay of Naples *through our act of reading*, Pliny's real letters are made real for us, too. This effect amounts to a sort of virtual reality *avant la lettre*, and the way it works in the *Epistles* is quite unparalleled. For while ancient epistolary discourse, as we saw above, is regularly envisioned as generating a simulated presence by (re)producing the speech of an absent person, Pliny's ekphrastic letters do something new and different when they materialize not the author but the addressee, transporting him to a setting created through detailed description.

And yet for all their vividness, these synaesthetic portrayals of Pliny's life remain just portrayals, as is hinted at by the last line in Pliny's letter to Sura which we discussed above (*Ep.* 4.30.11). Just as Sura has not *actually* seen the spring's trick, we have not *actually* enjoyed any of the delights offered by the author's seaside retreats, even if Pliny's textual tours so enthral us as to make us want to visit these villas in person. Ekphrasis, after all, is a mode of fiction; none of the sensations it conjures up, however lifelike, are real.[44] This fictitiousness of the ekphrastic experience is acknowledged by our rhetorical sources, which employ the vocabulary of approximation ('almost *but not quite*') when discussing the trope. For instance, Nikolaus, the author of one of our four sur-

---

44 See Webb 2009, 168–172.

viving *Progymnasmata* ('preliminary exercises' for students of rhetoric),⁴⁵ defines the workings of ekphrasis as 'bringing the subjects of the speech before our eyes and almost making speakers into spectators' (ὑπ' ὄψιν ἡμῖν ἄγοντα ταῦτα, περὶ ὧν εἰσιν οἱ λόγοι, καὶ μόνον οὐ θεατὰς εἶναι παρασκευάζοντα, Felten 1913, 70), and Quintilian describes *uisiones* (the mental elements whose transferal from speaker to audience was thought to enact ekphrasis' imaginative involvement) as confined to the realm of appearance (Quint. *Inst.* 6.2.30):

> *Quas φαντασίας Graeci uocant (nos sane uisiones appellemus), per quas imagines rerum absentium ita repraesentantur animo ut eas cernere oculis ac praesentes habere uideamur, has quisquis bene ceperit is erit in adfectibus potentissimus.*
>
> What the Greeks call *phantasiae* (let's call them, if you will, 'visions'), through which images of things that are absent are portrayed to the mind so that we *seem* to perceive them with our eyes and have them present, before us — whoever captures these [figures] competently shall be the most effective in the conveyance of emotions.

To quote Simon Goldhill, '[r]hetorical theory knows well that its descriptive power is a technique of illusion, semblance, of making to appear. This brings ekphrasis particularly close to the theatre—the space of seeing and illusion.'⁴⁶ Given what we saw above — *viz.* that Pliny is acquainted and engages with the theoretical thinking on ekphrasis in his letters 1.3 and 5.6, it should come as no surprise that he is well aware of this fictitiousness, too.

In the remainder of this paper, I will demonstrate that we are repeatedly invited by the *Epistles* to perceive the fallacy of the visions and sensations conjured up by ekphraseis, which offer 'almost *but not quite*' experiences of the places and events they so vividly describe. While we read forward in the collection, the reality of Pliny's all-encompassing descriptions is implicitly subverted as it is put forth, achieving a paradoxical effect that ultimately contemplates the analogously ambivalent status of the oeuvre itself. By highlighting the very elements of this rhetorical trope that indicate its artificial nature, the *Epistles* teases us with the unreality of ekphrasis in real letters to suggest the (possible) unreality of the entire collection as a true portrait of the author and his everyday life.

---

45 Our three other surviving *Progymnasmata* are by Theon, [Hermogenes] and Aphthonius. These range in date from the 1ˢᵗ c. to the 4ᵗʰ c. CE.
46 Goldhill 2007, 3.

3 PART II: The Fake Real

Criticism has long recognized that letters 2.17 and 5.6 form a diptych in Pliny's collection, a pair of texts whose common theme and approach ask us to read them together.⁴⁷ In light of my observations above that 1.3 not only prefigures these texts but rehearses their approach in miniature, we can see that rather than just a doublet what we in fact have is a triplet which constitutes a *tricolon crescens*: three ekphrastic missives transport us to a vacation spot (in alphabetic order, no less: Comum, Laurentum, Tifernum Tiberinum), which increase in length and discursive extent as well as in their self-awareness of the (literary) travel taking place through their lifelike descriptions.⁴⁸ But in addition to reading these three villa letters in a forward direction with the text's increasing ekphrastic momentum, we are also urged to read them backwards; that is, to reassess our understanding and indeed our experience of these immersive texts once we reach their culmination and fullest expression in Book 5. A cue to 'look' back comes in the final line of the introduction to letter 5.6 about Pliny's estate *in Tuscis* (Plin. *Ep.* 5.6.3):

> ...accipe temperiem caeli regionis situm uillae amoenitatem, quae et tibi auditu et mihi relatu iucunda erunt.
>
> Let me tell you about [the property's] climate, the lay of the land and the charm of the villa, all of which will be delightful for you to hear about and delightful for me to recount.

This sentence announcing the missive's topic closely echoes a line in the opening to letter 2.17 that has the same introductory function (Plin. *Ep.* 2.17.1) –

> ...desines mirari, cum cognoueris gratiam uillae, opportunitatem loci, litoris spatium.
>
> You'll stop marveling [at my love of the estate] when you come to know the grace of the villa, the fitness of the place and the extent of the shore.

– although 5.6's version of this sentence is presented as a mirror image of its model: a phrase about the charm of the villa to be described has been switched from first position in 2.17 to last in 5.6, whereas the *litoris spatium* in last place in the earlier letter has been replaced by *temperies caeli* in first place in the later

---

47 See Gibson/Morello 2012, 203–211.
48 This triplet is matched by another triplet of letters about villas — or at least about villa life, in Book 9, letters 9.7, 9.36 and 9.40. On letter 9.7, see n. 61.

letter — a swap that (incidentally?) reproduces the location of these two opposites (sea/sky) in the physical world. Expressions denoting the position of each estate remain in the middle of their respective triplets although the word order is chiastic, as it is for the two other word pairs:

> *gratiam uillae* (1st in 2.17)/*uillae amoenitatem* (3rd in 5.6)
> *opportunitatem loci* (2nd in 2.17)/*regionis situm* (2nd in 5.6)
> *litoris spatium* (3rd in 2.17)/*temperies caeli* (1st in 5.6)

In other words (although of the same words in Pliny's text!), by reading 5.6's text backwards and in the case of the *litus* and *caelum*, 'upside down', we 'get' the text of 2.17. In its turn, this sentence in 2.17 recalls the first letter in our ekphrastic triplet by categorizing the questions Pliny poses to Caninius Rufus in the opening sequence of 1.3 which inquire about architectural features of the villa (*porticus, gestatio, balineum, triclinia, cubicula*), features of the surrounding area (*platanon, euripus*) and of the shore specifically (*lacus*). Once we have connected these dots, sent back to 2.17 by 5.6 and then further back still to 1.3 by 2.17, the interpretive game begins: why does the epistle to Domitius Apollinaris ask us to return to its partners in the collection, and how does following its prompt to (literal and literary) *re*-vision change our reading?

The answer lies in the texture of letter 5.6's ekphrasis, which differs from and so invites us to rethink its predecessors via an insistent emphasis on its own fictitious nature. The epistle to Domitius Apollinaris makes plain the fictive pretense of ekphrastic discourse through what I shall call 'mimetic mimesis', a phenomenon whereby various features of Pliny's Tuscan villa evoked through ekphrasis themselves evoke something else (yet another image, or a sensation) *inside the ekphrasis*. So, for instance, we shall see (and 'see') that a view of the landscape resembles a painting and a plant's leaves feel as if they are liquid. This internal replication of ekphrasis' main mechanism of imitation pushes us deeper into the text's perceptual mimesis while reminding us of it by staging the act of conjuring within a conjured scene, but also by the very nature of those sights and sensations conjured on the secondary level. For what *seems* to inhabit 5.6's illusory mirror of reality (a picture, water etc.) is often itself an illusory mirror of reality and therefore exists as an analogue to the descriptive trope in which it originates — a reflective entity inside of a reflection. It will emerge that these *mises-en-abyme* serve ultimately to underscore the fictitiousness of ekphrastic discourse, prompting us to recognize the *un*reality of our seemingly very realistic experience of a life through letters.

Pliny's description of his Tuscan estate begins with a panoramic overview of the area which tells of its climate and natural environs. The shape of the landscape is portrayed as follows (Plin. *Ep.* 5.6.7):

> *Regionis forma pulcherrima. Imaginare amphitheatrum aliquod immensum, et quale sola rerum natura possit effingere. Lata et diffusa planities montibus cingitur, montes summa sui parte procera nemora et antiqua habent.*

> The shape of the region is really beautiful. Imagine some enormous amphitheatre, such as only the natural order of things could forge. A wide and extensive plain is surrounded by hills, and on their peaks the hills have tall and ancient forests.

In order to 'see' the Tuscan countryside, we are asked to picture something else that it evokes. The *regionis forma*, that is, whose sight is generated only through the literary mimesis of sight, itself mimics the sight of something else. In this light, Pliny's use of *imaginari* and *effingere* is pointed: although Nature herself is its artist, this 'amphitheatre' is nevertheless doubly imaginary, for we cannot *really* see it nor the landscape that recalls its form. Neither is the choice of an amphitheatre to depict the subject of the letter's depiction casual: as the locus of drama — that most illusory medium analogous to ekphrasis, but also of other sorts of entertainment that involve pretense and performance, this building is where mimesis happens.[49] In this way, the area's comparison to an amphitheatre 'sets the scene', making Pliny's Tuscan *suburbanum* into a 'stage' for this ekphrastic tour that will put on an imitation of reality. The metaphor takes immediate effect. Just a few sentences later, we are invited to 'see' a bird's eye view of Pliny's estate and its surrounding countryside not for what it is, but for what it resembles (Plin. *Ep.* 5.6.13):

> *Magnam capies uoluptatem, si hunc regionis situm ex monte prospexeris. Neque enim terras tibi sed formam aliquam ad eximiam pulchritudinem pictam uideberis cernere: ea uarietate, ea descriptione, quocumque inciderint oculi, reficientur.*

> You'll get a real delight if you glimpse the lay of the land from the mountain. Nor will it seem to you that you're seeing a landscape but some image painted to exquisite beauty. Such is the diversity, such is the arrangement that wherever your eyes look they shall be made as if new.

---

[49] See, e.g., Coleman 1990 on the public punishment of criminals in amphitheatres which involved an element of mythological enactment and an explicitly dramatic context (for example, we hear in our sources of a criminal castrated as if he were Attis, or a *damnatus* forced to burn off his own hand in imitation of the myth of Muscius Scaevola). Coleman terms this phenomenon 'fatal charades'.

Chinn has explained these lines as serving to establish 5.6's equation of reading about the Tuscan villa with actually seeing it ('[i]n this way visual and descriptive acts are merged into a single perceptual experience'),[50] but he misses much of the point. For painting exists as the embodied doublet of ekphrastic discourse, doing with images what ekphrasis does with words in that both media seek to (re)create reality, if deceptively.[51] And in fact, the speaker or author of an ekphrastic depiction may be compared to a painter and his depiction to a painting.[52] So by suggesting that the landscape will appear to the 'viewer' (=reader) not as a real landscape but as a painted landscape — i.e. as a medium *which itself mimics reality*, Pliny acknowledges the fictive nature of this 'sight' he proposes while asking us to ponder whether mimesis can actually outstrip reality in its portrayal of reality. Can a natural landscape *actually* be forged more perfectly by the brush (or the word) than by Nature herself?[53] The question is especially confounding since the scene too 'picture perfect' to be real is *actually real*: Pliny's villa really did exist when this letter reached its addressee. Reality and its imitations are here exchanged and confused, although it is by that very blurring that the text's fictive premise is made obvious; by posing the problem of representation Pliny draws our attention to representation and thus to the fundamentally fictive discourse in which the current representation originates.

Some paragraphs later, the analogy between mimetic modes (written and painted) suggested by our 'sight' of the Tuscan landscape is realized when we enter into a bedroom shaded by trees which is decorated with a painting of the same (Plin. *Ep.* 5.6.22–23):

Est et aliud cubiculum a proxima platano uiride et umbrosum, marmore excultum podio tenus, nec cedit gratiae marmoris ramos insidentesque ramis aues imitata pictura.

---

50 Chinn 2007, 271.
51 For the notion of painting as deceptive, see (e.g.) the proem to Philostratus' *Imagines* in which the art of the master painter is described thus (Philostr. *Im. pref.* 25.4): ἡδεῖα δὲ καὶ ἡ ἐν αὐτῷ ἀπάτη καὶ οὐδὲν ὄνειδος φέρουσα· τὸ γὰρ τοῖς οὐκ οὖσιν ὡς οὖσι προσεστάναι καὶ ἄγεσθαι ὑπ' αὐτῶν, ὡς εἶναι νομίζειν, ἀφ' οὗ βλάβος οὐδέν, πῶς οὐ ψυχαγωγῆσαι ἱκανὸν καὶ αἰτίας ἐκτός;
52 See Webb 2009, 27.
53 The ancients were evidently intrigued by this idea. Take, for instance, the *agon* in naturalism between master painters Zeuxis and Parrhasius that is reported by the Elder Pliny (Plin. *HN* 35.65). While Zeuxis painted grapes so real that birds were attracted to feed on them, Parrhasius outdid this feat of realism by painting a curtain over the grapes which succeeded in deceiving Zeuxis himself when he (Zeuxis) attempted to pull it back.

> There is also another bedroom — green and shady from the nearest plane-tree and constructed from marble up to the balcony; nor does a painting representing branches and birds sitting upon those branches yield to the charm of the marble.

Rather than the reader's materialization (or, textualization) inside the ekphrasis as occurs in *Epistles* 4.30, here the subject of ekphrastic description itself is reified as the subject of a representation inside the primary representation, crossing between two analogous media to become a creation in paint that is embedded within a creation in words. As much is emphasized by the word order in the Latin text, which makes us wait until the very end of the sentence to discover that the branches and the birds sitting upon them are only pretend, inhabiting a painting that imitates the 'natural' scene that surrounds it. Existing as portrayal of something that already exists for us in a literary portrayal (surely Pliny's use of *imitor* here is not incidental), the fresco once again invites us to perceive the fiction of our perception and to wonder whether it (the fresco) exists at all. The imitation of nature in yet another bedroom on our tour has a similar effect. This *cubiculum* whose exterior walls are covered in vines contains a small alcove (Plin. *Ep.* 5.6.38–40):

> ...*zothecula refugit quasi in cubiculum idem atque aliud. Lectus hic et undique fenestrae, et tamen lumen obscurum umbra premente. Nam laetissima uitis per omne tectum in culmen nititur et ascendit. Non secus ibi quam in nemore iaceas, imbrem tantum tamquam in nemore non sentias.*

> ...a little alcove recedes [from the bedroom] which exists almost as part of it but also separate. Here there is a bed and windows on all sides, and yet the light is made dim by a dense shade that bears upon [the room]. For a most pleasing vine rests upon and ascends the whole building up to the roof. In this place it's just as if you were lying in a wooded grove, only that you would not feel the rain as you would in a grove.

To imagine that we are lying in a forest where we would, however, not feel the rain (the mimetic paradox is thus accentuated: the reader cannot really feel the feeling of *not feeling* the rain), we need *first* to imagine that we are lying in the alcove of a bedroom in Pliny's villa — a doubly envisioned vision that uncoincidentally has its setting in not only a bedroom, the place where dreams immerse us in mimeseis of reality night after night, but in a room within a room. The location where 'mimetic mimesis' happens reflects its own ekphrastic framework.

This self-subverting tendency recurs throughout letter 5.6, which again and again employs the words of semblance and illusion to refer to various features of the villa evoked in ekphrastic description but also to refer to the semblance and illusion of the ekphrasis itself. So, for instance:

A latere aestiua cryptoporticus in edito posita, quae non adspicere uineas sed tangere uidetur. In media triclinium saluberrimum adflatum ex Appenninis uallibus recipit; post latissimis fenestris uineas, ualuis aeque uineas sed per cryptoporticum quasi admittit.

Plin. *Ep.* 5.6.29

From the side placed on high ground is a covered arcade for summertime use, which seems not to look down on but be actually touching the vineyards. In the middle a dining room receives the most invigorating breeze from the Apennine valleys; by its very wide windows [it looks out on] the vineyards, and so, too, by its folding doors, but through the covered arcade it almost lets the vineyards in.

...et in opere urbanissimo subita uelut inlati ruris imitatio.

Plin. *Ep.* 5.6.35

...and then in the middle of most ornate workmanship suddenly [you come upon] what seems like a patch of rural country, as if planted there.

Ex stibadio aqua uelut expressa cubantium pondere sipunculis effluit...

Plin. *Ep.* 5.6.36

Water flows out through little pipes from under the couch as if pressed out by the weight of people reclining on it...

Particularly interesting for our purposes is a description of a colonnade (*xystus*) laid out in front of a covered portico and its surroundings (Plin. *Ep.* 5.6.16):

Ante porticum xystus in plurimas species distinctus concisusque buxo; demissus inde pronusque puluinus, cui bestiarum effigies inuicem aduersas buxus inscripsit; acanthus in plano, mollis et paene dixerim liquidus.

In front of the portico is a colonnade separated into many patterns and bordered by boxwood; from there descends a sloping ridge which figures of animals, cut out of boxwood, inscribe on both sides; on the level below is an acanthus so soft that I would almost call it liquid.

This animal-themed topiary presents us with yet more imaginary objects that mimic something else — Nature no less, much like the paintings (real and imagined) that populate Pliny's letter/estate.[54] As for the acanthus, our vicarious

---

54 Elsewhere on our tour of the estate we 'see' shrubs trimmed into words (Pliny's name and that of the gardener: Plin. *Ep.* 5.6.35), drawing our attention to the analogy of text and villa.

'touching' of this soft, glossy plant which description *almost* puts before us (the vocabulary of approximation again pulls us back as we are drawn in: *paene dixerim*) prompts the impression that it is liquid. More 'mimetic mimesis', then, since water and its reflective surface are emblematic of ekphrasis — a conceit Philostratos will cleverly play upon in his *Imagines* via the painted figure of Narcissus, whose deception by his own reflection depicted in water is mirrored by the deception of the viewer, tricked into thinking that the painting is *real*.[55] But Pliny plays upon it, too. I argued above that *Epistles* 4.30 exploits the similarity of water and ekphrasis as two media both capable of producing likeness; water's reflective potential is further elaborated upon in two missives in Book 8, my final examples of Pliny's 'mimetic mimesis'.

Bodies of water are 'enargetically' described in *Epistles* 8.8, 8.17 and 8.20 which together compose another ekphrastic triplet in the collection. The first and last of these texts take their cue from 5.6 by implicitly undermining the reality of the depiction they so vividly set forth, using ekphrasis to say something about ekphrasis and thus about the ekphrastic experience offered to us by Pliny's oeuvre.[56] In this way letter 5.6 is pivotal, the subversion of its own literary fiction reverberating not only backwards to its ekphrastic predecessors in the collection but also forwards to those that follow; once the artifice of this rhetorical mode is put on display, it cannot be withdrawn and continues to be flaunted throughout the *Epistles*.

A metaliterary dynamic is apparent from the very first lines of letter 8.8 to Voconius Romanus, which opens by pointing directly to its capacity to make the addressee 'see' (Plin. *Ep.* 8.8.1):

> *Vidistine aliquando Clitumnum fontem? Si nondum (et puto nondum: alioqui narrasses mihi), uide; quem ego (paenitet tarditatis) proxime uidi.*

Chinn 2007, 272 comments: 'Literally fashioned into discourse, the gardens of the villa offer themselves as a textual supplement to an actual tour, mirroring the role of Pliny's own description'.

55 On this episode and its self-reflexivity, see (e.g.) the analysis of Elsner 2007, 143–146.
56 Although letter 8.17 on the floods of the Tiber and the Anio also employs the vocabulary of semblance in its ekphrastic portrayal (Plin. *Ep.* 8.17.3: *Anio, delicatissimus amnium ideoque adiacentibus uillis uelut inuitatus retentusque, magna ex parte nemora quibus inumbratur fregit et rapuit*), this text does not contain the same kind of internal reflection (what I have been calling 'mimetic mimesis') as letters 8.8 and 8.20. The nature of the bodies of water described must be the reason. For these swollen, rushing waters are not reflective but the opposite; rather than mirroring back the world around them, the Tiber and Anio destroy and thus change whatever lies in their path.

Let's Get Real: Ekphrasis, Reality and Fiction in Pliny's *Epistles* — **233**

Have you ever seen the source of the Clitumnus? If you haven't yet (and I think that you haven't yet, for you would have told me so), then *see it* which I only just saw (I regretted the delay).

Just like the invitations to presence that both occur in and are realized by the three villa letters, Pliny here unambiguously announces what the following missive will do — *viz.* show its reader the source of the Clitumnus. And see it we do: this river, located in modern-day Umbria, appears before our eyes via Pliny's detailed description which encompasses not only the sight of it but also its feel: the water is as clear as glass (Plin. *Ep.* 8.8.2) and cold as snow (Plin. *Ep.* 8.8.5), and the current is so strong that crossing it by boat is difficult (Plin. *Ep.* 8.8.4). But this letter also takes our vision beyond what 'is' in the ekphrasis to what *seems* to be within it. Here is what Pliny writes about the Clitumnus' banks (Plin. *Ep.* 8.8.4):

> *Ripae fraxino multa, multa populo uestiuntur, quas perspicuus amnis uelut mersas uiridi imagine adnumerat.*
>
> The banks are dressed with many ash trees and poplar trees galore, which the clear stream counts with their green reflection, as if they were submerged.

We have 'seen' this sort of *mise-en-abyme* before. Like the bedroom fresco in Pliny's Tuscan estate, the river's waters reflect back an image of trees which inhabit the very same depiction as the waters themselves, creating a portrait within a portrait that is a fiction twofold. What is more, like the forest-conjuring-alcove within a bedroom we considered above, these trees seem to be *embedded* in the Clitumnus (*uelut mersas*) — a nod towards their status on the inside of an inside. And once again, this self-reflexive/self-*reflective* ekphrasis reminds us that what we 'see' is just another rhetorical conjuring trick: the trees mirrored by the Clitumnus appear only *as if* they were planted under water, just as our experience of the Clitumnus itself is only *as if* we were seeing it ourselves. All of this is pointed up by the adjective *perspicuus* which in its double meaning as 'transparent' but also 'clearly seen', 'manifest', lays bare (as it were) the illusion's multiplicity: the trees appear to be below the water because of the river's 'transparency' which is itself so 'clearly seen' via ekphrastic description. And yet the reflection inside of the ekphrasis is an illusion (it is anything but *perspicuus*) — a fact which, thanks to Pliny's metaliterary teasing, is 'manifest' to the reader. Speaking of reading, letter 8.8 concludes with yet another *mise-en-abyme* that reinforces its games of seeing and *not* seeing the subjects of Pliny's depiction. The missive's second part describes a temple to Jupiter Clitumnus and its surrounding scenery which is populated by chaplets, secondary springs, the odd villa and a public bath built by the people of Hispellum (Plin. *Ep.* 8.8.5–6). Recalling the gardens of Pliny's Tuscan villa which are dotted with topiary in the shape of not only animals but also words — the medium of ekphrastic deception (Plin. *Ep.* 5.6.35), the landscape of *Ep.* 8.8 is likewise a written one (Plin. *Ep.* 8.8.7):

> *Nam studebis quoque: leges multa multorum omnibus columnis omnibus parietibus inscripta, quibus fons ille deusque celebratur.*

> [While there] you'll even be able to do some studying: you'll read the many inscriptions of many people on all the columns and all the walls, by which the spring and the god himself are worshipped.

Once again, we are sucked into the epistolary scene where, by our very act of reading, we can 'read' these texts in praise of Jupiter and his river — except that we *can't really*. But we *can* read the letter within which these inscriptions are inscribed — a text which, like the texts it describes, likewise praises Jupiter and his river.[57]

Letter 8.20 also acknowledges its ekphrastic *modus operandi* right from the start. In the opening of a second letter to Gallus which this time describes a *thauma* located near a country estate belonging to Calpurnia's grandfather, Pliny points out that while we travel far and wide to see marvels of the world, we do not appreciate those that are before our very eyes (Plin. *Ep.* 8.20.1):

> *Ad quae noscenda iter ingredi, transmittere mare solemus, ea sub oculis posita neglegimus...*

> We are accustomed to embarking on journeys and crossing the sea to sightsee, but those attractions placed before our eyes we overlook.

In what must be an echo of *subiectio sub oculis*, the theoretical term for ekphrasis also alluded to in letter 5.6,[58] Pliny here prepares us to *see* something (and thus to go somewhere) through his ekphrastic text; in fact, the vocabulary of hearing (*auris, audire*) and seeing (*oculi, uidere*) repeated insistently throughout the letter's opening lines draws our attention to ekphrasis' equation of words and pictures.[59] Having thus alerted us to be on the look-out (literally) for self-

---

57 On these texts, see, too, Morello 2015, 165–166 who reads them in juxtaposition with those in Plin. *Ep.* 8.7.
58 On the play with this theoretical term in Plin. *Ep.* 5.6, see Chinn 2007, 272.
59 Plin. *Ep.* 8.20.2–3: *...permulta in urbe nostra iuxtaque urbem non oculis modo sed ne auribus quidem nouimus, quae si tulisset Achaia Aegyptos Asia aliaue quaelibet miraculorum ferax commendatrixque terra, audita perlecta lustrata haberemus. Ipse certe nuper, quod nec*

referentiality, Pliny proceeds to 'show' us this local marvel, the *lacus Vadimonis* found 60 kilometers north of Rome in what is now the province of Viterbo. Here, too, we encounter words and expressions that hint at the same 'almost *but not quite*' quality that is fundamental to ekphrastic discourse (Plin. *Ep.* 8.20.4):

> *Lacus est in similitudinem iacentis rotae circumscriptus et undique aequalis: nullus sinus, obliquitas nulla, omnia dimensa paria, et quasi artificis manu cauata et excisa. Color caerulo albidior, uiridior et pressior; sulpuris odor saporque medicatus; uis qua fracta solidantur. Spatium modicum, quod tamen sentiat uentos, et fluctibus intumescat.*

> The lake is as if drawn in a circle, similar to a wheel lying on the ground, and it is completely even: there is no dip in the circumference, no slanting; all the measurements are exactly equal, as if dug out and shaped by the hand of a craftsman. The colour is somewhat paler than sea-blue - greener and gloomier; it has the smell of sulphur and a medicinal taste — a property whereby fractures are healed. Its size is moderate and yet it is large enough that it feels the winds and swells with waves.

Similar to the landscape surrounding the Tuscan villa, Lake Vadimon is so perfect in its form that it resembles something wrought by man (an *artifex*, no less) rather than by nature. What makes this body of water wondrous, however, is not its shape but what lies on its surface. The lake contains floating islands that from above look like land (on their surface grow the same sorts of plants one finds on the lakeshore, Plin. *Ep.* 8.20.5) and like ships below (their roots resemble the keels of ships, Plin. *Ep.* 8.20.5) and yet each is different in shape (*sua cuique figura ut modus*, Plin. *Ep.* 8.20.5). These itinerant landmasses are also protean in their arrangement on the lake's surface, creating different patterns as they are driven together and then apart again (Plin. *Ep.* 8.20.6–8):

> *Interdum iunctae copulataeque et continenti similes sunt, interdum discordantibus uentis digeruntur, non numquam destitutae tranquillitate singulae fluitant. Saepe minores maioribus uelut cumbulae onerariis adhaerescunt, saepe inter se maiores minoresque quasi cursum certamenque desumunt; rursus omnes in eundem locum adpulsae, qua steterunt promouent terram, et modo hac modo illa lacum reddunt auferuntque, ac tum demum cum medium tenuere non contrahunt.*

> Sometimes when joined together and bound they are similar to a tract of land, whereas at other times they are driven apart by the winds blowing in different directions, and occasionally, when the lake is still, they float around singly and separately. Often the smaller islands cling onto the larger ones, like small boats to freight ships; often, too, the bigger

---

audieram ante nec uideram, audiui pariter et uidi. Exegerat prosocer meus, ut Amerina praedia sua inspicerem. Haec perambulanti mihi ostenditur subiacens lacus nomine Vadimonis; simul quaedam incredibilia narrantur.

and smaller islands amongst themselves engage in a race — a sort of contest; then again they're all driven into the same spot, where they stand and form an extension to the shore. Now on this side and then on that side they increase and decrease [the size of] the lake and only when located in the middle they don't make it smaller.

The floating islands of Lake Vadimon compose different pictures as they are variously arranged on the water's surface (to be sure, Pliny's use of the word *figura* — 'shape', but also 'sketch' or 'drawing', to describe the islands' shape is not incidental),[60] imitating, now as 'boats' and now as 'land', different settings and scenarios that are all entirely probable for a lake. By their behaviour, the islands are not only marvelous but also inherently deceptive, seeming to be what they are not. This is illustrated by their frequent beguilement of the cattle which grazes nearby (Plin. *Ep.* 8.20.8–9):

> *Constat pecora herbas secuta sic in insulas illas ut in extremam ripam procedere solere, nec prius intellegere mobile solum quam litori abrepta quasi inlata et imposita circumfusum undique lacum paueant; mox quo tulerit uentus egressa, non magis se descendisse sentire, quam senserint ascendisse.*

> It's well known that herds of cattle, seeking plants to graze on, often walk right onto the islands as if onto the edge of the shore, nor do they perceive the ground's mobility until, torn from the bank as if transported and planted [there], they are terrified at the lake surrounding them on all sides. Soon, when they have stepped off where the wind has brought them, they no more perceive that they have 'disembarked' than they perceived that they had 'embarked' in the first place.

Tricked by the islands' very real appearance as land, the cows are transported onto the lake when these turn into 'boats' and float away. And yet they remain unaware of their transportation once returned to the shore, just as if they had never gone anywhere at all.

Lake Vadimon's floating islands and sailing cows inhabit the final *descriptio regionum* in Pliny's *Epistles*,[61] bringing his ekphrastic collection, itself enclosed

---

[60] But incidental (perhaps) is the fact that Lake Vadimon's floating islands are not unlike the texts in a literary collection, whose arrangement affects the reader's perception of both the individual parts and the whole.

[61] It should be noted, however, that letter 9.7 describes the Pliny's villas 'Tragedy' and 'Comedy' in some ekphrastic detail. These estates are so called because of their respective positions — the former is perched on a high ridge as if upon *cothurni* whereas the latter 'wears' *socci* in its position on a curved bay. Here, too, we find an admission of the vivid description's fundamental fiction: Pliny claims that whereas from a bedroom window of 'Tragedy' one can look upon the fishermen, from 'Comedy' one can cast a line for fishing *as if* one were in a boat

within a collection, to a close. It is a fitting *sphragis*. By making the surface of a lake which is itself described in and exists as an analogue to ekphrasis the scene of the same sort of mimetic deception that ekphrasis produces *but made real* (within the text, at least), Pliny stages the mechanism of this rhetorical mode and, crucially, his exposition of it, more pointedly than anywhere else in the *Epistles*. For these islands that imitate various states and scenarios typical for a lake (one big island, the lakeshore, boats racing or smaller boats being towed by larger boats) are the reflections produced by water's surface reified, existing as 'real' versions of letter 8.8's trees that only *seem* to be submerged in the Clitumnus but also concretizing other sights and sensations conjured up via imitation: a landscape that resembles an amphitheatre, or a *cryptoporticus* that appears to be touching the vineyard below. That is, letter 8.20's tableau is like an exploded ekphrasis whose traces of fictitiousness have exceeded their bounds from what *seems* to be inside the description to what *is* inside the description. It is no 'wonder', then, that the ekphrastic viewer, represented in this text by the herd of cows, is duped into believing the deception regularly played out on Lake Vadimon's surface. Unable to tell the difference between reality and representation, the cows take the islands for *terra firma* and are accordingly swept away onto the water. More significant still is the fact that the cows remain entirely unaware of their voyage into the lake's portrait of a lake as the islands become 'boats' and then 'land' again, thereby exemplifying precisely the effect of ekphrastic representation which Pliny's 'mimetic mimesis' works to expose.

4 Conclusion

This chapter began by arguing that we do not have to choose between a historical or literary reading of the *Epistles*, but that neither should we entirely dismiss this old controversy. Rather, we ought to reframe the debate as one that picks up on a tension central to Pliny's oeuvre arising from its novelty in Graeco-Roman epistolography. As an authorially curated collection of everyday correspondence which is the very first of its kind, the *Epistles* inhabits a contested territory between raw documentation and literature, suspended between the real and the fake and self-consciously so, since this collection contemplates its own problematic ontology from the start. At least one way this paradox mani-

---

(Plin. *Ep.* 9.7.4): *ex illa possis despicere piscantes, ex hac ipse piscari, hamumque de cubiculo ac paene etiam de lectulo ut e naucula iacere.*

fests itself throughout the *Epistles* is via ekphrastic description. The ekphraseis which bring the letters and, thereby, the author's daily existence, to life in the reader's mind are similarly positioned to the texts they inhabit by virtue of the fact that these evoke very real places, things and events but nevertheless inhabit the realm of fiction by virtue of the fundamentally illusory experience they offer. Pliny repeatedly invites us to perceive this equivocal dynamic through what I have called 'mimetic mimesis', the exposition of ekphrasis' artifice in its representation of objects and surfaces that themselves produce representations of reality. This analogy between the letters' contents and the ontological status of letters themselves points to something rather important, I think, namely that however real its parts and all that is described therein, Pliny's collection — and therefore his self-portrait that it constructs — is literary.

It turns out, then, that real letters can be literature. Pliny's *Epistles* employs rhetorical tropes and figures, engages in *imitatio* and presents the texts it contains in a most deliberate order to create an equally deliberate (or, perhaps more precisely, *curated*) depiction of the author — what amounts to a vivid and yet nevertheless fundamentally mimetic and un-real experience of the people, places and events of Pliny's everyday existence. After all, we're only 'seeing' what the author 'shows' us. So, too, then, does it then turn out that real letters can also be fictive. That is, the *Epistles*' self-subverting ekphraseis point us towards the fact that in spite of the medium's claim to authenticity as a 'low', everyday genre which is a locus for its correspondents' innermost thoughts and emotions (the epistolary theorist Demetrius calls the letter 'a mirror of the soul' at *Eloc.* 227), all letters can nevertheless be containers of what isn't exactly true. Indeed, a tension between epistolary discourse as authentic and yet somehow also deceptive and lying runs throughout ancient literature; what functions as a veracity-lending *Beglaubigungsapparat* in genres like theatre and the novel is from its very first appearances in Greek literature an especially apt means of sowing confusion and of transacting deceit.[62] But just like the old debate of real *vs* fake, the question of whether letters are purveyors of truth or a medium for lies is one better cast as a productive paradox that makes the epistle such a versatile and intriguing genre. As we have 'seen' in all that precedes, Pliny already knew that.

---

[62] The ancients were wary of graphic communication *tout court*, fretting about a mode of communication that travelled without its author and could be kept secret; see Steiner 1994. Rosenmeyer 2001 and Ceccarelli 2013 discuss the (potential) deceitfulness of letters specifically.

List of Contributors

Roy K. Gibson is Professor of Classics at Durham University and has published widely on Latin poetry and prose from Cicero to late antiquity, particularly Ovid, Pliny the Younger and Sidonius Apollinaris. He is Co-Director of the Ancient Letter Collections project, which researches Greco-Roman letter collections from Isocrates to Augustine.

Claire Rachel Jackson is a postdoctoral researcher on the ERC-funded *Novel Echoes* project (principal investigator Prof. Koen De Temmerman) at Ghent University, Belgium. Her research focuses on theories and practices of fiction in ancient Greek novels and their early reception in Late Antiquity and Byzantium, as well as concepts of fiction in Greek epistolography. She has published on the reception of fiction in Heliodorus' *Aithiopika*, letters in Iamblichus' *Babyloniaka*, and the pseudonymous *Letters* of Chion of Heraclea.

Catharine Edwards is Professor of Classics & Ancient History at Birkbeck, University of London, and a Fellow of the British Academy. Her publications include *The Politics of Immorality in Ancient Rome* and *Writing Rome*. Seneca's *Epistulae Morales* have been her particular focus in more recent years (she edited *Seneca: Selected Letters* for CUP) but she has also written about Ovid's *Fasti* (in *Eugesta* 2021).

Michael Trapp is Professor of Greek Literature & Thought at King's College London. His publications include *Greek and Latin Letters. An Anthology with translation*, *Philosophy in the Roman Empire: ethics, politics and society*, and articles and chapters on philosophical culture, Socrates, Dio Chrysostom, Plutarch, Lucian and Aelius Aristides. He is now editing and translating the complete works of Aristides for the Loeb Classical Library.

Serena Cammoranesi obtained a PhD in Classics and Ancient History from the University of Manchester in 2022. The title of her project is 'Cicero's *Epistulae ad Familiares*: Narratives of the Civil War'. She has also worked on Cicero's reception in Fronto's correspondence. Her other research interests include: Latin epistolography, Horace, and narratology in Classical literature.

Kathryn Tempest is Reader in Roman History and Latin Literature at the University of Roehampton. She has published extensively on the literature, history, and political life of the late Roman republic, with particular interests in oratory and rhetoric, all aspects of Cicero, and ancient letters. She is the author of *Cicero: Politics and Persuasion in Ancient Rome* and *Brutus: The Noble Conspirator*, as well as co-editor, with Christos Kremmydas, of *Hellenistic oratory: Continuity and Change*.

Janja Soldo is Lecturer in Latin Language and Literature at Edinburgh University. She is the author of *Seneca, Epistulae Morales Book 2. A Commentary with Text, Translation, and Introduction*. Her research focuses on ancient epistolography and Roman Stoicism.

Ruth Morello is Senior Lecturer in Classics at the University of Manchester. She has published extensively on the non-Ciceronian letters of the *Ad Familiares*, on exemplarity in Martial's epigrams, on the letters of Caesar, Pliny the Elder, Livy and Vergil. She is the co-author, with Roy Gibson, of *Reading the Letters of Pliny the Younger: An Introduction* and she has co-edited, with Andrew Morrison, *Ancient Letters: Classical and Late Antique Epistolography*, and, with Roy Gibson, *Pliny the Elder: Themes and Contexts* and *Re-Imagining Pliny the Younger*.

Emilia A. Barbiero is an Assistant Professor of Classics at New York University. She has published extensively on Roman comedy and on ancient letters both Greek and Latin.

Bibliography

Allen, Pauline/Neil, Bronwen (eds.) (2020), *Greek and Latin Letters in Late Antiquity. The Christianisation of a Literary Form*, Cambridge.
Altman, Janet G. (1982), *Epistolarity: Approaches to a Form*, Columbus.
Barbiero, Emilia A. (2019), "Time to Eat: Chronological Connections in Alciphron's *Letters of Parasites*", in: Michèle Biraud/Arnaud Zucker (eds.), *The Letters of Alciphron: A Unified Literary Work?*, Leiden, 42–58.
Barbiero, Emilia A. (2023), *Letters in Plautus: Reading Between the Lines*, Cambridge.
Barchiesi, Alessandro (2005), "The Search for the Perfect Book: A PS to the New Posidippus", in: Kathryn Gutzwiller (ed.), *The New Posidippus: A Hellenistic Poetry Book*, Oxford, 320–342.
Barlow, Claude (ed.) (1938), *Epistolae Senecae ad Paulum et Pauli ad Senecam <quae vocantur>*, Rome.
Barthes, Roland (1968), "L'Effet de Réel", in: *Communications* 11, 84–89.
Basore, John W. (1932), *Seneca: Moral Essays*, Vol. 2, Loeb Classical Library 254, Cambridge, MA.
Beard, Mary (2002), "Ciceronian Correspondences: Making a Book out of Letters", in: Timothy P. Wiseman (ed.), *Classics in Progress: Essays on Ancient Greece and Rome*, Oxford, 103–144.
Beard, Mary (2004), "Writing ritual: the triumph of Ovid", in: Alessandro Barchiesi/Jörg Rüpke/Susan A. Stephens (eds.), *Rituals in Ink: A Conference on Religion and Literary Production in Ancient Rome*, Stuttgart, 115–126.
Beard, Mary (2009), *The Roman Triumph*, Cambridge/London.
Beaujeu, Jean (1996), *Cicéron. Correspondance*, vol. xi, Paris.
Beebee, Thomas (1999), *Epistolary Fiction in Europe. 1500–1850*, Cambridge.
Berno, Francesca Romana (2006), *L. Anneo Seneca. Lettere a Lucilio, libro VI: Le Lettere 53–57*, Bologna.
Berry, Dominic H. (2008), "Letters from an advocate: Pliny's 'Vesuvius' narratives (*Epistles* 6.16, 6.20)", in: *Papers of the Langford Latin Seminar* 13, 297–313.
Bing, Peter/Höschele, Regina (2014), *Aristaenetus, Erotic Letters*, Atlanta.
Biraud, Michèle/Zucker, Arnaud (eds.) (2019), *The Letters of Alciphron: A Unified Literary Work?*, Leiden.
Blanck, Horst (1992), *Das Buch in der Antike*, Munich.
Bloomer, W. Martin (1992), *Valerius Maximus and the Rhetoric of the New Nobility*, Berkeley.
Bocciolini Palagi, Laura (1985), *Epistolario apocrifo di Seneca e San Paolo*, Florence.
Bodel, John (2015), "The Publication of Pliny's Letters", in: Ilaria Marchesi (ed.), *Pliny the Book-Maker: Betting on Posterity in the Epistles*, Oxford, 13–108.
Bolzan, Jacopo (2009), *Socratis et Socraticorum Epistolae: studi preliminari, traduzione, commento*, diss. Padova.
Booth, Charles/Clark, Peter/Delahaye, Agnès/Procter, Stephen/Rowlinson, Michael (2009), "Modal narratives, possible worlds and strategic foresight", in: Laura A. Costanzo/Robert B. Mackay (eds.), *Handbook of Research on Strategy and Foresight*, Cheltenham, 113–127.
Bowersock, Glenn (1967), "A new inscription of Arrian", in: *GRBS* 8, 279–280.
Bowie, Ewen L. (1993), "Lies, fiction and slander in early Greek poetry", in: Christopher P. Gill/Timothy P. Wiseman (eds.), *Lies and Fiction in the Ancient World*, Exeter, 1–37.

Bowie, Angus (2013), "'Baleful Signs:' Letters and Deceit in Herodotus", in: Owen Hodkinson/ Patricia A. Rosenmeyer/Evelien Bracke (eds.), *Epistolary Narratives in Ancient Greek Literature*, Leiden/Boston, 71–83.

Braconi, Paolo/Uroz-Sáez, José (eds.) (1999), *La villa di Plinio il Giovane a San Giustino: primi risultati di una ricerca in corso*, Perugia.

Braconi, Paolo/Uroz-Sáez, José (2008), "La villa di Plinio il Giovane a San Giustino", in: Filippo Coarelli/Helen Patterson (eds.), *Mercator Placidissimus: the Tiber Valley in Antiquity*, Rome, 93–108.

Bradley, Keith R. (2010), "The exemplary Pliny", in: Carl Deroux, (ed.), *Studies in Latin Literature and Roman History 15*, Brussels, 384–422.

Brink, C.O. (1971), *Horace on Poetry 2. The Ars Poetica*, Cambridge.

Brook, Adriana (2016), "Cicero's Use of Aeschylus' *Oresteia* in the *Pro Milone*," in: *Ramus* 45.1: 45–73.

Brownlee, Marina Scordilis (1990), *The Severed Word: Ovid's Heroides and the novela sentimental*, Princeton.

Bruner, Jerome (1987), *Actual Minds, Possible Worlds*, Cambridge.

Calboli, Gualtiero (2015), "Two letters by Brutus and Cassius to Mark Antony: different people, different times, different styles", in: *Journal of Latin Linguistics* 14.2, 241–267.

Camiciotti, Gabriella D.L. (2014), "Letters and letter writing in early modern culture: an introduction", in: *Journal of Early Modern Studies* 3, 17–35.

Cammoranesi, Serena (2022), *Cicero's Epistulae ad Familiares: Narratives of the Civil War*, diss. Manchester.

Cappello, Orazio (2016), "Everything you wanted to know about Atticus (but were afraid to ask Cicero). Looking for Atticus in Cicero's *Ad Atticum*", in: *Arethusa* 49, 463–487.

Carlsson, Gunnar (1929), Review of Guillemin 1927–8, in: *Gnomon* 5, 134–144.

Casali, Sergio (1997), "*Quaerenti plura legendum*: the necessity of "reading more" in Ovid's exile poetry", in: *Ramus* 26, 80–112.

Cavarzere, Alberto (ed.) (2016)², *Lettere ai familiari*, 2 vols., Milano.

Ceccarelli, Paola (2013), *Ancient Greek Letter Writing: A Cultural History (600 BC–150 BC)*, Oxford.

Chinn, Christopher (2007), "Before Your Very Eyes: Pliny *Epistulae* 5.6 and the Ancient Theory of Ekphrasis", in: *CPh* 102 (3), 265–80.

Citroni-Marchetti, Sandra (2000), *Amicizia e Potere nelle Lettere di Cicerone e nelle Elegie Ovidiane dell'Esilio*, Florence.

Claassen, Jo-Marie (1999), *Displaced Persons: The Literature of Exile from Cicero to Boethius*, London.

Clarke, Martin L. (1981), *Brutus: The Noblest Roman*, London.

Cohn, Dorrit (2000), *The Distinction of Fiction*, Baltimore/London.

Coleman, Kathleen (1990), "Fatal charades: Roman executions staged as mythological enactments", in: *JRS* 80, 44–73.

Coleman, Kathleen M. (2012), "Bureaucratic language in the correspondence between Pliny and Trajan", in: *TAPhA* 142, 189–238.

Connolly, Joy (2007), *The State of Speech: Rhetorical and Political Thought in Ancient Rome*, Princeton.

Corbeill, Anthony (2020), "How not to Write like Cicero: *Pridie quam in exilium iret oratio*", in: *Ciceroniana On Line* 4.1, 17–36 (https://doi.org/10.13135/2532-5353/4664).

Cordes, Lisa (2017), *Kaiser und Tyrann. Die Kodierung und Umkodierung der Herrscherrepräsentation Neros und Domitians*, Berlin.
Costa, C.D.N. (2002), *Greek Fictional Letters: A Selection with Introduction, Translation, and Commentary by C.D.N. Costa*, Oxford.
Crawford, Michael (1974), *Roman Republican Coinage*, 2 vols., Cambridge.
Cugusi, Paolo (1983), *Evoluzione e forme dell'epistolografia Latina*, Rome.
Čulík-Baird, Hannah (2022), *Cicero and the Early Latin Poets*, Cambridge.
Curry, Susan A. (2018), "Seneca rising: epistolary self-recreation in the *ad Helviam*", in: *BICS* 61, 45–55.
Damon, Cynthia (2021), "Situating Catullus", in: Ian du Quesnay/Tony Woodman (eds.), *The Cambridge Companion to Catullus*, Cambridge, 7–25.
Davies, Mark (2014), "Living with Seneca through his Epistles", in: *G&R* 61, 68–90.
Davisson, Mary H.T. (1985), "*Tristia* 5.13 and Ovid's use of epistolary form and content", in: *CJ* 80, 238–246.
De Giorgio, Jean P. (2015), *L'écriture de soi à Rome. Autour de la correspondance de Cicéron*, Brussels.
Deißmann, Adolf (1908), *Licht vom Osten: das Neue Testament und die neuentdeckten Texte der hellenistisch-römischen Welt*, Tübingen.
De Lacy, Phillip (1943), "The logical structure of the ethics of Epictetus", in: *CPh* 38, 112–125.
De Pourcq, Maarten/Roskam, Geert (2012), "'Always to Excel'! Some Observations and Reflections on φιλοτιμία in Greek Literature and Culture', in: Geert Roskam/Maarten de Pourcq/L. van der Stockt (eds.), *The Lash of Ambition: Plutarch, Greek Literature, and the Dynamics of Philotimia*, Louvain, 1–8.
De Pretis, Anna (2003), "'Insincerity', 'facts' and 'epistolarity': approaches to Pliny's letters to Calpurnia", in: *Arethusa* 36.2, 127–146.
Derrida, Jacques (1987), *The Post Card: From Socrates to Freud and Beyond*, translated by Alan Bass, Chicago.
De Temmerman, Koen (2016), "Ancient Biography and Formalities of Fiction", in: Koen de Temmerman/Kristoffel Demoen (eds.): *Writing Biography in Greece and Rome: Narrative Technique and Fictionalization*, Cambridge, 3–25.
De Temmerman, Koen/Demoen, Kristoffel (eds.) (2016), *Writing Biography in Greece and Rome: Narrative Technique and Fictionalization*, Cambridge.
Dickey, Eleanor (2002), *Latin Forms of Address: From Plautus to Apuleius*, Oxford.
Dobbin, Robert (1998), *Epictetus. Discourses Book 1*, Oxford.
Doležel, Lubomír (1998), *Heterocosmica: Fiction and Possible Worlds*, Baltimore/London.
Drago, Anna Tiziana (2013), "Su alcuni (presunti) casi di imitazione letteraria: le epistole di Eliano e di Alcifrone", in: Onofrio Vox (ed.), *Lettere mimesi, retorica. Studi sull'epistolographia letteraria greca di età imperiale e tardo antica*, Brescia, 71–86.
Drago, Anna Tiziana/Hodkinson, Owen (eds.) (2023a), *Ancient Love Letters: Form, Themes, Approaches*, Berlin/Boston.
Drago, Anna Tiziana/Hodkinson, Owen (2023b), "Introduction", in: Anna Tiziana Drago/Owen Hodkinson (eds.), *Ancient Love Letters: Form, Themes, Approaches*, Berlin/Boston, 1–20.
Du Prey, Pierre de la Ruffinière (2018), "Conviviality versus seclusion in Pliny's Tuscan and Laurentine villas", in: Annalisa Marzano/Guy P.R. Métraux (eds.), *The Roman Villa in the Mediterranean Basin: Late Republic to Late Antiquity*, Cambridge, 467–475.
Duncan-Jones, Richard (1990), *Structure and Scale in the Roman Economy*, Cambridge.

Ebbeler, Jennifer (2010), "Letters", in: A. Barchiesi/W. Scheidel (eds.), *The Oxford Handbook of Roman Studies*, Oxford, 464–476.
Edwards, Catharine (2005), "Epistolography", in: Stephen Harrison (ed.), *A Companion to Latin Literature*, Oxford, 270–283.
Edwards, Catharine (2018), "On not being in Rome: Exile and displacement in Seneca's prose", in: William Fitzgerald/Effrosini Spentzou (eds.), *The Production of Space in Latin Literature*, Oxford, 169–194.
Ehrman, Bart (2013), *Forgery and Counter-forgery: the Use of Literary Deceit in Early Christian Polemics*, Oxford.
Elsner, Jás (2002), "The Genres of Ekphrasis", in: *Ramus* 31, 1–18.
Elsner, Jás (2007), *Roman Eyes: Visuality and Subjectivity in Art and Text*, Princeton.
Erasmo, Mario (2020), "The Theatre of Pompey", in: *MAAR* 65, 43–69.
Evans, Harry B. (1983), *Publica Carmina: Ovid's Books from Exile*, Lincoln.
Fairweather, Janet (1987), "Ovid's autobiographical poem: *Tristia* 4.10", in: *CQ* 37, 181–196.
Fantham, Elaine (2013), "The First Book of Letters", in: Hans-Christian Günther (ed.), *Brill's Companion to Horace*, Leiden, 407–430.
Favret, Mary A. (1993), *Romantic Correspondence: Women, Politics, and the Fiction of Letters*, Cambridge.
Fedeli, Paolo/Dimundo, Rosalba/Ciccarelli, Irma (eds.) (2015), *Properzio: Elegie. Libro IV*, Nordhausen.
Feeney, Denis (1993), "Towards an account of the ancient world's concepts of fictive belief", in: Christopher P. Gill/Timothy P. Wiseman (eds.), *Lies and Fiction in the Ancient World*, Exeter, 230–44.
Fehrle, Rudolf (1983), *Cato Uticensis*, Darmstadt.
Feldherr, Andrew (2010), *Playing Gods. Ovid's Metamorphoses and the Politics of Fiction*, Princeton.
Fezzi, Luca (2019), *Crossing the Rubicon: Caesar's Decision and the Fate of Rome*, trans. Richard Dixon, New Haven.
Fisher, Nick (2013), "Erotic *Charis*: What Sorts of Reciprocity?", in: Ed Sanders (ed.), *Erôs and the Polis: Love in Context*, BICS 119, 39–66.
Fitton-Brown, A.D. (1985), "The unreality of Ovid's Tomitan exile", in: *LCM* 10.2, 18–22.
Fletcher, Richard/Hanink, Johanna (eds.) (2016), *Creative Lives in Classical Antiquity: Poets, Artists, and Biography*, Cambridge.
Fludernik, Monika (2007), "Letters as Narrative: Narrative Patterns and Episode Structure in Early Letters, 1400 to 1650", in: Susan M. Fitzmaurice/Irma Taavitsainen (eds.), *Methods in Historical Pragmatics*, Berlin/New York, 241–266.
Formicola, Crescenzo (2017), *P. Ovidio Nasone: Epistulae ex Ponto, Libro III. Introduzione, testo, traduzione e commento. Vichiana, 1*, Pisa.
Foss, Pedar (2022), *Pliny and the Eruption of Vesuvius*, London.
Fowler, Don (1991), "Narrate and Describe: The Problem of Ekphrasis", in: *JRS* 81, 25–35.
Frampton, Stephanie (2019), "Ovid's two body problem", in: Matthew Loar/Sarah Murray/Stefano Rebeggiani (eds.), *The Cultural History of Augustan Rome: Texts, Monuments, and Topography*, Cambridge, 141–159.
Frazier, Françoise (1988), "À propos de la "philotimia" dans les *Vies*: Quelques jalons dans l'histoire d'une notion", in: *RPh* 62, 109–127.
Frenschkowski, Marco (2009), "Erkannte Pseudepigraphie? Ein Essay über Fiktionalität, Antike und Christentum", in: Jörg Frey/Jens Herzer/Martina Janßen/Clare K. Rothschild (eds.),

Pseudepigraphie und Verfasserfiktion in frühchristlichen Briefen. Pseudepigraphy and Author Fiction in Early Christian Letters, Tübingen, 181–232.
Freudenburg, Kirk (ed.) (2009), *Horace: Satires and Epistles*, Oxford.
Frey, Jörg/Herzer, Jens/Janßen, Martina/Rothschild, Clare K. (eds.) (2009), *Pseudepigraphie und Verfasserfiktion in frühchristlichen Briefen. Pseudepigraphy and Author Fiction in Early Christian Letters*, Tübingen.
Froesch, Hermann (1968), *Ovids Epistulae ex Ponto I–III als Gedichtsammlung*, diss. Bonn.
Fuentez González, Pedro (2000), "Epictète", in: Richard Goulet (ed.), *Dictionnaire des philosophes antiques* III, 106–151.
Fuhrer, Therese (forthcoming), "Vom "Lehrer des Kaisers" zum "neuen Verkünder Christi": Persuasive Strategien im Briefwechsel 'Seneca' – 'Paulus'", in: Émeline Marquis/Peter von Möllendorff (eds.), *Brief und Macht. Pseudonyme Briefsammlungen der Antike/Letters and Power. Pseudonymous Letter Collections*.
Fürst, Alfons (1998), "Pseudepigraphie und Apostolizität im apokryphen Brief zwischen Seneca und Paulus", in: *JbAC* 41, 77–117.
Fürst, Alfons (2006), *Der apokryphe Briefwechsel zwischen Seneca und Paulus. Zusammen mit dem Brief der Mordechai an Alexander und dem Brief des Annaeus Seneca über Hochmut und Götterbilder*, Tübingen.
Futre Pinheiro, Marília P. (2018), "Thoughts on *Diēgēma* (*Narratio*) in Ancient Rhetoric and in Modern Critical Theory", in: Kathryn Chew/J.R. Morgan/Stephen M. Trzaskoma (eds.), *Literary Currents and Romantic Forms: Essays in Honour of Bryan Reardon*, Groningen, 19–32.
Gaertner, Jan-Felix (2005), *Ovid, Epistulae ex Ponto book I*, Oxford.
Gaertner, Jan-Felix (2006), "Ovid and the poetics of exile", in: Gaertner, Jan-Felix (ed.), *Writing Exile: The Discourse of Displacement in Greco-Roman Antiquity*, Leiden, 155–172.
Galasso, Luigi (2009), "*Epistulae ex Ponto*", in: Peter Knox (ed.), *A Companion to Ovid*, Oxford, 194–206.
Gallia, Andrew B. (2012), *Remembering the Roman Republic: Culture, Politics and History under the Principate*, Cambridge.
Gamberini, Federico (1983), *Stylistic Theory and Practice in the Younger Pliny*, Hildesheim.
Gäth, Stephan (2011), *Die Literarische Rezeption des Cato Uticensis*, Frankfurt.
Gibson, Roy K. (2011), "Elder and better: the *Naturalis Historia* and the *Letters* of the younger Pliny", in: Roy K. Gibson/Ruth Morello (eds.), *Pliny the Elder: Themes and Contexts*, Leiden, 287–306.
Gibson, Roy K. (2012), "On the Nature of Ancient Letter Collections", in: *JRS* 102, 56–78.
Gibson, Roy K. (2013), "Letters into Autobiography: The Generic Mobility of the Ancient Letter Collection", in: Theodore D. Papanghelis/Stephen J. Harrison/Stavros A. Frangoulidis (eds.), *Generic Interfaces in Latin Literature: Encounters, Interactions and Transformations*, Berlin/Boston, 387–416.
Gibson, Roy K. (2015), "Not dark yet … : reading to the end of Pliny's nine-book collection", in: Ilaria Marchesi (ed.), *Pliny the Book-Maker: Betting on Posterity in the Epistles*, Oxford, 185–222.
Gibson, Roy K. (2018), "The *Epistulae Heroidum* and the epistolographical tradition", in: Paolo Fedeli/Gianpiero Rosati (eds.), *Ovidio 2017. Prospettive per il terzo millennio*, Teramo, 215–235.
Gibson, Roy K. (2020), *Man of High Empire: The Life of Pliny the Younger*, Oxford.

Gibson, Roy K. (2022), "*Pro Marcello* without Caesar: grief, exile and death in Cicero *Ad Familiares* 4", in: Roy K. Gibson/Ruth Morello (eds.), *The Epistolary Cicero: Further Readings in the Letters*.

Gibson, Roy K. (forthcoming a), *Pliny the Younger. Epistles Book VI*, Cambridge.

Gibson, Roy K. (forthcoming b), "Intertextuality in Pliny, *Epistles* 6", in: Margot Neger/Spyridon Tzounakas (eds.), *Absorbing Genres in Letters: Intertextuality and Interdiscursivity in Pliny's Epistles*, Cambridge.

Gibson, Roy K./Morello, Ruth (2012), *Reading the Letters of Pliny the Younger: An Introduction*, Cambridge.

Gibson, Roy K./Morello, Ruth (eds.) (2022), *The Epistolary Cicero: Further Readings in the Letters*, Hermathena 202–203.

Gibson, Roy K./Morrison, Andrew D. (2007), "Introduction: What is a Letter?", in: Ruth Morello/Andrew D. Morrison (eds.), *Ancient Letters: Classical and Late Antique Epistolography*, Oxford, 1–16.

Gibson, Roy K./Morrison, Andrew (forthcoming), *Ancient Letter Collections*.

Gibson, Roy K./Steel, Catherine (2010), "The indistinct literary careers of Cicero and Pliny the Younger", in: Philip Hardie/Helen Moore (eds.), *Classical Literary Careers and their Reception*, Cambridge, 118–137.

Gibson, Roy K./Whitton, Christopher L. (eds.) (2016), *The Epistles of Pliny: Oxford Readings in Classical Studies*, Oxford.

Gibson, Roy K./Whitton, Christopher L. (eds.) (2023), *The Cambridge Critical Guide to Latin Literature*, Cambridge.

Gigante, Marcello (1989), *Il fungo sul Vesuvio*, Rome = (1979), "Il racconto Pliniano dell'eruzione del Vesuvio dell' a. 79", in: *La Parola del Passato* 34, 321–376.

Gildenhard, Ingo/Zissos, Andrew (2000), "Ovid's Narcissus (*Met.* 3.339-510): Echoes of Oedipus", in: *AJPh* 121, 129–147.

Gildenhard, Ingo (2018), "A Republic in Letters: Epistolary Communitites in Cicero's Correspondence, 49–44 BCE", in: Paola Ceccarelli et al. (eds.), *Letters and Communities: Studies in the Socio-Political Dimensions of Ancient Epistolography*, Oxford, 205–233.

Gilroy, Amanda/Verhoeven, W.M. (2000), "Introduction", in: Amanda Gilroy/W.M. Verhoeven (eds.), *Epistolary histories: letters, fiction, culture*, Charlottesville, 1–25.

Goldberg, Sandor M. (1997), "Melpomene's declaration (rhetoric and tragedy)", in: William J. Dominik (ed.), *Roman Eloquence. Rhetoric in Society and Literature*, London/New York, 166–181.

Goldhill, Simon (1991), *The Poet's Voice: Essays on Poetics and Greek Literature*, Cambridge.

Goldhill, Simon (2007), "What is Ekphrasis For?", in: *CPh* 102 (1), 1–19.

Goldhill, Simon (2009), "Constructing Identity in Philostratus' Love Letters", in: Ewen Bowie/Jás Elsner (eds.), *Philostratus*, Cambridge, 287–305.

Goldsmith, Elizabeth (ed.) (1989), *Writing the Female Voice: Essays on Epistolary Literature*, Boston.

Gösswein, Hans-Ulrich (1975), *Die Briefe des Euripides*, Meisenheim am Glan.

Gotter, Ulrich (1996), *Der Diktator ist tot! Politik in Rom zwischen den Iden des März und der Begründung des Zweiten Triumvirats*, Stuttgart.

Gowers, Emily (2012), *Horace: Satires. Book I*, Cambridge.

Gowing, Alan (2005), *Empire and Memory. The Representation of the Roman Republic in Imperial Culture*, Cambridge.

Graf, Franz (1995), "Ekphrasis: Die Entstehung der Gattung in der Antike", in: Gottfried Boehm/ Helmut Pfotenhauer (eds.), *Beschreibungskunst– Kunstbeschreibung: Ekphrasis von der Antike bis zur Gegenwart*, Munich, 143–55.
Grafton, Anthony (1990), *Forgers and Critics: Creativity and Duplicity in Western Scholarship*, Princeton.
Graziosi, Barbara (2002), *Inventing Homer: The Early Reception of Ancient Epic*, Cambridge.
Green, Peter (2005), *Ovid: The Poems of Exile Poems: Tristia and the Black Sea Letters*, Berkeley.
Grillo, Luca (2015), "Reading Cicero's Ad Familiares 1 as a Collection", in: *CQ* 65(2), 655–668.
Grillo, Luca (2016), "The Artistic Architecture and Closural Devices of Cicero's Ad Familiares 1 and 6", in: *Arethusa* 49(3), 399–413.
Gruen, Erich S. (1995), *The Last Generation of the Roman Republic*, Berkley/Los Angeles/London.
Gudeman, Alfred (1894), "Literary Frauds among the Romans", in: *TAPhA* 25, 140–164.
Gudmundsdóttir, Gunnthórunn (2003), *Borderlines: Autobiography and Fiction in Postmodern Life Writing*, Amsterdam.
Guillemin, Anne-Marie (1927–8), *Pline le Jeune, Lettres I–IX*, 3 vols., Paris.
Guillemin, Anne-Marie (1929), *Pline et la vie littéraire de son temps*, Paris.
Günther, Hans-Christian (2013), "The Second Book of Letters", in: Hans-Christian Günther (ed.), *Brill's Companion to Horace*, Leiden, 467–498.
Gunderson, Erik T. (2003), *Declamation, Paternity and Roman Identity: Authority and the Rhetorical Self*, Cambridge.
Gunderson, Erik T. (2007), "S.V.B.; E.V.", in: *ClAnt* 26(1), 1–48.
Gunderson, Erik T. (2016), "Cicero's Studied Passions: The Letters of 46 B.C.E.", in: *Arethusa* 49(3), 525–547.
Gurlitt, Ludwig (1883), "Die Briefe Ciceros an M. Brutus", in: *Philologus* Supplementbände iv, 551–630.
Gutzwiller, Kathryn (ed.) (2005), *The New Posidippus: A Hellenistic Poetry Book*, Oxford.
Hanink, Johanna (2008), "Literary Politics and the Euripidean Vita", in: *CCJ* 54, 115–135.
Hanink, Johanna (2010), "The *Life* of the Author in the Letters of 'Euripides'", in: *GRBS* 50, 537–564.
Hanink, Johanna (2016), "What's in a *Life*? Some Forgotten Faces of Euripides", in: Richard Fletcher/Johanna Hanink (eds.) (2016), *Creative Lives in Classical Antiquity: Poets, Artists, and Biography*, Cambridge, 129–146.
Hardie, Philip (2002), *Ovid's Poetics of Illusion*, Cambridge.
Harrison, Stephen (2007), "The Primal Voyage and the Ocean of Epos: Two Aspects of Metapoetic Imagery in Catullus, Virgil and Horace", in: *Dictynna* 4 (https://journals.openedition.org/dictynna/146).
Hartmann, Karl (1905), "Arrian und Epiktet", in: *Neue Jahrbücher für das Klassische Alterthum, Geschichte und deutsche Literatur* 15, 248–275.
Harvey, Paul B. (1991), "Cicero Epistulae ad Quintum Fratrem et ad Brutum: Content and Comment; II. Epistulae ad Brutum et Invicem", in: *Athenaeum* 69, 17–29.
Haugen, Kristine (2011), *Richard Bentley: Poetry and Enlightenment*, Cambridge, MA.
Heine, Rudolph (1875), *Quaestionum de M. Tullii Ciceronis et M. Bruti mutuis epistolis capita duo*, diss. Leipzig.
Helzle, Martin (1988), "Ovid's poetics of exile", in: *ICS* 1, 73–83.
Helzle, Martin (2003), *Ovids Epistulae ex Ponto: Buch I–II: Kommentar*, Heidelberg.
Henderson, John (2002), *Pliny's Statue: The Letters, Self-Portraiture and Classical Art*, Exeter.
Henderson, John (2004), *Morals and Villas in Seneca's Letters: Places to Dwell*, Cambridge.

Hendrickson, George L. (1939), "Brutus *De Virtute*", in: *AJPh* 60(4), 401–413.
Hercher, Rudolf (1873), *Epistolographi Graeci*, Paris.
Heyworth, Stephen J. (1995), "Notes on Ovid's *Tristia*", in: *PCPS* 41, 138–152.
Highbie, Carolyn (2010), "Divide and edit: a brief history of book divisions", in: *HSCPh* 105, 1–31.
Hinard, François (1985), *Les Proscriptions de la Rome républicaine*, CEFR 83, Rome.
Hinds, Stephen (1985), "Booking the return trip: Ovid and *Tristia* 1", in: *PCPhS* 31, 13–32.
Hinds, Stephen (2005), "Dislocations of Ovidian time", in: Jürgen Schwindt (ed.), *La représentation du temps dans la poésie augustéenne*, Heidelberg, 203–230.
Hinds, Stephen (2007), "Ovid among the conspiracy theorists", in: Stephen J. Heyworth (ed.), *Classical Constructions: Papers in Memory of Don Fowler*, Oxford, 194–220.
Hine, Harry M. (2017), "Seneca and Paul: The first two thousand years", in: Joseph R. Dodson/ David E. Briones (eds.), *Paul and Seneca in Dialogue*, Leiden, 22–48.
Hodkinson, Owen (2007) "Better than Speech: Some Advantages of the Letter in the Second Sophistic", in: Ruth Morello/Andrew D. Morrison (eds.), *Ancient Letters: Classical and Late Antique Epistolography*, Oxford, 283–300.
Hodkinson, Owen (2010), "Some Distinguishing Features of Deliberate Fictionality in Greek Biographical Narratives", in: Koen De Temmerman/Pieter Borghart (eds.), *Biography and Fictionality in the Greek Literary Tradition*, Phrasis 51(1), 11–35.
Hodkinson, Owen (2013), "Aelian's Rustic *Epistles* in the context of his corpus: a reassessment of Aelian's literary programme and qualities", in: Onofrio Vox (ed.) (2013), *Lettere, mimesi, retorica. Studi sull'epistolografia letterariagreca di età imperiale e tardoantica*, Lecce, 257–310.
Hodkinson, Owen (2019), ""Les lettres dangereuses": epistolary narrative as metafiction in the *Epistles of Chion of Heraclea*", in: Ian Repath/Fritz-Gregor Herrmann (eds.), *Some Organic Readings in Narrative, Ancient and Modern. Gathered and Originally Presented as a Book for John*, Ancient Narrative Supplementum 27, Groningen, 127–153.
Hodkinson, Owen/Rosenmeyer, Patricia A./Bracke, Evelien (eds.) (2013), *Epistolary Narratives in Ancient Greek Literature*, Leiden/Boston.
Hoffer, Stanley E. (1999), *The Anxieties of Pliny the Younger,* Atlanta.
Høgel, Christian/Bartoli, Elisabetta (eds.) (2015), *Medieval Letters: Between Fiction and Document*, Turnhout.
Hölkeskamp, Karl-Joachim (2011), "The Roman Republic as theatre of power: the consuls as leading actors", in: Hans Beck/Antonio Duplá/Martin Jehne/Francisco Pina Polo (eds.), *Consuls and Res Publica: Holding Office in the Roman Republic*, Cambridge, 161–181.
Holzberg, Niklas (1994a), "Der griechische Briefroman. Versuch einer Gattungstypologie", in: Niklas Holzberg (ed.), *Der griechische Briefroman: Gattungstypologie und Textanalyse*, Tübingen, 1–52.
Holzberg, Niklas (ed.) (1994b), *Der griechische Briefroman: Gattungstypologie und Textanalyse*, Tübingen.
Höschele, Regina (2012), "From Hellas with Love: The Aesthetics of Imitation in Aristaenetus's *Epistles*", in: *TAPhA* 142(1), 157–186.
Huskey, Samuel (2006), "Ovid's (mis)guided tour of Rome: some purposeful omissions in *Tr.* 3.1", in: *CJ* 102(1), 17–39.
Hutchinson, Gregory O. (1998), *Cicero's Correspondence: A Literary Study*, Oxford.
Hutchinson, Gregory O. (ed.) (2006), *Propertius: Elegies Book 4*, Cambridge.
Hutchinson, Gregory O. (2008), *Talking Books: Readings in Hellenistic and Roman Books of Poetry*, Oxford.

Ingleheart, Jennifer (2006), "Ovid, *Tristia* 1.2: high drama on the high seas", in: *G&R* 53, 73–91.
Ingleheart, Jennifer (2010), *A Commentary on Ovid Tristia Book 2*, Oxford.
Innes, Doreen (1995) (tr.), *Poetics. Longinus: On the Sublime. Demetrius: On Style*, Cambridge, MA.
Isnardi Parente, Margherita (2002), *Platone: Lettere*, Milano.
Jackson, Claire Rachel (forthcoming a), "Epistolary and Philosophical Narratives in the *Letters of Chion of Heraclea*", in: Ruth Morello/Jenny Bryan (eds.), *Philosophical Letters*, under review with Oxford University Press.
Jackson, Claire Rachel (forthcoming b), "Letters, Mirrors, and Fiction in Iamblichus' *Babyloniaka*", in: *Mnemosyne*.
Jansen, Laura (2012), "Ovidian paratexts: editorial postscript and readers in *ex Ponto* 3.9", in: *MD* 68, 81–110.
Jenkins, Thomas E. (2006), *Intercepted Letters: Epistolarity and Narrative in Greek and Roman Literature*, Lanham, MD.
Jones, Christopher P. (2017), "Greek Letter Collections Before Late Antiquity", in: Cristiana Sogno/Bradley K. Storin/Edward J. Watts (eds.) (2017), *Late Antique Letter Collections: A Critical Introduction and Reference Guide*, Oakland, 38–53.
Jouan, Francois/Auger, Danielle (1983), "Sur le Corpus des "Lettres d'Euripide", *Melanges Eduoard Delebecque*, Aix-en-Provence, 183–199.
Kauffman, Linda S. (1986), *Discourses of Desire: Gender, Genre, and Epistolary Fictions*, Ithaca.
Keeline, Tom (2018), *The Reception of Cicero in the Early Roman Empire: The Rhetorical Schoolroom and the Creation of a Cultural Legend*, Cambridge.
Keith, Alison (2011), "Lycoris Galli/Volumnia Cytheris: a Greek Courtesan in Rome", in: *Eugesta* 1, 23–53.
Kennedy, Alex (2016), "*Haec nobis fingebamus*: Tibullus, Ovid and the power of imagination", in: *Classical Outlook* 91, 52–54.
Kennedy, Duncan (1984), "The epistolary mode and the first of Ovid's *Heroides*", in: *CQ* 34, 413–422.
Kennedy, Duncan (1993), *The Arts of Love: Five Studies in the Discourse of Roman Love Elegy*, Cambridge.
Klauck, Hans-Josef (2006), *Ancient Letters and the New Testament: A Guide to Context and Exegesis*, Waco.
Knöbl, Ranja (2008), *Biographical Representations of Euripides. Some Examples of Their Development from Classical Antiquity to Byzantium*, unpublished PhD thesis, Durham University.
Kolb, Anne (2000), *Transport und Nachrichtentransfer im römischen Reich*, Berlin.
König, Jason (2007), "Alciphron's Epistolarity", in: Ruth Morello/Andrew D. Morrison (eds.), *Ancient Letters: Classical and Late Antique Epistolography*, Oxford, 257–282.
Konstan, David (1998), "The Invention of Fiction", in: Ronald F. Hock/J. Bradley Chance/Judith Perkins (eds.), *Ancient Fiction and Early Christian Narrative*, Atlanta, 3–17.
Koselleck, Reinhart (2004), *Vergangene Zukunft: Zur Semantik Geschichtlicher Zeiten*, Frankfurt am Main.
Kovacs, David (1994), *Euripidea*, Leiden.
Krauter, Stefan (2009), "Was ist "schlechte" Pseudepigraphie? Mittel, Wirkung und Intention von Pseudepigraphie in den Epistolae Senecae ad Paulum et Pauli ad Senecam", in: Jörg Frey/Jens Herzer/Martina Janßen/Clare K. Rothschild (eds.), *Pseudepigraphie und Ver-*

fasserfiktion in frühchristlichen Briefen. Pseudepigraphy and Author Fiction in Early Christian Letters, Tübingen, 765–785.

Kurke, Leslie (1991), *The Traffic in Praise: Pindar and the Poetics of Social Economy*, Ithaca.

La Bua, Giuseppe (2020), "Man of Peace? Cicero's Last Fight for the Republic in Greek and Roman Historical 'Fictions'", in: Christoph Pieper/Bram van der Velden (eds.), *Reading Cicero's Final Years*, Berlin, 79–95.

La Penna, Antonio (2018), *Ovidio: Relativismo dei valori e innovazione delle forme*, Pisa.

Laignoux, Raphaëlle (2012), "Le monnayage de Brutus et Cassius après la mort de César", in: Nicholas Holmes (ed.), *Proceedings of the XIVth International Numismatic Congress* (Glasgow 2009), Glasgow/London, 785–793.

Lanciani, Rodolfo (1888), *Ancient Rome in the Light of Recent Discoveries*, London.

Laughton, Eric (1964), *The Participle in Cicero*, Oxford.

Lavan, Myles (2023), "Latin literature and Roman history", in: Roy K. Gibson/Christopher L. Whitton (eds.) (2023), *The Cambridge Critical Guide to Latin Literature*, Cambridge.

Leach, Eleanor W. (1999), "Ciceronian Bi-Marcus: Correspondence with M. Terentius Varro and L. Papirius Paetus in 46 B.C.E.", in: *TAPhA* 129, 139–179.

Leach, Eleanor W. (2000), "The *spectacula* of Cicero's *Pro Sestio*: patronage, production and performance", in: Sheila K. Dickison/Judith P. Hallett (eds.), *Rome and Her Monuments: Essays on the City and Literature of Rome in Honour of Katherine A. Geffcken*, Wauconda, 369–398.

Lee, Benjamin T. (2008), "The potentials of narrative: the rhetoric of the subjunctive in Tibullus", in: Genevieve Liveley/Patricia Salzman-Mitchell (eds.), *Latin Elegy and Narratology: Fragments of Story*, Columbus, 196–220.

Lefèvre, Eckhard (2009), *Vom Römertum zum Ästhetizismus: Studien zu den Briefen des jüngeren Plinius*, Berlin.

Leonard, Emelan (2020), "Perversions of the Epistolary Instinct: Desire and Form in the *Letters* of Philostratus", in: *TAPhA* 150.1, 115–141.

Létoublon, Françoise (2003), "La lettre dans le roman grec ou les liaisons dangereuses", in: Stelios Panayotakis/Maaike Zimmerman/Wytse Keulen (eds.), *The Ancient Novel and Beyond*, Leiden, 271–288.

Lévy, Carlos (2012), "Other followers of Antiochus", in: David Sedley (ed.), *The Philosophy of Antiochus*, Cambridge, 290–306.

Lintott, Andrew (2013), *Plutarch: Demosthenes and Cicero*, Oxford.

Long, Anthony (2002), *Epictetus: A Stoic and Socratic Guide to Life*, Oxford.

Ludolph, Matthias (1997), *Epistolographie und Selbstdarstellung. Untersuchungen zu den 'Paradebriefen' Plinius des Jüngeren*, Tübingen.

Ma, John (1994), "Black hunter variations", in: *Proceedings of the Cambridge Philological Society* 40, 49–80.

Macedo, Gabriel N. (2021), *Ancient Latin Poetry Books: Materiality and Context*, Ann Arbor.

MacLachlan, Bonnie (1993), *The Age of Grace: Charis in Early Greek Poetry*, Princeton.

MacMullen, Ramsay (1966), *Enemies of the Roman Order: Treason, Unrest, and Alienation in the Roman Empire*, Cambridge.

Malcovati, Henrica (1976), *Oratorum Romanorum Fragmenta*, 4th ed., Turin.

Malherbe, Abraham J. (1988), *Ancient Epistolary Theorists*, Atlanta.

Malik, Shushma (2020), *The Nero-Antichrist. Founding and Fashioning a Paradigm*, Cambridge.

Malosse, Pierre-Louis (2005), "Éthopée et fiction épistolaire", in: Eugenio Amato/Jacques Schamp (eds.), *Ethopoiia: la représentation de caractères entre fiction scolaire et réalité vivante à l'époque impériale et tardive*, Salerno, 61–78.

Manuwald, Gesine (2019), *Fragmentary Republican Oratory: Part 3, Oratory*, Loeb Classical Library 542, Cambridge, MA.

Marchesi, Ilaria (2008), *The Art of Pliny's Letters: A Poetics of Allusion in the Private Correspondence*, Cambridge, MA.

Marchesi, Ilaria (2015a), "Uncluttered Spaces, Unlittered Texts: Pliny's Villas as Editorial Places", in: Ilaria Marchesi (ed.), *Pliny the Book-Maker: Betting on Posterity in the Epistles*, Oxford, 225–254.

Marchesi, Ilaria (ed.) (2015b), *Pliny the Book-Maker: Betting on Posterity in the Epistles*, Oxford.

Marquis, Émeline (ed.) (2023), *Epistolary Fiction in Ancient Greek Literature*, Berlin.

Martelli, Francesca (2013), *Ovid's Revisions: The Editor as Author*, Cambridge.

Martelli, Francesca (ed.) (2016), *New Readings in Cicero's Letters*, in: *Arethusa* 49(2).

Martelli, Francesca (2017), "The Triumph of Letters: Rewriting Cicero in ad Fam 15", in: *JRS* 107, 90–115.

Martelli, Francesca (forthcoming), "Letters to the Editor: A reading of *ad Fam.* 16", in: Tom Geue/Claire Rachel Jackson/Francesca Middleton/(eds.), *The Medium of Empire: Unstable Text in Rome's Imperial Literature*, forthcoming special issue of *Hermathena*.

Mayer, Roland (1994), *Horace. Epistles I*, Cambridge.

McConnell, Sean (2014), *Philosophical Life in Cicero's Letters*, Cambridge.

McDermott, William C. (1972), "M. Cicero and M. Tiro", in: *Historia* 21(2), 259–286.

McGill, Scott (2005), *Virgil Recomposed: The Mythological and Secular Centos in Antiquity*, Oxford.

Mellet, Sylvie (1988), *L'imparfait de l'indicatif en latin classique: temps, aspect, modalité*, Louvain.

Mendelssohn, Ludwig (1893), *M. Tulli Ciceronis Epistularum Libri Sedecim*, Leipzig.

Messmer, Marietta (2001), *A Vice for Voices. Reading Emily Dickinson's Correspondence*, Amherst/Boston.

Meyer, Paul (1881), *Untersuchung über die frage der echtheit des briefwechsels Cicero ad Brutum*, Stuttgart.

Millar, Fergus (1965), "Epictetus and the Imperial court", in: *JRS* 55, 141–148.

Miller, Paul A. (1999), "The Tibullan dream text", in: *TAPhA* 129, 181–224.

Miller, Paul A. (2013), "The *puella*: accept no substitutes", in: Thea S. Thorsen (ed.), *The Cambridge Companion to Roman Love Elegy*, Cambridge, 166–179.

Moles, John L. (1987), "Politics, Philosophy, and Friendship in Horace "Odes" 2,7", in: *Quaderni Urbinati di Cultura Classica* 251, 59–72.

Moles, John L. (1997), "Plutarch, Brutus and Brutus' Greek and Latin Letters", in: Judith Mossman (ed.), *Plutarch and his Intellectual World*, London, 141–168.

Moles, John L. (2017), *A Commentary on Plutarch's Brutus*, with updated bibliographical notes by Christopher B.R. Pelling, *Histos Supplement* 7, Newcastle upon Tyne.

Mollea, Simone (2019), "*Naturales quaestiones* 4a *praef.* 20 and *ep.* 34.2: approaching the chronology and non-fictional nature of Seneca's *Epistulae Morales*", in: *CQ* 69, 319–334.

Mordine, Michael J. (2010), "Sine me, liber, ibis: the poet, the book and the reader in Tristia 1.1", in: *CQ* 60, 524–544.

Morello, Ruth (2013), "Writer and addressee in Cicero's Letters", in: Catherine Steel (ed.), *The Cambridge Companion to Cicero*, Cambridge, 196–214.

Morello, Ruth (2015), "Pliny Book 8: Two Viewpoints and the Pedestrian Reader", in: Ilaria Marchesi (ed.), *Pliny the Book-Maker: Betting on Posterity in the Epistles*, Oxford, 146–186.

Morello, Ruth (2022), "Further voices and familiar perspectives in Cicero's *Letters*", in: Roy K. Gibson/Ruth Morello (eds.), *The Epistolary Cicero: Further Readings in the Letters, Hermathena* 202–203.

Morello, Ruth/Morrison, Andrew D. (eds.) (2007a), *Ancient Letters: Classical and Late Antique Epistolography*, Oxford.

Morello, Ruth/Morrison, Andrew D. (2007b), "Preface", in: Ruth Morello/Andrew D. Morrison (eds.), *Ancient Letters: Classical and Late Antique Epistolography*, Oxford, v-xii.

Morrison, Andrew D. (2013), "Narrative and Epistolary in the 'Platonic' Epistles", in: Owen Hodkinson/Patricia A. Rosenmeyer/Evelien Bracke (eds.) (2013), *Epistolary Narratives in Ancient Greek Literature*, Leiden/Boston, 107–131.

Morrison, Andrew D. (2014a), "Authorship and Authority in Greek Fictional Letters", in: Anna Marmodoro/Jonathan Hill (eds.), *The Author's Voice in Classical and Late Antiquity*, Oxford, 287–312.

Morrison, Andrew D. (2014b), "Pamela and Plato: Ancient and modern epistolary narrative", in: Douglas Cairns/Ruth Scodel (eds.), *Defining Greek Narrative*, Edinburgh, 298–313.

Morrison, Andrew D. (2019), "Order and Disorder in the *Letters* of Alciphron", in: Michèle Biraud/Arnaud Zucker (eds.), *The Letters of Alciphron: A Unified Literary Work?*, Leiden/Boston, 24–41.

Morrison, Andrew D. (2023), "Lookin' for Love (in Plato's *Epistles*)", in: Anna Tiziana Drago/Owen Hodkinson (eds.), *Ancient Love Letters: Form, Themes, Approaches*, Berlin/Boston, 103–119.

Morson, Gary S. (1998), "Side-shadowing and tempics", in: *New Literary History* 29, 599–624.

Nagle, Betty R. (1980), *The Poetics of Exile: Program and Polemic in the Tristia and Epistulae ex Ponto of Ovid*, Brussels.

Neger, Margot/Tzounakas, Spyridou (eds.) (forthcoming), *Intertextuality in Pliny's Epistles*, Cambridge.

Nesselrath, Heinz-Günther (2023), "Der "alte, gute" Euripides der "Euripidesbriefe", oder: Sinn und Zweck einer korrigierten Biographie", in: Émeline Marquis (ed.), *Epistolary Fiction in Ancient Greek Literature*, Berlin, 139–150.

Nicholson, John (1998), "The survival of Cicero's letters", in: Carl Deroux (ed.), *Studies in Latin Literature and Roman History* 9, Brussels, 63–105.

Nilsson, Ingela (2023), "Greco-Roman Love Letters and Modern Genre Theory", in: Anna Tiziana Drago/Owen Hodkinson (eds.), *Ancient Love Letters: Form, Themes, Approaches*, Berlin/Boston, 23–37.

Nipperdey, Karl (1865), *Die Leges Annales der Römischen Republik*, Leipzig.

O'Donnell, James J. (1992), *Augustine, Confessions*, 3 vols., Oxford.

Oliensis, Ellen (1997), "Return to sender: the rhetoric of *nomina* in Ovid's *Tristia*", in: *Ramus* 26(2), 172–193.

Oliensis, Ellen (2004), "The power of image-makers: representation and revenge in Ovid *Metamorphoses* 6 and *Tristia* 4", in: *CA* 23, 285–321.

Oliver, James (1970), "Arrian and the Gellii of Corinth", in: *GRBS* 11, 335–338.

Orlemanski, Julie (2019), "Who has fiction? Modernity, fictionality and the middle ages", in: *New Literary History* 50, 145–170.

Ortmann, Ursula (1988), *Cicero, Brutus und Octavian – Republikaner und Caesarianer: Ihr gegenseitiges Verhältnis im Krisenjahr 44/43 v. Chr.*, Bonn.

Ottway, Sheila (1996), "Dorothy Osborne's love letters: novelistic glimmerings and the Ovidian self", in: *Prose Studies* 19, 149–159.
Pandey, Nandini B. (2018), *The Poetics of Power in Augustan Rome: Latin Poetic Responses to Early Imperial Iconography*, Cambridge.
Papalas, Anthony J. (1992), *Ancient Icaria*, Mundelein.
Peirano, Irene (2012), *The Rhetoric of the Roman Fake: Latin Pseudepigrapha in Context*, Cambridge.
Peirano Garrison, Irene (2021), "Epistolary Collaboration in Ovid's *Heroides*", draft paper circulated for the 2021 Laurence Seminar *Collaboration and Ancient Literature*, University of Cambridge.
Pelling, Christopher B.R. (1979), "Plutarch's Method of Work in the Roman Lives", in: *JHS* 99, 74–96.
Penwill, John L. (1978), "The Letters of Themistocles: An epistolary novel?", in: *Antichthon* 12, 83–103.
Pepe, Luigi (1958), "Petronio conosce l'epistolario di Plinio", in: *Giornale Italiano di Filologia* 11, 289–294.
Phillips, John J. (1986), "Atticus and the Publication of Cicero's Works", in: *CW* 79, 227–237.
Poltera, Orlando (2013), "The Letters of Euripides", in: Owen Hodkinson/Patricia A. Rosenmeyer/Evelien Bracke (eds.) (2013), *Epistolary Narratives in Ancient Greek Literature*, Leiden/Boston, 153–165.
Pontani, Filippomaria (2013), "Noblest *Charis*: Pindar and the Scholiasts", in: *Phoenix* 67.1–2, 23–42.
Poster, Carol (2007), "A Conversation Halved: Epistolary Theory in Greco-Roman Antiquity", in: Carol Poster/Linda C. Mitchell (eds.), *Letter-Writing Manuals and Instruction from Antiquity to the Present*, Columbia, 21–51.
Powell, Anton/Hardie, Philip (eds.) (2017), *The Ancient Lives of Virgil: Literary and Historical Studies*, Swansea.
Power, Tristan J. (2010), "Pliny, *Letters* 5.10 and the literary career of Suetonius", in: *JRS* 100, 1–23.
Prost, François (2001), "L'éthique d'Antiochus d'Ascalon", in: *Philologus* 145, 244–268.
Radt, Stefan (1990), "Zu Epiktets Diatriben", in: *Mnemosyne* 43, 364–373.
Ramelli, Ilaria E. (2013), "The pseudepigraphical correspondence between Seneca and Paul: a reassessment", in: Stanley E. Porter/Gregory P. Fewster (eds.), *Pauline Studies: Paul and Pseudepigraphy*, Leiden, 319–336.
Ramelli, Ilaria E. (2014), "A pseudepigraphon inside a pseudepigraphon? The Seneca-Paul correspondence and the letters added afterwards", in: *Journal for the Study of Pseudepigrapha* 23.4, 259–289.
Ratti, Stéphane (2015), "Relire le *Satyricon*: Pline le Jeune et les chrétiens, cibles du roman secret d'un affranchi cultivé", in: *Anabases* 22, 99–114.
Rawson, Elizabeth (1986), "Cassius and Brutus: The Memory of the Liberators", in: Ian S. Moxon/John D. Smart/Anthony J. Woodman (eds.), *Past Perspectives*, Cambridge, 101–119.
Reinhardt, Tobias/Winterbottom, Michael (2006), *Quintilian,* Institutio Oratoria, *Book 2*, Oxford.
Revermann, Martin (1999–2000), "Euripides, Tragedy, and Macedon: Some Conditions of Reception", in: *BICS* 24–25, 451–467.
Reynolds, Leighton D. (1983), *Texts and Transmission: A Survey of the Latin Classics*, Oxford.
Ricoeur, Paul (1980), "Narrative time", in: *Critical Inquiry* 7, 169–190.
Riehle, Alexander (2020), *A Companion to Byzantine Epistolography*, Leiden.

Riggsby, Andrew M. (1995), "Pliny on Cicero and oratory: self-fashioning in the public eye", in: *AJP* 116, 123–135.
Rimmell, Victoria (2015), *The Closure of Space in Roman Poetics*, Cambridge.
Rimmell, Victoria (2019), "After Ovid, after theory", in: *International Journal of the Classical Tradition* 26, 446–469.
Rohrbacher, David (2016), *The Play of Allusion in the 'Historia Augusta'*, Madison/London.
Ronen, Ruth (1994), *Possible Worlds in Literary Theory*, Cambridge.
Rosenmeyer, Patricia A. (1994), "The Epistolary Novel", in: John Morgan/Richard Stoneman (eds.), *Greek Fiction: The Greek Novel in Context*, London/New York, 146–165.
Rosenmeyer, Patricia A. (1997), "Ovid's *Heroides* and *Tristia*: voices from exile", in: *Ramus* 26, 29–56.
Rosenmeyer, Patricia A. (2001), *Ancient Epistolary Fiction: The Letter in Greek Literature*, Cambridge.
Rosenmeyer, Patricia A. (2006), *Ancient Greek Literary Letters: Selections in Translation*, London.
Roskam, Geert/De Pourcq, Maarte/Van Der Stockt, L. (eds.) (2012), *The Lash of Ambition: Plutarch, Greek Literature, and the Dynamics of Philotimia*, Louvain.
Roth, Ulrike (2016), "Liberating the *Cena*", in: *CQ* 66, 614–634.
Rowan, Clare (2013), *Under Divine Auspices: Divine Ideology and the Visualisation of Imperial Power in the Severan Period*, Cambridge.
Rudd, Niall (ed.) (1989), *Horace: Epistles Book II*, Cambridge.
Ruete, Edmund (1883), *Die Correspondenz Ciceros in den Jahren 44 u. 43*, Marburg.
Saïd, Edward (2000), *Reflections on Exile and Other Essays*, London.
Salzman, Michele (2017), "Latin Letter Collections before Late Antiquity", in: Cristiana Sogno/Bradley K. Storin/Edward J. Watts (eds.), *Late Antique Letter Collections: A Critical Introduction and Reference Guide*, Oakland, 13–37.
Santangelo, Federico (2012), "Authoritative Forgeries: Late Republican History Re-Told in Pseudo-Sallust", in: *Histos* 6, 27–51.
Sarri, Antonia (2017), *Material aspects of letter-writing in the Graeco-Roman world c. 500 BC – AD 300*, Berlin.
Scharffenberger, Elizabeth (2015), "The Life of Euripides", in: Rosanna Lauriola/Kyriakos Demetriou (eds.), *Brill's Companion to the Reception of Euripides*, Leiden/Boston, 292–319.
Schenkl, Heinrich (1916), *Epictetus. Dissertationes ab Arriano digestae*, Stuttgart.
Schmidt, Friedrich (1884), "Zur Kritik und Erklärung der Briefe Ciceros an M. Brutus", in: *Neue Jahrbücher für Philologie und Paedagogik* 129, 617–644.
Schmitz, Thomas (2000), "Plausibility in the Greek Orators", in: *AJP* 121.1, 47–77.
Schmitz, Thomas (2017), "The Rhetoric of Desire in Philostratus's Letters", in: *Arethusa* 50, 257–282.
Schulz, Verena (2019), *Deconstructing Imperial Representation. Tacitus, Cassius Dio and Suetonius on Nero and Domitian*, Leiden.
Scodel, Ruth (2017), "The Euripidean Biography", in: Laura McClure (ed.), *A Companion to Euripides*, Chichester, 27–41.
Sedley, David (1997), "The Ethics of Brutus and Cassius", in: *JRS* 87, 41–53.
Selle, Hendrik (2001), "Dichtung oder Wahrheit – der Autor der epiktetischen Predigten", in: *Philologus* 145, 269–290.
Setaioli, Aldo (1976), "On the Date of Publication of Cicero's Letters to Atticus", in: *Symbolae Osloenses* 51, 105–120.

Setaioli, Aldo (2014), *"Epistulae Morales"*, in: Gregor Damschen/Andreas Heil (eds.), *Brill's Companion to Seneca*, Leiden, 191–200.
Shackleton Bailey, David R. (1977), *Cicero: Epistulae ad Familiares*, 2 vols., Cambridge.
Shackleton Bailey, David R. (1980), *Cicero: Epistulae ad Quintum Fratrem et M. Brutum,* Cambridge.
Shackleton Bailey, David R. (1987), *Epistulae ad Familiares: Libri I–XVI*, Berlin/Boston.
Shackleton Bailey, David R. (2001), *Cicero: Letters to Friends*, 3 vols., Cambridge, MA.
Shackleton Bailey, David R. (2002), *Cicero: Letters to Quintus and Brutus; to Octavian; Invectives; Handbook of Electioneering,* Loeb Classical Library 462, Cambridge, MA.
Sharrock, Alison R. (2000), "Intratextuality: Texts, Parts, and (W)holes in Theory", in: Alison R. Sharrock/Helen Morales (eds.), *Intratextuality: Greek and Roman Textual Relations*, Oxford, 1–39.
Sharrock, Alison R. (2013), "The *poeta-amator, nequitia,* and *recusatio*", in: Thea S. Thorsen (ed.), *The Cambridge Companion to Roman Love Elegy*, Cambridge, 151–165.
Sherwin-White, Adrian (ed.) (1966), *The Letters of Pliny. A Historical and Social Commentary*, Oxford (with corrected reprint, 1985).
Smith, Mariah E. (2020), "Composing the Puella: Pliny the Younger's Elegiac Experimentation", in: *ICS* 45(1), 132–157.
Smolak, Kurt (2010), "Three Latin Paratexts from Late Antiquity and the Early Middle Ages ("Sulpicia", "Seneca" – "Paulus", Carmen Navale)", in: Philip Alexander/Armin Lange/ Renate Pillinger (eds.), *In the Second Degree: Paratextual Literature in Ancient Near Eastern and Ancient Mediterranean Culture and its Reflections in Medieval Literature*, Leiden, 219–237.
Sogno, Cristiana/Storin, Bradley K./Watts, Edward J. (eds.) (2017a), *Late Antique Letter Collections: A Critical Introduction and Reference Guide*, Oakland.
Sogno, Cristiana/Storin, Bradley K./Watts, Edward J. (2017b), "Greek and Latin Epistolography and Epistolary Collections in Late Antiquity", in: Cristiana Sogno/Bradley K. Storin/Edward J. Watts (eds.), *Late Antique Letter Collections: A Critical Introduction and Reference Guide*, Oakland, 1–10.
Soldo, Janja (2021), *Seneca: Epistulae Morales Book 2. A Commentary with Text, Translation & Introduction*, Oxford.
Speyer, Wolfgang (1971), *Die literarische Fälschung im heidnischen und christlichen Altertum*, Munich.
Squire, Michael (2009), *Image and Text in Graeco-Roman Antiquity*, Cambridge.
Squire, Michael (2013), "Apparitions Apparent: Ekphrasis and the Parameters of Vision in the Elder Philostratus' *Imagines*", in: *Helios* 40(1–2), 97–140.
Stadter, Philip (1980), *Arrian of Nicomedia*, Chapel Hill.
Steel, Catherine E.W. (2005), *Reading Cicero: Genre and Performance in Late Republican Rome*, London.
Steiner, Deborah T. (1994), *The Tyrant's Writ: Myths and Images of Writing in Ancient Greece*, Princeton.
Stellwag, Helena (1933), *Epictetus. Het eerste boek der Diatriben*, Amsterdam.
Stevenson, Tom (2015), *Julius Caesar and the Transformation of the Roman Republic*, London/ New York.
Stirewalt, M. Luther (1993), *Studies in Ancient Greek Epistolography*, Atlanta.
Stockton, David (1971), *Cicero: A Political Biography*, Oxford.
Stone, Martin (1980), "*Pro Milone*: Cicero's Second Thoughts", in: *Antichthon* 14, 88–111.

Stover, Justin (2022), "The Ciceronian book and its influence: a statistical approach", in: *Ciceroniana On Line* 5.2 (https://doi.org/10.13135/2532-5353/6522).
Sykutris, Johannes (1933), *Die Briefe des Sokrates und der Sokratiker*, Paderborn.
Syme, Ronald (1958a), "Pseudo-Sallust", in: *MH* 15, 46–55.
Syme, Ronald (1958b), *Tacitus*, Oxford.
Syme, Ronald (1972), "Fraud and Imposture", in: *Pseudepigrapha I*, Entretiens Hardt 18, Geneva, 3–17.
Syme, Ronald (1978), *History in Ovid*, Oxford.
Syme, Ronald (1985), "The Dating of Pliny's Latest Letters", in: *CQ* 35, 176–185.
Syme, Ronald (1991), *Roman Papers* VII (ed. A.R. Birley), Oxford.
Tarrant, Richard (1983), "Ovid", in: L.D. Reynolds (ed.), *Texts and Transmission: A Survey of the Latin Classics*, Oxford, 257–284.
Tatum, Jeff (2020), "A Great and Arduous Struggle: Marcus Antonius and the Rhetoric of *Libertas* in 44–43 BC", in: Catalina Balmaceda (ed.), *Libertas and Res Publica in the Roman Republic: Ideas of Freedom and Roman Politics*, Leiden, 189–215.
Tempest, Kathryn (2017), *Brutus: The Noble Conspirator*, New Haven/London.
Tempest, Kathryn (2023), "Remembering M. Brutus: From Mixed and Hostile Perspectives", in: Martin Dinter/Charles Guérin (eds.), *Cultural Memory in Republican and Augustan Rome*, Cambridge, 218–238.
Thraede, Klaus (1970), *Grundzüge griechisch-römischer Brieftopik*, Munich.
Tissol, Garth (2014), *Ovid Epistulae ex Ponto book I*, Cambridge.
Trapp, Michael (1997), *Maximus of Tyre. The Philosophical Orations*, Oxford.
Trapp, Michael (2003), *Greek and Latin Letters: An Anthology with Translation*, Cambridge.
Trapp, Michael (2006), "Biography in Letters, Biography and Letters", in: Brian McGing/Judith Mossman (eds.), *The Limits of Ancient Biography*, Swansea, 335–350.
Trapp, Michael (2009), "Lucian's Nigrinus and the anxieties of philosophical communication", in: Mustafa Çevik (ed.), *International Symposium on Lucianus of Samosata, 17–19 October 2008*, Adıyaman, 113–124.
Treggiari, Susan (2019), *Servilia and her Family*, Oxford.
Tyrrell, Robert Y./Purser, Louis C. (1933), *The Correspondence of Cicero*, Vol. VI: Second Edition, Dublin/London.
Tyrrell, William B. (2020), "Life of Euripides", in: Andreas Markantonatos (ed.), *Brill's Companion to Euripides*, Leiden/Boston, 11–28.
Tzounakas, Spyridon (2012), "Pliny and his elegies in Icaria", in: *CQ* 62, 301–306.
Underwood, Ted (2019), *Distant Horizons: Digital Evidence and Literary Change*, Chicago.
Van der Velden, Bram (2019), "J.J. Hartmann on Ovid's non-exile", in: *Mnemosyne* 73, 336–342.
Van der Velden, Bram (2020), "Ciceronian Reception in the *Epistula ad Octavianum*", in: Christoph Pieper/Bram van der Velden (eds.), *Reading Cicero's Final Years*, Berlin, 121–136.
Van Hoof, Lieve (2016), "Falsification as a Protreptic to Truth: The Force of the Forged Epistolary Exchange between Basil and Libanius", in: Peter Gemeinhardt/Lieve Van Hoof/Peter Van Nuffelen (eds.), *Education and Religion in Late Antiquity: Genres and Discourses in Transition*, London, 116–130.
Van Sickle, John (1980a), "The book roll and some conventions of the poetic book", in: *Arethusa* 13, 5–42.
Van Sickle, John (1980b), "Reading Virgil's Eclogue book", in: *ANRW* II.31.1, 576–603.

von Möllendorff, Peter (2006), "Camels, Celts, and Centaurs: Lucian's Aesthetic Concept – the *Charis* of the Hybrid", in: Ruurd R. Nauta (ed.), *Desultoria Scientia: Genre in Apuleius' Metamorphoses and Related Texts*, Leuven, 63–86.

Vox, Onofrio (ed.) (2013), *Lettere, mimesi, retorica. Studi sull'epistolografia letteraria greca di età imperiale e tardoantica*, Lecce.

Watt, William S. (1958), *M. Tullii Ciceronis Epistulae, Vol. 3: Epistulae ad Quintum Fratrem, Epistulae ad M. Brutum, Fragmenta Epistularum*, Oxford.

Waugh, Patricia (1984), *Metafiction: The Theory and Practice of Self-conscious Fiction*, London.

Webb, Ruth (2009), *Ekphrasis, Imagination and Persuasion in Ancient Rhetorical Theory and Practice*, Farnham/Burlington.

Weinstock, Stefan (1971), *Divus Julius*, Oxford.

Weyssenhoff, Christina (1966), *De Ciceronis epistulis deperditis*, Wrocław.

White, Peter (2010), *Cicero in Letters: Epistolary Relations of the Late Republic*, Oxford.

Whitmarsh, Tim (2013), *Beyond the Second Sophistic Adventures in Greek Postclassicism*, Berkeley.

Whitmarsh, Tim (2020), *Achilles Tatius: Leucippe and Clitophon Books I-II*, Cambridge.

Whittaker, John (1974), "Parisinus graecus 1962 and the writings of Albinus", in: *Phoenix* 28, 320–354.

Whitton, Christopher L. (ed.) (2013), *Pliny the Younger, Epistles Book II*, Cambridge.

Whitton, Christopher L. (2015a), "Grand Designs: Unrolling Epistles 2", in: Ilaria Marchesi (ed.), *Pliny the Book-Maker: Betting on Posterity in the Epistles*, Oxford, 109–145.

Whitton, Christopher L. (2015b), "Pliny's progress: on a troublesome Domitianic career", in: *Chiron* 45, 1–22.

Whitton, Christopher L. (2019), *The Arts of Imitation in Latin Prose. Pliny's Epistles/Quintilian in Brief*, Cambridge.

Whitton, Christopher L. (2022), "Last but not Least: *Ad M. Brutum*", in: Roy K. Gibson/Ruth Morello (eds.), *The Epistolary Cicero: Further Readings in the Letters*, Hermathena 202–203.

Whitton, Christopher L./Roy K. Gibson (2016), "Introduction: readers and readings of Pliny's *Epistles*", in: Roy K. Gibson/Christopher L. Whitton (eds.), *The Epistles of Pliny: Oxford Readings in Classical Studies*, Oxford, 1–48.

Wilcox, Amanda (2022), "Cicero the *scurra*? Modal satire in the *Letters*", in: Roy K. Gibson/Ruth Morello (eds.), *The Epistolary Cicero: Further Readings in the Letters*, Hermathena 202–203.

Williams, Gareth D. (1992), "Representation of the book roll in Latin poetry: Ovid, *Tr.* 1.1.3–14 and related texts", in: *Mnemosyne* 45, 178–189.

Williams, Gareth D. (1994), *Banished Voices: Readings in Ovid's Exile Poetry*, Cambridge.

Williams, Gareth D. (2002a), "Ovid's exile poetry: *Tristia, Epistulae ex Ponto* and *Ibis*", in: Philip Hardie (ed.), *Cambridge Companion to Ovid*, Cambridge, 233–245.

Williams, Gareth D. (2002b), "Ovid's exilic poetry: worlds apart", in: Barbara Boyd (ed.), *Brill's Companion to Ovid*, Leiden, 337–381.

Winsbury, Rex (2009), *The Roman Book: Books, Publishing and Performance in Classical Rome*, London.

Wirth, Theo (1967), "Arrians Erinnerungen an Epiktet", in: *MH* 24, 149–189, 197–216.

Wiseman, Timothy P. (2015), *The Roman Audience. Classical Literature as Social History*, Oxford.

Wohl, Victoria (1998), "Plato Avant La Lettre: Authenticity in Plato's *Epistles*", in: *Ramus* 27(1), 60–93.

Wohl, Victoria (2014), "Play of the Improbable: Euripides' Unlikely *Helen*", in: Victoria Wohl (ed.), *Probabilities, Hypotheticals, and Counterfactuals in Ancient Greek Thought*, Cambridge, 142–159.
Woolf, Greg (2015), "Pliny/Trajan and the poetics of empire", in: *CPh* 110, 132–151.
Woytek, Bernhard (2003), *Arma et Nummi. Forschungen zur römischen Finanzgeschichte und Münzprägung der Jahre 49 bis 42 v. Chr.*, Vienna.
Zadorojyni, Alexei V. (2006), "Plutarch's Themistocles and the Poets", in: *AJP* 127(2), 261–292.
Zeiner-Carmichael, Noelle (2013), *Roman Letters: An Anthology*, Chichester.

General Index

Aeschines Socraticus 100–104
Allusion 13, 22, 29–30, 37, 42–44, 56, 62–63, 132, 139, 148, 150–154, 156–158, 162, 164, 167, 169, 174, 177–178, 193–194, 211, 234, *see also* intertextuality
– As 'checklist' 151, 154
– Playfulness of 139, 151, 154
Altman, J. 76, 79, 53, 115, 196–197
Anachronism 2, 4, 47–48, 51, 163, 174, 193
Anonymity 13, 16, 46–47, 71, 75–76, 108, 164–168, 173, 182
Apocryphal 161–178
ἀπομνήμόνευμα/ἀπομνήμονεύματα 93, 101–102
Archelaus 45, 48, 50–55, 58–63
Aristippus 101–102
Aristophanes 55
Arrian (L. Flavius Arrianus) 89–106
Athens 45–46, 48, 53–55, 61, 103, 105, 213
Augustan poetry book 26–32, 37, 44, 210–211
Authenticity 1–9, 11–14, 16–17, 21–26, 31–32, 45–51, 56–57, 62, 65–68, 85–86, 91–95, 105–106, 107–110, 114–116, 128, 131–136, 138–144, 149, 154–158, 162–164, 169, 177–178, 181–182, 184–185, 189, 191, 199, 204–205, 207–208, 210–211, 238

Bentley, R. 2, 51
Biography 1, 4, 8–9, 21–25, 30–38, 41–51, 54–57, 63–67, 108, 112, 139, 144–145, 150–158, 162, 168–169, 184
– Alternative versions of 51, 54, 56, 65, 67, 144–145
– Rehabilitative approach to 50–56
Book units (epistolography) 26–28, 72
Brevity 37, 166
Brutus, Marcus Iunius 16–17, 131–159, 211
– As champion of liberty 146

– As parricide 137, 152, 157
– As subject of interest in Imperial period 157–159
– Philosophy of 140, 144–145, 148–150, 157
– Reception history of 156–159
– Temper, lack of 154–156

Caelius Rufus 182, 197–200, 202
Caesar, C. Iulius 97, 109, 112–114, 116–117, 119–120, 124, 131, 134, 136–138, 140, 142–147, 151–153, 159, 182, 184, 187, 190, 195, 200, 203–205, 211
Caninius Gallus, L. 123, 188, 201, 205
Caninius Rufus 37, 217–220, 222, 227
Captatio beneuolentiae 97–98
Cephisophon 54–56, 61
Christianity 163, 170–172
Christian pseudepigrapha 1, 14, 163
Chronology 13, 18, 107–108, 111–112, 115–116, 124, 133, 150, 156, 174
Cicero, M. Tullius 6, 8, 12–13, 16–18, 22, 25, 28–29, 36, 73–74, 79, 82, 107–128, 131–159, 162, 181–205, 209, 211, 217,
– Boastfulness 136–137
– Periodic style 134, 143
– Support for Octavian 131, 137, 146, 153, 158
Civil War 107–109, 112, 114–116, 119, 127–128, 147
Consolation 66, 84–85, 100, 116–118, 148, 154
Corinth 35, 83, 103–104, 176–177
Cotta Maximus 27, 76, 79–80, 82, 85
Creative supplementation 140

Declamation 132
Declamatory classroom exercises 139, 158
Deißmann, G.A. 2–3
Demetrius 10–11, 52–53, 58, 161–162, 166, 174, 238
– Pseudo-Demetrius 57–58
Diatribe 94, 96
Dionysius I 103

Dionysius II 7, 62
Distance between letter writer and addressee 11, 18, 53, 69, 74, 78–79, 84, 86, *see also* separation
Dobbin, R. 93, 95
Documentary letters and fictionality 2–4, 6–7, 10, 16–17, 183–184, 202
Domitius Ahenobarbus, Cn. 117

Editor 11–13, 16–17, 28, 58, 89, 105, 107–128, 181, 184–185, 191, 193, 202–203, 211, 217
Effet de réel see reality effect
Ekphrasis 53, 207–238
Emperor 40, 86, 169–172, 176
Enargeia 207, 211–212, 220
Epictetus 16, 18, 89–106
Epistolary dialogue 10–11, 14, 53, 58–61, 161, 178, 201
Epistolary etiquette 77, 163, 166, 173
Epistolary exchange 9, 11, 56–62, 67, 86,
Epistolary fiction
– Definitions of 4–7, 14, 18, 30, 45–48, 67–68, 105–106, 194–196
Epistolary format 56–57, 62–63, 79, 86, 108, 196, 207
Epistolary genre 1–7, 12–14, 39, 47, 67, 106, 111–112, 115, 162, 189–196, 201, 210–212, 238
Epistolary novel 1–7, 9, 45–48
– Definitions of 4–5, 7, 48
Epistolary typologies 4, 10, 12, 57, 59, 196
Erasmus of Rotterdam 163
Euclid 102–103
Euripides 1, 3, 17–18, 35, 45–68
Exile 15–16, 31, 36–38, 48–49, 69–70, 74, 78–82, 85, 109, 112–113, 116, 124, 146–148, 150, 182–184, 192, 201

Fabius Maximus 17, 76–77
Failure 31, 58–62, 69–70, 109–110, 112, 116–119, 124–126, 138, 164, 171, 187, 195, 200, 216
Fiction *see* epistolary fiction, historical fictions, epistolary novel, fictionalising strategies

Fictionalising strategies 6–7, 9–10, 15, 17, 21–23, 32–44, 92–94, 124, 184, 188, 191, 200, 205
φιλοτιμία 65–66
Fire of Rome 171–172
Flaccus 80
Forgery 1–3, 8–9, 12, 14, 16–17, 23, 45–47, 57, 133–138, 140–141, 149, 156–157, 162–164, 173
Friendship 59, 64–67, 75–76, 78–79, 84, 100–102, 107, 109–110, 112–114, 116, 119–120, 124–127, 131, 153–155, 163–166, 168, 173–174, 192–193, 207–211

Gallio 84–85
Games 120–124, 128, 186–187, 189, 200, 203
Gardens of Sallust 165–166, 169, 175
Gellius, Lucius (? L. Gellius Menander/Iustus) 89–106
Genre 36, 37–38, 40, 138, 159, *see also* epistolary genre
Getae 78, 81
Guillemin, A.-M. 23–26

Handwriting 82
Historical fictions 7, 15–16, 132, 139, 150, 152, 188
Holzberg, N. 3–5, 62–63
Horace 6, 27, 29, 31, 36, 40, 71, 211

Imagined/possible worlds 167–168, 187–189, 194, 200, 205
Imitatio 217, 238
Impersonation 56–57, 131–132, 139–140, 144–150
Intertextuality 22–26, 30, 34–35, 42–44, 138–144, 156, 181, 185, 193–196, 201–205, 208, *see also* allusion
– As fictionalising strategy 187–188, 193–196

Laudatio loci 213, 219
Lecture notes 89–106
Letter book 28, 69, 75, 111, *see also* Augustan poetry book
Letter collections

– Coherence of 5, 9–10, 60–61, 63, 76
– Differences between Latin and Greek 5–7
– Manuscript ordering of 26, 46
Letter-writing manual 10, 58–59, 161, 165, 173–174
Literary criticism 23–26, 47, 92–100, 207–211
Long, A.A. 94
Lucian 92

Macedon 46, 48–50, 54–56, 61
Macer 81–82
Marius, M. 107, 109, 115–116, 119–128, 185–189, 196–197, 200–202
Massalenus 97
Materiality 15, 82, 190–191
Messalinus 76, 78–79, 81
Meta-epistolary discourse 161, 165, 173–177
Meta-fictionality 191
Meta-literariness 36–38, 81, 131, 141–142, 232–233
Metre, elegiac 69, 83
Mimesis 207, 212, 215, 227–230, 232, 237–238
Mise-en-abyme 227, 233
Money 49–50, 54, 62–63
Munatius Plancus Bursa, T. 125–126
Musonius Rufus, C. 96, 98

Naming 55, 71, 75–76
Narrative, fragmented 9–10, 60–61, 110, 115, 201–202
Negotium 119, 122, 124, 186
Nero 165, 169, 173
Nigrinus 92

Odysseus/Ulysses 73–74, 184, 194
Otium 117, 119–120, 122, 124, 185, 189, 198, 203–204
Ovid 5, 21–22, 26–29, 31–32, 36–38, 69–86, 97, 181–183, 188
Ovid's wife 71, 74, 80, 82, 84

Painting 227, 229–232
Paul 2, 6, 17, 23, 161–178

Pella 51–53
Penelope 70, 73–74
Phaedo 101–102
Philosophical discourse 103, 105, 169
Philosophy 8, 65, 89, 92, 124, 144–145, 148, 192
Pisonian conspiracy 173
Plato 13, 97–98, 101–3, 192, 198
Platonic *Letters* 3, 5, 7–8, 11, 13, 26, 46, 51, 62–63, 67, 101, 115, 170
Plausibility 64–65, 92–99, 162–164, 175, 184, 193
Pliny the Younger 8–9, 13, 15, 17, 18, 21–44, 81, 207–238
Polish 81, 97, 104, *see also* style
Pompeius Magnus, Cn. 107, 109, 112–113, 115–120, 122–124, 126–128, 145–147, 151, 185, 187–189, 198–200, 202, 205
Poppaea Sabina 170
'Postcard effect' 213–214, 223
Preface 77, 89, 95, 97, 99
Privacy 71, 76, 86, 90–91, 114, 117, 123–124, 162, 174, 183–185, 210–211, 224
Pseudepigrapha 1–3, 5, 7–8, 14, 16–17, 45, 48, 100, 103–105, 131–159, 161–178, 193
– As literary game 131, 143
– Methodological challenges in identifying 140, 143

Quintus Sextius the Elder 167

Reading 72, 143, 161, 165, 173–177, 209–210, 213, 215–217, 223–224, 234
Realism 4, 31–32, 37, 53–54, 136, 141, 162, 185–193, 200–204, 212, 216, 227–229, 237–238
Reality effect/*effet de réel* 75, 212, 224
Recusatio 97–98
Reunion 107, 109, 120, 125, 127–128
Rhetoric 3–4, 6, 22, 25, 37, 40, 52–53, 132–134, 137–140, 151–152, 158, 163, 195, 211–212, 219–220, 224–225, 232–233, 237–238
Rome 27, 30–33, 35, 44, 46, 69, 72–74, 78–79, 81–86, 121–122, 127, 133, 137, 145–149, 155, 168–169, 171–172, 181,

183, 185, 187–188, 197, 199, 201, 209, 216, 235
Rosenmeyer, P.A. 3–4, 47, 70, 114–115, 143, 162
Rumour 44, 48–50, 54–56, 172, 182–183, 197–198, *see also* slander

Salus/health 61–62, 75, 78, 80, 109, 120, 125, 127–128, 133, 153–154
Self-reflection 11, 38–41, 147–148, 193–196, 215, 233
Seneca, L. Annaeus 17, 23, 28, 36, 44, 66, 140, 146–148, 157, 161–178, 211, 213
– Pseudo-Seneca 172
Separation 11, 74, 78–79, 83, 109, 119, 124–128, 167, *see also* distance between letter writer and addressee
Severus 85–86
Sextus Pompeius 83
Sherwin-White, A.N. 23–26
Shipwreck 43–44, 64, 66–67
Simon (the Cobbler) 101–102
Slander 49, 67, *see also* rumour
Socrates 3, 96–98, 100–103, 105–106
Sophocles 54, 62–67
Spectacle 121–124, 126, 196–200, 202–203
Sphragis 78, 237
Stadter, P. 94–96
Stellwag, H. 92–93, 95
Stoicism 36, 63, 89, 117, 148–149, 157, 163, 167
Style 24–25, 37–39, 52, 82, 94–98, 103, 133–135, 141–143, 156, 161–164, 169, 174, 176–177, 210, 217, *see also* polish

subiectio sub oculis 212, 234
συγγράφειν/σύγγραμμα 101

Tears 82, 85
Telamon 194, 201
Temporal dynamics 82–85, 185, 189–192, 196–202
Theatricality 181, 188, 199–200
Theophilus 176
Time-lag 82–83
Tomis 16, 31, 69, 72–75, 83, 85
Toranius, C. 116, 118
Tragedy 34, 61–62, 121, 145, 193–195, 236
Trebatius Testa, C. 113, 119, 203–204

Unreality 17, 193, 196, 200–201, 204, 212, 225, 227
ὑπόμνημα/ὑπομνήματα 97, 98

Vernacular ('diatribe') style 94
Victor, Iulius 166
Villa description 30, 32–33, 185–189, 218–222
Vulnerability of letters 57, 86

Water 35, 38, 43–44, 83–84, 214–217, 223–224, 227, 231–237
Weather 34, 69–70, 78
Wirth, T. 95–99

χάρις 56–62
Xenophon 96–97, 100–105

Index Locorum

Achilles Tatius
– *Leucippe and Clitophon*
1.19.1   62

Aelian
– *Ep.*
1–6   178
7–8   178
11–12   178
13–16   178

Anthologia Palatina
7.499   34
7.651   34
7.699   34

Appian
– *B. Civ.*
4.136   154

Aristophanes
– *Eq.*
664   55
– *Nu.*
1475   55

Aristotle
– *Poet.*
1460a18–19   36
– *Pol.*
1311b   49

Arrian
– *Anabasis*
1.12.4–5   97
– *Comm. In Epict. Ench.*
praef. init. (= Test. III Schenkel)   97
– *Discourses of Epictetus*
Prefatory epistle   95, 105
1.11   92
1.13–15   92
2.4   92
3.11   92
3.14   92
3.22   92
3.23.27–32   98
3.24   92
4.1   92
– *[Recollections of Epictetus]*   93

Augustine
– *Conf.*
2.4.9   36
6.6.9   40

Aulus Gellius
– *NA*
1.22.19   111
12.13.21   111
19.1.14   92

Caesar
– *Bell. Gall.*
8 *praef.* 5   97

Cassius Dio
40.55.1   126
47.25.3   140
47.49.2   145
47.79.3   154

Catullus
10   187
16   39, 41
55   187

Cicero
– *Att.*
1.2   209
1.18.2   147
2.1.8   198
2.23.1   82
3.5   28
3.12.2   91
3.15   85
5.7.1   82
6.8–7.9   109
7.17.3   119

8.12.1	82	1.16.1	131, 141–142, 144, 156
9.4	203		
9.10.7	184	1.16.2	145
9.11.2	184	1.16.3	134, 143
9.18.2	184	1.16.5	143
12.1	191	1.16.6	146, 153
12.1.2	191	1.16.8	133, 148
13.21	91	1.16.9	45, 149
14.6.2	136	1.17	133, 153–154, 156
14.9.2	142	1.17.1	144
14.11.1	136	1.17.1–2	136, 139
14.12.2	136	1.17.2	135, 138
14.14.2	142	1.17.3	153
14.15	136	1.17.4	149
14.17a.2	143	1.17.5	144, 153
15.11.1–2	147	1.17.7	154
16.3–4	184	1.18.2	147
16.5.5	108	1.18.13	155
16.7	155	2.5	136
16.7.3	155	2.5.5	153
16.7.4	155	11	146
16.7.5	155	– *Brutus*	
16.14.2	143	262	97
16.15.1	82	– *Fam.*	
– *Brut.*		2.4.1	52, 174, 195
1.2a.2	153	2.8–16	197
1.3	133	2.8.1	197
1.3.1	132	2.8.2	198
1.4	155	2.11.2	203
1.4a	155	2.19	119
1.4a.2	142	4.4	111, 144
1.4a.3	142	4.4.4	144
1.6.3	132	4.8.2	142
1.9	154	4.12	113
1.10.4	146	4.13.1	52
1.10.5	146	6.1	117
1.11.2	146	6.6	199
1.14.1	155	6.20	118
1.15	146	6.20.1	119
1.15.2	146	6.20.2	119
1.15.4	146	6.20.3	119
1.15.5	146	6.21	118
1.15.6	146	6.21.1	117
1.15.7	143	6.21–7.4	116–128
1.15.10	153	6.22	117–119
1.15.11	153	6.22.1	118
1.16	153, 156		

7.1	119–120, 123–124, 128	9.5	189
		9.7.1	142
7.1.1	120	9.16.4	195
7.1.1–2	120	9.21.1	81
7.1.2	121	9.22	193
7.1.2–3	121–122	9.26	185, 189, 191, 194, 196, 201, 203–205
7.1.3	121–122		
7.1.4	122	9.26.1	193
7.1.4–5	122	9.26.2	194
7.1.5	122, 127	10.33	111
7.1.6	123, 125	11.14.3	133
7.1–3	124	12.1.1	142
7.1–4	124, 128	12.3.1	142
7.2	119	12.13.1	152
7.2.1	125	12.30.1	10
7.2.2	125	13.15	195
7.2.4	125, 127	13.15.3	195
7.3	127	14.3	85
7.3.2–3	127	15.9.4	28
7.3.6	127	15.19	110
7.4	120, 127–128, 188	15.19.4	142
7.5	113, 119	15.21	204
7.9.3	203	16.16.2	11
7.16.2	203	– *Fin.*	
7.20	203	1.3.8	140
7.22	203	1.8	146
7.26	203	2.56	150
7.33	204	– *Inv.*	
7.33.2	204	1.27	195
8.1.2	197	– *Orat.*	
8.2.2	203	208	186
8.4.1	199	– *Phil.*	
8.4.5	203	2.28	137
8.6.5	203	2.31	152
8.9.2	198	2.114	136
8.9.3	203	3.3	143
8.10	198	13.24	143
8.11.3	199	– *Pro Flacco*	
8.14	199	37	12
8.14.1	199	– *Pro Sestio*	
8.14.2	199	120f.	194
8.14.3	199	– *Qfr.*	
8.14.4	199	2.9.5	187
9.1	189, 205	– *Tusc.*	
9.2	181, 205	1.4	145
9.2.5	197	3.29	194
9.3	205	4.46	150

5.1	140	5.4	54
5.30	140	5.6	56

Cornelius Nepos
– *Att.*

8.4	153
16.3	158
16.3–4	184

Demetrius
– *Eloc.*

223	53, 58
223–224	10
226	11
227	11, 161–162, 238
228	166
232	166
234	52, 174
235	58

Dio Chrysostomus
– *Or.*

42.4–5	91

Diogenes Laertius

2.9	102
2.13	102
2.62	102
2.83–5	102
3.61	8
4.8	50

Erasmus
– *Ep.*

2092	163

Euripides
– *Ep.*

1.1	49
1.2	51–52, 58
2.1	66
3.1	52
3.2	59
4.1	59
5.1	54, 61–62
5.2	54–55

Galen
– *De libr. propr.*

9	91
14	91
41–3	91

Gregory of Nazianzus
– *Ep.*

51.5	58

Herodotus
– *Hist.*

1.123.3–4	10
5.35.3	10

Homer
– *Il.*

6.168	10

Horace
– *Ars*

151–2	37

– *Ep.*

1.1	27
1.2	27
1.13	27
1.18	27
1.19	27
1.20	27
2.1.187–93	187
2.1.252–4	24

– *Sat.*

1.5	83

Inscriptions

– *CIL* III 7269	105
– *Corinth* VIII.3.124	104

Isidore of Seville

1.40	203

Iulius Victor
– *Ars Rhetorica*

27	166

Letters of the Socratics
(Socraticorum Epistulae):
15	100–101
18	100, 101–102
22	100, 102

Libanius
– *De forma epistolari/Ep. Char.*
1	10
10	58
58	53

Life of Aratus
I pg. 10.16–19	46

Livy
3.42.6	42
26.9.5	42
26.42.8	24
27.2.10	42
38.29.3	42

[Longinus]
– *Subl.*
15.9	220
26.2	213

Lucan
2.616–18	24

Lucian
– *Nigrinus*	92

Musonius
– *fr.*
48–49	98

Ovid
– *Am.*
1.2.34	183
2.10.23	36
2.18	82
3.12.19–20	37

– *Ars Amatoria*
1.227–8	183
3.538	37

– *Her.*
4.1	80
13.1	80
15.1–4	82
16.1	80
18.1	80
19.1	80

– *Met.*
9.530	80

– *Pont.*
1.1	27, 75, 77, 80
1.1.1	73, 81
1.1.11	81
1.1.17	71
1.1.17–20	76
1.1.18	75
1.1.28	75
1.1.29–30	75
1.2	27, 77
1.2.5–6	77
1.2.7–8	77
1.2.23–24	74
1.2.129–36	78
1.3	85
1.3.1	80
1.3.1–2	79
1.4	80
1.5	27, 80
1.5.3	80
1.5.59–60	81
1.5.61	81
1.5.71–6	84
1.5.83	81
1.7	73, 76, 78, 81
1.7.1	80
1.7.1–6	78
1.7.6	79
1.7.18	79
1.7.55	79
1.8	80
1.8.1	80
1.9	27, 85
1.9.1–4	85
1.10	73, 80
1.10.1	80
2.2	73, 76
2.2.3	80

2.2.121	79	– *Tr.*	
2.3	27	1.1.3–14	75
2.4	27, 73	1.1.11	81
2.5–6	27	1.2.9	74
2.6	73	1.5	71, 74
2.7	27	1.5.7	71
2.8	27, 82	1.5.79–80	74
2.10	82	1.6.21–22	74
2.10.1–4	81	1.7.9	82
3.1.53	74	1.7.15–28	97
3.2	27	1.10	83
3.2.1	80	1.11.1–2	83
3.4	73, 76	2.339–40	37
3.4.1	80	3.1	72
3.4.57–60	84	3.1.11–12	83
3.5	27, 76	3.1.13	82
3.5.1–4	79	3.3	71
3.5.5	80	3.3.1–2	82
3.6	73, 76	3.4.63–68	71
3.7.6	82	3.4.63–74	71
3.8	27, 76	3.5	71
3.9	27, 75–76	3.7	71
3.9.2	76	3.7.46–47	28
3.9.51–3	29	3.10	84
3.9.53–4	211	3.10.25–39	84
4.2	85	3.11.61	74
4.2.5–6	86	3.12.31	84
4.2.26	183	3.14	71
4.2.37–46	183	3.14.48–52	70
4.2.57–64	182	4.1.99–102	193
4.2.65	183	4.2	181–182, 188–189, 193
4.2.69–70	182		
4.2.67–68	182	4.2.16	183
4.4.8	73	4.2.27–46	200
4.5	83–84	4.2.57–64	182
4.5.3–8	83	4.2.67–68	182
4.9	73, 76, 80, 181	4.2.69–72	182
4.9.1	80	4.5.9–10	71
4.10.9–34	74	4.7.3–10	85
4.11	84	4.9	73
4.11.15–16	84	4.10	36, 78
4.13	71	4.10.59–60	37
4.13.11–16	82	5.1.2	73
4.13.18	70	5.2	71
4.14.5	80	5.2.1–2	72
		5.2.63	73
		5.4	72, 82–83

Index Locorum — **269**

5.4.1	73	**Pliny the Elder**	
5.4.1–3	72	– *NH*	
5.4.5–6	85	1.14	80
5.5.3–4	74	17.5	172
5.5.57–80	74	35.65	229
5.9.1–2	71	36.24	187
5.9.25–34	71		
5.9.33–34	71	**Pliny the Younger**	
5.10	83	– *Ep.*	
5.11.1–2	85	1.1	9, 29, 209–211, 217, 222
5.12.1–2	85	1.1.1	29, 35, 85
5.12.58	70	1.2	217–219
5.13	71, 80	1.2.2	217
5.13.1–2	80	1.3	217–220, 222, 225–227
5.13.9–16	85		
5.13.27–30	78	1.4.1	33
		1.11	209
Petronius		2.1	22
– *Sat.*		2.17	32, 212, 216, 219–220, 222, 226–227
115.6	43		
		2.17.1	24, 226
Philostratus		2.17.13–19	220
– *Im. pref.*		2.17.29	222
25.4	29	2.19.6	39
		3.6	214
Photius		4.14.4–5	39
– *Bibl.*		4.20.2	38
codex 58	92	4.30	214–216, 219–220, 230, 232
Plato		4.30.1–3	214
– *Apol.*		4.30.3–4	215
17b–18a	97	4.30.7–10	216
– *Ep.*		4.30.11	216, 224
1, 309b8–c2	63	5.6	30, 32, 216, 219, 220, 222–223, 225–234
2.314c	101		
– *Phaedr.*		5.6.3	226
274c–277a	98	5.6.7	228
275e	98	5.6.13	228
276d	98	5.6.16	231
276d–277a	98	5.6.17	38
– *Symp.*		5.6.19–21	223
215b	97	5.6.22–23	229
– *Tht.*		5.6.29	231
142a–143c	103	5.6.35	231, 234
		5.6.36	231
		5.6.38–40	230

5.6.41	223	8.20.5	235
5.16.2	32	8.20.6–8	235
6.1	29	8.20.8–9	236
6.2	29	9.7	236
6.10	30	9.7.4	237
6.14	30	9.36	226
6.16	30	9.38	37
6.16.4	32	9.40	226
6.16.18–21	43	– *Paneg.*	
6.16.20	44	15.3	41
6.18	30	95.3–4	40
6.20	30, 37, 42		
6.20.5	42	**Plutarch**	
6.20.12	42	– *Brut.*	
6.20.15	42	6.10	153
6.20.19	42	18.4.5	153
6.20.20	42–44	26.6	153
6.25	30	29.3	153
6.28	30	32	153
6.30	30	34.3	154
6.31	30	45.4–5	153
6.31.15	24	45.9	154
6.32	29	52.4–6	145
6.33	29	53.5	154
6.34	29	– *Caes.*	
7.4	33–34	63.7	190
7.4.2–3	34	– *Cat. Min.*	
7.4.4–6	35	48	126
7.9.8	38	– *Cic.*	
7.9.10–11	34	45.1	153
7.27	214	– *Cimon*	
7.31.2	33	1–2	24
8.4.2	24	– *De aud.*	
8.8	232–234, 237	9.42c–e	98
8.8.1	232	– *Mor.*	
8.8.2	233	38b	219
8.8.4	233	– *Pomp.*	
8.8.5	233	16.2–5	151
8.8.5–6	234	55	126
8.8.7	234		
8.10–11	209	**Priscian**	
8.17	232	– *Inst. Gramm.*	
8.17.3	232	6.7	140
8.20	232, 234, 237		
8.20.1	234	**Propertius**	
8.20.2–3	234	3.4.14	183
8.20.4	38, 235	4.3	6

Ps.-Demetrius
– *Ep. Typ.*
proem. 52
3 57–58

Ps.-Seneca
– *Oct.*
831 172

Quintilian
– *Inst.*
4.3.12–14 213
6.2.30 225
8.3.67 220
9.1.45 212

Seneca the Elder
– *Suas.*
1.1.5 28
1.5 110

Seneca the Younger
– *Ep. Mor.*
6.6 176
7.5 169
8.2 13
12 168
14.3 169
15.7 169
20.9 167
21 13
21.4 28
21.5 167, 169
29 168
32.1 173
40.1 11, 53
49.1–2 167
51 213
53 168
55 213
56 168, 213
64 167
64.1 167
75.1 81
75.2 176
86 213
95.45 140

97.3–6 28
108.5–7 98
115.12–13 169
118.1–2 28
– *Helv.*
8.1 147
9.4 140, 148
9.7 148

Seneca and Paul
– *Ep.*
1 165–167, 173–175
2 170
3 174, 176
4 173
6 174
7 170, 174, 176–177
8 170
9 170–171, 176
10 174
11 171–172, 174
12 174
13 174
14 174

Suetonius
– *Aug.*
12.1 143
– *Iul.*
56.5–7 211

Tacitus
– *Ann.*
1.8 136
4.34 152
13.47 169
16.19 171
15.44.2 172
– *Dial.*
18.5 158

Terence
– *Heaut.*
77 35

Theon
– *Prog.*
2.118.7–8   53

Thucydides
1.22.1   94

Tibullus
1.3   35

Valerius Maximus
1.5.7   152
1.8.8   152
1.6.13   152
2.6   187
4.5.6   152
4.6.5   154
6.2.8   151
6.4.5   152
6.8.4   152
14   97

Varro
– *LL*
6.60   194

Vergil
– *Aen.*
1.159   24
2.765   187
6.156–235   42
– *Georg.*
4.285–6   35

Xenophon
– *Ep.*
15   100
18   100
– *Mem.*
1.2.

www.ingramcontent.com/pod-product-compliance
Lightning Source LLC
Chambersburg PA
CBHW020225170426
43201CB00007B/316